THE
LETTERED
BARRIADA

THE LETTERED BARRIADA

Workers, Archival Power, and the Politics of Knowledge in Puerto Rico

JORELL A. MELÉNDEZ-BADILLO

Duke University Press   *Durham and London*   2021

© 2021 DUKE UNIVERSITY PRESS. *All rights reserved*
Designed by Courtney Leigh Richardson
Typeset in Elephant and Arno Pro by Westchester Publishing Services

Library of Congress Cataloging-in-Publication Data
Names: Meléndez Badillo, Jorell A., author.
Title: The lettered barriada : workers, archival power, and the politics of
knowledge in Puerto Rico / Jorell A. Meléndez-Badillo.
Description: Durham : Duke University Press, 2021. | Includes bibliographi-
cal references and index.
Identifiers: LCCN 2021002275 (print)
LCCN 2021002276 (ebook)
ISBN 9781478013853 (hardcover)
ISBN 9781478014782 (paperback)
ISBN 9781478022091 (ebook)
Subjects: LCSH: Partido Socialista (P.R.)—History. | Working class—
Political activity—Puerto Rico—History—20th century. | Labor
movement—Puerto Rico—History—20th century. | Press, Labor—Puerto
Rico—History—20th century. | Press and politics—Puerto Rico—
History—20th century. | Intellectuals—Puerto Rico—Attitudes. | Puerto
Rico—Politics and government—1898-1952. | Puerto Rico—Historiography. |
BISAC: HISTORY / Latin America / General | SOCIAL SCIENCE / Ethnic
Studies / American / Hispanic American Studies
Classification: LCC HD8238 .M45 2021 (print) | LCC HD8238 (ebook) | DDC
322/.2097295—dc23
LC record available at https://lccn.loc.gov/2021002275
LC ebook record available at https://lccn.loc.gov/2021002276

Publication of this book is supported by Duke University Press's Scholars of
Color First Book Fund.

Cover art: Kelvin Santiago Valles, cover art from the pamphlet "Juana Colón:
La Juana de Arco Comerieña," published by the Secretaría de prensa y
propaganda del comité local de Comerío del Partido Socialista
Puerto-rriqueño ("Juana Colon: the Joan of Arc of Comerío," published by
the Press and Information Committee of the Puerto Rican Socialist Party
of Comerío), 1972. Courtesy of Colección Gilberto Arias González.

Para abuela Ada y abuelo Carlos,
esto es fruto de su cosecha.

Para Aurora y Libertad,
mis fuentes de inspiración.

Para mis madres,
Iris y Robin.

Para todxs mis maestrxs,
en el salón de clases,
en la calle o en el texto.

Para quienes no aparecen
en este libro.

CONTENTS

ACKNOWLEDGMENTS

On a warm May afternoon in 2014, my family came together at the home of one my great-aunts in Moca, Puerto Rico. Since my *abuela* (grandmother) had fourteen siblings, growing up with my grandparents meant that family celebrations were massive. I had just come back from finishing my first year of doctoral studies in the United States. Suddenly, I found myself in the balcony surrounded by all the men. They were trying to figure out what I was doing *allá 'fuera* (abroad). "What? A doctor? In history? Ha!" Struggling with my words, I tried to explain that I was a historian, which meant that I was trying to write stories just like the ones they had told me on multiple occasions about long shifts in tobacco factories, about train rides in search of work, or about the blistering sun in the sugarcane fields.

I was finishing an article about an agricultural strike that took place in 1905 and told them all about it. They attentively listened until my great-uncle Guilo interrupted me and said, "Strikes? Papá [my great grandfather] was an expert. He was called every time there was one. Papá was a *rompe huelga* [scab]." When I asked him to clarify what he meant, he just replied with a smile, "Of course, Papá would travel throughout the island on the train. Whenever a strike broke out, that meant he had work." And right there, on that balcony, my conception of history was profoundly altered. I had spent years doing research about the most radical segments of the Puerto Rican working classes, written a book on anarchism, and dedicated countless hours to the study of strikes. While I had taken an interest in these topics because of my working-class background, I had failed to understand that my family were those on the other side, the ones anarchists and striking workers fought against, the *rompe huelgas*.

Hearing my great-uncle was a lesson about the multiple protean identities that people like them often negotiated. Learning about Papá's scab days did not make his stories about labor migration, exclusions, and exploitation less real. In fact, it added another layer to the already complicated histories that had been passed down to me by my great-aunts and great-uncles. On that day, I also understood that I wanted to write a history that was attentive to how identities were forged, negotiated, and mobilized at different historical moments. To be sure, the people that inhabit this book had access to things my family lacked: unions, self-managed pedagogical projects, and, eventually, political power. I came to understand these complexities, not by reading hundreds of books—which I did read—but through conversations like the ones that took place in that balcony. My family also taught me about the importance of community. Thus, I consider the production of history to be a collective endeavor.

This book was first conceptualized in that balcony with my family in Moca, Puerto Rico. It was written in between Storrs, Connecticut; Amherst, Massachusetts; and Hanover, New Hampshire. I finished it in another balcony, this time overlooking the Atlantic Ocean in Manatí, Puerto Rico. In the journey of transforming an idea into a book, I have inherited many debts that I will never get to fully repay. I have been very privileged to share conversations, laughs, and ideas with many colleagues and friends on different continents. In that sense, this book is my young self's wildest dream. It is a tribute to the people from the La Charca neighborhood, where my family comes from; the housing project Las Muñecas, where I spent the first years of my life; and the barriada Cabán, where I came of age. It is a tribute to all those—like my family—who remain unnamed and absent in history books.

At the University of Connecticut, a community of scholars and colleagues were crucial in conceptualizing the first drafts of this work. I am grateful to Matt Guariglia, Shaine Scarminach, Nathan Braccio, Eddie Guimont, Jessica Strom, Danielle Dumaine, Matt Perse, Erica Willis, Marc Reyes, Maggie Stack, Gabrielle Westcott, Aimee Loiselle, Mike Limberg, Allison Horrocks, Carla Silva Muhammad, Andrea Chunga, and Yesha Doshi. My time in cold Storrs, Connecticut, was made bearable by the warmth of Carlos Gardeazábal, Fatima K. Espinoza, Orlando Deavila, Claudio Daflon, Tania Torres, Gabriel Martínez, Marianna Todd, Ilán Sánchez, Luisa Arrieta,

Jenn and Christina Honeycutt, Nick Bannon, Guillermo Irizarry, Anne Lambright, and Ángel A. Rivera.

This book would not have been possible without the support of the University of Connecticut's History Department, including Kathy O'Dea, Jessica Muirhead, Heather Parker, Janet K. Watson, Chris Clark, Peter Baldwin, Cornelia H. Dayton, Michael Dintesfass, Melina Pappademos, Sylvia Schafer, Nancy Shoemaker, Fiona Vernal, and Emma Amador. El Instituto: Institute of Latina/o, Caribbean, and Latin American Studies not only served as a source of funding but also became an oasis for Latinx folks to connect, get together, and create knowledges. There, I am grateful to Anne Theriault, Anne Gabbelein, Samuel Martínez, and Charles Venator. I am forever indebted to Mark Overmyer-Velázquez and Mark Healey for all their support, mentorship, and friendship. I am especially thankful to my mentor and friend, Blanca G. Silvestrini. Her work has redefined the field of Puerto Rican history and has greatly informed my ideas.

The research for this book was funded by the Mellon Faculty Fellows Program at Dartmouth College, the Ford Foundation, and the University of Connecticut's Humanities Institute. In the latter I became part of an interdisciplinary community of scholars that greatly influenced this book. I am thankful for all the conversations with Michael Lynch, Alexis Boylan, Deirdre Bair, Rebecca Gould, Eleni Coundouriotis, Ruth Glasser, Kenneth Gouwens, Jeffrey O. G. Ogbar, Harry Van Der Hulst, Sarah Berry, Laura Wright, Alycia LaGuardia-LoBianco, and Tracy Llanera. During my time in Amherst, I was made to feel at home by a group of scholars at the University of Massachusetts and the Holyoke Public Library. I am particularly grateful to Gloria Bernabe, Agustín Lao-Montes, Roberto Alejandro, Yuri Gama, and Manuel Frau.

At Dartmouth College I have been fortunate to be part of a vibrant scholarly community. I am grateful for the intellectual dialogue, collegiality, and laughs with Bethany Moreton, Pamela Voekel, Matt García, Annelise Orleck, Israel Reyes, Udi Greenberg, Jennifer Miller, Rashauna Johnson, Golnar Nikpour, Yumi Lee, Robert Bonner, Leslie Butler, Cecilia Gaposchkin, Jeremy Dell, Dave Petruccelli, Stefan Link, Soyoung Suh, Matt Delmont, Mingwei Huang, Jacqueline Wernimont, Eng-Beng Lim, Desirée García, Kyle Booten, Mary Coffey, Tatiana Reinoza, Eman Morsi, Marcela Di Blasi, Yana Stainova, Yui Hashimoto, Becky Clark, Jorge Cuéllar, and Cristina Tedman-Lezcano.

The first person to read my initial book manuscript was Montse Feu, for whom I am very grateful. She gave me careful comments and suggestions that allowed me to morph the text into what it is today. Margaret Power and Aura Sofía Jirau read earlier versions of chapter 5 and were of enormous help, for which I am very grateful. This book also greatly benefited from a manuscript review workshop sponsored by Dartmouth College's Department of History and the Mellon Faculty Fellows Program. In the workshop, Eileen Findlay, Jorge L. Giovannetti, Matt García, Israel Reyes, and Pamela Voekel read the full manuscript and gave me invaluable comments, suggestions, and critiques.

This book would not have been a reality without the support of Gisela Fosado at Duke University Press. She believed in the project from its early stages and supported me throughout the editorial process. I am also thankful for all the help and support provided by Alejandra Mejía and Ellen Goldlust. Likewise, the book benefited from the careful reading and suggestions offered by Duke University Press's anonymous reviewers.

I am beyond privileged for having the following people in my personal, professional, and political life: Michael Staudenmaier, Ileana Rodríguez-Silva, Sandy Plácido, Solsiree del Moral, Jorge Duany, Adriana Garriga-López, Claudia Sofía Garriga, Joaquín Villanueva, José Fusté, José Atiles, Sarah Molinari, Mónica Jiménez, Roger Reeves, Daniel Nevárez Araújo, Pedro Lebrón, Nicole Cruz, Karrieann Soto Vega, Marisol LeBrón, Jenny Kelly, J. Kehaulani Kaunui, Lord Lewis, Reynaldo Lastre, Eilyn Lombard, Mark Bray, Yesenia Barragán, Enrique Alejandro Vargas Rivera, Mariel Acosta, Julio Ramos, Jesse Cohn, Silvia Álvarez Curbelo, Sandra Pujals, Juan José Baldrich, Ángel (Chuco) Quintero-Rivera, María Dolores Luque, Luis Agrait, Albeyra Rodríguez, Jorge Nieves Rivera, Javier Alemán, Pablo L. Crespo, Bianca Medina, Kenyon Zimmer, Dave M. Struthers, Kirwin R. Shaffer, Raymond Craib, Kevan Antonio Aguilar, Anna Elena Torres, George Ciccariello-Maher, Eileen Findlay, Jorge L. Giovannetti, Gladys Jiménez-Muñoz, Kelvin Santiago Valles, Rodney Lebrón Rivera, Glorimarie Peña, Nelson Pagán Butler, Mayra Vélez Serrano, Rachell Sánchez, Raymond Laureano, Jacqueline Villarrubia-Mendoza, Roberto Vélez, and Alexis Lorenzo Ruiz. I am enormously grateful for the PFNKR Reading Collective, which fostered a lively intellectual space and a community of care during the global COVID-19 pandemic.

In every archive and library consulted throughout my research, I have only found the most helpful and amiable people. I am thankful to all of them, but especially to Evelyn Solá and Milagros Rodríguez. In Puerto Rico, *tierra de mi corazón*, a network of people have kept me grounded throughout this process. I am grateful for friends like Hommy Cabrera, Paola Sánchez, Zevio Schnitzer, Paola Maisonet, Francis Rosario, and Lucas Noble. My family-in-law, Blanca Ortiz, Julio Santana, Guadalupe Santiago, and Freida Borges, have supported me every step of the way. My mothers, Iris Meléndez and Robin Guzzo, have always been there for anything that I have needed, and I will be forever thankful. My abuela Ada Roldán and my abuelo Carlos Nieves (may he rest in power) are the reason I wrote this book; it is a tribute to them.

Libertad Brouhns Santiago is the ray of sun that lights my every day. Libertad, this is the book I told you so much about, the one that stole many hours of play from you. Thank you for your patience, your joyfulness, and your love. Aurora, there are no words to describe how grateful I am for your everyday acts of solidarity. You have been patient and supportive with all my endeavors, but, most importantly, you fill my life with joy and happiness. This book is also the product of all our late-night conversations, theorizations, and debates. You have always challenged me to push my intellectual boundaries and to test the limits of my historical imagination. I am grateful for all you do and hope that the rest of our lives continue to be full of laughter, music, and happiness. Your love, *cariño*, and friendship are my bedrock, *te amo más de lo que las palabras pueden expresar.*

Every morning at the break of dawn, vendors flocked to Arecibo's *plazuela del mercado* (market square) hoping to sell some of their goods, produce, or livestock. Even before the plazuela's daily hustle and bustle began, the smell of coffee filled the air as Nemesio Morales opened his *cafetín* (small café) to the public. There, customers could enjoy a cup of coffee, order breakfast, or have lunch. Cafetines were also places where people came together to gossip about events in their neighborhoods, engage in debates about politics, or simply buy their newspapers. In December 1910, Nemesio's patrons were exposed to a recently published daily newspaper called *El combate* (The combat), dedicated, according to its subtitle, to dignifying labor.[1] Anyone that came into the cafetín and glanced at the newspaper's masthead could easily perceive its rhetoric. Besides its socialist grandiloquence and its confrontational tone, the paper's header portrayed labor as honorable and presented education as an instrument to achieve dignity and freedom.[2]

When asked by his clients about the newspaper, Nemesio might have answered that he did not know much but that it was the product of three young idealists from the Federación Libre de Trabajadores (FLT; Free Federation of Workingmen) guided by Esteban Padilla.[3] People might have recognized Padilla's name because of his activism. After all, he was one of organized labor's most vocal advocates in the northern town of Arecibo. *El combate* had a short life of six months. In one article, its editors criticized the town's mayor, causing an uproar in Arecibo's political establishment.

The mayor sued the paper for libel, and Padilla took the blame. He spent a few days imprisoned until he sent a letter to the mayor asking for forgiveness. At a time when the lines between public and private life were often blurry, Padilla's arrest or his involvement in the creation of Arecibo's Partido Obrero Insular (Insular Labor Party) might have put his name in the townspeople's mouths.[4]

Those of Nemesio's patrons who disagreed with *El combate*'s radical rhetoric but still flipped through its pages could at least find some usefulness in its announcements of cultural events taking place in Arecibo, or in the news section, which covered all of Puerto Rico and beyond. Some might have been puzzled as to how these three workingmen were able to document events taking place in faraway places, such as Sweden, Spain, and the United States. Beyond its fiery political rhetoric, the workingmen behind *El combate* also carved a space to experiment with their literary sensibilities by publishing poems, short essays, and philosophical commentaries. And while unfamiliar readers might have found these intellectual pursuits odd, *El combate* was hardly an exception.

By 1910, *El combate* was one in dozens of labor newspapers published throughout Puerto Rico.[5] Different forms of print media (including books, pamphlets, and single-page leaflets) allowed a small group of self-educated workingmen to produce knowledge and ideas in the margins of Puerto Rico's cultural elite. At a moment when workers started organizing unions and venturing into partisan politics, a handful of people that self-identified as *obreros ilustrados* (enlightened workingmen) crafted a makeshift intellectual community, which I refer to as the lettered *barriada*. Physical barriadas were poor neighborhoods usually interconnected by a system of alleys that allowed people to move from one place to another. These narrow passageways between houses were less streets than trails made with asphalt, stones, or dirt. Resembling the veins of a cardiovascular system, alleys were also added on the go as housing structures were built, creating spatial unity among the barriada dwellers. The lettered barriada came alive through the nexus of literary production and print culture, political participation, and labor rituals that reconfigured social and physical spaces. Newspapers became its alleyways, books became its houses, and social study centers were its public plazas.

The Lettered Barriada tells the story of how a cluster of self-educated workingmen were able to go from producing knowledge within their workshops and labor unions in the margins of Puerto Rico's cultural and intellectual elite to becoming highly respected politicians and statesmen. It is a story of how this group of workingmen produced, negotiated, and archived powerful discourses that ended up shaping Puerto Rico's national mythology. By following a group of ragtag intellectuals, this book demonstrates how techniques of racial and gender silencing, ghosting, and erasure also took place in the margins. Ultimately, it is a book about the intersections of politics, knowledge, and power relations in Puerto Rican working-class intellectual production at the turn of the twentieth century.

WHAT OTHER NEWSPAPERS were sold at Nemesio Morales's cafetín? Would *El combate* sit next to national papers like *La correspondencia de Puerto Rico* (Puerto Rico's correspondence), or were there other working-class newspapers being sold? Would people actually buy *El combate*, or would Esteban Padilla collect a packet of unsold newspapers at the end of every week? Since we lack the sources to answer these questions, we must resort to the realm of speculation and imagination. Some questions posed in this book will remain unanswered because they did not fit any of the competing archives that generated what we have inherited as historical knowledge. By "archive," I am referring not only to physical repositories of documents but, following historian Antoinette Burton, to any "traces of the past that are collected either intentionally or haphazardly as 'evidence.'"[6]

Puerto Rican workingmen did create material archives by housing their institutional documents in union venues and locales. They built a decentralized national network of makeshift libraries, night schools, and social study centers that stored books, newspapers, and photographs. Obreros ilustrados also participated in the creation of nonmaterial archives that came to life through the print word and that I refer to as "ideational archives." The nature of these archives was twofold. On the one hand, they came alive through print media and workers' intellectual production. On the other, the discourses and narratives produced in their pages acquired power beyond the text and often operated autonomously. While I am attentive to the materiality of working-class archives, I am also interested in unpacking the ways in which particular historical narratives and discourses operated as archives in themselves—archives of particular desires, ideas, and political projects.

Workers' ideational archives were not created in a vacuum. In the late nineteenth century—as literary scholar Lorgia García Peña argued in relation to the Dominican Republic—Puerto Rican liberals built the "archive of *puertorriqueñidad* (Puerto Ricanness)" through "historical documents, literary texts, monuments, and cultural representations sustaining national ideology."[7] Beyond the hegemonic national archive, minor ones served the structure and logic of the archive of puertorriqueñidad; that is, in early twentieth-century Puerto Rico, multiple competing archives operated simultaneously. Each archive sought to establish its own "truth" to shape "history." After all, "the archive," as philosopher Michel Foucault argued, "is the first law of what can be said, the system that governs the appearance of statements as unique events."[8]

There were also "counterarchives" that challenged such logic and oftentimes were silenced from the historical record by those that controlled the modes of working-class knowledge production. One such case was the feminist counterarchive created by the anarchist Luisa Capetillo, who stormed the male-dominated lettered barriada with the publication of various books and newspapers. Perhaps more radical were the counterarchives created by the Black laundress Paca Escabí or the Black illiterate labor organizer Juana Colón (further discussed in chapter 3). While paying attention to multiple archives, The Lettered Barriada focuses on the archive—both physical and ideational—created by the FLT and the Socialist Party because it acquired hegemonic dimensions within working-class history. These organizations had the financial, material, and intellectual resources to create long-term editorial projects, publish books, and create physical repositories.

This book began as an attempt to find the voices of those people like my family—my great-grandparents, grandparents, and great-aunts and great-uncles—who were not unionized, did not aspire to become modern or "civilized," and might have even opposed unions. Since I was not able to find them in the historical record, I began to pay attention to a question that ended up guiding this book's narrative: why were they absent? Following Michel-Rolph Trouillot's argument that archives are neither neutral nor natural, and that silences are always actively produced, added another layer: how were they silenced? Seeking to answer these questions, this book explores obreros ilustrados' worldviews but also takes into consideration how they became historical narrators.

Because obreros ilustrados eventually dominated the means of working-class knowledge production through their leadership positions within Puerto Rico's premier labor organizations, the narratives they created have oftentimes been equated with history itself.[9] That is, obreros ilustrados got to dictate what was deemed important enough to become history. In the process, and to be legible in the archive of puertorriqueñidad—an archive crossed by centuries of colonialism, slavery, and imperial violence—they silenced those that did not fit their whitened and male idealized worker identity.[10] Thus, racial discourses, workingwomen, and nonunionized workingmen were rendered invisible. This was, as Trouillot argued, "archival power at its strongest, the power to define what is and what is not a serious object of research and, therefore, of mention."[11]

NEMESIO MORALES'S CAFETÍN was located in Arecibo's plazuela del mercado, an important space for socializing. The plazuela was the town's commercial center. While people from the countryside could get copies of working-class newspapers only at labor-related events, city dwellers could buy them in specific stores, cafetines, or union venues. Indeed, the lettered barriada's physical space was undoubtedly urban, embodied in social study centers, printing houses, and union halls. Yet its social space was not geographically limited to Puerto Rico.

Let us imagine a workingman who had never traveled outside Puerto Rico or the northern region of Arecibo deciding to stop for a coffee at Nemesio Morales's cafetín. If he was one of the fortunate few who knew how to read, he could take a sip from his drink as his eyes flitted through *El combate*'s pages. There, he could read about massive mobilizations in Belgium or about the assassination of Catalan anarchist pedagogue Francisco Ferrer i Guardia. Perhaps he could feel connected to others who, in his mind, suffered the same oppression as his. Maybe, for a second, he could also imagine that he was part of a movement that transcended national borders. He could imagine himself as a global subject, all without ever leaving the cafetín.

The expansion of capitalism, new technologies, and travel routes made the turn of the twentieth century a heyday of labor's globalization. Since the 1860s, workers from around the world had made a concerted effort to connect with each other through international congresses, migration, correspondence, and the circulation of the labor press and other cultural products. During the first decade of the twentieth century, Puerto Rican obreros ilustrados became active participants in that global phenomenon. They read and published in international newspapers, celebrated labor rituals of remembrance like May Day, and established contacts with comrades in different countries. Through global interactions, they joined what one workingman described as "the concert of advanced nations."[12] That transnational subjectivity, or global sensibility, is an underlying theme throughout this book.

This does not mean, however, that the barriada was disconnected from broader political and social processes in Puerto Rico. It was created and developed in tension with the country's political and cultural establishments. During the first decade of the twentieth century, and as a new polity emerged after the US occupation and colonization of Puerto Rico, obreros ilustrados used print media to craft protean identities that allowed them to establish proximity to the populace at times and distance at others—all while becoming workers' self-assigned interlocutors.

After the creation of the Socialist Party in 1915, obreros ilustrados moved to centralize working-class knowledge production with the aim of attracting workingmen to the ballot. By the 1930s, after the Socialist Party became an undeniable political force in Puerto Rico, many of those who had been in charge of producing knowledge and organizing labor unions had turned into career politicians. Meanwhile, as tensions within the party increased, and as a generational relay began to take place, it became imperative for aging labor leaders to write the movement's historical narratives. The publication of three books by the movement's most recognized leaders in the late 1920s and the 1930s (Santiago Iglesias Pantín, José Ferrer y Ferrer, and Rafael Alonso Torres) consolidated the ideational archive that began at the turn of the century and that would later shape historical production about Puerto Rico's working classes. To be sure, workers had been publishing books and pamphlets for decades, but these three books became foundational texts for Puerto Rican labor historiography.

The obreros ilustrados this book focuses on—a group mostly composed of urban and skilled workingmen—were also successful in crafting their political identities through their participation in the lettered barriada. They were deemed legitimate political subjects, as they occupied seats in Puerto Rico's senate and legislature. The cultural elite, however, saw workingmen's intellectual credibility as dubious at best. Nonetheless, at a moment when the labor movement had not been a serious object of academic study, these workingmen understood the power of crafting their own historical narratives. Those who published newspapers like *El combate* and distributed them in cafetines, on public corners, or at rallies perhaps never imagined the impact they would later have in Puerto Rican history and society. This book is the story of how that handful of ragtag intellectuals who stole time off their nights to study, debate, and educate other workers were able to successfully influence Puerto Rico's politics, national mythology, and, later, historical interpretations of the "Puerto Rican reality."

Conceptualizing the Lettered Barriada

Producing history is a collective effort. My work builds on and is indebted to scholars who pioneered working-class studies in Puerto Rico decades ago and have reimagined the field several times since. Under the name of *nueva historia* (new history), in the 1970s a group of scholars set out to analyze what until then were understudied social sectors. Most of the other books and articles published about the labor movement were centered on the figure of Santiago Iglesias Pantín and reproduced the idea that he "created" the organized labor movement.[13] Influenced by trends in social history, this new generation of academics from the nueva historia was skeptical of grandiose historical narratives and sought to rewrite Puerto Rican history from below.[14] Since then, scholars of Puerto Rican labor have paid attention to workers' theatrical plays, literature, and social study centers as part of their class struggle, demonstrating that most literary and cultural production was created as organizing propaganda. Yet workers' cultural production also reveals the emergence of an intellectual project and community. Thus, looking at obreros ilustrados as part of that community allows a deeper understanding of the power relations among the working classes.[15]

In this book I use the concept of the lettered barriada in dialogue with a key text in Latin America's intellectual tradition, *La ciudad letrada* (*The Lettered City*), by the Uruguayan literary critic Ángel Rama. In *La ciudad letrada*, Rama mapped the urban dimensions of Latin American cultural production, the relationship between elite intellectuals and the state, and the centrality of reading and writing to the creation of urban (social and political) life. The workers that inhabited Puerto Rico's lettered barriada participated in similar processes but did so in the margins of the country's cultural and intellectual elite. These mostly self-educated workingmen used their makeshift libraries, improvised pedagogical projects, and public events to build the lettered barriada.[16]

Rama argued that in Latin America, "there were more real links between *letrados* [men of letters] and labor organizations at the turn of the century than in the 1930s (when such links became so central to left ideology)."[17] While this was true in some Latin American countries, as exemplified by thinkers like Manuel González Prada in Peru or Rafael Barrett in Paraguay, this was not the case in Puerto Rico. Both González Prada and Barrett were raised in wealthy families but later in life became militant anarchists, publishing several incendiary books and articles.[18] Intellectuals that came from the Puerto Rican professional classes sought to articulate a national project in the late nineteenth century and excluded workingmen from such conversations. I do not want to imply that it was a firm binary, but like any social process, interactions were porous at times. There were intellectuals, albeit few, that sympathized with the socialist program of the FLT, including Rafael López Landrón and Matienzo Cintrón, both lawyers.[19] Unlike

Rama's assertion, it was precisely in the 1920s and 1930s—after the Socialist Party facilitated the entrance of workingmen into Puerto Rico's political spheres—that the imaginary line between intellectuals and workingmen began to dissipate, but not entirely. By then, books written by working-class authors circulated more widely and ceased to resemble those rustic pamphlets produced within the lettered barriada at the turn of the twentieth century.

Similarly, Rama contended that a new *letrado* emerged in early twentieth-century Latin America and joined the ranks of professional writers. This new letrado, "usually from a lower class," lacked "contact with the most esteemed instruments of formal education" and "necessarily developed a less disciplined and systematic, but also more liberated, intellectual vision."[20] While the process of intellectual formation described by Rama resembled what Puerto Rican workingmen went through, they did not end up joining the rank of professional writers. Most people did not have the privilege of pondering the muses of leisure and had to dedicate most of their time to work. Many of the obreros ilustrados that I follow through the lettered barriada abandoned the workshop as they became full-time organizers and politicians, not writers.

The creation of makeshift intellectual communities in the margins of a country's cultural elite was not a process exclusive to Puerto Rico. If we understand the development of the lettered barriada as the convergence between print media, alternative social spaces, and political participation (broadly defined), then workers, radicals, and intellectuals across the Americas had been building their intellectual communities since the last decades of the nineteenth century. For example, ever since the 1860s, workers in Buenos Aires and Havana published dozens of newspapers and books; opened social study centers, rational schools, and bookstores; and sought representation in political processes from the war for independence in Cuba to the consolidation of academic disciplines in Argentina. Nonetheless, these processes were tied to the particularities of the historical moment in which they developed. This book explores how Puerto Rico's lettered barriada was forged in a Caribbean country at a colonial crossroads, from Spanish colonialism (1493–1898) to US imperialism (1898 to present day).[21]

In early twentieth-century Puerto Rico, access to the printed word, either through writing or reading, was a marker of social power and authority among the laboring masses. That is why Rama's formulation about the relation between letters and power is crucial to my conceptualization of Puerto Rican workers' intellectual production. Furthermore, understanding the lettered barriada not only as a physical space, but also as a social one allows me to look at the transnational dimensions of local processes. While there has recently been a shift toward a transnational scope in Latin American labor and working-class histories, it has been rooted in the migration of peoples through national borders. In the following pages, I engage in conversation with recent literature on the topic, yet I shift the emphasis toward understanding how the circulation of ideas transformed the subjectivities of those who did not necessarily move outside Puerto Rico.[22]

In recent years, the field of Puerto Rican labor history has also moved toward much needed nuanced analyses of gender and race, which have added different interpretations to the previous class-based studies.[23] As Ileana Rodríguez-Silva has argued, the silencing of race was crucial for the making of class and nation building in turn-of-the-twentieth-century Puerto Rico.[24] When nineteenth-century liberals began to discursively articulate the Puerto Rican nation, workingmen were racialized and feminized, and thus excluded from those imaginaries. Instead of challenging these discourses, the nascent labor movement and its cadre of intellectuals reproduced them in their writings, cultural production, and historical narratives. In the process, they enacted many layers of exclusion and silencing. Workingwomen also actively participated in the organized world of labor since its beginnings. When obreros ilustrados wrote their histories of the movement, however, workingwomen were largely absent. Obreros ilustrados erased not only workingwomen but femininity in itself, as well as blackness.

The exclusion of blackness was not necessarily tied to Black bodies, as some were allowed participation in different echelons of the labor organizations these workingmen created. Yet they were allowed only if they practiced a de-Africanized and "respectable" form of blackness. That is, they were allowed participation if they aspired to become "civilized" and "modern," if they aimed to become whitened. The obreros ilustrados affiliated to the FLT and the Socialist Party sought to silence the histories of those who partook in practices racialized as Black and thus coded by the elites as backward, foreign, and uncivilized. These exclusions were not deviances but integral to the creation of labor's ideational archive and still operate with great transhistorical power in present-day Puerto Rico.[25]

Lastly, this book takes into consideration the significant role the geopolitics of knowledge play in how research questions are articulated. Although there are outstanding exceptions, oftentimes works produced in Puerto Rico are not in dialogue with those published in the United States, and vice versa. By paying attention to both historiographical strands, this book engages in conversations happening not only within Puerto Rico and the United States but also in the Caribbean and Latin America. As literary scholar Arcadio Díaz-Quiñones has argued, Puerto Rico is often overlooked by the institutional knowledge produced in North American universities. Since it is neither Latin America nor the United States, it ends up disappearing.[26]

Recognizing such dichotomy, this book situates Puerto Rican working-class knowledge production within the Caribbean and Latin America but also pays attention to the US empire's regional power at the beginning of the twentieth century. Although the lettered barriada emerged in the early years of US colonialism in Puerto Rico, in the following pages I resist the urge to make colonialism or empire the book's central analytical axis. Several scholars have done an excellent job exploring how imperialism and empire operated in Puerto Rico and how they shaped policies toward education, sexuality, and labor.[27] By not centering empire or colonialism, I am not negating the archipelago's colonial condition, which is still sustained with great transhistorical violence as I write these words.[28]

This book explores the complexities and contradictions of obreros ilustrados' ideational worlds beyond their opinions about the island's political status. It seeks to move away from a binary logic of "resistance or integration" that obscures other political processes, desires, and sociabilities. In fact, there's a nationalist-infused historiographical strand that has accused early twentieth-century socialists of being traitors or expounding "empty rhetoric of principles."[29] That binary logic not only downplays the agency of historical subjects, but also limits our analysis of what can be considered radical politics. As philosopher Jacques Rancière argued, "A worker that had never learned how to write and yet tried to compose verses to suit the taste of his times was perhaps more of a danger to the prevailing order than a worker who performed revolutionary songs."[30]

While it is true that the Socialist Party's leadership supported the annexation of Puerto Rico to the United States, this book aspires to think what it meant for self-educated workingmen—most of them also ex-convicts—to enter intellectual and political spaces that had been denied to them in the past.[31] Ultimately, the binary logic of "resistance or integration" also ignores the fact that colonialism and coloniality should not be solely defined by political status. The violence of these systems of power permeated (and still permeate) social relations, regimes of knowing, and often-indiscernible modes of societal control.[32] This book, then, pays attention to how the obreros ilustrados negotiated, challenged, and reified those systems of colonial power through their praxis, discourses, and shifting positionalities.

Weaving the Barriada into Puerto Rico's Historical Fiber

The last three decades of the nineteenth century offered a whirlwind of changes for Puerto Ricans. Transformations in the Iberian Peninsula sent shockwaves through the Caribbean island, which had been a colonial possession of the Spanish empire for nearly four hundred years. After 1868, the crown was swayed by a series of revolutions that gave birth to a brief republican government in Spain and, later, a seemingly moderate reinstituted monarchy. In merely three years, from 1870 to 1873, Puerto Rico saw its first political parties, censorship eased away, and people could freely associate; slavery and the system of forced labor known as the *libreta de jornaleros* (laborer's notebook) were abolished; and new technologies that would alter agricultural production arrived at the scene.[33]

These transformations also refashioned Puerto Rico's societal fiber. Landowners (*hacendados*) and factory owners ranked highest in the country's social hierarchy. Meanwhile, toward the end of the nineteenth century, a new group composed of foreign-educated professionals (mostly lawyers and doctors) started to emerge. Both social groups had different political and ideological agendas. Their interactions were oftentimes porous, as they were connected through bonds of friendship and familial relations. Landowners wanted to implement a hegemonic project to control the island's polity and means of production while the new professional class aspired to set the foundations for a generalized national consciousness. Slavery produced such wealth that landowners could send their sons to study abroad in the United States and Europe's most important intellectual centers. Salvador Brau, one of the leading intellectuals among these professionals, noted that this young group was infused with modernizing and liberal ideas when they went to study abroad, only to arrive back to the island with the most fervent antislavery stances and political projects.[34] Other liberal thinkers, like Francisco del Valle Atiles, Alejandro Tapia y Rivera, and José Julián Acosta, joined Brau in establishing the intellectual foundations of the imagined Puerto Rican nation and the archive of puertorriqueñidad.[35]

These professionals created a cross-class project that sought to include landowners, professionals, and workers. The "Great Puerto Rican Family" was to be used as a powerful discursive tool to unify the country. Attesting to its power, sociologist Carlos Alamo-Pastrana suggests that it still operates nowadays "within the field of Puerto Rican studies, especially in literature, . . . as the major trope for framing the island's racial heterogeneity. The great Puerto Rican family (*la gran familia puertorriqueña*) discursively constructs Puerto Rico as a patriarchal, inclusive, and mestizo nation."[36] Although the Great Family aspired to civilize and modernize labor, workers were excluded from the conversations that created it.

After 1873, and following three years of conditioned liberty, freed formerly enslaved peoples entered the country's precarious labor market. Some became salaried workers in both agricultural and urban settings, while others used their previous labor experiences to become artisans and skilled workingmen.[37] Groups of urban workingmen started crafting their own cultural and societal projects, such as newspapers, mutual aid societies, and literary soirees. But, in a country that in 1899 had a total of 659,294 inhabitants over the age of ten and 328,850 who were unemployed and did not attend school, cultural projects were produced and enjoyed by few.[38] This gave way to the creation of several hierarchies within the laboring masses.

Ramón Romero Rosa, a printer and one of the most prolific writers among the early twentieth-century obreros ilustrados, wrote: "There was a time, very stupid for sure, in which what can be called a 'worker supremacy' (*supremacía obrera*) was established among the working class that attended [literary] soirees." He continued, "Printers, barbers, silversmiths, and people from other trades thought that the word 'workingman' was humiliating to their craft because they truly saw themselves as artists, organizing their racket centers which they called 'Artistic Casinos,' . . . denying access to bricklayers' assistants, non-skilled workingmen (*peones*), [and] dockworkers."[39] As Romero Rosa pointed out, workingmen were not a homogenous group. To the contrary, they created social hierarchies based on trade, remuneration, and access to cultural capital.[40] Even when excluded from Puerto Rico's cultural elite, those workingmen who had access to letters crafted an intellectual project that would seek to discursively unify workingmen from all trades. To do so, obreros ilustrados, most of whom were urban skilled workers, used print media, labor mobilizations, and cultural projects to create labor's historical narratives, collective aspirations, and masculine whitened identities.

On July 25, 1898, Puerto Rico was militarily occupied by the United States as part of the Spanish American–Filipino–Cuban–Puerto Rican War. Barely three months after the occupation—and three days after the US flag was officially hoisted in Puerto Rico—a group of workingmen created the archipelago's first labor federation, the Federación Regional de Trabajadores (FRT; Regional Federation of Workingmen) on October 23. Under its banner, workers held strikes throughout the island, published the newspaper *El porvenir social*, and organized the first public May Day celebration. The FRT leadership favored Puerto Rico's annexation to the United States. They believed that joining the northern nation would allow them to be protected by US laws. In their program, the FRT advocated for the eight-hour day, maternity leave, work safety laws, abolition of child labor, and the creation of public dining halls, as well as reforms in the educational system.[41]

Some FRT leaders also promoted the creation of a joint political strategy with the pro-statehood Republican Party.[42] A group steered by Ramón Romero Rosa, José Ferrer y Ferrer, and Santiago Iglesias Pantín, among others, fiercely opposed any political alliance. That dissident group created the FLT on June 18, 1899. In October of that year, members of the FLT also created the Partido Obrero Socialista (Socialist Labor Party). Santiago Iglesias Pantín was elected president and Ramón Romero Rosa, the party's secretary.[43] Nonetheless, military governor George W. Davis abolished universal male suffrage—established months before the US occupation—and did not allow the party's participation in the first local elections under US rule.[44] Two years later, in 1901, the FLT became affiliated with the American Federation of Labor.[45]

The people of Puerto Rico sought to make sense of the rapidly changing economic, social, and political landscapes. The US colonial government consolidated its control over Puerto Rico and paved the way for transnational corporations to dominate the island's two major exports: sugar and tobacco. The entrance of US capitalism also meant a sharp transformation in the modes of production, which materialized in different organizational structures within workshops. Cigarmakers, for example, went from being well-respected artisans who knew the "secrets of the trade" to replaceable units in a rapidly mechanizing system.[46]

The obreros ilustrados saw the moment as an opportunity, even amid their different approaches, ideologies, and political orientations. Using their newly created unions, they sought to leverage Puerto Rico's emerging polity. While some of them, such as Romero Rosa and Manuel F. Rojas, cautioned against colonialism, others, such as Santiago Iglesias Pantín and Jesús María Balsac, promoted the incorporation of Puerto Rico into the United States as a step toward becoming legitimate political actors. Seeking to strengthen their unions' political bonds, the obreros ilustrados created alliances with local politicians and US government officials.

The Foraker Act of 1900 allowed Puerto Ricans to vote for members of the local House of Delegates, while the US president appointed the governor and his executive council. At times the governor and municipal authorities' relations were frail at best. For example, Manuel Egozcue Cintrón was the mayor of San Juan intermittently from 1900 to 1904. While in office, the mayor gave impunity to mobs that attacked anyone who opposed his Republican Party. Even when the FLT had cordial relations with the governor, and some labor leaders corresponded with high-ranking US officials, they were physically attacked and persecuted in the streets of San Juan by members of the mayor's political party.[47]

Throughout the first fifteen years of the twentieth century, the FLT sought to create an institutional identity that would allow its members to participate in the country's political, social, and intellectual life. To do so, labor leaders experimented with multiple short-lived political alliances that, even when not always effective, allowed labor leaders to articulate their demands in the political sphere. Furthermore, by 1905 the FRT became almost nonexistent beyond the San Juan area, allowing the FLT to project itself as Puerto Rico's leading labor federation.

With the FLT's growth also came attempts to centralize the diverse political visions and strategies within labor organizations. For example, Ramón Romero Rosa and four other FLT members participated in the 1904 elections through the Union Party ballot. The Union Party, which later became the Socialist Party's rival, represented the old landowning class and intellectuals, and was organized around patriotic lines in defense of the imagined Puerto Rican nation. All the FLT members who ran for the House of Delegates were elected. Yet the Unionists did not allow Santiago Iglesias Pantín, then president of the FLT, to participate in the elections. Enraged by his exclusion, Iglesias Pantín demanded that all elected FLT members resign from their political positions. When they refused, the elected workingmen were expelled from the labor federation. Romero Rosa had been one of Santiago Iglesias Pantín's most loyal defenders. He wrote Iglesias Pantín's first biography in 1901, elaborating what historian Gervasio L. García called the "Early Riser Myth," in which Iglesias Pantín was portrayed as the "creator" of the labor movement. Nonetheless, Romero Rosa became a persona non grata for refusing to follow Iglesias Pantín's orders.[48]

Around the same time, in 1905, Puerto Rico was rocked by a series of strikes in the northern and southern agricultural fields as well as in San Juan's docks. Since the FLT's beginnings, the organization had aspired to unionize the agricultural labor force, which was the country's overwhelming working majority. For labor leaders, the southern agricultural strike of

1905 gave hope of attaining such a possibility. Indeed, there were moments in which more than twenty thousand agricultural workingmen mobilized in joint actions throughout the region. Some of the striking workers' demands were met, but the FLT, which had invested most of its resources and money in the process, was severely weakened. As Andrés Rodríguez Vera, one of the FLT's harshest critics, argued, after the 1905 strikes the FLT was reduced to an office in San Juan. While that may have been an overstatement, the labor federation did struggle to maintain its numbers. After the strike, the FLT's numbers plummeted from 8,700 unionized workers in 1905 to 6,300 the following year.[49]

Labor leaders went from using strikes to attain their immediate goals toward a more conservative trade-unionist stance while also experimenting with municipal politics. The FLT's San Juan locale, led by Santiago Iglesias Pantín, created the Federación Libre Party and had little to no success. In the 1908 elections, for example, it barely gathered 1,326 votes, or 0.86 percent of all the ballots cast countrywide. Meanwhile, Esteban Padilla—who was one of the people behind the labor newspaper *El combate*—founded the Partido Obrero Insular (Insular Labor Party) in Arecibo. Despite its poor results in the 1908, 1910, and 1912 elections, the Partido Obrero Insular took everyone by surprise when it won the majority of votes in Arecibo during the 1914 elections. There had been a desire to enter the world of politics since the organized labor movement's early days, but it was this victory, along with a major strike that developed throughout the Puerto Rican countryside during the same year, that created the conditions for labor leaders to form the Socialist Party in 1915.[50]

Meanwhile, workingwomen fought to carve a space in the male-dominated labor organizations. They created several unions, from domestic unions, which served as umbrellas for women with different occupations, to trade-specific ones, like the Women Tobacco Stripper Union. The number of officially recognized workingwomen unions increased from nine in 1904 to thirty-five in 1909.[51] Their activism was not only labor related; they also generated broader social demands. For example, in 1908 workingwomen demanded universal suffrage in an FLT congress, something unprecedented that would not become a reality until 1935. When the Socialist Party was created in 1915, not a single woman occupied a position of power within its ranks.[52] By 1919, workingwomen played such a central role as organizers that the FLT and the Socialist Party sponsored the First Congress of Puerto Rican Workingwomen.[53] Nonetheless, they continued to be excluded from the party's leadership positions through the 1930s.

Although the Socialist Party was a distinct entity from the FLT, it was through the latter's unions that the party generated enough signatures to participate in the 1917 elections, the same year that the Jones Act granted US citizenship to Puerto Ricans. The party's program advocated land distribution; the creation and control over a Labor and Agricultural Department; a better educational system, with free food, clothing, and materials for children; eight-hour workdays; and the creation of *barriadas obreras* (working-class neighborhoods), among other progressive measures. The Union Party won every election from 1904 to 1924. Yet the Socialist Party quickly became a political powerhouse after its founding. In 1917, Socialists garnered 14 percent of the votes and won six municipalities. Likewise, in the following elections (1920), it attained 23.7 percent of the general vote, winning eight municipalities.[54] From 1924 onward, the Socialist presence in the political sphere was one of the reasons that traditional parties with different ideological orientations were forced to create alliances to win elections.[55] The Socialist Party was not exempt from this trend and created electoral partnerships with the Republican Party.

These political processes took place as Puerto Rico's economy was radically transformed during the first three decades of the twentieth century. The US occupation also created a "free trade zone," which prompted export activities in the sugar, tobacco, and needlework industries. Indeed, sugar production and tobacco manufacturing, practiced since Spanish colonial times, expanded greatly during these decades. Coffee production, on the other hand, plummeted. Needlework, which mostly employed working-women in factories or in their own houses, boomed after World War I, when the United States lost sources of embroidered cloth and drawn linen, such as France, Belgium, and Japan.[56]

These economic processes shaped and transformed Puerto Rico's social relations, spatial configurations, and intellectual spheres. During the last decades of the nineteenth century, a group of letrados started imagining how a process of modernization could look in Puerto Rico. After 1898, most of these letrados became members of the Union Party and articulated a patriotic discourse that resented US occupation while proposing independence or greater autonomy, as exemplified by intellectuals like Luis Muñoz Rivera, Rosendo Matienzo Cintrón, and José de Diego. This literary generation was followed by the modernists, who, according to literary critic Rafael Bernabe and sociologist César Ayala, articulated three defining elements: openness to cosmopolitanism and modernizing influences, an affirmation of Puerto Rican cultural identity and of its link with a Hispanic American cultural universe, and a challenge to US arrogance.[57]

A younger generation born after 1898, influenced by their readings of US, Latin American, and European literature, started articulating their aspirations and sensibilities. In the 1920s, avant-garde literature sought to break away from "older generations" and experimented with new literary forms and styles. People like Antonio Pedreira, Luis Muñoz Marín, Vicente Geigel Polanco, Pedro Albizu Campos, Juan Antonio Corretjer, and Luis Palés Matos were not only known within literary circles but would later become significant political actors throughout the twentieth century. The trends and literary developments of this newer generation owed much to the shift the University of Puerto Rico (UPR) had made from a teachers college to an institution of higher education.[58] From within the university, some of those intellectuals started to think of the Puerto Rican nation as a distinct cultural entity from the United States. Indeed, known as "the '30s generation," it is no exaggeration to say that they reimagined the Puerto Rican nation.[59]

These ideas about the nation were articulated in the 1930s as the country went, once again, through enormous economic and social transformations. The US government's New Deal program created a series of agencies through which technocrats sought to modernize Puerto Rico, such as the 1933 Puerto Rican Emergency Relief Administration (PRERA) and later the Puerto Rican Reconstruction Administration (PRRA) in 1935. Meanwhile, other marginal intellectual communities tied to specific political projects started to emerge.[60] The Nationalist Party abandoned electoral politics and became a militant movement; the Communist Party lured former Socialists into its ranks; and new labor organizations challenged the FLT's hegemony over the organized labor movement. These groups, organizations, and parties housed cadres of intellectuals who imagined the nation from vastly different positions. In this context, several splits within the Socialist Party and the FLT took place, and the newly created Partido Popular Democrático (Popular Democratic Party) eventually became a hegemonic force in Puerto Rican politics.

This is the texture that weaved together the world navigated by obreros ilustrados during the first three decades of the twentieth century. As I demonstrate in the pages that follow, workingmen made their way into partisan politics but were not allowed into Puerto Rico's intellectual and literary spheres. Nonetheless, they created their own social and cultural spaces, from which they imagined, theorized, and sought to transform their reality. Ultimately, this book is not a history of the FLT or the Puerto Rican working classes. It is the story of a small group of obreros ilustrados that used knowledge production to create a makeshift archive and intellectual community with its internal contradictions, global aspirations, and local exclusions.

The Creation of Workers' Intellectual Community

Understanding an intellectual community's historical development is a daunting and complicated endeavor. You must take into consideration many relations, practices, and individuals. Like culture, "if you are to understand the relationship between different practices," argued cultural theorist Stuart Hall, "you have to know something about economics, social history, literature, and so on."[61] To tackle such complexity, each chapter represents a different moment in the emergence of Puerto Rico's lettered barriada.

Chapter 1 explores the moment of creation. Through its pages I follow workers into evening meetings to discuss the creation of newspapers, trace the development of their first publications, and explore who these obreros ilustrados were. The chapter begins in 1897, with the publication of the newspaper *Ensayo obrero*, and analyzes the development of the lettered barriada in tune with the FLT's expansion as it became the island's most important labor federation. It also explores how obreros ilustrados used print media to establish proximity to the laboring masses at some moments and distance at others. Chapter 2 focuses on how obreros ilustrados imagined themselves as part of a global community at a moment when the labor movement was expanding and as some of its leaders ventured into politics. It explores the uses of print media and private correspondence to take part in international conversations that gave them cultural referents to theorize about their social conditions, struggles, and everyday lives. This imagined global labor community was deeply Eurocentric and allowed obreros ilustrados to locally articulate anti-Black narratives that silenced any race-based discourse.

Chapter 3 pays attention to the voices and the counterarchives of anonymous *obreras ilustradas* (enlightened workingwomen). While they did not create a literary corpus, workingwomen did pen their ideas in newspaper articles and spread them by speaking in *mítines* (public meetings). Thus, this chapter also problematizes the notion of who was considered a worker. To do so, I follow the labor organizing of Black laundress Paca Escabí and the transnational activism of anarcho-feminist Luisa Capetillo, while also tracing the life of Juana Colón, a Black illiterate labor organizer from the town of Comerío. The story of Colón challenges obreros ilustrados' silencing power. Although she was consciously omitted from Comerío's history, the community remembered her through corner conversations, songs, and poems. Such acts of remembrance saved Juana Colón from the lingering penumbra of historical silence.

Chapter 4 analyzes the Socialist Party's establishment and how it became a moment of consolidation for the lettered barriada's political project. Like any institution, different political, intellectual, and cultural opinions coexisted within the party. The chapter explores how obreros ilustrados who held positions of power sought to promote a homogenous political agenda and to centralize working-class knowledge production. Further, it shows how most obreros ilustrados, who came out of workshops, later held powerful positions in San Juan and Washington, which granted access to spaces that had been denied to them in the past.

Historians and social scientists have meticulously explained how even though the Socialist Party attained electoral victories in 1932 and 1936, it suffered significant setbacks throughout the 1930s. The scholarship has paid attention to dissidence, the breach of trust between the rank and file and its leadership, and the rise of other progressive political parties.[62] Nonetheless, Puerto Rican labor scholars have overlooked the 1933 student strike at the UPR as a watershed moment for the Socialist Party. The strike, explored in depth in chapter 5, was the first of several major public blows that debilitated Puerto Rico's premier labor organizations throughout the rest of the decade, leading to the FLT's disappearance and the Socialist Party's electoral insignificance. The 1933 student strike took place at a moment when the UPR became the archipelago's leading center for intellectual production. Workingmen were considered legitimate politicians by the country's cultural elite, but, as the strike demonstrated, they were not deemed legitimate intellectuals.

As these processes were taking place in the late 1920s and 1930s, it became imperative for aging labor leaders to narrate their role in the movement's creation. Chapter 6 explores how three books became an ideational archive capable of reproducing the historical narratives created within the lettered barriada at the turn of the twentieth century. Ultimately, these books, written by some of the movement's most important leaders, became the barriada's discursive consolidation. Following Siraj Ahmed's argument about the intersections of print media and the historical method,

I argue that these "texts became vessels of historical knowledge only on the condition that their own historicity be rendered invisible."[63] Thus, this chapter not only analyzes these books as constitutive pieces of labor's ideational archive, but also understands each book as the product of specific historical moments. Doing so allows an exploration into how dominating the means of knowledge production became an important political tool as the FLT and the Socialist Party's hegemony over the organized labor movement began to shatter in the 1930s. The book's epilogue traces how some of the myths created by labor's ideational and material archives later became tools in the realm of mid-twentieth-century politics, nation building, and history making.

A Note on Language and Terminology

At the turn of the twentieth century, the neighborhoods of La Perla (figure I.1) and Puerta de Tierra, both located outside San Juan's fortified walls, were the quintessential archetypes of barriadas. Their houses and living quarters were frequently improvised and lacked the most basic sanitary infrastructure. Yet their affordability and location—a stone's throw away from the island's capital—made them ideal for those coming from all around Puerto Rico in search of work. Some artisans and urban skilled workingmen earned enough to live inside the enclosed city, but their housing conditions were not ideal either. Most lived precariously to the point that we can consider their damp and dusky apartments as extensions of the extramural barriada. Indeed, although barriadas existed in the margins of power, they were constituted in relation to it. In this book, barriadas are not merely physical spaces but also represent the social worlds its dwellers forged through print media, cultural products, and literary works.

Taking such complexities into consideration, how can we translate the term barriada without losing its many layers? Expressions such as "slum," "shanty town," or "poor working-class neighborhood" reproduce negative connotations that obscure the vibrant conversations, interactions, and desires of those that lived in them. Furthermore, barriada's multifaceted meaning embodies all the above-mentioned definitions. Barriadas were often overcrowded, making them slums. Their buildings were crude, improvised, and for the most part created from scraps. Its inhabitants were those who did not own anything and who worked for those who enjoyed European and later North American luxury furniture and architecture. In

FIGURE I.1. Edwin Rosskam, *In the Workers' Quarter of La Perla, San Juan, Puerto Rico*, 1937. Courtesy of the Library of Congress.

sum, barriadas were the homes of those in the bottom of the social hierarchy. Hoping to maintain some of these nuances, I use the term in Spanish.

Similarly, I use the phrase "obreros ilustrados" (enlightened workingmen) in Spanish when referring to those behind the creation of the intellectual community I call the lettered barriada. For these urban skilled workingmen who started producing knowledge at the beginning of the twentieth century, the word "intellectual" was associated with the upper classes and carried negative undertones. After the French Dreyfus Affair (1896–1906)—where a Jewish military officer was unfairly imprisoned, and a host of well-respected thinkers came to his defense, including, most famously, Émile Zola—the word "intellectual" acquired new currency throughout the Western world.[64] Not until the late 1910s did Puerto Rican obreros ilustrados start using it without a negative connotation. Nonetheless, the term "intellectual" still maintained a class dimension. For obreros ilustrados, "intellectuals" were professionals who possessed higher education, not workers.

Workers' knowledge production was not only political and rooted in their class experiences but also revealed their literary, cultural, and self-making aspirations. It is up to the reader, then, to decide which is the noun and which is the adjective that best describes the subjects that populate the following pages. Were people like Romero Rosa, Ferrer y Ferrer, and Capetillo workers who were enlightened, or were they enlightened individuals who had to work? Using the phrase "obreros ilustrados," in Spanish, invites readers to arrive at their own conclusions.

Another word used in Spanish throughout the text is "mítines." Although it is an anglicism that roughly translates to "public meeting," it had a deeper meaning in early twentieth-century Puerto Rico. As I have noted elsewhere, "Mítines generally took place in spaces, such as empty lots, town plazas, or street corners. In the countryside they were organized in crossroads, in the patios of the peasant's humble huts or in wastelands."[65] Beyond their propagandistic nature, mítines were social events. "While the orator gave his or her speech, other workers handed out pamphlets, leaflets or newspapers. People interrupted speeches with applauses or by contradicting, challenging, or cursing at the speaker. Conversations, debates, and insults filled these spaces with vibrant life."[66] Hence, mítines were spaces where people came together to share ideas, construct knowledges, and forge collective identities.

One of this book's underlying arguments is that workingwomen were actively erased from the archives obreros ilustrados created. Attentive to such exclusions and erasures, I have decided to use the male "workingmen" when translating *trabajadores,* instead of the genderless "workers." It is very common to find "trabajadores" as a genderless noun in labor historiography, but that inevitably centers men. That is, using "workers" when referring to "workingmen" epistemically perpetuates the silencing processes I seek to untangle in the following pages.

For the obreros ilustrados that populate this book, knowledge production—from editing books and newspapers to writing poetry and theatrical plays—was a very serious affair. Attentive to obreros ilustrados' intellectual desires and aspirations, each section's subhead is accompanied by an epigraph from the working-class literary magazine *Luz y vida* (Light and life). One of the magazine's main editors was Rafael Alonso Torres, who becomes a crucial character in the second part of this book. While his opponents accused him of being as ignorant as an ox, this subtle action of using his magazine's quotations throughout the book is a way of problematizing the delegitimization of workers' intellectual production.

I also capitalize "Black" when referring to people of African descent. I recognize that the use of capitalization is part of a broader debate in the US African diaspora, and I do not wish to impose imperial academic modes of thinking to the study of Puerto Rico. Using capitalization in the context of early twentieth-century Puerto Rico allows me to center and forefront blackness at a moment in which the archives this book explores sought to silence and erase it.[67] I also use Spanish words whenever I feel that their English translation does not encompass their full meaning, and I leave any book and newspaper title in its original language. Nonetheless, every Spanish word is followed by an English translation in the text. Lastly, this book understands Puerto Rico as a Caribbean and Latin American country colonized and occupied by the United States. Thus, I use the terms "country" and "nation" interchangeably to refer to Puerto Rico, unless otherwise noted. I hope the following pages serve as a map to navigate the lettered barriada. Let's start our journey through its alleys.

CHAPTER 1. **WORDS AS BRICKS AND PAGES AS MORTAR**
Building the Lettered Barriada

In February 1897, carpenter Eusebio Félix Santiago invited José Ferrer y Ferrer, a printer, to an evening meeting. San Juan was still an enclosed city, its fort and walls a testament to the Spanish Crown's imperial ambitions. Possibly tired from his day's work, Ferrer y Ferrer walked down cobblestone streets, under the light of the moon and the old lampposts, as he probably felt the Atlantic Ocean's cool salty breeze. Within three months, those city walls would be torn down; within a year, the city would be occupied by the US military. Dramatic change was coming to Puerto Rico from without. But the meeting Ferrer y Ferrer was headed to would also launch dramatic change from within.[1]

Ferrer y Ferrer arrived at 5 San José Street (figure 1.1) and entered a long, narrow hallway. Upstairs was an elegant colonial house, the residence of a wealthy family. In contrast, artisans and workers occupied the downstairs tiny and damp apartments. The meeting was in one of those rooms, which served as carpenter Fernando Gómez Acosta's living space. As Ferrer y Ferrer entered the room, a group of artisans and skilled workingmen, consisting of Gómez Acosta, Norberto Quiñones, José Rivera, and Ramón Romero Rosa, greeted him. A few minutes later, there was another knock on the door. It was the meeting organizer, Eusebio Félix, along with a foreigner by the name of Santiago Iglesias Pantín. In the coming years, some of the workingmen who participated in this meeting would become central figures in Puerto Rico's labor movement and political spheres.[2]

FIGURE 1.1. San José Street, San Juan, Puerto Rico, ca. 1900. Courtesy of the Library of Congress.

In Gómez Acosta's damp and dim room, these men began a conversation—and a movement—to transform Puerto Rican workers' conditions, politics, and social life. On that night, they gave birth to the idea of publishing a newspaper by the name of *Ensayo obrero*. The meaning of *ensayo* is twofold. It suggests trial and experimentation. Likewise, it can refer to "essay" as a literary genre that encourages and defends personal opinion. Its ambiguity reflects the world of contradictions inhabited by workers at the turn of the twentieth century. Those who met in San José Street undertook a project that was both political and literary. From the margins of Puerto Rico's polity and cultural institutions, these workingmen tried new ways to promote and defend their opinions and ideas. They experimented with different ways of producing knowledge. Yet they were not the first to do so.

Artisans and urban skilled workingmen had published newspapers since the 1870s. In the southern city of Ponce, then commonly referred to as the island's "alternate capital," artisans created *El artesano* (The artisan) in 1874.[3] During the 1870s the press consolidated its propagandistic role, facilitating and even encouraging the foundation and development of political parties.[4] *El artesano*'s masthead demonstrated the editors' liberal orientation; it called itself "a republican, federalist newspaper."[5] Beyond its political affiliation, through its pages, *El artesano* called for the union of all artisans. It argued that rivalries between artisan associations were frivolous. According to the paper, artisans complained about their attendance at social events, the popularity of their orators, or the number of their associations' members. These "insignificant rivalries" were nothing, an editorial suggested, as "the only useful division, is the division of labor." The editors argued that notwithstanding their differences, all artisans should treat each other as equals.[6]

El artesano's correspondence documented an emerging island-wide audience. It had readers in the western towns of Mayagüez, Aguadilla, Quebradillas, Cabo Rojo, San German, and Sábana Grande, as well as in the southern municipalities of Villa de Coamo, Juana Díaz, and Guayama.[7] While the first cluster of labor newspapers appeared in Ponce—*El heraldo del trabajo* (Labor's herald, 1877), *El trabajo* (Labor, 1882–84), *El obrero* (The workingman, 1889), and *Revista obrera* (Labor magazine, 1893)—workingmen in the capital city of San Juan started to publish the newspaper *Eco proletario* (Proletarian echo) in 1892. Hence, when the 1897 meeting to create *Ensayo obrero* took place, the project could draw on recent precedents.

The publication of *Ensayo obrero* became a foundational moment, not in the broader tradition of working-class newspapers but in the historical narratives its editors began crafting. It was the first publication linked to a wider print production that ideologically sustained, promoted, and legitimized the labor organizations its editors eventually created. This group of workingmen would come to use their positions of power within those organizations to dominate labor's modes of knowledge production, reproduction, and documentation. This archival power allowed them to decide what would be considered legitimate working-class knowledge and what was deemed important enough to be part of their history, as well as what and whom would be cast outside, excluded, and erased. In the process, they imagined themselves as historical subjects, that is, in the words of anthropologist Michel-Rolph Trouillot, "voices aware of their vocality."[8] Just as its name suggested, *Ensayo obrero* was a testing ground for these urban skilled workingmen on how to assert their claim to historical importance, demand rights as citizens at a moment when the concept of citizenship itself was being contested, and become self-assigned interlocutors of the working classes.

Ensayo obrero hit the streets of San Juan on May 1, 1897. The publishing date was highly symbolic. After 1889, May 1, or May Day, became known worldwide as a workers' holiday in commemoration of Chicago's labor martyrs, executed for allegedly placing a bomb at a demonstration demanding the eight-hour workday. The first public celebrations of May Day in Latin America took place in the cities of Buenos Aires and Havana in 1890. Since then, every year thousands of workers occupied public plazas and marched through their cities to demonstrate the power of organized labor. It was also a showcase of international collaboration and solidarity. Those that organized these May Day activities were aware of the transnational dimensions of capitalism and understood that only an international response could potentially challenge it.[9]

At a moment when labor unions were not legal in Puerto Rico and public mítines were frowned on, the workingmen behind *Ensayo obrero* used print media to honor the Chicago martyrs' memory. Publishing their paper on May Day without an accompanying public event was a gesture that evaded local censorship while connecting these Puerto Rican workingmen to an international radical tradition that upheld these martyrs as symbols of global unity and resistance.[10] Launching newspapers on May 1 to commemorate the Chicago martyrs was not a strategy exclusive to Puerto Rican workingmen. For example, a year after the publication of *Ensayo obrero*, on May 1, 1898, the members of Brazil's Centro Operario Internacional (International Workers' Center) also launched their newspaper, *1ro de Maio* (May 1).[11]

Ensayo obrero proudly called itself the "Organ [*órgano*] of the working class," as stated in its masthead. But in the absence of any labor union and at a moment when artisans and workers were socially divided by trade and cultural capital, how was that "class" defined? What gave them the authority to speak on behalf of the laboring masses? What were they going to talk about in its pages? Who was their intended audience? How were they going to fund it? And, most importantly, who were the people behind this project? These are some of the questions that guide this chapter's analysis. I follow a cluster of artisans and urban skilled workingmen who self-identified as obreros ilustrados and used print media—specifically newspapers and books—to produce knowledge on behalf of Puerto Rico's laboring masses. I use the term "knowledge" as an active form of producing meaning and as a category of analysis to explore the ways in which people on the margins of society created notions of self and their social surroundings.[12] Lacking legitimizing traits like academic degrees, access to scientific publications, or social status, workers used their lived experiences to validate their intellectual production.

Within the lettered barriada, workers "did not play the spectator but intervened actively" in the production of knowledge, in the words of Walter Benjamin.[13] What follows is a mapping of lettered barriada's materiality. To do so, I explore how books and pamphlets discussed in social study centers (hereafter referred to as centros), or read in factories, workshops, and public plazas, were crucial to the development of workers' unique worldviews, self-fashioning, and political demands. Moreover, although the lettered barriada emerged in the margins of the island's cultural elite, some of the ideas produced within it eventually became part of Puerto Rico's national mythology.

Our Turn to Speak

And, what is a writer? He is the painter or narrator of a tradition, of a real scene or an imaginary generation. —LUZ Y VIDA, January 20, 1910

The first Puerto Rican newspaper, *Gaceta oficial* (Official gazette), was published in 1806. Since then, other papers appeared, but they had to be sanctioned by and loyal to the Spanish colonial government. Authorities strictly monitored any book that circulated or was printed in Puerto Rico.[14] From 1868 to 1873 a series of revolutionary processes shook Spain and its last two colonial enclaves in the Americas: Puerto Rico and Cuba. After a brief republican moment in Spain, from February 1873 to December 1874, the reestablished crown enacted a series of laws that produced profound changes in Puerto Rico, including the liberalization of the press, the abolition of slavery, and the free association of individuals under certain limitations. After 1870, Puerto Rican newspapers multiplied and openly expressed different ideological and partisan political positions.[15]

The Ateneo Puertorriqueño (Puerto Rican Athenaeum) opened its doors in 1876 in the capital city of San Juan. It was a physical space where individuals came together to discuss civic matters in hopes of influencing public opinion and action, quickly becoming Puerto Rico's main cultural and intellectual center. Inside its walls, members of the island's lettered elite discussed topics that ranged from Hegelian phenomenology to contemporary trends in science, history, and medicine.[16] The Ateneo was one in a series of intellectual hubs around the capital, like the Colegio Seminario Conciliar (Seminary Council College) and the Instituto Civil de Segunda Enseñanza (Civil Institute of Secondary Education). These spaces served as the decentralized edifice of the country's emergent lettered city.[17]

The nineteenth century came to an end with Puerto Rico at a colonial crossroads, as the Caribbean became a theater of war between the United States and Spain. In the weeks that followed *Ensayo obrero*'s publication, San Juan was radically transformed. In less than two weeks, on May 12, the US

Navy bombed the city on the eve of the 1898 war. Four military men and five civilians were killed. Later that month, on May 29, authorities decided to tear down the city walls that had been erected more than three centuries before. The occupation of the country by the United States on July 25, 1898 (barely nine months after Spain had granted autonomy to the island), propelled a series of changes. The local currency was devalued, a military government was established, and social imaginaries clashed as four centuries of Spanish colonization came to an end, giving way to US colonialism in Puerto Rico, which persists until the present day. Nonetheless, as historian Rubén Nazario Velasco has documented, the meanings of 1898 were not fixed; they changed during the first three decades of the twentieth century.[18] Bands of peasants attacked Spanish hacendados, and most obreros ilustrados celebrated the end of what they understood as "four hundred years of ignorance." Some intellectuals and former elites who felt their power was being challenged lashed out against US intervention and later upheld romantic visions of the past, evoking the Great Puerto Rican Family of yesteryear.[19]

The organized labor movement in Puerto Rico became a reality after 1898, but it was not the product of the US occupation. Similar to the labor effervescence throughout the hemisphere, the earliest workers' organizations in Puerto Rico were mutual aid groups and artisan societies.[20] The newspapers that workers and artisans published since the 1870s also set the intellectual foundations for the turn of the century's trade union movement. In this, Puerto Rico was hardly an exception. For example, the Portuguese Royal House of Braganza ruled the Brazilian empire from 1822 until 1889. While authorities were hostile toward labor organizing, forty-eight working-class newspapers were published in Brazil during the 1860s and 1870s. Trade unions began to emerge shortly after the establishment of First Brazilian Republic in 1899. Much like the Puerto Rican case, the proliferation of Brazilian trade unions and other labor organizations took place at the turn of the twentieth century, but it was facilitated by decades of theorizations in the margins through working-class print media.[21]

By then, a large group of Puerto Rico's cultured elite had been educated in Europe and the United States. They engaged in conferences and seminars and produced literary works, while also setting the discursive foundations for Puerto Rican history and literature, projecting their modernizing desires as the country's future.[22] Even if some artisans, like Sotero Figueroa and Francisco Gonzalo (Pachín) Marín, had been able to participate in the late nineteenth-century public sphere, obreros ilustrados felt that the working classes had not been part of the conversation.[23] The group of self-educated workingmen behind *Ensayo obrero*—including people like Ferrer y Ferrer, Romero Rosa, and Iglesias Pantín, among others—hoped to change this at the turn of the twentieth century with the creation of their own intellectual community.

While the country's lettered elite paid little attention to workers' print media, the government immediately took notice.[24] In December 1897, the same year *Ensayo obrero* hit the streets, colonial governor Sabás Marín wrote an alarmed letter to the Spanish crown. He warned about radical ideas entering Puerto Rico through the expanding labor press. "Although [*Ensayo obrero*] does not spill overtly anarchist ideas," Marín cautioned, "it tends to prepare the masses to receive them at any moment." He asked the crown to implement harsher laws in Puerto Rico, emulating those enacted in Barcelona and Madrid after the Italian anarchist Angiolillo assassinated the Spanish prime minister, Antonio Cánovas del Castillo, earlier that year.[25] Nonetheless, colonial fears were greater than the actual threat.

Through the pages of *Ensayo obrero*, the paper's editors disputed these accusations. They argued that their ideas were sustained through the force of reason and not by reason through force. This entailed stealing time "from our leisure and dedicating it to sharing our ideas with our comrades while teaching them the path they should take."[26] And that was precisely the tone promoted and transmitted to future publications affiliated with *Ensayo obrero*'s editorial group: they held a knowledge that differentiated them from the rest of the laboring masses. This paternalistic logic operated in a least two different yet interconnected ways. The workingmen behind *Ensayo obrero* distanced themselves from the "ignorant" laboring masses while asserting their claim to citizenship, honor, and civility.

In an article published in December 1897, an author using the pseudonym of D'Gualfiricio asked for people not to confuse "dignified workingmen" like the obreros ilustrados, who were using "reason and logic" to make the island prosper, with others who were "slackers and miserables."[27] That was a constant theme throughout the newspaper's lifespan. For example, Rodolfo López Soto, a workingman from the hill town of San Sebastían, wrote in *Ensayo obrero* about his desire to transform the laboring masses. After citing the works of Jean-Jacques Rousseau to legitimize his ideas in the article, López concluded: "We want [workingmen] to be citizens with equal rights. . . . Men and not pariah! Workingmen and not slave or miserable helot. Ultimately, we want to see the light of knowledge shining on their foreheads."[28] These references to civilization, enlightenment, and progress were articulated from a deeply hierarchical stance. Those who wrote in *Ensayo obrero* imagined themselves as possessing enlightenment, which they needed to share with the rest of the laboring masses to save them from themselves. Resembling the nineteenth-century liberal project that sought to transform laborers without incorporating them into the conversation, obreros ilustrados articulated a paternalistic logic toward the "ignorant" working classes.

Possessing knowledge could distance obreros ilustrados from the masses, but it did not provide proximity to the intellectual and literary elite. José Ferrer y Ferrer, whom we followed through the streets of San Juan and who later became one of the lettered barriada's main architects, published a fictional piece in the pages of *Ensayo obrero* in which he highlighted these tensions. The short story took place at midnight in the streets of San Juan. A young man by the name of Anselmo arrived at his fiancée Marianita's house to serenade her. After he finished singing, a crowd of onlookers that had gathered in front of the building asked him to say a few words. He demonstrated his oratory skills by giving a toast to the country's illustrious dead (*muertos ilustres*) and his fiancée's domesticity.

Through the words of Anselmo, Ferrer y Ferrer articulated two nineteenth-century codes of conduct tied to contemporaneous notions of honor: male civility and female domesticity. "[This is] for my loved one, so she will be true to her promise, and I shall not allow my desired fortune [of having you] to end, no!" Anselmo continued, "For our illustrious dead . . . forever blessed be their names because they paved the way for progress, fighting for our liberties, fighting with fervor the ultramontane colossus that sought to make men slaves." The crowd cheered for Alejandro Tapia y Rivera, Román Baldorioty de Castro, José Gautier Benítez, Manuel Corchado y Juarbe, and José Gualberto Padilla. All the men being praised were part of the nineteenth-century liberal elite. José Ferrer y Ferrer was radicalized shortly after the piece was published, and he became active in socialist and anarchist circles. In the story, however, published in 1897, he enunciated a prevalent notion among nineteenth-century artisans, which historian Ileana Rodríguez-Silva has coined as "the politics of gratitude." It was a discourse promoted by Puerto Rican liberals in which "everyone should be morally indebted to abolitionists and their successors" because abolition was understood as an effort to modernize the island.[29]

Shortly after the crowd cheered for all the "illustrious dead," Ferrer y Ferrer's story took an unexpected turn. An onlooker arrived at the scene and began screaming "mambí" at Anselmo, accusing him of trying to destroy the nation with subversive ideas. It is just then that the author provides an important insight: Anselmo, just like Ferrer y Ferrer, is Black. Although race is not explicitly mentioned in the text, it is presented through the use of "mambí." As historian Eileen Suárez Findlay has argued, in the nineteenth century, "race was openly addressed in Puerto Rico" without "directly naming racial distinctions," but by using codes and discourses around honor, sexuality, and morality, among other things.[30] The term "mambí" had been used to refer to members of the Cuban Liberation Army fighting against the Spanish government in the neighboring Caribbean island. Since many Cuban fighters were of African descent, the use of the term in Puerto Rico was racially and politically charged.[31]

Ferrer y Ferrer published this story at a moment of great political discord between those who defended liberal ideas and autonomy (represented by Anselmo) and those who clung to more conservative and promonarchical sentiments (embodied in the enraged onlooker). Yet the story also highlighted the racial and class undertones workingmen needed to navigate. Obreros ilustrados may know the names and the work of nineteenth-century liberals, but they were still "mambises." In fact, the story presented an ending to which workingmen could relate: "And it goes without saying that Anselmo went to the *cacharro* (prison)."[32] It did not matter if they were enlightened. Their class positionality guaranteed them time in prison if workers spoke out of turn, and more so if they were Black.

An article published in an 1889 edition of *El obrero* (The workingman) argued that since the early 1870s, "the working class started moving toward enlightenment."[33] Andrés Rodríguez Vera, a working-class author who would become one of the FLT's harshest critics, argued that well before 1898, the idea of "proletarian redemption had sprouted in the minds of many Puerto Ricans." He noted, "Fernando Gómez Acosta, Zoilo Betancourt, Sandalio Sánchez, Ramón Romero Rosa, Eduardo Conde, Juan Guerra, and José Ferrer y Ferrer, among other less significant [thinkers], were all obreros ilustrados."[34] The first generation of early twentieth-century obreros ilustrados also self-identified as "leaders." Used in English, this term was probably appropriated from the American Federation of Labor (AFL) after the FLT joined its ranks in 1901.[35] A *leader* was at once an agitator, labor organizer, and intellectual. While workers lacked the intellectual authority of the cultured elite (university titles, formal education, or political positions), they used other means to legitimize their knowledge production, such as their ties to labor organizations, their print media, and their oratory skills.

Leaders affiliated with the FLT were not the only people disseminating their ideas. Anarchists and other radicals who were critical of the labor movement's leadership also published books and newspapers without any financial support from labor unions. These tensions also materialized in insults toward those who did not follow union or party lines. For example, when the anarcho-feminist writer and activist Luisa Capetillo passed away in 1922, the FLT's newspaper *Justicia* (Justice) published an obituary that clearly demonstrated their contempt toward radicals. The article compared Capetillo to a child and argued, "She was not a true militant in the realm of labor or socialist ideas. Her rebellious temperament towards any discipline led her to certain ideology that formed her character, [and] formed her semi-erratic personality . . . distancing her from the ideas expressed by Karl Marx and Miguel Bakounine [*sic*]."[36] Although she was a longtime FLT member, the paper's editors articulated a disdainful tone to highlight her "irrationality" and "non-labor" ideas.

While working-class print media proliferated, its producers were a minority in Puerto Rico's early twentieth-century social composition. Access to the print word was a commodity enjoyed by few. In 1899, the population of Puerto Rico was 951,835. About 15 percent (143,472) could read and write, while 16.5 percent (156,852) were able only to read; that is, approximately 651,511 (roughly 69 percent of the population) were illiterate.[37] Furthermore, much like turn-of-the-twentieth-century Puerto Rican society, the production of knowledge was highly gendered. Women started organizing unions and became active within the labor movement in its early days, but they were excluded from official positions within the FLT.[38] Workingwomen like Paca Escabí, Soledad Gustavo, and Juana Colón published articles in the press, wrote letters, or used *mítines* to express their ideas and grievances. Nonetheless, Luisa Capetillo was the only workingwoman that we know of to edit a newspaper and publish books during the first two decades of the twentieth century. Besides the exceptional case of Capetillo, women were silenced in the historical archive created by *obreros ilustrados*.[39]

Since printers and cigarmakers occupied the highest positions in Puerto Rico's cultural division of labor, they dominated the production of print media. At the turn of the twentieth century, very few people had the privilege of attending the Instituto Civil de Segunda Enseñanza. Most received their education by reading in San Juan's public library or in their workshops. Rafael Alonso Torres, a printer, argued that the capital's municipal library "practically constituted a popular university at the service of all inhabitants, free of registration or enrollment, with each of its volumes constituting a *cátedra* [professorship] that could voluntarily educate any mind that had such noble eagerness."[40] For many, workshops also served, in the words of cigarmaker Epifanio Fiz Jiménez, "as a school and a university."[41]

Alonso Torres recalled that printers "had the privilege of being admitted into the *forums* or salons of the newspapers they worked in."[42] Besides occasionally drinking wine, chatting, and socializing in their workshop, printers spent their days typesetting books, newspapers, and other print materials. Their trade was "essential and fundamental in their [intellectual] formation and enlightenment."[43] Printing workshops were spaces where people from different cultural backgrounds came together, resembling something similar to what literary scholar Mary Louise Pratt has coined as "contact zones," or "social spaces where disparate cultures meet, clash, and grapple with each other."[44] In other words, for some workingmen and apprentices, workshops were perhaps the first place they interacted on equal terms with people from other class upbringings. Alonso Torres, for example, was an apprentice at José Julián Acosta's print shop in San Juan. Although he began his apprenticeship a year after Acosta's death, the latter was considered one of the main architects of late nineteenth-century Puerto Rican liberalism. Thus, his workshop undoubtedly was an intellectual hub in Puerto Rico's cultural cartography. One can only imagine how much Alonso Torres enjoyed those wine-fueled workshop intellectual debates. Inhabiting those spaces also legitimized his intellectual authority among other obreros ilustrados while socially distancing him from the "ignorant" laboring masses.[45]

Like printers, cigarmakers were another vastly literate group. They were better remunerated than most workers, which gave them access to certain commodities, such as print media. Cigarmakers were also highly cultured in part because of the practice of having *lectores* (readers) in their factories. They would collect money and pay for someone to read to them for two hours in the morning and two hours in the afternoon. In the morning, the lector read local and foreign newspapers, and the evening was dedicated to philosophical, political, and scientific works, followed by novels. Without having to leave their workbench, cigarmakers were exposed to a wide variety of Western writers, such as Émile Zola, Alexandre Dumas, Victor Hugo, Gustave Flaubert, Jules Verne, Fyodor Dostoyevsky, Maxim Gorky, and Leo Tolstoy.[46]

Nonetheless, the obreros ilustrados' lack of formal instruction caused them deep anxiety. They dedicated many pages to theorizing about being intellectuals in the margins and their role within the labor movement and broader society. Using satire, the printer Ramón Romero Rosa wrote in 1898, "They say that workingmen are ignorant . . . that we belong to the weird class . . . and that we complain without causes."[47] For Romero Rosa, writing and publishing were wagers against those who deemed workingmen ignorant or weird. Similarly, almost all their books opened by warning the reader about the author's "little-fostered intelligence."[48] Conversely, their lack of education and cultural capital also bolstered their legitimacy as obreros ilustrados. Unlike those nineteenth-century intellectuals who sought to understand (to transform) the conditions of the working classes, their literary authority stemmed from lived experiences.

For these workingmen, being enlightened was inherently political, notwithstanding the different discourses (socialist, anarchist, or conservative) they articulated. Most obreros ilustrados, except for anarchists, were opposed not to workingmen's participation in electoral politics but to bourgeois politicians. In fact, they understood the creation of a labor party as an important step toward passing legislation that would improve workers' lives while also advancing their socialist agenda. Yet as an anonymous workingman wrote in the pages of *Ensayo obrero*, "An obrero ilustrado, a workingman that feels and knows how to think becomes ... politicians' major enemy, a wall of resistance against their diabolical plans."[49] And he was right. Thirteen years later, in 1911, just as workingmen began entering Puerto Rico's political sphere, Mariano Abril y Ostaló, a politician and one of the country's leading intellectuals—who would become the first director of Puerto Rico's Academy of History in 1931—lashed out against them for trying to form a workers' party.[50]

Abril y Ostaló attacked workingmen's political capabilities in his book *El socialismo moderno* (Modern socialism). In its pages, he mocked workingmen for trying to enter the political arena carrying a socialist banner without being able to understand the scientific nature of such ideology: "Their limited mentality is not prepared for such elevated ideas that require intellectual preparation. If those coryphaei have read any socialist work, they have not known how to digest them."[51] This sort of condescending and arrogant attitude led obreros ilustrados to claim that bourgeois politicians and the lettered elite were their enemies. José Ferrer y Ferrer, under the pseudonym of Rabachol, asked in the pages of the newspaper *La miseria* (The misery), "What difference is there between a scientific and a manual workingman? ... Take the son of a carpenter; pay him for a scientific career, and you will see how that son of the People will nourish from knowledge's sap like any mister's [*señorón*] son."[52]

For Ferrer y Ferrer, lack of access to education, not intellectual deficiency, kept workingmen from producing knowledge. He continued, "those *obreros de la inteligencia* [intellectual workingmen] are our biggest enemies" because the people's ignorance was their fault. By obreros de la inteligencia, he was referring to those who did not have to do manual labor to survive but could spend their time thinking and writing, a reference to elite intellectuals.[53] Ferrer y Ferrer was interested not in transforming knowledge but in attaining it. In that sense, he was not advocating the creation of new solidary forms of knowledge that were historically specific to their Puerto Rican reality, but his critique was framed in the context of his class positionality, and the lack of access that entailed.

As literary scholar Julio Ramos has argued, the "new [worker] intellectual" that emerged in early twentieth-century Puerto Rico "was a writer and a speaker, and far from being inspired by the muses of creative leisure, it emerged as a union cadre, propagandist, and agitator."[54] But their worker identity was not the only thing they forged and negotiated. As Jesús María Balsac and Santiago Valle, a printer, argued in 1905, "The mistake made by bosses and journalists is to presume that all [workers] live the same way, that they have the same necessities and aspirations."[55] Balsac and Valle's words demonstrated a desire to not be homogenized, which echoed obreros ilustrados' broader impetus of distancing themselves from the "ignorant masses." Yet it also pointed toward the creation of plural identities not necessarily centered on labor. In print media and in their artistic expressions, obreros ilustrados projected themselves not only as politicians and labor leaders, but also as poets, social scientists, journalists, litterateurs, playwrights, and teachers.

In 1903, cigarmaker, essayist, and radical activist Venancio Cruz published a *poemario* (poetry book) titled *Fragmentos* (Fragments). Fernando Gómez Acosta, whose apartment was used in the February 1897 meeting that led to the publication of *Ensayo obrero*, wrote the book's prologue. "Poets are not born, they are made," wrote Gómez Acosta. He argued that Venancio Cruz possessed only the most basic rudimentary knowledge of "Rhetoric and Poetics" because he was raised in an environment of privation, receiving no more education than the one given in the workshop. Cruz had learned to read and write autodidactically. Given his class positionality, Cruz's desire to publish a poemario was a disruption in Puerto Rico's world of letters.

After claiming that Cruz's "poor intellect" did not allow him "to make a critical analysis of the poems," Gómez affirmed in the prologue that Cruz possessed "the three conditions [French intellectual Alphonse de] Lamartine thought necessary to be a great poet in his study of Alfredo de Musset: love, faith, and character."[56] Various intersecting assertions operate in Gómez's comment. He was claiming intellectual modesty or humility because of Cruz's underprivileged upbringing. This may have stemmed from Cruz's anxiety about not possessing official instruction. It also served as a way of legitimizing his knowledge through lived experiences. By citing French intellectuals, Gómez made another important claim. Cruz may not have attended school or received any formal instruction, but he assessed his poetic production through his understanding and awareness of European cultural production. In that sense, demonstrating his familiarity with thinkers such as Lamartine was a way of claiming intellectual legitimacy and status.

Labor newspaper editors and contributors, on the other hand, projected themselves as journalists. They addressed other established newspapers as their peers and had networks of correspondents throughout the island. For example, when *Ensayo obrero* covered local San Juan news stories, they would commonly write, "we are interested, and as journalists, we will continue to investigate."[57] And the island's press community saw them as journalists as well. When Julio Aybar, editor of *Unión obrera* (Labor union), was arrested for libel in 1910, many nonlabor newspapers protested his arrest. The editors of Arecibo's *El combate* applauded the actions of *La voz de la patria* (The nation's voice), a conservative newspaper that had criticized *Unión obrera* in the past but joined the campaign for Aybar's release. *El combate*'s editors wrote, "On the day of a colleague's disgrace, solidarity towards the comrade in disgrace makes them forget old resentments." Not only was Aybar considered a labor leader, but he also garnered the respect of the island's press community.[58]

Besides poets and journalists, some obreros ilustrados projected themselves as litterateurs. From 1909 to 1910, while serving as the FLT's general secretary, Rafael Alonso Torres edited the magazine *Luz y vida* (Light and life), dedicated to literature, culture, and aesthetics.[59] He sustained: "A daily newspaper, notwithstanding its size, represents four, six, ten or more pages written on the run with the pen of humanity's history. . . . A magazine summarizes a series of occurrences, moments, or human events that disrupt the life of communities."[60] Obreros ilustrados used the magazine to discuss literary works, publish poems, write short stories, and reprint biographies of foreign intellectuals, such as French radical philosopher Pierre-Joseph Proudhon and Filipino nationalist thinker José Rizal. They also kept track of cultural happenings in San Juan. Each number, for example, publicized visiting foreign theatrical companies and gave a summary of their plays. Similarly, they announced movie screenings at the "Puerto Rican" and "Cuban" theaters in San Juan. As one of *Luz y vida*'s advertisements read, only "the most enlightened workingmen from the country and abroad collaborate[d] in it."[61]

Luz y vida sought to produce a medium where workingmen could learn about, and criticize, art and literature. Although obreros ilustrados had been producing poetry, theater, and novels for decades, this was the first publication solely dedicated to its analysis and distribution. The magazine did serve the propagandistic purposes of the FLT. It was publicly affiliated to the labor federation and even shared the same physical space. Yet through its pages it aspired to promote another type of working-class sensibility, one that understood art as part of their political repertoire but could also appreciate art for art's sake. *Luz y vida*'s uniqueness did not translate into sustainability, which may also point toward a lack of interest from its idealized working-class readership. It became the only publication of its kind and had a short run of about two years, even with financial support from the FLT.

While using print media to craft these protean identities as poets, journalists, and litterateurs, workingmen used "different tactics to speak to a variety of audiences."[62] The cigarmaker Alfonso Torres argued in his book *Solidaridad* (Solidarity): "When two workingmen talk about their organizations, one worker would say to the other, I belong to the Federation of Shoemakers or whatever trade he possessed." But "when a bourgeois and a workingman talk about the same affair, the workingman would say to him, I belong to the Federation of Workingmen."[63] Speaking to multiple audiences, then, was important. That is why an obrero ilustrado like Fernando Gómez Acosta prefaced a book warning its readers about his lack of instruction but immediately proceeded to cite European intellectuals. That discursive trope highlighted the tension between distancing themselves from the laboring masses and their aspired proximity to the country's intellectual elite. Print media was not the only place where these frictions took place, but it was the means through which obreros ilustrados self-fashioned their identities and built their (material and nonmaterial) archives.[64]

Newspapers as the Barriada's Alleyways

A newspaper is a vehicle of communication among the masses. Besides being an element of moral and intellectual progress, it is an agent of combat, of struggle.
—LUZ Y VIDA, January 20, 1910

For some obreros ilustrados, newspapers were part of their everyday activism. For example, Ferrer y Ferrer's labor organizing and agitation granted him jail time on multiple occasions. He also became a famed soapbox orator, dispatched by the FLT to numerous towns across the country to promote strikes and workers' unionization. He was a member of the FLT's executive council by 1910 and became a militant member of the Socialist Party after it was established in 1915. In the meantime, Ferrer y Ferrer actively participated in the lettered barriada's expansion by publishing at least nine different newspapers in San Juan, Caguas, and Humacao.[65]

As historian David S. Struthers has noted for radical print media in Los Angeles, which was also true of working-class newspapers produced throughout the Americas, "The financial realities of publishing a newspaper included generating the funds to purchase or lease a printing press, buy ink, paper, and postage, possibly rent an office, and support financially a limited staff of maybe a few people."[66] With the notable exceptions of *Unión obrera* and *Justicia*, affiliated to the FLT and the Socialist Party respectively, most Puerto Rican labor newspapers lasted only a few months, which speaks volumes about their precarious existence. Nonetheless, the high number of newspaper titles published (at least four dozen different newspapers in the first two decades of the twentieth century) also indicates workers' persistence to spread their ideas. Through their pages, editors begged their readers and subscribers to pay their dues, for as one newspaper argued, "ink and printing materials are not free yet."[67] Some, like *El porvenir social* (The social future), had runs of three thousand copies, while others, like *Ensayo obrero*, *La miseria*, and *El pan del pobre*, eventually shifted toward single-page leaflets to offset costs.[68] In 1898, each run of one thousand leaflets would cost eight dollars, whereas in 1908, a four-page newspaper with a run of five thousand copies cost eighty dollars.[69]

While sources about the actual print process in Puerto Rico are scarce, the case of *El eco del torcedor* (The roller's echo) is quite telling. Published from 1908 to 1909 by Alfonso Torres and Julio Quiñones, it called itself the "weekly organ of Puerto Rican cigarmakers." The year the newspaper came out, there were at least 892 unionized cigarmakers in Puerto Rico; 166 of those were from San Juan, and 127 from Bayamón.[70] Ever since November 1908, *El eco del torcedor* documented the precarious conditions in which the newspaper was produced. Not only was Alfonso Torres facing libel charges, but the paper was also struggling financially.[71]

On November 9, 1908, the paper published a compelling front-cover editorial arguing in favor of acquiring its own printing press. Owning one would allow the editors to publish the newspaper without interruptions— a symptom suffered by most labor newspapers—and to reach Puerto Rico's seven thousand cigarmakers. The editorial also accused Emilio Crespo Molina, a cigarmaker from San Juan, of appropriating a former union's printing press without permission. The paper argued that it had been bought with donations of hundreds of cigarmakers and that after their union dissolved, he kept the press, which did not belong to one person but to "the cause." They were not able to retrieve the printing press, however, demonstrating some unions' vulnerability.[72]

While *El eco del torcedor* was published in the FLT's San Juan venue, after November 1908, lack of funds forced them to shut down. Two months later, they relocated to Bayamón, a "tobacco workers' stronghold," where "the generous and disinterested comrade Pedro Moreno put his typographic workshop at EL ECO DEL TORCEDOR's disposal."[73] Moreno was a self-educated workingman and had been employed as a reader in a tobacco factory. He later became a printer and opened his workshop in the town of Bayamón.[74] While financial considerations might have weighed heavily in Moreno's decision, solidarity could have done so as well. It seems very plausible that Moreno was part of Bayamón's radical cigarmakers' community. Whatever the reasons, the paper's editors celebrated the newspaper's reappearance while continuing to condemn Emilio Crespo Molina for the appropriation of the printing press. While they had to move their newspaper, they complained, "Crespo Molina's machine was rusting in his apartment." There are no existing copies of the paper after this number, suggesting its disappearance shortly after. The case of *El eco del torcedor* also highlights the battles over the ownership of printing presses and the means of knowledge production.[75]

While labor newspapers flourished throughout Puerto Rico, it was a mostly urban phenomenon. Twenty-three of the forty-one workers' newspapers I have been able to trace from 1897 to 1920 were published in San Juan. The rest came from smaller cities and towns like Caguas (four), Mayagüez (two), Bayamón (four), Arecibo (two), Ponce (one), Cataño (one), and Utuado (one). Perhaps that is why some workingmen, like those behind Arecibo's *El combate*, developed a discourse of urban spaces as civilized. According to *El combate*'s editors, who self-identified as city dwellers that studied "sociological texts," those who "do not live near cities cannot receive the influx of civilizing currents and are thus ignorant."[76]

Puerto Rico's instructional system gradually improved after 1900. Nevertheless, most adult workers had received only the most basic education, if any.[77] To some obreros ilustrados, the press became a pedagogical tool. Newspapers like *El centinela* (The sentinel) published definitions of what they called "sources to form cadres," where they explained concepts such as "socialism," "proletariat," and "politics."[78] Others also published short, easy-to-remember phrases throughout their pages and in between articles.

"The emancipation of workingmen must be the task of workingmen themselves," for example, was constantly repeated in leaflets, newspapers, and books. *Luz y vida* had a section titled "Cosas y casos" (Things and situations), where editors offered readers tidbits on how to become enlightened. Other newspapers filled their pages with short phrases by foreign intellectuals, such as Karl Marx, Piotr Kropotkin, and Francisco Ferrer i Guardia.[79]

According to a workingman whose nom de plume was Acabá de Franco, the FLT in Arecibo had served as a school to create soapbox speakers. "Even if the speakers are not that good, we do not have to import them [from San Juan] anymore to start a political or economic campaign." Franco advocated for the use of newspapers as schools because with the advancements of print media, Arecibo's labor movement now needed writers. He argued that using newspapers, the "scribblers today" would become "writers tomorrow." To do so, Franco suggested that workers study and then write their ideas, and *El combate* or any other labor newspaper would publish them. In sum, he believed that workers simply needed a desire to write, and they would become educated in the process.[80]

While Acabá de Franco imagined a far-reaching grassroots educational project through the press, most newspapers' influence was limited. Each paper had its own small group of contributors and readers, either regionally or by trade. The same way *El eco del torcedor* was the cigarmakers' print organ, *El tipógrafo* served printers, and *Unión obrera* was the FLT's newspaper until the foundation of the Socialist Party in 1915, when *Justicia* became the party's mouthpiece. Other newspapers represented political parties, such as *El Trabuco* and *La voz del obrero*, which supported the Puerto Rican Republican Party. Others, like *Voz humana*, were openly anarchist. Newspapers created a space for workers to articulate and experiment with multiple ideas, but they had a precarious existence. Books, on the other hand, allowed obreros ilustrados to deepen some of the ideas elaborated in newspaper columns. Unlike newspapers, which were ongoing economic projects, books were one-time financial affairs.

Books as the Barriada's Buildings

A book is an illuminating headlamp that attracts humanity towards a position, towards more freedom, more health, more humanity.—LUZ Y VIDA, September 30, 1909

In 1901, José Ferrer y Ferrer published a series of articles explaining why *La miseria*, a newspaper he edited with Ramón Romero Rosa, distrusted partisan politics. Under his nom de plume of Rabachol—an ode to a late nineteenth-century Italian insurrectionist anarchist—*La miseria* published a total of thirteen articles under the title of "¿Por qué no somos politicos?" (Why are we not politicians?). They also published readers' letters responding to it. A workingman from Ponce stated how influenced he was by Ferrer y Ferrer's ideas and affirmed that he was going to make copies and share them among his comrades. A few weeks later, *La miseria* announced that they had compiled all of Ferrer y Ferrer's articles into a book sold at the FLT offices in San Juan.[81] And just as in Ferrer y Ferrer's book, both forms of print media—newspapers and books—often overlapped.[82]

From 1897 to 1915, workers published dozens of books and pamphlets, and there was no clear distinction between these two formats. This would change by the 1930s, when some of the books by obrero ilustrados were published in hardcover and became lengthier, reaching hundreds of pages. The books that built the lettered barriada, however, were mostly pocket size, with an average of thirty to fifty pages, and their price ranged anywhere from one cent to a dollar. Workers sold them through the press and at rallies, union venues, or any labor-related activity. The profit generated from selling these books served various purposes. Some were sold to fund printing presses, unions, or workers' centros. Other obreros ilustrados used books as a source of income, as was the case for Luisa Capetillo.

Capetillo complained about the precarity of financially depending on her literary production through the pages of the Cuban anarchist newspaper ¡*Tierra!*: "What I have said is true, I have never charged for my propaganda [referring to public speeches]. I have sold my books and pamphlets. Now I cannot even sell them at my propaganda [events], because I get there tired with my brain disoriented from all the discussion and their diverse opinions, and as a reward they do not buy anything unless you revolutionize their workshop to get them to buy some pamphlets for 10 cents."[83] As Capetillo complained, it was almost impossible to generate a living wage from their publications. Beyond commercial considerations, these books also resembled what cultural theorist Magalí Rabasa has coined as "organic books"; that is, "a particular kind of book that doesn't necessarily act like commercial, academic, elite, private, or other books." Rather, it is an object and a practice that "is always connected to other books, other objects, other spaces, other actors."[84]

From literature to poetry, congressional proceedings to official union documents, and history to sociology, the books written by Puerto Rican workers at the turn of the century covered a wide range of topics and genres.

While most books sought to propagate what Ramón Romero Rosa identified as "labor's universal ideas" (*obrerismo universal*), when analyzed as a body of literature, difference and plurality defined them.[85] Yet two very different books, Alfonso Torres's *Solidaridad* (Solidarity) and Américo Arroyo's *Cabezas* (Heads), demonstrate how notwithstanding their disparity, these books' point of contact was not their political rhetoric but, instead, workers' intellectual and literary aspirations. That is, these books shared their authors' desire to produce and consume knowledge.

Published in 1905, *Solidaridad* was an ambitious book. Alfonso Torres, a cigarmaker who eventually became the Socialist Party's general secretary for more than two decades, stated his thesis in the cover page: "Anyone that consumes but does not produce is a thief." On that same page he also emphasized: "Any workingman and every sympathizer *must* buy this pamphlet . . . its revenues will be used to acquire a printing press, with the aim of publishing a genuinely working-class newspaper." Again, there was a recurring concern over owning the means of knowledge production, just as there was for the workingmen behind the *Eco del torcedor* newspaper.

Torres, who later developed the first clearly defined Marxist analysis in Puerto Rico in his second book, *Espíritu de clase* (1917), sought to interweave his theoretical production and his political organizing, all while trying to fund a printing press for the purposes of propaganda.[86] Beyond *Solidaridad*'s political discourse and rhetoric, dedicating various chapters to explaining how to form labor unions as well as their usefulness in bringing about revolution, Torres presented his book as a "humble work of Sociology."[87] He criticized political science, which he equated with governance, because it had maintained worker exploitation. Torres argued that three different states had emerged out of political science: absolutism, monarchy, and the republic. He proposed a "necessary fourth state" that would emerge as a contradiction and abolish itself. Besides some actual quotations from Marx in his book *Solidaridad*, this "fourth state" solution demonstrated the author's exposure to Marxist theory. Thus, the solution to "the social problem," argued Torres, could be found in the social sciences.[88]

In its disciplinary post-Enlightenment origins, the discipline of sociology as well as radical ideas like Marxism and anarchism were influenced by classical liberalism, positivism, and the rise of industrialism out of feudalism. Before its more conservative disciplinary shift in the early 1900s, sociology focused "on the amelioration of social problems."[89] This made it attractive to radicals and workers from around the world. Torres framed his book as a work of sociology thirty-seven years before the opening of the country's first social sciences academic department at the University of Puerto Rico (UPR) in 1941.[90]

Torres used sociology as a scientific framework to validate his theory on solidarity. Indeed, for the author, solidarity could be explained using science, as Russian anarchist and scientist Piotr Kropotkin had done in his book *Mutual Aid*, which Torres cited multiple times. Within a teleological historical narrative, Torres argued, "the empire of peace and love, of freedom and rights, equality and universal fraternity, will sooner or later be human redemption's creation, and realized through solidarity."[91] According to Torres, "solidarity is the product of civilized nations" and stems from workers' shared misery, which was believed to be a prerequisite for international workers' solidarity.[92] He argued, "Organization is the principle of solidarity, and solidarity has to always be the common end pursued by us."[93] In his narrative, unionization was inevitably linked to progress, as had been demonstrated by workers in revolutionary France, England, and the United States. He articulated a political discourse that aspired to transform society, but underneath was a desire to become modern. Even when workers' intellectual production had been denied access to Puerto Rico's emerging lettered city, Torres's rationalist orientation put him in tune with positivist intellectual trends elsewhere.

In 1904, a year before the publication of *Solidaridad*, Américo Arroyo Cordero, a barber from the town of Mayagüez, published his novel *Cabezas*. Similar to most of the books produced during the first decade of the twentieth century, the prologue, written by Carmelo Honoré, demonstrated workingmen's anxieties about writing. When the book was published, Honoré was a clerk from Mayagüez. He later moved to San Juan and became a lawyer.[94] In the prologue, Honoré argued, "I am but a humble workingman born in the terrible struggles for existence, without having the chance in the course of my life of having a prodigious hand to help me attain the only thing I ambition: knowledge."[95] While he recognized that a prologue should be a synthesis or summary of the work that followed, he refrained from doing so. Honoré also argued that the book might be criticized because of its literary shortcomings, but readers could not object "that what it portrays is true, and very true."[96]

Américo Arroyo Cordero used the first pages of his book to publish short fictional conversations with obreros ilustrados from around the island. All of them expressed that they were impatiently waiting for his novel. In one of these fictional exchanges, a workingman named Lacourt asked the author about the novel's publishing date, as it had received rave reviews in the Puerto Rican and US press.[97] These fictional short conversations served as a trope for the author to establish himself as an authority even before the reader set eyes on the novel's actual text. In the last of these interventions, the author's false modesty becomes evident. He asked the book's printer for his opinion. The fictional printer replied: "Do not pay attention to the envious who hope to mortify you through criticism. Pride should be your norm in this case, because *Cabezas* is a gem. In evidence there is triumph, and that is what awaits you. . . . [You should] feel big among the vain, and a Hero of your pride."[98]

Truth was a recurring theme in Arroyo Cordero's prologue. In fact, the novel's subtitle situates it in the broader naturalist literary tradition, which upheld material objectivity as one of its core tenets. The front page of Arroyo Cordero's book described it as a "Novela de corte naturalista" (Novel of naturalist style). Unlike other prominent and contemporaneous naturalist writers in Puerto Rico, such as Manuel Zeno Gandía or Juliá Ramón Marín, Arroyo Cordero used his class positionality to claim access to the truth he sought to portray in its pages. Although those elite intellectuals wrote about the miseries of the laboring masses, they were disconnected from "the truth" and "the facts" possessed by laboring people. For obreros ilustrados, no university title could substitute the knowledge granted by lived experiences. As the prologue made clear, however, Arroyo Cordero also desired to be closer to the intellectual elite. In fact, the copy I consulted for this book had a handwritten note from Arroyo Cordero to Manuel Fernández Juncos, one of the most prominent journalists and poets of his time. "To my friend and distinguished Spanish writer, don Manuel F. Juncos in evidence of fellowship [*prueba de compañerismo*]." Although I do not know if they were, in fact, friends, the note does point toward Arroyo's desire to be legible to one of the most prominent contemporaneous intellectuals.

Arroyo's novel takes place in the fictional city of Crons. It follows two labor leaders who reside in Washington, Juan Antonio and another workingman known as Trivillé. They are sent to Crons to study the conditions of the city's thousands of organized workers. Through its pages the author presents urban Puerto Rican workingmen as civilized, while reproducing xenophobic and sexist stereotypes of women and foreign non-Western cultures. While waiting in a hotel, Juan Antonio and Trivillé read in the press about "internal revolutions in Santo Domingo while Puerto Rican workingmen sought to make their revolution to conquer socio-political regeneration through their honest word."[99] Similarly, Juan Antonio and Trivillé described Siberian nations as barbaric, uncivilized, polygamous, and lawless.

What they needed in those countries, according to Arroyo Cordero, were people like the Puerto Rican lawyer José de Diego. Arroyo Cordero claimed that the reason Asian people were enslaved and rude was because women were ignorant in those nations. Puerto Ricans should follow Europe's example, where "women are men's loyal partners, and love the softest culture and the best civilization."[100] He argued, "I recognize Puerto Rican women's love for instruction; I believe so! But that instruction should be harmonized with their intellectual capacity."[101] Reproducing a patriarchal and religious logic, Arroyo Cordero understood that the role of women was to educate children so they can learn to "love and respect God and society."[102]

Toward the end of the novel, the setting moves from the city of Crons to the Puerto Rican countryside, where Arroyo Cordero describes how men searched for jobs while women lived with their children in filth. Drawing from the naturalist tradition, the author depicts a scene where two women in rags cook a poor soup and they talk about superstition, while their children play in residual water. As these poor workingwomen go about their uncivilized lives, a copy of the Qur'an lies open on a nearby table. Much like Juan Facundo Sarmiento's famous 1845 dictum, *Civilización i barbarie* (Civilization or barbarism), in Arroyo's novel, European cities symbolize progress and civilization, while the poorly educated women who read the Qur'an represent barbarism.[103] Arroyo's novel provides a vista into the ideational worlds of an obrero ilustrado who was not a labor leader. Through the novel's pages, he makes an explicit argument about workingmen's need to become more civilized and enlightened, like the inhabitants of the fictional city of Crons. By equating non-Western cultures with backwardness, Arroyo Cordero was echoing the lettered barriada's broader ethos of attaining knowledge and enlightenment to become part of the global (i.e., Western) labor community.

Reading was also imagined as crucial for attaining progress and emancipation. This became clear in acclaimed writer and FLT member José Limón de Arce's 1906 play *Redención* (Redemption). Pedro, the main character, is struck by a fever. The acquisition of knowledge is symbolized by an illness that takes over his body. After reading out loud from a book the often-used phrase "La emancipación de los trabajadores obra ha de ser de ellos mismos" (The emancipation of workingmen must be achieved by workingmen themselves), Pedro goes on to say, "It is precise, and an absolute necessity that all of us who live from our labor unite . . . and more than that, it is indispensable that I take all the knowledge of that redemptory ideal to my comrades."[104] Later in the play, Pedro becomes a labor organizer and successfully leads a heroic strike. Meanwhile, he condemns the abuse of women, vices, and wage exploitation. Limón de Arce used this fictional character to present his ideal workingman: a moralist who used education as an organizing tool.[105]

Similarly, printers Jesús María Balsac and Santiago Valle argued in their 1910 book *Revolución* (Revolution) that if workingmen wanted to "quench their thirst for knowledge" they needed to read. "Let's find light in books that enlighten; let's drink from the fountain of knowledge."[106] In *Revolución*'s prologue, Julio Aybar, the editor of *Unión obrera*, described the authors as "studious young workingmen that take advantage of their resting hours by having books in their hands to nourish their intelligence and give back that product to suffering humanity."[107] Balsac and Valle probably "stole time off their nights" by visiting the FLT's venue in the town of Mayagüez, which opened their library to its members from 8:00 to 10:00 PM. There, workers had access to, as an ad in the newspaper *Obrero libre* (Free workingman) read, "newspapers from all around the island and labor literature to relax."[108] This book collection was part of a broader network of libraries and centros created by workers in different municipalities and towns.[109]

Centros as the Barriada's Public Squares

To create a beautiful composition in verse or prose is to produce, to work like a mason, a carpenter, a blacksmith, a helper in a building's construction.
—LUZ Y VIDA, February 15, 1910

If newspapers were the barriada's alleyways and books were its buildings, then centros became its public squares, a space were bodies converged and ideas were collectively created. As early as March 6, 1898, two workingmen by the names of Esteban Rivera and Gabino Moczó used the pages of *Ensayo obrero* to argue in favor of the creation of a centro for the "intellectual emancipation of our class through learning and the social education of all of us who produce, and all of us who are society's vigor."[110] Shortly after, the editorial group behind *Ensayo obrero*—all of them FRT members at the time—opened a centro in San Juan by the name of Los Hijos de Borínquen (Borínquen's Sons). It was located at the intersection of San Justo and Luna Streets and served as a library where workers could read foreign publications and socialize. The centro's bookshelves were filled with translated works from authors like Piotr Kropotkin (*The Conquest of Bread; Fields, Factories, and Workshops;* and *To the Young*) and Jean Grave (*The Future Society* and *Moribund Society*), along with international newspapers.[111] Most of these books were translated in Barcelona, imported through the mail or smuggled by sailors, and then distributed in Puerto Rico through centros, newspapers, and public events.[112]

Following San Juan's centro, workingmen in Caguas opened theirs in 1902. Later, in 1905, Washington's Department of Labor donated a complete library with all the documents and books the department had published to the FLT.[113] Two years later, a group of workingmen that had been expelled from the FLT because of their affiliation with the Union Party created a centro called Círculos Obreros: Instrucción, Moralidad y Economía (Workers' Circles: Instruction, Morality, and Economy). This centro was a night school and a social space to keep workingmen away from vices like drinking and gambling. In 1910, the editors of *Luz y vida* opened their Club Ideas Nuevas (New Ideas Club). Radical cigarmakers created Once de Marzo (March eleventh) in Bayamón and Solidaridad (Solidarity) in Caguas. The latter changed its name in 1909 to Trece de Octubre (October 13) to commemorate the assassination of Spanish radical pedagogue Francisco Ferrer i Guardia and was eventually renamed Juventud Estudiosa (Studious Youth).[114]

Beyond these centros' political differences, all were rooted in the desire to attain and produce knowledge. For example, in the northern town of Arecibo, workingmen used the newspaper *El combate* to call for the opening of various centros. Acabá de Franco—who had advocated for the use of the press as a pedagogical tool—delineated how and why they needed centros in Arecibo. To start one, they needed just "a few benches, a pair of oil lamps, another pair of big chalkboards, and some books and office supplies; all of its installation should not cost more than 8 or 10 dollars." He also proposed having at least twenty-five members that pay ten cents weekly and argued that there were enough workingmen in Arecibo to open six or seven centros in various neighborhoods (La Puntilla, Guaryabal, Punta Braya, Palmarito, Playa, and Santo Domingo). Yet "the only thing needed," argued de Franco, "is good will."[115]

In de Franco's words, the purpose of having a centro in Arecibo was to "strip more comrades from vices and corruption, to better enlighten ourselves everyday toward sociological questions and its constitutive ramifications." To do so, they would have to dedicate "two hours each night to teach reading and penmanship to those that do not know how to do it, and another hour to reading socialist books and making sense of each of their paragraphs."[116] While I have not been able to confirm if de Franco succeeded in such an endeavor, the town had precedents they could draw from. For example, on January 1, 1907, workers in Arecibo inaugurated a centro called El Lazo Social (The Social Link).[117]

Centros served as a decentralized system of makeshift libraries where reading out loud exposed workers to books written by Puerto Rican and international comrades. But these centros were not exclusive to Puerto Rico. They were part of a longer and broader tradition of radical spaces that emerged in the 1870s and rhizomatically expanded throughout the Americas.[118] Deeply influenced by, and in dialogue with, members of the International Workingmen's Association (IWA), workers in Buenos Aires created the Centro de Propaganda Obrera (Workers' Propaganda Center) in 1878. While not much is known about this center, affiliated workers promoted the Russian anarchist Mikhail Bakunin's theories. Shortly after its opening, the centro members actively produced print media to propagate their ideas. In 1879, for example, the centro published a pamphlet titled *Una idea* (An idea), where they reproduced not only the IWA's principles but also the pact signed by members of the Antiauthoritarian International, a group of anarchists that had split from the IWA.[119] Other centros soon followed and created the radical fabric of Buenos Aires's cultural landscape.[120]

In Havana, the Junta de Artesanos de la Habana (Central Board of Havana's Artisans), commonly referred to as the Centro de Artesanos (Artisans' Center), opened its doors in 1883. The centro was important not only because of its labor orientation—most unions regularly used its space in Dragones 39 to meet—but also because it became a cultural hub in Havana. It was the headquarters of two widely read labor newspapers, *El obrero* (The worker) and later *El productor* (The producer).[121] Through the pages of *El productor*, centro members advised readers about incoming publications, making the centro a makeshift library and bookstore for workers to buy or simply read pamphlets. On October 6, 1887, for example, they announced that they had received the following newspapers: *Le revolté* and *Revolution cosmopolite* (France); *Humanitas* (Naples); *Freedom* (London); *Gleichect* (Vienna); *Revoltado* (Lisboa); *Acracia, El Productor*, and *El obrero* (Barcelona); *El Socialista* (Madrid); *El Socialismo* (Cadiz); and the *Labor Inquirer* and the *Leader* (United States).[122]

Organized around their bookshelves, and much like other centros across the Americas, Puerto Rican centros had tables for workers to sit around and debate, and they were decorated with red flags and pictures of foreign radical thinkers. For example, the walls of Bayamón's Once de Marzo had pictures of Piotr Kropotkin, Karl Marx, and Anselmo Lorenzo, among others. The centro in Caguas had pictures of Spanish anarchists, such as Francisco Ferrer i Guardia, Soledad Villafranca, Mateo Morral, and Fermín Salvochea. When reading or talking about these international authors, Puerto Rican workers had visual references of who they were. Centros were also night schools for workers who lacked formal education. They were self-managed pedagogical projects that provided a service the state had denied to workers in the past.

Reading and discussing foreign books and newspapers were an essential part of San Juan's Club Ideas Nuevas, founded on February 4, 1910, by the editorial group behind *Luz y vida*. The club shared the building with the FLT's national headquarters, located on San Juan's Allen Street 11. The capital city became a hub for labor unions and obreros ilustrados' knowledge production. For example, during the first decade of the twentieth century, the FLT organized mítines and cultural events in theaters, plazas, or workers' houses around the capital.[123] The Club Ideas Nuevas became a node in San Juan's cultural world of labor, and it advocated the study and discussion of ideas through rational education.

In the Club Ideas Nuevas's foundational statement, its members wrote, "This is not novel, it is simply a continuation of groups and centers that have been promoting modern ideals in Europe and America for a few years now."[124] While the club's main goal was to democratize knowledge— advocating for the creation of a library, the celebration of public meetings and literary soirees, the participation of its members in protests, and the creation of night schools—it was still highly inaccessible for most workingmen. For example, club members chose different volumes "of the best universal thinkers"; then, two or three workingmen were commissioned to study those works and write a summary to be read out loud for the benefit of other comrades. This way, they argued, "members would stay mentally active, preparing to take part in social, economic, political, or religious struggles." Yet in a highly illiterate society, reading "universal thinkers" and writing a summary, which resembled an academic paper presentation, was something not every worker could do. While sources are scarce and do not allow us to know who participated in these encounters, it seems highly unlikely that these meetings catered to people outside the small group of urban skilled workingmen behind the *Luz y vida* magazine or those affiliated with the FLT. Nonskilled workingmen and women were probably ignored and absent from these conversations.

Club Ideas Nuevas members hoped to fill its library with "the best classic and modern authors for its members' use, analysis, controversy, and study of diverse procedures, schools, principles, and ideas that are currently unraveling inside the universal (intellectual and manual) labor movement."[125] The books donated from some of the members' personal libraries are also quite telling about their intellectual interests. Rafael Alonso Torres donated the two volumes of *My Trip Around the World*, by Charles Darwin; Severo Cirino donated *El Doctor Pascal*, by Émile Zola; and Francisco R. Febres donated *El arroyo*, by Élisée Reclús. The club members were not interested in transforming knowledge but in making it accessible to others. Possessing these books might have provided cultural capital to self-educated working-men who were not supposed to be reading them. The simple act of owning these books could have been understood as a transgression. Donating them to be shared collectively also signaled the value these books had for them. They were probably imagined as civilizing tools.[126]

Contrary to other centros' open revolutionary rhetoric and aspirations, the members of Club Ideas Nuevas wanted to be cultured, educated, and civilized. They wrote in their program, "Ideas Nuevas is created to spread its beliefs amongst the (intellectual and manual) working classes." They continued, "It [the club] will always make an effort to create strong and conscious beings, capable of sustaining, governing, and dignifying themselves through the study and analysis of altruist and elevated ideas that predominate the minds of the modern world nowadays."[127] Its members envisioned the club as a vehicle to become modern, which they equated with European intellectual culture.

Knowledge was intended to move freely and not be contained in a single physical space. Instead of reading in the privacy of their homes, obreros ilustrados conceived books as mobile, and the ideas contained within their pages had to be socialized. As Epifanio Fiz Jiménez argued, centros were not only schools for its members but spaces to train orators who would go out and give daily public speeches in their town's plazas.[128] Centros, then, also served the purpose of creating leaders to excel in the production of knowledge, labor organizing, and politics.

THE COPIOUS PRINT MEDIA produced by obreros ilustrados not only created an intellectual community but also laid the foundations for labor's ideational archive, an archive of feelings, anxieties, and desires. The pages written, printed, and distributed by obreros ilustrados serve as a window to explore the multiple ways in which they fashioned their identities, crafted historical narratives, and understood their place in the colonial polity that emerged after the US occupation. It was also in newspapers, books, and centros that obreros ilustrados created solidarity campaigns, propagated their union's agendas, and began theorizing a political project that eventually led to the Socialist Party's creation.

The obreros ilustrados who wrote newspaper columns and essays, and gave fiery speeches, complained about how they lacked access to knowledge. As Ferrer y Ferrer demonstrated using the example of the carpenter's son, they believed that knowledge had been denied to them because of their class position. Since they lacked formal instruction and university titles, obreros ilustrados created and dominated their own means of knowledge production. In the process, new voices and discourses entered the public sphere through workers' print media. Nonetheless, obreros ilustrados sought to access knowledge but did not attempt to transform it. They oftentimes did not challenge but reproduced the elites' discourses and logics. In the process, they created their own set of erasures, silences, and exclusions. Furthermore, they also used print media to distance themselves from the laboring masses while claiming to speak on their behalf.

To be sure, the lettered barriada was not representative of all workers in Puerto Rico, as only a cluster of them controlled the modes of knowledge production. Print media, however, allowed for obreros ilustrados to imagine themselves as part of a global labor community. While the subjectivities created through print media took place locally, they were informed by the turn of the century's international circulation of labor ideas, cultures, and aesthetics.

CHAPTER 2. **THE WORKSHOP IS OUR HOMELAND**

Global Communities, Local Exclusions

At 1:30 PM, on December 28, 1909, Guillermo Delgado López, manager of *Luz y vida* magazine, sent a postal card from San Juan's Allen Street, 11, where both the FLT and the magazine's headquarters were located (figure 2.1). It was addressed to "Mr. M. Nettlau and/or Newspaper Freedom" at 127 Ossulston Street in London, England. Max Nettlau was a world-renowned Austrian historian and anarchist intellectual. When Delgado López sent the letter, Nettlau lived in London and was part of the editorial collective behind *Freedom*. The latter is perhaps the world's longest-running anarchist newspaper, published from 1868 until the present day. Nettlau was also an avid collector and archivist, which led him to create a network of correspondents from across the globe. In the process, he became a node inside the turn of the twentieth century's global cartography of radical ideas.[1]

The letter sent by Delgado López read: "Dear Fellow: Replying your postal card, I send in a different package, some numbers of *Luz y Vida* of different date. I hope, that you will send us by return mail, some numbers of Freedom. Happy new year wish to you."[2] In its January 20, 1910, edition, *Luz y vida* announced they had received "Freedom, revolutionary magazine from London."[3] It was through interactions like the ones between Delgado López and Nettlau that obreros ilustrados got in touch with their international peers to share books, ideas, and aspirations. During the first decade of the twentieth century, obreros ilustrados took an active role in the global circulation of labor ideas. Puerto Rican workers published articles

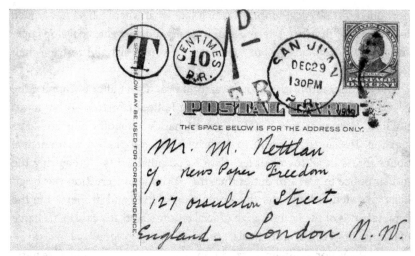

FIGURE 2.1. Guillermo Delgado López to Max Nettlau, December 29, 1906, Max Nettlau Papers. Courtesy of the International Institute of Social History, Amsterdam.

in New York City's *Cultura obrera*, exchanged publications with European anarchists, and collectively discussed newspapers coming from different parts of Latin America.

While the circulation of labor and radical ideas was global in scope, print media traveled through particular networks and circuits that were not always connected with one another. The obreros ilustrados affiliated to the FLT and the Socialist Party actively participated, often interchangeably, in at least two international circuits. One stemmed from the United States and was facilitated by the Puerto Rican labor movement's relationship to the American Federation of Labor (AFL), which granted them access to funds, publications, and labor congresses provided that they advanced their agenda. The other, broader in depth and scope, was part of the Spanish-speaking world of labor and included nodes in Barcelona, Madrid, New York City, Havana, Tampa, and Buenos Aires, among others.

Foreign publications became windows offering Puerto Rican workers a glimpse of different realities and distant nations. By participating in the international circulation of print media, obreros ilustrados were exposed to articles written by people like them who also used a language of solidarity, shared misery, and the idea of belonging to a universal labor community. By reading, distributing, and discussing local and international print media, workers started crafting a transnational subjectivity that was not dependent on physical mobility. Much like what Micol Seigel has argued for the case of Brazil, in Puerto Rico "not only did non-elites develop large-scale social imaginations, but they used them to resist and reshape their local worlds."[4]

Meanwhile, authorities kept a watchful eye. A year after occupying the island, the United States created the Insular Police of Porto Rico, but it was not until January 31, 1901, that Governor Charles Allen officially ratified its creation. The law that gave life to the insular police abolished "all municipal police forces in all towns of less than 6,000 inhabitants . . . requiring the insular police to perform duties therein."[5] Although its creation was originally intended to look after the "protection of lives and properties in the rural sections of the island," as an official report stated, it was also in charge of monitoring radical individuals, events, and publications.[6]

In 1908, Major Wilhelm Lutz, the insular police's acting chief, secretly corresponded with the governor of Puerto Rico, Regis Post, and with Graham Rice, the United States commissioner of immigration. The insular police was following a group of anarchists from the northern towns of Bayamón and Cataño. According to their report, two of the group's members were foreign agitators Manuel Escalona from Mexico and Pablo Hernández from Venezuela. The report also stated that they routinely organized meetings and that these groups received their mail through the coastal town of Cataño. Major Rice wrote: "I enclose herewith copies of anarchist publications, such as the 'Tierra y Libertad,' and 'El Rebelde,' published in Barcelona, Spain, and received here weekly."[7]

The distribution of foreign publications, such as those cited by the insular police, was neither a secret nor limited to those two newspaper titles. Puerto Rican labor newspapers published lists with the names of overseas books and newspapers received, obreros ilustrados cited them in their writings, and police officials kept them in record. Newspapers like *Rebelión* (Rebellion) from Cuba, *Verdad* (Truth) from Uruguay, *El intercontinental* (The intercontinental) from Florida, *Le temps nouveaux* (The new times) from France, and *Humanidad nueva* (New humanity) from Spain, along with other publications from around the Western world, circulated in Puerto Rico.[8]

The scholarship on early twentieth-century Puerto Rico has yet to explain how these transnational interactions took place; why workers risked police repression to read these newspapers to their comrades; and, most importantly, how foreign print media shaped workers' perceptions of self. This chapter explores how even when excluded from the conversations held by Puerto Rico's cultured elite, obreros ilustrados joined international exchanges through a global network of information anchored in the circulation of the labor press, correspondence, and the celebration of rituals, such as May Day and Labor Day. Participating in that imagined global community allowed obreros ilustrados to craft, project, and enforce the notion of an ideal worker (always male and raceless) in tune with Western rational projects and colonial logics. Ultimately, since obreros ilustrados dominated the local means of working-class knowledge production, they decided not only who got to speak but also who would be remembered.

Shortly after 1898, government officials promoted the relocation of workers from Puerto Rico to other US-dominated territories. United States officials saw Puerto Rico as a small, poor, and backward country with few natural resources. Thus, early government efforts facilitated the mobility of laborers to places such as Hawaii, Cuba, the Dominican Republic, and the US Virgin Islands.[9] Meanwhile, workers migrated to the United States in search of work, especially after 1917, when Puerto Ricans became US citizens. A small group of labor leaders had the economic privilege of visiting other countries and sharing their experiences upon their return. Luisa Capetillo traveled to Cuba, the United States, and Mexico; José Ferrer y Ferrer and Saturnino Dones took part in organizing the Dominican Republic's first labor association; and some cigarmakers from Bayamón, Utuado, and Caguas often moved between Puerto Rico, New York, and Tampa. They brought back new understandings and worldviews, which they shared through print media and mítines.[10]

The Circulation of Print Media

Reading is not enough[;] it is indispensable to digest what you read.
—LUZ Y VIDA, September 15, 1909

In the late nineteenth century, Puerto Rican labor leaders began corresponding with socialists in Spain, which was probably facilitated by Cuba and Puerto Rico being Spain's last two colonial possessions in the Americas. In Cuba, workers were highly influenced by, and in conversation with, members of the Federación Regional de Trabajadores de España (Regional Federation of Workers of Spain), which had an openly anarcho-collectivist ethos. These interactions took place through the press, particularly through two newspapers published in both Spain and Cuba with the same name but not officially related, El productor (The producer).[11]

While anarchist ideas began circulating in Puerto Rico around the 1890s, those that formed *Ensayo obrero* and later took control over the FLT corresponded with Pablo Iglesias, one of the founders of the Spanish Socialist Labor Party (PSOE; Partido Socialista Obrero Español). Pablo Iglesias was interested in the possibility of establishing a branch of the PSOE in Puerto Rico. While this never materialized, the obreros ilustrados behind *Ensayo obrero* often published articles related to the situation in Spain and sustained correspondence with socialists in the Iberian Peninsula. With the US occupation, the FLT's leadership had easier access to ideas and conversations taking place in the North.[12]

Since its foundation in June 1899, the FLT and its political arm, the Partido Obrero Socialista (Socialist Labor Party), established relations with the US-based Socialist Labor Party of America. On April 1, 1900, the FLT circulated a document among its ranks calling for the organization of an international congress on May Day: "The time has come to stretch our bonds of solidarity, union, and affection with all Puerto Rican workingmen as well as those in the American continent and Europe."[13] The obreros ilustrados behind the international congress proposed the celebration of two events: an economic forum and a socialist one. They also hoped to receive visiting comrades from the United States.[14] While sources do not allow us to identify whether the congress did in fact take place—and it seems highly unlikely—the desire to organize such an event demonstrates obreros ilustrados' yearning to emulate their international peers.[15]

Meanwhile, Puerto Rico's political and social fiber was quickly changing. On the same day the labor congress was supposed to take place, May 1, 1900, the United States ended their military government in Puerto Rico. The Foraker Act (also known as the Organic Law of 1900) came into effect, and although the president of the United States maintained the right to select the governor and his executive council, Puerto Ricans could now elect the House of Delegates' thirty-five members. As these events unraveled, workingmen were not passive observers. They wanted to take part in the island's emerging polity. Their incursion into partisan politics, however, took place not only in the political sphere but also in the streets.

During this period a group of people mostly composed of workingmen affiliated with the FRT created the Republican Party's Defense Committee, colloquially known by its detractors as the "Republican Mobs." They attacked anyone who was seen as a Republican Party enemy. Since they enjoyed a host of political connections, including the support of San Juan's Republican mayor Manuel Egozcue Cintrón (1900, 1901–3), these mobs acted with impunity. Card-carrying FLT members became recurrent targets. On multiple occasions the federation's San Juan venue was trashed and showered with bullets. For example, during the 1900 May Day celebrations, Republican Mobs attacked FLT members and effectively halted the event. The night ended with multiple shots fired at the FLT venue. Santiago Iglesias Pantín was constantly harassed; José Ferrer y Ferrer spent a month imprisoned after being beaten by a Republican police officer who argued that the labor leader had insulted him; and Ramón Romero Rosa and his daughter were attacked and severely wounded while strolling through the streets of San Juan.[16]

After facing persecution and serving time in prison, Santiago Iglesias Pantín traveled to the United States in September 1900 with hopes of formalizing the FLT's relationship with the AFL.[17] The contacts Iglesias Pantín made in the United States secured him a meeting with the AFL's president, Samuel Gompers. After talking with US President Theodore Roosevelt, Gompers gave Iglesias Pantín a charter officially affiliating the FLT to the AFL on October 14, 1901.[18] The AFL poured money, resources, and political support for workers into Puerto Rico.[19] It also granted Puerto Rican labor leaders access to new peoples and ideas. In return, Puerto Rico needed to become a colonial hub. The FLT was in charge of promoting trade unionism and advancing the AFL's program in both Puerto Rico and Cuba.[20] Yet that was not always the case. For example, the FLT's leadership promoted the creation of the Socialist Party in 1915 in conscious opposition to the AFL's stance against its unions' participation in electoral politics.[21]

After the FLT was affiliated with the AFL, some labor leaders could travel to the United States on business trips. For the AFL's Twenty-Second Annual Convention (1902), Santiago Iglesias Pantín, Eugenio Sánchez López, and Julio Aybar traveled to the city of New Orleans. According to internal FLT communications, lodging, food, and fares added up to $102.93, a hefty sum for 1902. Santiago Iglesias Pantín paid the amount with his "particular funds," along with money borrowed from the Union of Carpenters in San Juan and Ponce. The three labor leaders signed a letter that called for an immediate recollection of funds to pay back the unions.[22] Afterward, they supplied Unión obrera with official reports and communications from these conventions.[23] Although in later years Santiago Iglesias Pantín was the only Puerto Rican labor leader who traveled annually to these meetings, Unión obrera published reports from every AFL congress. Julio Aybar, Unión obrera's editor-in-chief, had firsthand experience with these international events as he had attended AFL's conventions in 1902 and 1905.[24]

Traveling outside Puerto Rico gave labor leaders new perspectives and worldviews. This was the case for Jesús María Balsac, a Mayagüez-based printer and obrero ilustrado who served as the general secretary of his town's Central Labor Union and was also a published author. In 1900, he coauthored a book titled *Revolución* (Revolution), which included a series of essays he wrote with Santiago Valle. Ten years later, Balsac published his already cited book *Unión y fuerza* (Union and strength). It was a compilation of essays, opinions, and propaganda that also displayed the author's internationalist aspirations and sensibilities.

Balsac opened *Unión y fuerza* with a common trope used by obreros ilustrados to assert their authenticity and authority as organic intellectuals; he highlighted his lack of education.[25] "The sociological works you will find in this small volume are the result of the studies we have made and we present them without any type of pretentiousness, because we are humble workingmen, which have not had the opportunity of acquiring the painstaking education we desire because of our daily labor."[26] Most of the book's chapters were dedicated to explanations and definitions of labor terms, such as "strikes," "lockouts," and "mediation." The book also reproduced the FLT's program and an essay titled "The use of *la estampilla* [tobacco stamp]," which won honorable mention at a cigarmakers' literary competition.[27]

Besides its propagandistic nature, Balsac's book also dedicated five chapters to a visit he had made to Montreal and New York. Balsac wrote about his "brief stay in [Montreal,] the King of England's beautiful countryside." There, he participated in the celebration of Labor Day. To describe the event, he used words like "superb," "imposing," "cultured," and "artistic." After braving Canada's "rough cold" for a few months—something he described in detail, as some of his readers might have never felt anything beyond Puerto Rico's warm Caribbean weather—Balsac made his way to the "upper part of the progressive city of New York."[28]

A year had gone by since Balsac had arrived in North America, and Labor Day celebrations were about to take place again, this time in New York. He described the magnitude of the event, along with spatial descriptions of Central Park, Fifth Avenue, and the subway system. Thousands of workers took to the streets representing their different trades. Two things stood out for Balsac: the participation of women and that of employers. "The pleasant presence of women always contributes to complete success, and in this event, they wore their elegance like the most beautiful flowers." Women, then, were not active participants in Balsac's narrative but, instead, became decorative elements. Employers, on the other hand, were symbols of "order

and harmony." In his descriptions, Balsac used a discourse of class concili-
ation and industrial peace—embodied in the participation of employers
in the Labor Day parade—similar to the one the FLT promoted from the
1910s onward.[29]

After listening to soapbox speeches in English, Italian, French, German,
and Russian, Balsac meticulously described the food he ate for lunch at
a Hungarian restaurant. Afterward, he made his way to "an elegant building called 'Cooper Union;' a temple of knowledge." With much "difficulty
[because of his rustic English] and using diplomacy," Balsac introduced
himself to a few comrades and picked a seat to enjoy a meeting about "Socialist Philosophy." There, libertarian socialists, anarchists, and capitalists
debated for a while before the podium was taken over by speeches alluding
to Labor Day. Balsac left the meeting at six in the evening thinking, "the
world was becoming one sole society, where everyone is simultaneously
employer and employee."[30]

Through the book's pages, Balsac promoted and propagated the FLT's
agenda and offered a window into distant countries, foods, and customs for
those readers who had never traveled outside Puerto Rico. Reading, either
individually or out loud, became a way of getting to know about people
like them who believed in the possibility of another world. It was a way of
positioning themselves within an imagined "universal labor community."
Nonetheless, these books' local propagandistic nature should not be overlooked. Labor propaganda was not mutually exclusive with obreros ilustrados' global aspirations.

There was not much direct oversight from the AFL over the FLT. Puerto
Rican organizers submitted reports during the AFL's annual congress, maintained direct communication with Gompers when pressing issues arose,
and periodically published notes and updates in the American Federationist
magazine. During the FLT's first twenty years, it struggled to keep steady
numbers. From 8,700 affiliates in 1905, it shrank to 6,300 in 1906, not making
it to five digits until 1917.[31] The situation was so alarming that Samuel Gompers wrote a letter to Santiago Iglesias Pantín asking for an explanation.[32]
Gompers wrote: "The amount expended in organizing in Porto Rico is not
the amount paid to anyone else. . . . Your attention is also called to the fact
there are now affiliated to American Federation of Labor, by charter, in Porto
Rico, but 13 (?) local unions, paying per capita tax on 387 members, when
as a matter of fact in 1904 there were 42 local unions."[33] It seemed that obreros ilustrados had been more successful in creating an intellectual community
than a mass union movement. To address the situation, in 1915 Iglesias Pantín

published a book titled *¿Quiénes somos? Organizaciones obreras* (Who are we? Labor organizations). It was to be used as a training manual. The book mixed propaganda, bylaws, and frequently asked questions.

The book had important administrative and bureaucratic information on how to form, run, and maintain unions, with specifics related to different trades. It also provided organizers with discursive tools to use when addressing workers. The core argument made by Iglesias Pantín was that only through unionization and labor organizing could workingmen create "a free, happy, and completely civilized country."[34] According to Iglesias Pantín, Puerto Rican workingmen needed to join their international peers in the modern world. "What is true and tangible is that a great part of humanity, maybe the most conscious and moral, is transforming the world intellectually with great success." And it is labor, argued Iglesias Pantín, that "is steering humanity to a new social orientation evolving through the force of reason and justice towards an organized existence."[35]

In its last two pages, *¿Quiénes somos?* provided organizers with a table summarizing what Iglesias Pantín called "global revolutionary forces." This information was made available so labor organizers could give concrete examples when addressing workers. The statistics were from June 1914. They were divided into seventeen countries and documented a total of 8,432,504 "socialist votes," 10,465,289 "unionized workers," 711 "Congress members," and 227,800 "libertarian anarchists." The only information provided about the source was that it came from "an official statistic [made] by a special London office."[36] Labor leaders, as Iglesias Pantín's book demonstrates, were trained to present their project as global. They needed to convince the rank and file that by becoming members of their local FLT-affiliated trade union, workingmen were not only striving to change their immediate reality but also joining and emulating millions of workers in the "civilized" and "moral" world.

Locally produced print media, such as Iglesias Pantín's manual or Balsac's *Unión y fuerza*, was a way of getting to know and learning about distant countries, but it was not the only one. Workers also accessed these ideas by reading foreign books and newspapers. Meanwhile, Puerto Rican obreros ilustrados locally censored, erased, and silenced those discourses that ran counter to the AFL's program. Print media was monitored by the FLT and the Socialist Party as well as by local authorities who feared the expansion of radical ideas. Nonetheless, it was not difficult for workers to get their hands on international working-class books and newspapers.

At the turn of the twentieth century, there were six active ports throughout Puerto Rico, and the docks in San Juan were the busiest. Vessels entered the capital city full of produce, manufactures, and merchandise, while dockworkers emptied incoming cargo under the blistering Caribbean sun. For example, on January 14, 1897 (a month before *Ensayo obrero*'s foundational meeting, a year before Puerto Rico's first labor union, and twenty-two years before the Russian Revolution), a group of dockworkers received a shipment that they hid from view and smuggled through San Juan's streets. Since workingmen were aware of the Spanish Civil Guard's practice of arbitrarily stopping and harassing them, one can only imagine the cold sweat trickling down the forehead of the person carrying the mysterious parcel.[37]

The package was delivered to a prearranged safe space, probably the apartment of an artisan or skilled workingman, which served as meeting space before the advent of union halls. The parcel contained anarchist, socialist, and labor-oriented ideas written, printed, and produced by workers from different parts of the world. Newspapers and pamphlets had made it all the way from Madrid, Barcelona, Buenos Aires, Havana, and New York. After opening the package, some literate workingmen read them out loud to their comrades. All incoming print media was destroyed immediately after, because, as Rafael Alonso Torres, the founder of the *Luz y vida* magazine, argued, "In any search made by police authorities, it [the parcel] would constitute evidence of pernicious materials or could initiate a process of conspiracy against any workingman or group of workingmen for trying to alter the established order."[38]

During the first decade of the twentieth century, censorship eased, and it became easier for workers to access foreign publications. Those interested could buy books and newspapers from workingmen who served as distributors or by directly subscribing to their favorite international paper. These publications were also available in workers' libraries and centros. The Cuban anarchist newspaper *¡Tierra!* became popular among Puerto Rican cigarmakers and other skilled workingmen. *¡Tierra!* became, as historian Kirwin R. Shaffer has argued, "the journalistic hub for anarchists throughout the Caribbean, serving a key communicative and financial role that linked a far-flung, fledging regional network."[39] Being 1,162 miles from Havana and located in the eastern district of Puerto Rico, Caguas was a node inside that network in part because of the town's radical cigarmakers.[40]

While sugar and coffee had been the country's leading exports, the US occupation significantly expanded tobacco production and manufacturing.

The Valley of Caguas (which also includes the town of Gurabo and parts of Aguas Buenas) had been known for the quality of its tobacco crops since Spanish colonial times.[41] Yet as North American markets and investments became a reality, tobacco export grew exponentially. Indeed, the export of tobacco in 1901 was valued at $375,000, while in 1930, it was worth $11,916,505.[42] Tobacco workshops became the first big manufacturing centers in Puerto Rico, and they also led to urban development. In the first decade of the twentieth century, at least ten tobacco-producing factories opened their doors in the eastern town of Caguas. Seven were created with US capital, while local elites owned three. As an example of tobacco production's expansion and power, the Porto Rico Leaf Tobacco Company transformed Caguas's city center when it built ten steel-reinforced cement buildings for warehouses, offices, and housing for workers. These changes triggered a migration from the countryside to the urban center, which forced the city to take a $50,000 loan to create an aqueduct and a sewer system.[43]

Although most cigarmakers did not attend schools, they created their own pedagogical and cultural projects. As previously mentioned, cigarmakers became highly educated as a result of their higher acquisitive power and the practice of having someone read to them as they worked. Thus, various obreros ilustrados came out of tobacco workshops and factories. Caguas became a hotbed for radicals, socialists, and anarchists, who forged different social, cultural, and educational projects anchored in the advancement of their utopian ideas. Some of these enlightened cigarmakers were members of Solidaridad (Solidarity), a centro in Caguas's Celis Aguilera Street. Pablo Vega Santos was one them.[44]

On June 24, 1905, Vega Santos used the pages of Cuba's ¡Tierra! to announce the birth of the Caguas newspaper Voz humana. Sketching out the paper's editorial line, Vega Santos argued: "Voz humana comes to the battlefield to preach great ideals, redemptory ideals, ideals of human improvement. . . . Without a doubt, it will have a long-lasting life because it is sheltered and sustained by a group of altruistic comrades that will selflessly fight for the cause of labor."[45] Being supported by altruistic and selfless workingmen, however, did not translate into sustainability. For example, most of Voz humana's contributors were cigarmakers.[46] In 1906, various tobacco workshops in the eastern district of Puerto Rico went on strike, demanding better salaries. Left out of work, most of the newspapers' dues-paying subscribers could not keep up with their payments. While supporting those on strike and trying to keep the presses rolling, Voz humana called for international support. On September 30, 1906, the newspaper's editors made a proposal for the open exchange of newspapers with *Tierra y libertad* (Land and freedom, Madrid), *La voz del cantero* (The stonecutter's voice, Madrid), *El porvernir del obrero* (The workingman's future, Mahón), *El proletario* (The proletarian, San Feliú de Guixols), *El productor literario* (The libertarian producer, Barcelona), and *¡Tierra!*[47]

The following month, workers in Caguas received various newspapers as part of the exchange. José Guillermo Osorio, another member of Solidaridad, sold the international newspapers among Caguas's radical community to generate some much-needed income. Osorio complained from the pages of *Voz humana* about comrades who ordered and received such publications but were not diligent with their payments. "It is through these means that I advise all of the comrades who receive the newspapers '*¡Tierra!*,' '*El productor literario*,' and '*El porvenir del obrero*,' to pay me the amount owed, because having to go to their houses two or three times to cash a miserable nickel is not working." He continued with a commonly used phrase: "I also have to let these comrades know in detail that we still have not been able to get free printing, ink, paper, and shipping."[48]

José Guillermo Osorio's complaints were not unfounded. Later that year, on December 2, 1906, Solidaridad distributed a communiqué announcing their newspaper's suspension. The lack of a printing press and scarce economic resources forced them to pause their project. Filled with optimism, the communiqué asked international comrades to continue sending newspapers "until we happily come back to the *palestra*" (a wrestling school in ancient Rome and Greece). Notwithstanding their hopefulness, arguing they would eventually succeed in acquiring "Guttenberg's admirable invention," *Voz humana* never saw the light of day again.[49]

The editorial group behind *Voz humana* was composed of a cluster of obreros ilustrados, all of whom were active in the labor movement throughout the first two decades of the twentieth century. Two of its most energetic members were the already-mentioned José Ferrer y Ferrer and Juan Vilar. The latter was a young cigarmaker who became the centro's intellectual pillar. Their venue in Caguas's Celis Aguilera Street became their base of operations. The space, which changed names multiple times (from Solidaridad to Trece de Octubre to Juventud Estudiosa), was open to the public, and its interiors were decorated with red flags and pictures of European radical intellectuals.[50] It had some rustic tables and bookshelves, an editorial office for their newspaper, and a stage to practice and present theatrical plays. Indeed, two of the most important working-class playwrights in Puerto Rico came out of this centro: Enrique Plaza and Magdaleno Gómez.[51] They also had a children's theater group called El Cuadro Rojo de Niñas (Red Girls' Cadre). While *Voz humana* lasted only one year (1905–6), the centro kept running until at least 1911. Solidaridad's editorial group later published other newspapers, such as *La humanidad libre* (Free humanity), *Adelante* (Onward), and *Avante* (Forward).[52]

Influenced by the ideas of Catalan rationalist pedagogue Francisco Ferrer i Guardia, the centro offered night classes to workers. Their pedagogical program was twofold. Juan Vilar taught natural history, while reading, grammar, and math were taught by Rosa Álvarez, whenever she had free time.[53] Although a young woman was partly in charge of the centros' teaching curriculum, women were not part of its organizational structure. In tune with the labor movement's masculine ethos, women participated in Solidaridad as teachers or actresses in some of the centro-sponsored plays, but they did not occupy positions of influence.[54]

Solidaridad's group of obreros ilustrados was also part of a broader international network of knowledge and ideas. Not only did they use the Cuban anarchist press to announce the creation of *Voz humana*, but it was not uncommon for Puerto Rican workers to use the Havana-based *¡Tierra!* or New York City's *Cultura obrera* to inform their international peers about local struggles or to vent their frustrations.[55] Similarly, the communiqué announcing *Voz humana*'s culmination made its way to Max Nettlau's London office.[56] In fact, the communiqué's only known copy is part of Nettlau's massive collection located in Amsterdam's International Institute of Social History.[57] Ultimately, while print media and centros were crucial in the construction of an imagined global community, they were not the only method used. It was quite common for obreros ilustrados to take over public spaces and polish their soapbox oratory through mítines, which transformed houses, union halls, or town plazas into the lettered barriada's alleyways.

Participating in a Global Community:
Public Events and Labor Rituals

Gaze over the globe and you will find humans destroying themselves. Deep inside that struggle, nothing benefits humanity.—LUZ Y VIDA, August 30, 1909

Just as the sun started to set on Friday, August 27, 1909, at 7:00 PM, around five hundred workers and onlookers began flooding San Juan's Plaza Baldorioty. A labor mitin was about to take place. Some attendees might have wondered if the day's thunderstorms were an indicator of rain. So far this had been the rainiest August since 1899, when hurricane San Ciriaco devastated the island, and three storms had just missed Puerto Rico in previous weeks. To the ease of both mitin organizers and their public, the day's thunderstorms did not turn into precipitation. The outdoor event went on as planned.[58]

For police detective Felipe Maldonado, it was a typical night. He recounts, "I was strolling along San Francisco St. and on arriving at the Plaza Baldorioty I saw that a meeting was being held, and on getting nearer to the platform I noticed that Santiago Iglesias [Pantín] was making a very fiery speech."[59] Three other police officers were also present. Meanwhile, various obreros ilustrados—including Francisco R. Febres, Rafael Alonso Torres, Prudencio Rivera, P. Luciano, Eduardo Conde, and Eugenio Sánchez López—addressed the crowd from the tribuna (soapbox used for public speaking at mítines). The event lasted until 11:00 PM.[60]

Within two weeks, what seemed like a normal labor activity would be the subject of great controversy. The Spanish prime minister, the US chief of the Bureau of Insular Affairs, and the governor of Puerto Rico all called for an investigation into what took place that night. But why did a local, ordinary public event become a matter of foreign policy? What was discussed that evening in the tribuna might provide a partial answer. As the editors of Luz y vida commented: "The discourse made by comrade Iglesias [Pantín] raised welts amongst the Spanish reactionaries [in Puerto Rico]."[61]

In his report, Detective Maldonado noted that Iglesias Pantín "was explaining the cause of the war in Morocco which he stated was due to the Moroccains having requested higher wages, which had been refused them, and the substitution of Spanish workmen, some of which were killed by the Moroccains and this started the war."[62] Corporal Torres Quintero reported that Santiago Iglesias "cited the atrocities recently occurred in Barcelona and the shooting down of the people by the soldiers."[63] They were referring to a general strike that had started in Barcelona on July 26, 1909, to protest the arbitrary draft of soldiers to fight in Morocco, which ended up in a rebellion that was heavily repressed by the Spanish government. Puerto Rico's obreros ilustrados used the tribuna to voice their opinions, to protest, and to express solidarity with Catalan workers. After a few days, the Barcelona events became known as the Semana trágica (Tragic Week) and acquired global dimensions.[64]

Liberal, labor, and radical newspapers around the world condemned the Spanish government's repressive actions. Spain's prime minister, Antonio Maura y Montaner, a man of letters who was a member and later president of the Royal Spanish Academy, understood the importance of public opinion and wanted to shape his government's image on the international stage.[65] On September 11, 1909, Maura's government sent a cable to the United States' chief of the Bureau of Insular Affairs complaining about "representations made to the Spanish Minister relative to a meeting held in San Juan on August 27." The Spanish government also inquired about "whether there is not a municipal regulation in San Juan that would justify the withholding of a permit for the holding of open-air meetings that are calculated to create riotous disturbance."[66] There were indeed municipal regulations, but since different political factions frequently used San Juan's public spaces, they had been a dead letter.[67]

Two months before leaving office, Governor Regis H. Post ordered an investigation into what had happened that night. The results were four police reports that confirmed that the mitin did take place but without disturbances. Contrary to Spain's claims, police officers affirmed that the meeting was neither anarchistic nor against the monarchy. According to one officer, at one point in his speech, Santiago Iglesias Pantín did make Minister Maura responsible for the repression, but he did not mention the king's name.[68]

But how did the Spanish prime minister find out about this ordinary mitin from the other side of the Atlantic Ocean? If news traveled fast, gossip did as well. Different social groups and political factions used Plaza Baldorioty to celebrate outdoor activities. The Casino Español, located on San José Street, in front of the plaza, had a balcony that offered a front-row view of these events. As the FLT's open-air mitin took place on the night of August 27, Detective Maldonado recalled, "The Casino Español's balcony was packed with people." Some of those onlookers probably did not like when Iglesias Pantín "called Spanish residents in Puerto Rico 'mantequeros,' an expression of contempt."[69] The casino not only was a cultural center for Spaniards in Puerto Rico but at times also became Spain's eyes and ears in its former colony. Unionist politician Cayetano Coll y Cuchi later recalled in his memoirs that it was there, in the casino, where he met Santiago Iglesias Pantín in 1897. Hence, Iglesias Pantín was no stranger to the club members who came to scorn him.[70]

Meanwhile, obreros ilustrados kept using print media and public events to condemn Prime Minister Maura and the repressive events taking place in the Iberian Peninsula. After the Tragic Week, five people—José Miguel Baró, Antonio Malet, Eugenio del Hoyo, Ramón Clemente, and world-renowned rationalist pedagogue Francisco Ferrer i Guardia—were detained, convicted, and sentenced. Because of Ferrer i Guardia's national and international fame, he became the Spanish government's scapegoat. On October 9, 1909, Ferrer was charged with being the rebellion's chief and mastermind. He was sentenced to death. Four days later, the Spanish government executed Ferrer i Guardia in Barcelona's Montjuich Castle.[71]

Francisco Ferrer i Guardia promoted rational education through his modern school movement. During his lifetime, eight modern schools opened in Spain, and after his death in 1909, the project expanded around the world. In Latin America, workers, radicals, and intellectuals had been building a movement based on his ideas a few years prior to his death. In Brazil, for example, workers organized several rational schools based on Ferrer i Guardia's model. In 1906, workers in Porto Alegre opened the country's first rational school named after Ferrer's friend and collaborator Élisée Reclus.[72] After Ferrer's death, the modern school movement spread widely throughout the Americas. In Cuba, for example, rational schools mushroomed in Pinar del Río, El Cobre, Sagua la Grande, Cruces, Manzanillo, Matanzas, and Havana. The same was true in Chile, Mexico, Argentina, Brazil, and the United States.[73]

A handful of Puerto Rican workers had been influenced by Ferrer i Guardia's ideas and carefully followed all the developments in Spain. When Ferrer was first arrested in 1906 for allegedly participating in an assassination attempt against the king of Spain, cigarmakers in Caguas used the pages of *Voz humana* to raise funds. A note on their front page demonstrated their international solidarity: "For Ferrer: In Paris a Ferrer Committee has been constituted to avoid a barbaric action against the founder of the Modern School and Liberal Spaniards persecuted by the reactionary ire. The address of the Ferrer Committee is: Bouisson, 11 rue des Petites-Ecuries, Paris."[74]

When news of Ferrer's death broke out, the FLT's executive committee called for an ad hoc meeting. They crafted a manifesto and an invitation to a *mitin de protesta* (protest meeting) at Plaza Baldorioty on Monday, October 18, at 7:00 PM. The FLT's manifesto was a declaration of modernist self-affirmation. Ferrer's rationalist philosophy was presented as a symbol of progress and the advancement of modern ideas. "His assassination," argued the manifesto, "was the most iniquitous and coward[ly] act ever registered in the annals of the modern world."[75] For event organizers, the ritual of martyrdom connected local participants with workers on a global scale. The manifesto read: "Today Ferrer is a monument of great universal teachings. Immortality has covered his white head with the crown of martyrdom. . . . The virile and energetic protest of the Puerto Rican people needs to emerge that night.... Human liberty deserves our most fervent enthusiasm.... Let's place a crown of siemprevivas [houseleek] over his tomb! Let us send and stretch the extent of our proletarian solidarity and fraternity through the sea of protests against the Spanish government!"[76]

A few days before the scheduled mitin de protesta was to take place, the Casino Español filed a complaint with the insular police's Colonel Hamilton. The FLT took their protest to the governor, who authorized the event, and it took place as planned. Homages to Ferrer i Guardia were not limited to San Juan. In the town of Bayamón, a street was named after the martyr. To pay their respects, the obreros ilustrados behind Arecibo's El combate used their front page to publish Ferrer i Guardia's last letters. Caguas's centro was renamed Trece de Octubre (October 13), after the day he was executed. Furthermore, on the first anniversary of Ferrer i Guardia's death, Caguas's workers took over Palmer Plaza for a "great anarchist meeting." The festive event included political speeches and revolutionary poetry, as well as a children's choir singing "Towards Progress," and the stage was later taken over by Primero de mayo, a play by the Italian anarchist Pietro Gori.[77] Puerto Rican obreros ilustrados used public actions to voice their opinions about events like Spain's Tragic Week and Ferrer i Guardia's death, as well as other atrocities committed by "dictatorial, monarchical, and republican governments throughout the world," as a May Day leaflet argued in 1912. By attending these events, workers protested their local situation but also "all of those [global] injustices" suffered by their international comrades.[78]

Most obreros ilustrados believed that the only solution to Puerto Rican workers' ignorance and backwardness was rational and secular education like the one proposed by the late Ferrer i Guardia. Jesús María Balsac wrote in his already cited book, Unión y fuerza, "Everywhere around the world, the organized proletariat marches towards civilization.... Puerto Rico is no exception.... In the past fourteen years, the advantages of unionizing were preached in cities, hills, and villages. If the results have not been abundant, it is because of the previously received education."[79] Balsac conceived unions as symbols of civilization and progress. Nonskilled workingmen, he believed, resisted unionization because they lacked adequate education.

Following that same logic, Ramón Romero Rosa—one of the lettered barriada's most prolific writers and perhaps the FLT's first ideologue—published a book titled Musarañas (Musings) in 1904. Its subtitle summarized his opinion: "Brief Treatise about Certain Worries and Customs that Are Obstacles for Puerto Rican Workers' Understanding of Universal Labor's Redeeming Ideals." Like most obreros ilustrados, Romero Rosa understood the term "universal" as a synonym for Western civilization. For him, people's intelligence was the product of their social surroundings. Like the Genevan philosopher Jean-Jacques Rousseau, who was well known among the lettered barriada dwellers, Romero Rosa believed that no one was born good or bad. He argued, "We owe everything to the environment created by this hypocrite and immoral society, based on injustice and pillage, and extends to poverty and misery."[80] In his opinion, it was religion that made people accept such conditions.

Women, Romero Rosa believed, were more susceptible to superstition and religious indoctrination. Since workingmen received their first and sometimes only education from their mothers at home, Rosa argued that women perpetuated the social cycle of ignorance. He wrote, "Having their brains filled with such ridicule and fatal concerns, it is not possible for a country to walk towards the path of economic emancipation, which is the only way of establishing happiness and joy in this world." But women were not the only thing Romero Rosa associated with ignorance; he did the same with blackness.[81]

According to Romero Rosa, after the Spanish exterminated the island's indigenous population, they imported "the poor [African] Black who was living in crass ignorance." He continued: "It is known that countries that live in ignorance only produce stupidity. Everything that the wretched African black brain produces has to be the daughter of fraud." In ignorance and superstition, Romero Rosa argued, "The white [man] was our father. The Black [woman] was our mother."[82] By equating blackness and womanhood with ignorance, Romero Rosa was producing not a deviant narrative but a prevalent discourse that permeated obreros ilustrados' literary and intellectual production.[83]

The racial logics articulated by Ramón Romero Rosa were complicated and porous. In 1901, three years before he published *Musarañas*, Romero Rosa used the pages of his newspaper *La miseria* to attack the blatant racism of Ramón de Castro Rivera, a white Spaniard from Ponce who advocated for the use of labor migration to whiten the island. Romero Rosa argued that enslaved Africans constituted Puerto Rico's first workforce, which produced all the wealth now enjoyed by the white bourgeoisie. "Now Ramón de Castro Rivera can see, as all the white bourgeois criminals can see," argued Romero Rosa with bitter irony, "it was the blood of the Black [worker] that is not needed anymore, that created all of the wealth enjoyed by yesterday's expropriating bourgeois and the present-day bourgeois hoarder."[84]

A few days later, Eduardo Conde, another obrero ilustrado, also used the pages of La miseria to attack Castro Rivera's racism. He published a satirical piece titled "A Niño Ramón Rivera" (To child Ramón Rivera). Using a rhetorical style that would become a literary trend decades later, he wrote the piece phonetically to resemble how Black people, according to Conde, talked in early twentieth-century Puerto Rico. "Oye, branco fasificao, branco a ra fuesa ¿porqué tu quere la epusion de nosoto? Que daño temo echo si e beda que abemo negro sinvergüenza tambien ai branco (como tu) ma canna I sinvergüenza que cuaquiera de nosoto" (Hey, false white, white by force, why do you want to expulse us? What have we done to you [?] if it's true that there are scoundrel Blacks, there are whites (like you) more scoundrel than any of us).[85]

Ramón Romero Rosa's and Eduardo Conde's positionalities were vastly complex as well. The surviving pictures of both labor leaders leave much to the imagination, as they can be read as phenotypically white or at least non-Black. Yet Conde signed this text as "Er nego Conde" (the Black Conde). Perhaps it was a play on words, as it could signify "the Black Count," or simply a race-conscious self-identification. Since they did not leave any written record about how they understood their identities beyond the overarching "worker" category, it is up for interpretation. The 1920 census identified Eduardo Conde as white, yet the above cited texts are part of an anthology of Black Puerto Rican literature edited by the playwright Roberto Ramos Perea.[86]

Beyond a critique of Ramón de Castro Rivera's racism, these obreros ilustrados also shared an understanding about certain traits they associated with blackness. Conde mockingly argued that even Castro Rivera had some African ancestry. He used a popular saying, "poque en Puertorico el que no tiene 'ringa' tiene 'manringa'" (because in Puerto Rico, those who do not have tinga, have mandinga). He continued, "Quiere conbenserte de que tu ere un nego? Cuando alla un baire re bomba asecateta a oí y me rejo cota ra cabesa si a pimé repiqueteo, no te enpiesa a bairá la piena" (Do you want to convince yourself that you're Black? When there's a bomba dance, get close and listen, and I'll let someone cut my head if at the first rattling your leg doesn't start dancing).[87]

Eduardo Conde was reproducing a logic shared by the country's elites. blackness was equated with the performance of Africanness, which they tied to what they considered sensual dancing and rhythms. Thus, it is in this context that we need to read Romero Rosa's Musarañas. Romero Rosa had not become in three years that which he criticized in "the criminal white bourgeoisie." Toward the end of Romero Rosa's 1901 article criticizing Castro Rivera, he mentioned something that would be consistent throughout his vast intellectual production: "The Black enriched the country through slavery, and they were denied the bread of instruction."[88] By equating education and instruction with enlightenment and Western modernity, Romero Rosa rendered blackness as foreign and as something that needed to be eradicated from the Puerto Rican laboring masses if they were to become civilized. Rational education would facilitate this by de-Africanizing Puerto Rican workingmen. Through this logic, obreros ilustrados enacted many layers of exclusion and silencing. But the erasure of blackness was not necessarily tied to Black bodies, as some were allowed participation in different echelons of the FLT and later the Socialist Party.

Instead, obreros ilustrados affiliated with those labor organizations silenced any racial discourse as well as the histories of those who partook in practices that were racialized as Black and thus coded as backward, uncivilized, and foreign. Ironically, for some obreros ilustrados who reproduced such logic, this meant participating in an intellectual project that rendered them invisible and outside history. Such was the case of Juan Vilar, who suffered at least two exclusions. On the one hand, he perpetuated the silencing of race in his intellectual work, which did not challenge but instead complemented the discursive tropes that erased people like him—a Black workingman—from Puerto Rican labor history. On the other, his anarchist politics made him a persona non grata in the labor organizations he was affiliated with and that eventually dominated the historical production of working-class narratives.

Rational Education: A Local Project with Global Aspirations

Sciences have become the fountain, the origin, or the point of departure to obtain all the secrets and all the mysteries hidden from the thinking mind for centuries.
—LUZ Y VIDA, December 13, 1909

In 1915, the annual celebration of May Day was cut short in the town of Caguas. At around 10:00 AM, Juan Vilar passed away. He was a widely respected working-class philosopher, rational pedagogue, and anarchist agitator. He had become involved in radical politics at an early age. When he was fourteen, in 1902, he joined José Ferrer y Ferrer and other radicals to establish his hometown's first centro. Three years later, he organized solidarity actions with agricultural workingmen on strike in southern Puerto

Rico. By 1906, he was a founding member of Caguas's longest running centro, Solidaridad.[89]

Juan Vilar's lungs surrendered to tuberculosis at the age of twenty-seven. As soon as the news broke out, dozens of people began making their way to his house to bid their last farewell. The following day, Vilar's funeral procession made its way to the town's necropolis, and the crowd marched to the tune of "La Marseillaise," the French national anthem, whose music the FLT appropriated for their own labor anthem.[90] True to Vilar's political inclinations, the event was closer to a public meeting or demonstration than to a funeral. Seven working-class speakers talked at length about Vilar's life and the need for people to emulate his work. One of his mentors, the Black printer José Ferrer y Ferrer, reminded those in attendance what Vilar had fought for: "A society without bosses, without slaves, without gods, without armies, without laws, without punishment, and without ignorance or hunger."[91]

Besides labor organizing, Vilar wrote many newspaper articles that can be traced throughout the Puerto Rican labor press. He also published several books of which there are no surviving copies.[92] Although there is no evidence that he ever traveled outside Puerto Rico, he was a truly cosmopolitan thinker, who theorized about France and London's "glacial nights and sumptuous streets." Vilar often cited philosophers, scientists, historians, sociologists, and radical thinkers including Socrates, Galileo, Jan Hus, Giordano Bruno, Emilio Castelar, Victor Hugo, Émile Zola, Francisco Ferrer i Guardia, Diogenes, Reclus, Louise Michel, Georg Büchner, and Carlos Malato, among others.[93]

In August 1911, Vilar compiled a 150-page book titled *Los sucesos de Caguas* (The events of Caguas). It documented the incidents of March 11, 1911, when the police burst into Caguas's centro after one of its members, Ventura Grillo, shot and killed two businessmen to avenge a defeated cigarmakers' strike. When journalists and police officers informed Grillo, behind bars, of his victims' passing, he shrugged his shoulders. The press portrayed Grillo as deranged. One newspaper called him a "human wild beast."[94] Santiago Iglesias Pantín, speaking on behalf of the FLT, told the *New York Call* that Grillo was mentally unstable, yet recognized that he had acted out of desperation.[95] When police officers seized Caguas's centro, they found pictures of Francisco Ferrer i Guardia, his wife, Soledad Villafranca, and Mateo Morral.[96] The police arrested thirty-four workingmen, framed as part of an anarchist scheme, and shut down their centro temporarily. Only Grillo and Vilar were convicted.[97]

Vilar was considered the centro's main organizer and was charged with running the conspiracy. When those charges were dropped, he was accused and sentenced for violating public morality because of two articles he had published in *Voz humana*.[98] Vilar became gravely ill and served part of his two-year sentence in the prison's infirmary. He had grown weak and could not rejoin the tobacco workshop where he had earned a living. Out of desperation, he wrote a series of public letters to the FLT's president Santiago Iglesias Pantín that were reproduced on the front pages of the labor newspaper *Unión obrera*. He reminded Iglesias Pantín about his militancy and loyalty to the FLT and asked for an explanation as to why he was being denied any support when he needed it the most.[99] Neither prison nor illness stopped Vilar's intellectual production. Although there are no surviving copies of his book *Los sucesos de Caguas*, Pedro Rosa, one of the centro's teaching assistants and a member of Vilar's group Juventud Estudiosa (Studious Youth), wrote about it in *Unión obrera*:

> Workingmen and altruists have to buy *Los sucesos de Caguas*, which will serve as a torch to illuminate the redeeming future of justice- and freedom-seeking humanity. Progressive men need to acquire this very interesting book that will bring to their homes the memories of those sad days that are worthy of being known and engraved in the annals of labor history. *Los sucesos de Caguas* should not be absent in any proletarian home because it teaches many scientific and humane things. *Los sucesos de Caguas* is the integral account of events that disgrace and stain civilization. That is why I invite every intellectual skilled workingmen to give his opinion on such an important book when it comes out. Its author will yield any necessary vindicating light and will not omit any detail so the book will have all the features of cultured and rational literature.[100]

Pedro Rosa targeted "intellectual skilled workingmen" and urged them to read and comment on the book. The text was not only a historical source, or a history-making document, but also worthy of being called "cultured and rational literature." More than journalistic reporting on sensationalist events, the book was considered a piece of literature in its own right. In that sense, it could sit next to the books of Charles Darwin or Élisee Reclus in any working-class centro. Claiming culture and rationality was perhaps another way to assert workingmen's proximity to the island's intellectual elite. The book documented how the state and the police turned against the Juventud Estudiosa and thus against civilization. But more importantly, by buying a copy, those living in proletarian homes could access scientific and rational ideas produced by workingmen themselves.

The centro that was raided in Caguas and that was at the center of Vilar's book did not have the prominence of the Ateneo Puertorriqueño or the Casino Español, but its members also imagined themselves as part of a vibrant yet alternative intellectual community. From the pages of the Cuban anarchist newspaper ¡Tierra!, Luisa Capetillo reported that others in Puerto Rico had been influenced by the events in Caguas. Far from being startled by the state's repressive response, Capetillo affirmed, "this unprecedented case will serve as a stimulus for other social study centers to appear throughout the island."[101]

Capetillo also announced that workers in San Juan were going to open another centro by the name of Luz, Más Luz (Light, More Light). According to her, the centro's motto would be: "The problem of misery will be resolved through anarchy: by which means? Through education and instruction in our anarchist philosophical centers that will make men freer, and will teach him to know his rights, educating his will and his energies."[102] I have not been able to confirm if Capetillo's centro became a reality. Nonetheless, Pedro Rosa's review of Vilar's book was in conversation with Capetillo's aims and ethos. Thus, Rosa's comments can be read not only as an advertisement but also as an affirmation of workers' literary production as cultured and its writers and readers as modern and civilized. That desire beat deep in Vilar's overall intellectual production.

It seems that because of Vilar's radical politics, the obreros ilustrados affiliated with the FLT or the Socialist Party—whose records and collections set the foundations for later Puerto Rican labor historiography—had no desire to archive or store Vilar's books for future consultation and history marking. The titles of the books that have disappeared are quite telling about Vilar's longing to participate in contemporaneous international conversations about rationality, ethics, and social reform: Ética social (Social ethic) and Racionalismo científico (Scientific rationalism). Vilar's sole surviving book, Páginas libres (Free pages), published in 1914, offers a window into the ideas he promoted in Caguas's centro.[103] The book's title pointed toward Vilar's anarchist tendencies and could have also been a subtle tribute to the Peruvian anarchist Manuel González Prada, who had published a book with the same name in 1894.[104]

Juan Vilar considered himself a disciple of Francisco Ferrer i Guardia's pedagogical philosophy.[105] Even though a proper modern school was never established in Puerto Rico, Vilar echoed Ferrer's ideas in Caguas's centro.

In *Páginas libre*, he emphasized the need for rational education among children and adolescents, while also arguing that adults should aspire to educate themselves to become modern men. "Education should not be pagan, nor Christian, nor deistic, nor spiritualist, education should be humane, cultured, [and] scientific."[106] In Vilar's understanding, this type of education aspired to create a "new Man" who would "be the spark of thought that will sustain progress and civilization." Failing to embrace such ideas would create what he called "ex-Men"—that is, those men that had vices, did not study, and did not associate (i.e., unionize) with other workingmen.[107]

In his book, Vilar argued that countries with strong spiritual traditions, like China or India, were more prone to ignorance. Science and the arts had flourished in Rome, Greece, and Carthage, but Vilar believed that they eventually declined because they all based their education in theology. Times were changing, however, and all the political rights that workingmen now enjoyed in the United States were possible because of secularism, inherited, according to Vilar, from France. Thus, in Vilar's understanding, Eastern cultures were superstitious, spiritual, and barbaric, while "secular" Western countries were the symbol of progress and civilization.

Because Puerto Rico's working classes lived in misery, Vilar believed that people did not want to be in solidarity with each other. Thus, "this country will never be prosperous, big, and progressive."[108] For Vilar, in Puerto Rico the social revolution could not be limited to the political and economic spheres. "Economic, political, and social transformation would not be a reality without the conquest of life." Only by dreaming, loving, and producing ideas could workingmen "revolutionize human thought and proclaim: EQUALITY AND LIBERTY!"[109] Vilar's utopian dreams of revolution were rooted in intellectual activity rather than solely in the realm of politics.

Juan Vilar's call for equality did not challenge the labor movement's patriarchal ethos. As historian Eileen Suárez Findlay has argued, "Many radical twentieth-century workingmen attempted to preserve some form of male-defined social order in Puerto Rico, even as they defended women's rights to equal pay, suffrage, and freedom from sexual harassment."[110] Much like the broader labor movement's intellectual production, women entered Vilar's pages as just mothers, naïve teenagers, or envious co-workers or as lacking their mental faculties. In his pedagogical vision, it was women's role to nurture and educate children in the realm of emotions, while men would take care of scientific instruction. Since he equated science with progress and civilization, his portrayal of women can be read as backward and childlike—that is, in need of guidance and education.

Even though Juan Vilar was himself a Black workingman, in *Páginas libres* and in his articles in the press, there is not a single mention of race. Even when he did mention slavery, he used it as a deracialized category. "There are internal and external slaves; the former belong to the realm [of] ideas and the latter to physical matter. He who moans in a cell is not free, [as] matter is imprisoned. He who is dogmatic has his thoughts enslaved." While he differentiated between material and ideological slavery, none was related or linked to race. He went further: "Divine slavery is the worst of all slaveries."[111] By positioning slavery in the ideological realm and arguing that the only way to break free from slavery is through progress, reason, hygiene, and civilization, Juan Vilar reproduced a Westernized positivist logic that sought to de-Africanize the labor movement. Obreros ilustrados like Vilar also reproduced the elite's perceptions of rural workingmen as too lazy, sensual, and superstitious—traits they associated with blackness. For the laboring masses "to join the concert of advanced nations," obreros ilustrados needed to promote rational ideas that would civilize (and whiten) the laboring masses.[112]

In the preface to *Páginas libres*, Diego Vázquez attested to Vilar's popularity among the working classes. He argued that there were "various literary works from this young socialist writer who is pretty well known in the genre that he nurtures because of the intense love he [Vilar] professes to his cause and his regular collaboration in the press."[113] A few years after Vilar's death, however, one of his pupils painted a different picture. Juan S. Márcano, a cigarmaker from Caguas, wrote in his 1919 book *Páginas rojas* (Red pages), "Here I am over your sacred dwelling, where you rest forever, forgotten by everyone but me, your disciple always remembers you."[114] After Juan Vilar's death, his name was forgotten.

Vilar took part in the creation of a discourse—and an archive—that had no space for him. He was an anarchist at a moment when the FLT promoted a depoliticized trade-unionist stance. Juan Vilar was also Black, at a moment when labor organizations (and their cadre of intellectuals) crafted and promoted a raceless (yet anti-Black) discourse. As historian María del Carmen Baerga has noted, ever since its early days, the FLT considered any discourse fixed on race, nationality, or gender as disruptive to unionization efforts.[115] It is no surprise, then, that the obreros ilustrados behind this labor organization sought to downplay those discourses in their writing and print media. Those silences also permeated workingmen's historical production and not only had power in the moment in which they were produced but still shape our historical understanding of the period.

Although Vilar did not leave any written record on his ideas about race, he might not have repudiated his blackness. In turn-of-the-twentieth-century Puerto Rico, workers, artisans, and even elite intellectuals oftentimes coded their references to race. While not explicitly mentioning it, they spoke about morality, sexuality, and honor through racialized understandings. Furthermore, many Puerto Ricans engaged in what anthropologist Isar Godreau identifies as "slippery semantics." That is, people used different racial markers and categories in everyday interactions, often interchangeably and in the same conversation. This created "classificatory practices [that] are not consistently or permanently verbalized as pertaining to fixed racial identities."[116] Being attentive to the fluidity of racial identifiers adds another layer to the already complicated task of knowledge archaeology in (nonmaterial) archives that actively silenced blackness.

It might be possible that Vilar aspired to create a de-Africanized and "dignified" Blackness rooted in contemporaneous perceptions of respectability. That was the case for other FLT members, like Mateo Pérez Sanjurjo. He was a Black agricultural worker-turned-landowner who dedicated his political life to the FLT and the Socialist Party. He propagated the FLT agenda in the eastern countryside by acting as a labor negotiator with other landowners and putting financial resources, cars, and horses at the FLT's service during strikes. In 1914, Pérez Sanjurjo unsuccessfully ran for mayor of Loiza through the Partido Obrero Insular (Insular Labor Party), accruing only fourteen votes. In the process, he befriended many powerful labor leaders, like Santiago Iglesias Pantín, who referred to him as *el gran Mateo* (the great Mateo).[117]

Pérez Sanjurjo did not leave any written record because he never learned how to read or write. In fact, the only things we know about Pérez Sanjurjo are from an unpublished oral history interview conducted by the late labor historian Kenneth Lugo del Toro (or one of his students) in the 1970s.[118] In the interview, Pérez Sanjurjo proudly referred to himself as a *negro parejero* (sassy Black) to explain how he negotiated with landowners during strikes. He also mentioned that he used clothes to transgress the era's racial stereotypes and to show off his economic success. He recalled, "There are times when I do not have anything to eat but I always have extra suits and shoes. People usually think that I have a laundromat because I have a different suit for every day."[119] Being well dressed was a constant source of anxiety for labor leaders. For example, Ramón Romero Rosa wrote about how after being elected to Puerto Rico's House of Delegates, he was mocked for not having appropriate clothing.[120] Articulating a respectability discourse, Pérez Sanjurjo recalled, "I was Black, but I was always well dressed."[121]

Just like Juan Vilar, Pérez Sanjurjo gave his life to labor organizations that erased him from the narratives its obreros ilustrados created of the movement. Perhaps it was because he was proud of being a negro parejero at a moment when the island's leading labor federation silenced any racial discourse among its intellectual ranks. Although he was wealthy and well dressed—two socially respectable traits—he was still Black, unskilled, and illiterate, which rendered him invisible within the archive of puertorriqueñidad and labor's ideational archive.

DURING THE FIRST DECADES of the twentieth century, obreros ilustrados actively participated in international conversations. These interventions took place through the circulation of print media and their participation in Puerto Rico's lettered barriada. In fact, in the first two decades of the twentieth century, the FLT seems to have had more success in creating an intellectual community (that produced discourses, historical narratives, and archives) than in building and sustaining a mass movement. After 1905, the FLT's numbers went down, and it was not until the following decades that they increased, although not substantially. Nonetheless, working-class histories of the period are often equated with the FLT, an important reminder of how much transhistorical power the archive that obreros ilustrados created still holds.

Obreros ilustrados participated in two broader international circuits. One was through the AFL in the United States and the other was a larger network of Spanish-speaking intellectual communities in Europe, the United States, the Caribbean, and Latin America. During this period, however, other vibrant networks and circuits were also being forged in the region. For example, Black Internationalism and Garveyism were attracting members throughout the Caribbean, and discourses of *antillanismo* magnetized intellectuals as a possible counterforce to US imperialism.[122] "Despite its middle-class leadership," historian Ashley Farmer notes, "Garveyism was a working-class movement"; workers were critical to its success.[123] Thus, it is very possible that some obreros ilustrados participated in these circuits and conversations, or were at least aware of them as the work of historians Reinaldo Román and Paul Cruz Rosa seem to suggest.[124] What seems clear is that the FLT and the Socialist Party's leaders were not interested in promoting these ideas. They could have seen them as threats to their class-based rhetoric, and more so if they centered race, ethnicity, or anti-imperialism. Any possible interaction between rank-and-file FLT members and these ideas was erased in the historical narratives obreros ilustrados created; these ideas were cast outside labor's archives.

Although labor's intellectual project was attentive to, and influenced by, international events and conversations, it also facilitated the exclusion of people on a local level. Juan Vilar participated in an intellectual project that rendered people like him invisible in the historical record. Furthermore, the stories of people like Mateo Pérez Sanjurjo were erased because obreros ilustrados did not deem the many people like Mateo as worthy of being represented in their archive at a moment when the majority of Puerto Rican workingmen were Black, illiterate, and from nonskilled trades. Yet this is a very porous and complex process. Pérez Sanjurjo continues to be invisible, while the people of Comerío created a popular archive that was able to rescue Juana Colón (a Black illiterate labor organizer) from the lingering penumbra of historical silence.

Race was not the only marker that rendered workers invisible in the archive forged by obreros ilustrados; gender was also actively invisibilized. To decentralize the archives created by a handful of male skilled workers who imagined themselves as the interlocutors of the laboring masses, we need to be attentive to the stories of those who were silenced. Politicians, labor leaders, and obreros ilustrados were not the only people who produced knowledge in the early twentieth century. In fact, it is important to emphasize that most Puerto Ricans did not fit those categories. Workingwomen like Paca Escabí, Luisa Capetillo, and Juana Colón wandered through the lettered barriada but were never allowed to settle there.

CHAPTER 3. IN THE MARGINS OF THE MARGIN

Workingwomen and Their Struggle for Remembrance

Juana Colón, a lifelong *planchadora* (ironer) who was also known as a barrio healer, died from heart complications at the age of eighty-one on January 17, 1967.[1] She lived by herself in a small house in the barriada Cuba Libre, one of Comerío's poorest sectors.[2] As was customary among peasant families, the wake took place in her living room.[3] But this was no humble wake; hundreds of people from different social groups came to bid their last farewell. When it was time to transfer her remains to the local cemetery, around one thousand people waited in front of her house and joined the procession. Although peasants' wakes were "a representation of everything they lacked and reaffirmed their social inferiority," Juana Colón's funeral procession became a testament to the respect and affection she had earned in her community.[4]

The coffin, as she had ordered, was covered with the flag of the then-extinct Socialist Party.[5] People took turns carrying it through the streets of Comerío, where she used to address workers on top of bank walls, crates, or anything that would elevate her five-foot body over the crowd's heads.[6] A group of women walked next to the coffin and sang the Socialist Party's anthem:

> La unión nos salvará
> la unión no cederá
> atrás burgueses
> infames y traidores

que estalle la revolución
y causará gran horror
al infame explotador,
y causará gran horror
al infame explotador.

The union will save us
the union will not cede
On the backs of the bourgeoisie
infamous and traitorous
let revolution burst
and it will cause great horror
to the infamous exploiter
and it will cause great horror
to the infamous exploiter.[7]

Workers and peasants were not the only ones in attendance. Members of Comerío's civil society gave a series of speeches at her burial ground. The president of Puerto Rico's Bar Association and former resident of Comerío William Fred Santiago took the stage to remember Juana Colón's life, recalling about her militancy, "Cuando hacían falta pantalones, a Juana Colón le sobraban faldas" (When pants were needed, Juana Colón had plenty of skirts).[8] The town's mayor also talked about the need to emulate Juana's strong will and character. Other prominent citizens, like retired teacher Eliseo Guerrero and the director of the town's Civil Defense, Nicolás Malavé, honored her memory. Her coffin was lowered to her final resting place below ground to an arrangement of "La Marseillaise." Comerío's Joan of Arc, as she was commonly called, was dead. But what life had Juana Colón led? Why was the celebration of the life of an illiterate Black workingwoman such an emotive event? And if so many people honored her memory, why was her name absent from the labor movement's official histories written by obreros ilustrados?

In William Fred Santiago's book about the history of Comerío, he stated, "Juana Colón had the *carimbo* [slave mark] on her four sides. She was Black, poor, slave descendant, and illiterate."[9] As a planchadora, Juana never worked in a factory and perhaps never even joined a union, but she dedicated her life to the advancement of the labor movement, the Socialist Party, and women's suffrage. Thus, Comerío's townspeople remembered Juana Colón as one of labor's most loyal defenders. Colón's lifelong activism became powerful in oral tradition, but when labor leader Epifanio Fiz

Jiménez wrote a book documenting the history of Comerío, he did not mention her name once.[10] Fiz Jiménez's omission of Juana Colón is not an isolated case. Most of the obreros ilustrados' historical narratives silenced workingwomen's role within the broader labor movement.

Following anthropologist Michel-Rolph Trouillot, I argue that perhaps these women were "silenced not only because some narrators may have consciously chosen not to mention [them], but primarily because most writers followed the acknowledged rules of their time."[11] By speaking, writing, and theorizing, these anonymous *obreras ilustradas* (enlightened workingwomen) posed a threat to the male-controlled labor movement and working-class knowledge production. Excluded from the intellectual community created by obreros ilustrados, workingwomen used labor unions to carve out spaces and articulate their demands. Women's participation in the labor movement entailed appropriating and challenging masculine notions of what it meant to be a worker. Thus, unionization not only became a way to gain better working conditions and salaries, but also offered a space to socialize with other women, create new ideas of self-worth, and challenge early twentieth-century Puerto Rico's gender roles.

Not all workingwomen had the privilege of being remembered by their communities and then written about, either by scholars or activists. Many had anonymous lives and have been overlooked by historians. If we could access what James C. Scott has called "hidden transcripts," we might well be able to document their acts of ideological or material resistance "that takes place 'offstage,' behind direct observation of powerholders."[12] While Scott used the term "powerholders" to refer to the dominant classes, for early twentieth-century Puerto Rican workingwomen, it might also have meant their husbands, neighborhood gossipers, or the obreros ilustrados that dominated the production of historical narratives.

It is imperative to recognize the importance of those who did not leave any written record. Their "hidden" acts of resistance might have been crucial in shaping their workshop dynamics, their communities, and even the labor movement as a whole. They might have not produced any historical trace because many, like Juana Colón, did not know how to read or write. But what about literate women who wrote articles in the press, spoke at mítines, or performed in makeshift theatrical plays? They were not silent, even when some decided to publish behind pseudonyms. Moreover, even when workingwomen did not produce a concrete literary corpus, their works were scattered throughout the press, becoming a testament to the existence of women who did not stay silent but used their pens to theorize about their realities. Many of their writings and speeches were not archived, thus disappearing from the histories we have inherited.

The three women we follow in this chapter—Paca Escabí, Luisa Capetillo, and Juana Colón—challenged obreros ilustrados by speaking on their own terms and articulating their own ideas. In the process, they created multiple distinct counterarchives. By "counterarchive" I refer to an assemblage or accumulation of knowledges that have been disqualified as inadequate to their task, an assemblage of what philosopher Michel Foucault coined as "subjugated knowledges."[13] In other words, these workingwomen engaged in varying degrees of working-class knowledge creation that was not legitimized by the FLT and the Socialist Party, which dominated the production of the labor movement's historical narratives. This chapter does not aspire to "rescue" silenced workingwomen from historical oblivion and incorporate them into a working-class canon. Rather, it is an exploration into the multilevel struggles for remembrance that workingwomen waged against the master codes created by obreros ilustrados, which eventually shaped Puerto Rican labor history.

Anonymous Obreras Ilustradas

In many cases, vanity and envy serve as the basis of criticism toward people's actions and writings.—LUZ Y VIDA, September 15, 1909

As early as February 1898—five months before the US invasion and eight before the first labor federation—a workingwoman named Dominica González took the tribuna in a mitin organized by the newspaper *Ensayo obrero* in San Juan. There, she argued, "The workingman has to educate his compañeras [female comrades]. [The w]oman serves more than just in the kitchen and household duties; redemption [of society] is impossible when the woman, the mother, continues to be enslaved."[14] In González's speech, however, "workers" was a synonym for men, and their role was to "educate" women. The pages of *Ensayo obrero* and its successor, *El porvenir social,* documented women's participation in the labor movement's early days, publishing lists of "compañeras" who donated money whenever the paper collected funds.[15] Likewise, they published accounts of "feminist congresses" and unionized workingwomen activities from around the world, probably because they were aware of an emerging female readership.[16]

Although labor newspapers published articles about women, it was not until José Ferrer y Ferrer's short-lived *El pan del pobre* (1901) that some workingwomen found a space to write and publish their opinions. Only four issues of Ferrer y Ferrer's paper have survived. In its second number, published on August 31, 1901, Josefa G. de Maldonado wrote a "Workers' Manifesto" dedicated and directly addressed to her compañeras. It called for women to raise their voices "that have remained muted for way too long . . . while weak by nature, we are strong enough to demand that we are provided with the same [rights] as our husbands, sons, and brothers." Josefa's rhetoric subverted the era's male-dominated narrative of workingwomen as fragile, docile, and in need of saving.[17] Instead, she called on women to exercise their agency in the process of emancipation. "As free citizens," she continued, "if we do not fight to achieve [emancipation], we will continue to be immersed in the most atrocious misery throughout our lives."[18]

The following month, in September 1901, another woman, under the pen name R. D. de Otero, insisted that "just because we are women [that] does not mean we cannot enter the beautiful lidia [fight] of ideas." Otero stated that this was the second time she had used the press, "neither with the exaltation of a fiery writer nor with the pretension of having my vanity praised," but simply to make her voice heard. She reproduced the labor movement's narrative about the need to fight for better conditions, workers as the lever toward a new society, and the importance of unity. Her article challenged the lettered barriada's masculine ethos in at least two ways. First, as she clearly stated, she used the paper to join in the "lidia" of ideas. Recognizing that women had been excluded from the literary world that workingmen were crafting, she demanded recognition even if she did not present herself as a "fiery writer." Second, unlike Josefa G. de Maldonado, who appealed only to women, Otero made a demand for recognition that allowed her to address both compañeros and compañeras, a practice that was highly uncommon during the first two decades of the twentieth century.[19] Unfortunately, the scarcity of sources does not allow us to determine the identity, trade, or union membership of these anonymous obreras ilustradas.

A few years after the articles in *El pan del pobre*, a young Black domestic workingwoman from Mayagüez named Francisca (Paca) Escabí started publishing her ideas while also carving out a space within her FLT locale. Born in the nearby town of Cabo Rojo in 1885, she moved to Mayagüez and in 1903 married Abraham Peña, a Black lawyer who had been affiliated with the FLT since its early days, becoming one of the town's most prominent obreros ilustrados.[20] Peña eventually held many executive positions in the FLT.[21] Meanwhile, Escabí earned her living as a laundress, which was a feminized trade that took place in the countryside streams or in munici-pally assigned fountains.

Although the role of laundresses in Puerto Rican society and within the labor movement is understudied—perhaps because they did not fit the tra-ditional (masculine) category of worker that has populated Puerto Rican labor historiography, and they were rarely unionized—most laundresses were Black and had been actively organizing their guilds since at least 1876.[22] In the last decades of the nineteenth century, laundresses actively demanded the state to construct safe and sanitary public fountains and washing places. Similarly, as a wave of strikes spread throughout the island in 1895 protesting precarious economic conditions, laundresses joined the struggle. While not always successful, their organizing and mobilization show how some of these women got together to defend their interests.[23]

By 1904 Escabí was a member of Domestic Union No. 11,663—which unionized laundresses, steamers, and workers from other trades often done by women—and was already a respectable member of the island-wide labor community.[24] To celebrate that year's May Day, Printers' Union No. 422 compiled a series of writings by Puerto Rico's most celebrated obreros il-ustrados in a book titled *Páginas del obrero: Artículos para conmemorar el Primero de Mayo* (The workingman's pages: Articles to commemorate May Day). It included a three-page essay written by Paca Escabí titled "Nuestra misión" (Our mission), which opened with an epigraph from Leo Tolstoy about using the lamp given to us to illuminate others' paths. Her interven-tion called on workers to continue struggling toward their emancipation.[25]

In her essay, Escabí stressed the importance of using a class-based dis-course to improve workers' "prejudicial social situation." Widespread igno-rance, Escabí argued, had led some workers to accept the misery they lived in without questioning it. In her opinion, fighting should be done not only through labor unions but also through education. It was labor leaders' obli-gation to "educate ourselves to be able to fight with knowledge of our cause, spreading truth, and helping those comrades who are in a worse position than us." She was reproducing the logic articulated by obreros ilustrados like Juan Vilar or Jesús María Balsac about the need to spread rational educa-tion to enlighten the laboring masses. Unlike male working-class discourses, however, Escabí's contribution ended with a gendered tone, articulating a discourse of care and domesticity: "Let's fight for workers' emancipation, for universal peace, for moral peace, and the good standing of our homes, for our children's education, and to secure our society's peacefulness."[26]

Escabí's text can be read in at least two ways. She differentiated between two types of workingmen, those who had started questioning their social situation in hopes of transforming it, and those who remained ignorant and, as she argued, were in a "worse position than us." Drawing this distinction allowed Escabí to locate herself among those who possessed knowledge and were obliged to help those who did not. In other words, Escabí positioned herself within the lettered barriada. Unlike those workingwomen who published in *El pan del pobre*, Escabí wrote from a masculine perspective. She did not use a feminine noun once. Her every use of the collective "we" or "workingmen" was male gendered (*nosotros* or *trabajadores*). Even so, her use of the era's masculine language of emancipation and comradeship was strategic, as her actions and militancy subverted the movement's masculine ethos.

In 1905, the FLT scheduled their third congress to take place on May Day in Paca Escabí's hometown, Mayagüez. It was the third-largest city in Puerto Rico and an FLT stronghold. Because of a massive strike that had developed on the southern coast in the months of March through May, however, the congress was postponed to a later date.[27] It finally convened on June 18 and lasted seven days. Out of more than eighty delegates, only four women were in attendance.[28] Paca Escabí was one of them, and she made her presence felt.

Escabí was the only woman to propose resolutions, three of them, and all were approved. Her resolutions were rooted in an understanding of women's precarious conditions, both intellectually and in their workspaces, something she experienced firsthand by her positionality as a Black laundress. The first one recommended the publication of the congress's proceedings; the second pushed the FLT to promote the education of all workingwomen, whether or not they were unionized; and the third urged the executive committee to lobby for the creation of safe and sanitary public fountains for laundresses in every town and municipality. Whenever she addressed congress members, Escabí used male nouns, such as "compañeros" and "hermanos." Perhaps the use of labor's masculine language was a way of employing the power holders' rhetoric to advance her agenda. It may have been a subtle act of resistance that eluded the gender binary of her times and, thus, our historical eye.[29]

Three months after the FLT congress, in September 1905, Paca Escabí wrote an article in the Cuban anarchist newspaper *¡Tierra!*, in which she described herself as a utopian who dreamed of universal equality and solidarity. For Escabí, all the misery that Puerto Rico was living through was the fault of the United States, whom she called "the blonde invaders." She wrote: "The invaders have mocked us; they have stepped on our most tender aspirations, and they overwhelm us with heavy taxes. The American invasion of Puerto Rico has only meant division among workers, controversy in the [government] administration, moral disorder and hunger, exodus and mourning for the people."[30] Such ideas were quite radical and contrary to the FLT's official institutional position, which sought to maintain a good relationship with US officials. That might have been one of the reasons Escabí chose the Cuban newspaper to publish her opinions about the social and political situation in Puerto Rico. Perhaps she was referring to the labor movement's leadership when she wrote, "Oh, wise ignorant! If it weren't for the thieves and murderers for whom you sacrifice yourselves, you would have work to earn your bread."[31]

Paca Escabí's paper trail disappears after that 1905 article in the Cuban press. Maybe she grew disillusioned with the labor movement; perhaps she kept organizing without necessarily writing about it; or she might have become ill and moved away from union-related work. While certainty might be impossible, the third seems plausible. Four years later, in 1909, Paca Escabí died of kidney failure, leaving behind her husband, two sons, and one daughter.[32] Yet Paca Escabí's trajectory was quite uncommon. Not many women were able to become valued participants in both labor organizing and the lettered barriada. The most extraordinary example of the time was Luisa Capetillo. As far as we know, she was the only workingwoman whom her male peers considered an obrera ilustrada. She toured extensively within and outside Puerto Rico and published several books.

Luisa Capetillo and the Performance of Radicalism

You cannot maintain and defend an idea without skillful character.
—LUZ Y VIDA, August 30, 1909

Luisa Capetillo's parents migrated from Europe to the northern town of Arecibo around the mid-nineteenth century. Her father, Luis Capetillo Echevarría, was from Barcelona, and her mother, Margarita Perón, was from France. They arrived in Puerto Rico with jobs that allowed them certain social prestige. He was to manage an amusement park, and she was the governess of a wealthy family. After a couple of years, they lost their jobs and experienced downward social mobility. Luis became a laborer and Margarita a *lavandera* (laundrywoman) and planchadora. Yet they still preserved some social capital. Luis would often joke that he was a count that worked as a laborer. Margarita kept attending *tertulias* (social gatherings) in Arecibo where the elite used French as their lingua franca.[33]

As Capetillo later acknowledged in her writings, her parents influenced her greatly. They were avid readers, heavily swayed by Romanticism, and never formalized their marriage, something that might have informed her later stance on free love. Luisa Capetillo was born in the town of Arecibo on October 28, 1879. Since she was Luis and Margarita's only child, they carefully looked after young Capetillo's instruction. Her father taught her how to read and write, as well as basic arithmetic. Later, she attended a private school in Arecibo where she excelled in most of her classes.[34] Capetillo did not attend any institution of higher education, probably because of her parents' precarious economic situation. As she later wrote, "I speak with perfect comprehension of what I am saying, with a profound intuition that guides me; but I have not been able to study according to the precepts of colleges, lectures, or higher education classrooms."[35]

While lacking access to those institutions of higher learning that legitimized intellectual production, Capetillo's upbringing allowed her to craft an impressive mental library as an autodidact. As her writings attest, she devoured the works of Victor Hugo, Émile Zola, Leo Tolstoy, Paul Vigne, Piotr Kropotkin, and John Stuart Mill, among many others. Capetillo gave birth to her daughter, Manuela, in 1897 and her son Gregorio two years later. Their father was Manuel Ledesma, a wealthy man who would later become the mayor of Arecibo. Although Capetillo and Ledesma never formalized their union and eventually took separate paths, he later recognized his children and took care of them financially.[36]

Early in 1905, agricultural workingmen in Capetillo's hometown of Arecibo started protesting low wages and harsh working conditions. It was in those strikes that took place across the northern coast that Capetillo debuted as a labor organizer, something that she continued practicing intermittently until her death in 1922. The following year, in 1906, Capetillo started working as a lectora (reader) in her hometown's tobacco factories. Lectores were paid to read out loud by those working in the shop. That way, the workplace was transformed into a space for learning, debating, and imagining other worlds. Workingmen also collectively decided what was to be read, ranging from novels and poetry to political treatises and current news.[37] As Epifanio Fiz Jiménez, a cigarmaker turned politician, wrote, "Workshops became schools, and they also became universities that gave the country a great number of men that, with no more education than our public schools' elementary education, excelled in the country's official and political life."[38]

In November 1907 Luisa Capetillo published a series of short essays as her first book, *Ensayos libertarios* (Libertarian essays). Much like the anonymous obreras ilustradas who published in *El pan del pobre*, Capetillo used the cover page to dedicate her work to "comrades of both sexes."[39] Through its pages, Capetillo developed socialist and anarchist ideas similar to those of other contemporaneous Puerto Rican radical obreros ilustrados, like Venancio Cruz, Ángel María Dieppa, and Juan Vilar. After the book's publication, she dedicated most of her time to advocating for universal suffrage and women's unionization, and to writing articles in the press. These endeavors meant traveling throughout the island and abroad, leaving her children to the care of her mother, a privilege not many workingwomen enjoyed.

The following years were of great activity for Capetillo. In 1909 she participated in the FLT-sponsored Cruzada del Ideal (Crusade for the Idea), a speaking tour throughout Puerto Rico. As literary scholar Julio Ramos has argued, the Cruzada was of great importance because it brought forms of knowledge located mostly in urban spaces to the rural world.[40] In 1910, she published her second book, *La humanidad en el futuro* (Humanity in the future), and edited the magazine *La mujer* (The woman). While there are no surviving copies of her magazine, a note published by Capetillo in the Cuban anarchist newspaper *¡Tierra!* demonstrates its vast international circulation. In it, Capetillo documented that she had sent copies of *La mujer* to Argentina, Switzerland, Brazil, Chile, and California as part of a newspaper exchange.[41] In 1911, Capetillo gave birth to her third and last child, Luis, and published her book *Mi opinión sobre las libertades, derechos y deberes de las mujeres* (My opinion on the liberties, rights, and obligations of women). Her fourth and last book, *Influencias de las ideas modernas* (The influences of modern ideas) appeared in 1915, the same year the Socialist Party was created.

Some scholars consider Capetillo's third book, *Mi opinión*, to be Puerto Rico's first feminist manifesto.[42] Like Paca Escabí, Capetillo favored the education of women to make them men's equals. She wrote, "If women were conveniently enlightened, educated, and emancipated from routine formalisms, nations' politics would be very different."[43] This was not limited to conventional schooling but also included sexual education, which would allow them to have greater control over their bodies, desires, and sexualities. For example, rooted in her anarchist philosophy, Capetillo strongly advocated for free love instead of marriage.[44]

Her ideas subverted the era's gender norms and presented radical notions of love and sexuality that were far from those shared by all workingwomen. In her four books and articles in the press, Capetillo also developed a critique of social inequalities and gender oppression, as well as advocating for libertarian socialism and the organization of the working classes. While her political project was anchored in the tenets of liberal modernity, she expressed them from her own experience as a Puerto Rican workingwoman.[45]

In 1917, after Puerto Ricans became US citizens, Capetillo applied for a passport to visit the neighboring country of the Dominican Republic to, according to her application, "sell books." Although she was censored and banned from speaking publicly by the Dominican government, she nonetheless helped raise funds for the families of striking workingmen from the Federación Libre de Trabajadores de Santo Domingo (Free Federation of Workingmen of Santo Domingo). Whether she really sold books or just used that as an excuse to evade US authorities, she did share the practical knowledge acquired through years of union organizing with her Dominican comrades, and vice versa. Such exchanges of knowledge might have also taken place elsewhere, perhaps in her tours through the United States to support universal suffrage; maybe while living in New York or Ybor City, Florida; or possibly when she spent time with Cuban anarchists in Havana and Cárdenas.[46]

Across the Americas, other workingwomen merged their activism with the print word to challenge labor's patriarchal ethos. Similar to Capetillo, Uruguayan and Argentinian workingwomen, such as Virginia Bolten and Salvadora Medina Onrubia de Botana, irrupted into labor's masculine world of letters and affirmed their place in the labor movement through their writings and militancy. In 1897, a group of anarchist workingwomen from the Argentinian cities of Buenos Aires and Rosario published *La voz de la mujer* (The woman's voice). It was one of the first anarcho-feminist newspapers in the Southern Cone. Through its pages, workingwomen challenged the era's notions of female domesticity that portrayed women only as producers in the household's private sphere. These workingwomen appropriated anarchism's masculine ethos and mockingly subverted it with phrases like, "Anarquía y libertad, y las mujeres a fregar" (Anarchy and liberty, and women to do the dishes).[47]

Another contemporary of Capetillo who traveled extensively and used the pen to express her ideas was Blanca de Moncaleano. Blanca and her husband, José Francisco Moncaleano, were anarchist educators heavily influenced by the ideas of the late Francisco Ferrer i Guardia. They were expelled from Colombia in 1909 because of their anticlerical newspaper *Ravachol*. The couple moved to Cuba, where they immediately joined anarchists behind the newspaper *¡Tierra!* In 1910, shortly after their arrival in Havana, Juan traveled to Mexico to join the unfolding revolution. His militancy made him a target of state authorities that proceeded to deport him to Spain, eventually making it back to Los Angeles. Meanwhile, the Cuban anarchist community made a collection to help Blanca travel to Mexico with their three children. She arrived after Juan had been deported and was forced to be on the move with her children, this time making the trip north to Los Angeles. Once reunited, the Moncaleanos moved to El Paso, Texas, where Blanca published her newspaper *Pluma roja* (Red pen) from 1913 to 1915. In the paper, Blanca and her collaborators "placed the emancipation of women at the center of the anarchist agenda."[48]

Luisa Capetillo, Blanca Moncaleano, Virginia Bolten, and the many workingwomen who used print media to articulate their ideas were consciously creating counterarchives that had power in the moment in which they were created and still do today. Their writings sought to challenge not only society's patriarchal structures, but also the regional and local labor movements from which they were operating. Much like Puerto Rico's lettered barriada, their writings were not limited to newspapers; they also published books and pamphlets that circulated throughout the region. A piece published by Capetillo in Cuba's *¡Tierra!* also points toward an understanding that these workingwomen were in conversation with one another even if they did not know each other. "I am proud," wrote Capetillo in 1912. "I feel happy and even powerfully indomitable when I see other women in the struggle joining the scene. Emma Goldman, Francisca de Mendoza, and now I read Julia Liusudill, and all the many more that will soon join us."[49]

It is worth emphasizing how rare it was for a woman, especially a workingwoman, to publish books in early twentieth-century Puerto Rico. Most of Capetillo's books were self-edited, and some appeared under her own publishing house, Biblioteca Roja (Red Library). For a workingwoman, it is very impressive how she was able to operate a publishing house—given the perennial struggles over access to printing presses—and travel extensively. While she argued that she did not receive any economic support from Manuel Ledesma, it is still unclear how she funded her travels, publications, and other living expenses. It seems uncertain that she could generate enough income from her work as a journalist in labor newspapers, as a union organizer, or as a lectora.

Capetillo was able to garner the respect of her peers through her militancy and literary production, but that respect was contingent on not transgressing the labor movement's patriarchal ethos. On September 30, 1909, working-class literary magazine *Luz y vida* announced: "Our friend and comrade, Luisa Capetillo, has given us a copy of her edited book, *Ensayos libertarios*. It is written in an elegant style. We wish her many sales and we send our congratulations."[50] Yet there were some conditions for belonging in workers' male-dominated intellectual community. Two years after the *Luz y vida* announcement, the editors of *El tipógrafo* wrote, "Our colleague in the press, Mrs. Luisa Capetillo, is introducing a new fashion style of falda-pantalón [trousers]. On many occasions, she has walked the streets with the abovementioned suit and has been bothered countless times by clueless youngsters. Do not pay attention comrade Capetillo and continue forward, always forward, provided that you do not intrude upon men's private matters."[51] For the men behind *El tipógrafo*, Capetillo was considered a "comrade," and they encouraged her to continue wearing her trousers. Nonetheless, this did not mean that they were going to treat her as an equal. She needed to know her place and "not intrude upon men's private matters." While what they referred to as "private matters" is uncertain, they were policing a clear gender divide that she did not have access to even when they supported some of her endeavors.

In 1915, Capetillo was detained in Cuba and tried in court for "causing a scandal" for the way she was dressed.[52] In court, she told the judge that pants "were more hygienic and comfortable and were also more appropriate for women in their new role."[53] Literary scholar Teresa Peña Jordán has argued that Capetillo "combined more traditional strategies—such as the creation of clubs to support the cause of women's vote—with (micro)political acts of an impure and performative nature, such as appearing in public dressed and groomed in ways only considered suitable for men."[54]

Perhaps Capetillo's performative act was an attempt not to challenge but to navigate male-dominated spaces.[55] Following literary scholar Julio Ramos's analysis, Luisa Capetillo's suit-wearing practice can also be read as a metaphor. For Ramos, Capetillo appropriated the dominant language like a costume without being submitted to its logic, the same way she wore masculine clothing.[56] Such a metaphor could also be useful for thinking not only of Capetillo's literary production but also about how she performed masculinity and was accepted into the male-dominated lettered barriada while advocating for women's rights and liberties through her writings. As the men of *El tipógrafo* suggested, however, this acceptance was dependent on her actions not altering the labor movement's patriarchal structure. Perhaps Capetillo's strategic act was not much different from Paca Escabí's, who used the masculine language of comradeship while promoting the advancement of women's rights and education through her labor organizing.

Luisa Capetillo and Paca Escabí were not the only workingwomen writing in early twentieth-century labor newspapers. At a moment when middle-class women, such as teachers and nurses, started to mobilize around universal suffrage and civil rights, workingwomen advocated similar things from within the labor movement. Some workingwomen, like Cándida Román, Carmen Rosario, and Elena Vázquez, used the pages of *Unión obrera* to voice their opinions about the double exploitation women faced because of unremunerated household work. Others theorized about the importance of organizing and participating in general strikes. They did not call themselves feminists, but their writings demonstrate that they were keenly aware of their gender and class positionality.[57]

Workingwomen had actively participated in the organized labor movement since its early days. Yet when the Socialist Party's foundational convention took place in 1915, there was not one workingwoman among the fifty-six delegates in attendance. "Members of both sexes attended the Congress," the official proceedings pointed out, but only men had a voice in discussions.[58] Eight months after the convention, a group of women wrote in the pages of *Unión obrera*: "We understand that any socialist that opposes women's participation in all the struggles for life or anyone that denies the free development of women's faculties, or prevents them of attending workshops to earn an honest living, the Socialist that does such thing is not a Socialist, and if he is, he stops being one the moment he does such things."[59]

After the Socialist Party's consolidation, exclusions became institutionalized, and some of the most active members in the working-class community were expelled, becoming personae non grata and erased from official labor histories. Yet the labor movement and the Socialist Party also offered workingwomen a space to subvert the era's patriarchal ethos through militancy and political participation. Even though most workingwomen could not enter the male-dominated lettered barriada or the FLT's spheres of power, some went to the grave proud of having belonged to the movement. Such was the case of Juana Colón. She dedicated her life to her community and her town's labor movement. Being illiterate did not allow her to use the same strategies employed by Escabí or Capetillo; and she did not have to. She was omitted from the historical narratives produced within the lettered barriada, but Comerío's townspeople and the community she served for so long made sure her name was not forgotten.

Comerío's Joan of Arc

In any state, individuals who are not members of the families that regulate power are slaves.—LUZ Y VIDA, December 13, 1909

Juana Colón was born on March 27, 1886, in barrio Río Hondo, Sábana del Palmar, in the center-eastern region of the island. The town was founded in June 1826 and rechristened with its current name of Comerío in 1894 by a royal decree.[60] Throughout the nineteenth century, Comerío's economy gravitated around agriculture, especially coffee and tobacco.[61] Juana Colón was born a generation away from slavery, and all of her relatives—from great-grandparents to her parents—had been slaves. Her last name, Colón, was that of her family's former master, Julián Colón Rivera—a reminder of a slave past that accompanied her throughout life.[62]

At the turn of the twentieth century, women—especially Black and mulatto women—often worked in agricultural fields or were employed as servants, laundresses, or seamstresses.[63] Back then, women held various jobs, often simultaneously. In Puerto Rico, of a total female population of 480,982, only 21.3 percent (around 102,449) were employed in what the 1899 census considered "gainful occupations." Out of those, 78.4 percent of the women who worked in domestic and personal services were their household's primary breadwinners.[64]

Tobacco production had been traditionally rooted in artisanal modes of production. As new technologies were introduced in factories, most tobacco workingmen clung to the "trade's secrets" as a way of negotiating with administrators in companies whose owners did not even live in Puerto Rico.[65] As a response, factory owners hired more women into these occupations to break the monopoly men held on the craft.[66] Hence, tobacco manufacturing also radically altered Puerto Rico's household composition and the organization of labor. Although cigarmaking was a highly gendered trade, the tobacco industry was the first that allowed women to become salaried workers. They were employed mainly as stemmers and leaf classers, often generating less income than their male counterparts.[67] Women also became militant in various strikes and rallies, as well as in expanding the reach of the FLT throughout the island. Their militancy also influenced other workingwomen beyond their workshops. Juana Colón was one among those inspired.[68]

Juana Colón came of age working in a coffee plantation in Comerío. Her family labored for their former master, Julián Colón Rivera, who by 1894 owned forty *cuerdas* (acres) of coffee and tobacco, twenty acres each.[69] In nineteenth-century Puerto Rico, many agricultural workers took part in the semifeudal systems known as *agrego* or *medianero*. This meant that a landowner granted a piece of land to someone who would be in charge of farming it to supply his or her family and the landowner.[70] Juana Colón's mother, who was the head of household, probably struck a deal with Colón Rivera to work the land as *agregados* (sharecroppers). Because her family was tied to their land via contractual agreements with their landowner, Juana Colón was not remunerated for her job; it was seen as part of her familial obligation.[71] While census records frequently omitted women's participation in agriculture, they were present in the fields. Women and children took care of chickens, pigs, cows, or guineas while also helping in the farming process, all while overseeing household duties imposed by the era's patriarchal ethos.[72]

In 1903, at the age of seventeen, Juana Colón got married and left her mother's household. She moved closer to the town's urban center with her husband, José Rosario, who was a farm worker. Between the years of 1903 and 1910 she gave birth to four sons. The 1920 census identifies her living with her mother in the barrio Cielito. Although she and her husband did not share the same household, she maintained an intermittent relationship with him, giving birth to one daughter and another son. Their marriage deteriorated and became plagued with domestic violence. One of their neighbors remembered an incident when Juana Colón and her spouse were fighting. Colón went outside the house, called her husband out, picked two sticks, and gave him one. They physically attacked each other until onlookers separated them. Afterward, both were taken to the town's judge, who advised them to break off their relationship.[73] The remembrance of such actions made Colón the antithesis of the docile and domesticated mother, educator, and wife that characterized obreros ilustrados' intellectual production.

When she married, Juana Colón began earning a living as a laundress and a planchadora. She charged twelve cents for a dozen pieces of clothing. Every morning Juana arrived at the river to start her work along with other laundresses. Each woman having previously agreed to bring something to eat, they would share lunch collectively. Since factory work in tobacco manufacturing took place only three or four months a year, women that worked in tobacco factories held multiple jobs, often as laundresses or planchadoras.[74] For laundresses, their workplaces (rivers or municipal fountains) became spaces where they could get to know each other, create community, and build solidarity across trades. At noon, Juana Colón would go back home to cook for her family and those in her barrio who lacked food, spending the rest of her day ironing until five or six in the evening.[75]

Having worked since her early years, Juana Colón never attended school or learned how to read or write. Nonetheless, she possessed other types of knowledges that were not legitimized by the intellectual elite or the educational system. Throughout Comerío she was known as a *santiguadora*, or barrio healer. Her biographers have encountered many testimonies of people attesting to her medical capabilities. One of her neighbors recalled, "She was a healer, like her brother Pablo Colón (known as Mechor), she tenía el conocimiento [had the knowledge] on how to prepare potions for different illnesses, including venereal. Santiguando she was a professional."[76]

At the turn of the twentieth century, the United States sought to institutionalize medical practices to modernize and civilize the country.[77] Yet Juana Colón maintained throughout her life the tradition of using alternate medicinal methods to cure illnesses. She had a room to receive patients in her house and did not formally charge for her services, only accepting donations that did not exceed five cents. Those who could not pay brought produce from their farmlands or chickens as a way of bartering goods for services. Despite her illiteracy, her practice was legitimized by the townspeople, who consulted her or brought their children when they lacked access to doctors.

While the scarcity of sources does not allow us to look deeper into Juana Colón's spirituality and how it connected to her medical practice, she frequently treated neighbors who believed they had been hexed. In an interview, one of them told historian Wilson Torres that his daughter "was dying [from an evil eye spell] and from there we took her to [Juana Colón] at dawn, at five in the morning . . . she started to santiguarla and to pray and she locked herself in the room with the nena [girl]. And to this day, the girl is bigger than me."[78] Thus, her medical practice was not limited to the physical world but also had spiritual coordinates that were illegible to medicine's scientific approaches. In this, Juana Colón was resisting not only state-sponsored medicine but also obreros ilustrados.

Ramón Romero Rosa lashed out against religion and spirituality. He wrote that "witchcraft, spells, curses, and the evil eye, among other nonsense," are "'products' imported to Puerto Rico through the poor African's brain, brought by colonization."[79] These practices were looked down on as mere superstition and symbols of backwardness. On the contrary, for Juana Colón, santiguar may have represented a way to connect with past ancestors, to negotiate other knowledges, and to give back to her community. Whatever her reasons, it was a site of resistance against civilizing agendas from both the state and the lettered barriada.

In addition to her healing practices, Juana Colón was known for her participation in a series of strikes that took place in 1917 and 1919. Even though she had never worked in a tobacco workshop, she was remembered as one of cigarmakers' most loyal defenders. Ultimately, she became a mythical figure in the town's folklore and popular archive.

From 1917 to 1919 a series of cigarmakers' strikes shook the town of Comerío to the core. These struggles were an island-wide effort to fight against the Puerto Rican American Tobacco Company (PRATC), which was formed shortly after the 1898 US occupation.[80] The PRATC established a monopoly over Puerto Rican cigar manufacturing, which was commonly referred to as a trust. They bought local companies or fixed prices by controlling production numbers so others could not compete, leaving local factories with the option of closing operations or being incorporated into the trust. By 1909, 79 percent of all the tobacco manufactured in Puerto Rico came out of trust-owned workshops.[81]

By 1917, unionized cigarmakers declared a series of nationwide strikes against the tobacco trust and asked for better salaries and working conditions.[82] Workers from the Porto Rico Tobacco Leaf Company (PRTLC) in Comerío went on strike for thirty-nine days in the summer months of June and July. In other municipalities, the strike started later in September and officially ended on December 27.[83] While most of the demands made by cigarmakers were met (including the right to have lectores, creating funds for those ill, and allowing the creation of representative committees in each workshop), the strike was also indispensable in setting the foundations for more militant strikes in the years that followed. The eight-page document announcing the agreements and calling an end to the 1917 strikes finished with a clear message to the trust: "Struggle is less painful with bread. Let us plant the seeds in our organization that we will harvest in 1919."[84]

The collective agreement reached in 1917 was valid until December 31, 1918. On that day, the workshops owned by the PRATC unexpectedly closed, and the company said they would reopen on January 10. When that day came, workers were left out of their shop. The company had no intention of reopening and started a lockout (factory strike). The FLT organized an extraordinary assembly that called for resisting the lockout, and its members ratified it nationally through telegrams. When the company decided to open their workshops in late February, workers refused to go back to their jobs until a collective agreement had been signed.[85]

In Comerío those tensions materialized on April 8, 1919, as workers from the PRTLC went on strike. The next day, one of the factory's foremen, Juan Bautista Carmona, attacked Manuela Soto when she was walking home in the evening. Soto was a workingwoman that acted as the local strike committee's treasurer. After cursing at Soto, he took her by the neck and threatened her with a gun, saying, "You are one of the bosses of this binge of a strike, if you do not end it soon, we will finish you with gunshots."[86] He was right on two counts: women were at the forefront of the strike-organizing efforts, and the strike did end after shots were fired.

The morning after the attack on Manuela Soto, on April 10, 1919, about twenty-five workingmen and women gathered in front of the factory gates to stop anyone from entering the building. Juana Colón was one of them. Although Colón had never worked in the tobacco industry, her proximity to the town's urban center and her friendship with tobacco strippers had marked her life and politics. She befriended many female tobacco strippers and cigarmakers outside their workshops, probably in the rivers where they worked as laundresses during off-seasons.[87]

When foremen approached, striking workers and their supporters tried to convince them not to enter. Foreman Juan Bautista Carmona angrily screamed that he would bring a few scabs "and break the crisma [head] of anyone that dared to get close." As police officers arrived, onlookers also approached to see what was happening. One of the officers, José Rosado, ordered people to leave the premises, and the police immediately started to violently remove everyone. The striking workers, including Juana Colón, reacted by throwing rocks or anything they could find at the officers, who turned their guns to the crowd. As the gunshots' loud bangs were heard, people ran for their lives. Three of the companies' foremen waited on top of a hill and started shooting at workers who were fleeing for safety. Vicente Rodríguez and Cirilo García, two onlookers who were not part of the strike, died from gun wounds while others were injured. Around three hundred people participated in the incident. Fourteen people were arrested, and four of them were women, including Juana Colón.[88]

While her arrest does corroborate her participation, sources about the 1919 strike are scarce. Besides police records documenting her arrest, in

Sangrienta tragedia en Bayamón.

FIGURE 3.1. *Justo Andrade kills Adolfo Reyes Torres*, front cover image of *La correspondencia de Puerto Rico*, March 11, 1911. Courtesy of the Colección Puertorriqueña, University of Puerto Rico, Río Piedras.

which she is identified as a thirty-year-old Black woman, the only other mention of Juana Colón was in the newspaper *Unión obrera*. The paper summarized the fateful events that took place in Comerío and dedicated a few lines to her: "We are told that Juana Colón, who has been in the municipal repository for having her mental faculties a bit disturbed, was directly shot by Carmona, but she was safe, and it appears that the purpose was to cause the greatest harm to striking women."[89]

The *Unión obrera* article highlights the labor movement's conception of gender and race. First, the article written by the FLT Investigation Committee portrayed Juana Colón as lacking her mental faculties. According to historian Bianca Medina Báez, "this was a common way of describing women that did not fit traditional roles."[90] There is also an implicit racial dimension in the paper's statement, however, specifically for a santiguadora who calls on spells and power beyond contemporaneous rational understandings. For example, after Ventura Grillo was arrested in Caguas for killing his boss on March 11, 1911, the press portrayed him as a deranged lunatic. Similarly, a day earlier, a workingman by the name of Justo Andrade had killed the radical labor leader Adolfo Reyes Torres in the town of Bayamón (figure 3.1). Reyes Torres had publicly called Andrade a rompe huelga (scab). According to some, this was the reason behind the assassination. Afterward, *La correspondencia de Puerto Rico* reported that Reyes "was white, cigarmaker, of about 25 to 28 years of age, and has always observed good behavior." On the other hand, they portrayed Justo Andrade as "tall, of color, of about 30 to 40 years of age, of quarrelsome character, and has been indicted on various occasions for aggression."[91] In sum, the press portrayed Reyes with traits associated with whiteness: honorable, with no police record, and a noble defender of his class. Justo Andrade, on the contrary, was presented as a Black rompe huelga, a troublemaker, with multiple charges of aggression. Both Grillo and Andrade, who were Black males, were depicted in the press as lacking their mental faculties.

The FLT Investigation Committee's note about Juana Colón sheds light on another important aspect of gender dynamics. It argued that women were targeted by foremen in the 1919 strike, as had happened to Manuela Soto. Female participation in the labor market had increased since the turn of the century. Yet women's work outside the household was still seen as a transgression for some men, who felt that they were disrupting the patriarchal home structure. As the editors of the newspaper *La federación obrera* (Labor federation) warned, if women continued leaving the house to work, "Where would we, the fathers who are head of families, end up?"[92]

After the 1919 strike, the townspeople started calling Juana Colón Comerío's Joan of Arc. The nickname highlighted Juana's daring audacity to put her body on the line for her cigarmaking comrades even when she did not work in the tobacco industry. But it also had undertones that emphasized her mental health. After all, Joan of Arc—who, like Capetillo, dressed as a man—was a heroine and a brave fighter, but she also had visions and heard voices.

The strike also launched Juana Colón into local politics. She was part of the Fundadores de la Primera Sección Socialista de Comerío (Founders of Comerío's First Socialist Section), which established the party's local branch. She also became a member of other socialist organizations, such as La fraternidad obrera de Comerío (Comerío's Labor Fraternity) and the Templo del trabajo de la sección socialista no. 36 de Comerío (Labor Temple of Comerío's Socialist Section No. 36).[93] It was perhaps Juana Colón's participation in these groups that allowed her to take her place among the town's most prominent socialist leaders. She collaborated with Perico Santiago, Manuel Arroyo, and Antonio Alvelo, as well as workingwomen such as Malela, Cayita, and Yuya. Unfortunately, we only know the first names of these workingwomen, as their lives have eluded historical records, and they are absent from the labor movement's histories. In fact, their names were mentioned in the *Comerío*, by William Fred Santiago, the president of the Bar Association of Puerto Rico, who delivered Colón's eulogy at her funeral.[94]

In the following decades, Juana Colón frequently used the tribuna to support labor struggles as well as to promote the political agenda of the Socialist Party. She actively participated in the party's 1932, 1936, and 1940 electoral campaigns.[95] Santiago remembered her as "a natural orator, witty, profound, and logical. Her grammar, diction, and rhetoric were obviously flawed, but her power of convincing and persuasion, as well as her sincerity, captivated her public and the stage."[96] Oral histories also attest to her participation in other municipalities' mítines, such as in Bayamón, San Juan, Barranquitas, and Cayey.[97]

Despite Juana Colón's militancy and political participation, she was excluded from the historical narratives produced by obreros ilustrados. Epifanio Fiz Jiménez's books are perhaps the clearest example. Fiz Jiménez was born in Comerío in 1886 and started working as a cigarmaker at a young age. After becoming radicalized by the assassination of Francisco Ferrer i Guardia in Spain, he turned into a labor organizer and later became the Socialist Party's vice president, as well as holding positions in Puerto Rico's House and Senate. After retiring from public and political life, he published two books: *Comerío y su gente* (Comerio and its people, 1957) and *Bayamón y su gente* (Bayamón and its people, 1960).

Through the books' pages, readers could find historical notes from the two towns that had served as Fiz Jiménez's home. He also included lists of the town's most prominent citizens. Notwithstanding having shared the tribuna with Juana many times, and despite her unbreakable support for the Socialist Party, which he led for some time, he did not mention Juana Colón once.[98] Yet while it might be true that she was excluded from the Socialist Party's spheres of power and intellectual circles, the party provided a space to become a local activist. It was in the Socialist Party's tribuna that a Black illiterate woman like Juana was allowed to speak her mind and project herself as a leader. Ultimately, even though she was ignored by obreros ilustrados, the town of Comerío never forgot her.

In 1972, five years after Juana Colón passed away, a group of young socialists affiliated with the newly established Partido Socialista Puertorriqueño published a fifteen-page pamphlet honoring her memory (figure 3.2).[99] It was divided into five chapters that included a biography, essays, art, poetry, and photographs. One of the essays was written by Mari V. de González. It documented how Juana Colón was remembered among Comerío's tobacco strippers. After several workingwomen were asked through a workshop window if they remembered Juana Colón, most replied with a common phrase, "How can I not?"

FIGURE. 3.2. Juana Colón pamphlet cover. Art by Kelvin Santiago Valles. In Hernández et al., *Juana Colón.* Courtesy of Colección Gilberto Arias González.

JUANA COLON 1875-1967

Colón was remembered not only for her militancy in labor struggles but also for her role as a barrio healer. One of the interviewees said: "Doña Juana Colón, the one from town, the one that worked in strikes and things? How can I not remember her? She was good, very good. Brave like there's no one today. I would take her my sons to santiguar." Another woman affirmed, before having to stop the interview because a foreman approached them, "She was called Joan of Arc. When there were big strikes, she joined and did not care if she was killed."[100]

Her participation in the 1919 strike had mythical proportions (figure 3.3). Most of the people interviewed remembered how she fought with rocks against police officers who were shooting at her. Mari V. de González

FIGURE 3.3. Juana Colón poster, ca. 1972. Art by Kelvin Santiago Valles, Taller El Seco. Courtesy of Colección Gilberto Arias González.

interviewed a group of older men on a street corner, and they all praised Juana Colón's militancy. Don Rafael Cruz Robles said, "It was in that corner that one day she fought against an officer, he used gunshots, and she used rocks. She had [her pants] where they belonged." Others told the same story but changed the date and the setting. A woman coming out of her shift in the tobacco factory remembered, "On a May Day celebration, she was even shot. Vidal Ríos, the tobacco workshop owner shot at her. . . . There is no one like her, there are no more people with her heart, they called her Joan of Arc."[101] With the publication of that pamphlet, the people of Comerío began creating a popular archive that preserved Juana Colón's memory. They kept alive the story of Juana as a woman who dedicated herself to the betterment of workers and her community. Those young socialists that published the 1972 pamphlet sought to propagate that myth of Juana Colón using memory as a political tool. Their work did not end with that publication. They continued their project of remembrance through civic activism. Because of it, along with the organizing efforts of local historian Wilson Torres, the town of Comerío nowadays has a public school and a cultural center named after their Black, illiterate, and socialist Joan of Arc: Juana Colón.

AS OBREROS ILUSTRADOS began crafting the lettered barriada, workingwomen were imagined as outside it; they were often ignored or distrusted at best. The workingwomen we have followed throughout this chapter, however, used different strategies to make their voices heard in labor congresses, print media, public protest, and mítines. In the process, they created a series of counterarchives; that is, workingwomen created ideational archives in the margins of the margins and against the will of those (men) who controlled the means of working-class knowledge production. Perhaps the most compelling case was that of Juana Colón, whose memory was recovered not by academics but by her hometown's popular folklore. The people of Comerío created, and politicized, an archive that is very much alive today.

But what made workingwomen like Paca Escabí or Juana Colón gravitate toward a party that silenced and excluded people like them from official positions of power? It seems that the Socialist Party offered other possibilities beyond electoral participation. It allowed, at least at a very local level, an illiterate woman to become part of a community of likeminded individuals. Perhaps that is why Juana Colón ordered for her coffin to be covered with the extinct party's flag. For obreros ilustrados, the Socialist Party's foundation became a moment of discursive consolidation. They had aspired to enter political office since the labor movement's early days; it now became a reality. As the following chapter demonstrates, the Socialist Party turned into a powerful force in Puerto Rican politics, granting obreros ilustrados access to spaces from which they had been excluded before.

CHAPTER 4. **BECOMING POLITICIANS**

The Socialist Party and the Politics of Legitimation

In early twentieth-century Puerto Rico, workers were not the only social group that used print media to intervene in the country's public sphere. Officers from the Insular Police of Porto Rico published a biweekly newspaper, *La fuerza pública* (The public force), that sought to influence public opinion and partake in political debates. Much like the conversations that took place in obreros ilustrados' lettered barriada, police officers projected themselves as active citizens and as learned minds. Yet in tune with the contempt felt by the country's elite toward the labor movement, police officers also used their pages to attack workers' political aspirations.[1]

The insular police's newspaper came out at a moment of great political upheaval and labor mobilizations. Governor Arthur Yager, appointed by US President Woodrow Wilson, waged war against the organized labor movement in Puerto Rico. During his administration, from 1913 to 1921, workers organized more than three hundred strikes. In 1915, when *La fuerza pública* began circulating, sugarcane fields throughout the island burned, as massive strikes organized by sugarcane workingmen spread like wildfire. Historians have yet to fully explore the depths of these strikes and understand if they signaled the FLT's increasing influence over agricultural workingmen or the unrecognized organizing work of local leaders like Juana Colón and Mateo Pérez Sanjurjo. What is certain, however, is that obreros ilustrados capitalized on the moment and successfully pushed for their entrance into the island's political sphere. The growing labor militancy was complemented by electoral victories that awed the island's political estab-lishment. In 1914, an electoral pact between Socialists and Republicans in the western town of Mayagüez launched Julio Aybar, the longtime editor of the newspaper *Unión obrera*, to Puerto Rico's House of Delegates. In the northern town of Arecibo, the Insular Labor Party—which was led by Es-teban Padilla, the editor of the labor newspaper *El combate*—won the local municipal elections. The following year, in March 1915, dozens of labor del-egates met in the hill town of Cayey and created the Socialist Party.[2]

La fuerza pública was published weekly for at least two years, an im-pressive run for most newspapers of the time. The only surviving copy is from March 21, 1916. By then, Julio Aybar had used his political platform to publicly denounce Governor Yager as solely responsible for police abuses against striking workingmen. Thus, as clashes between officers and work-ingmen took place in sugarcane fields, the insular police used its newspaper to attack Aybar. They criticized him not only for his public statements but also because he represented the labor movement in a space where it did not belong: the political arena.[3]

In its March 21, 1916, edition, most of *La fuerza pública*'s sixteen pages were dedicated to Aybar. Titled "A Brim of Dirt," the paper's opening ar-ticle accused the labor delegate of verbally assaulting Governor Yager, "the island's highest authority." For the paper's editors, Aybar's use of "vulgar words, loss of temper, excesses, and the abuses of charlatanism are a plague" that had no space in the political arena. The editors portrayed Aybar as dra-matically opposite to the way obreros ilustrados self-fashioned their iden-tities. Through its pages police officers associated the labor delegate with the "ignorant populace" and not with the "civic world of politics." They continued, "If they [workingmen] had power they would do like the Sans Culottes of La Marseilles and would kill anyone that does not think like them."[4] The editors also argued that although Aybar and the labor move-ment lacked civility, "reality will take care of it because . . . they are nothing, they never have been, and they never will be."[5]

To police officers' surprise and displeasure, by the 1920s the Social-ist Party had become a powerful force in Puerto Rico's polity, eventually winning the 1932 and 1936 elections through political alliances. Despite the political establishment's disdain toward organized labor, the Socialist Party became the consolidation of the obreros ilustrados' early twentieth-century political aspirations. The insular police were not alone in their cri-tique. Members of Puerto Rico's professional classes and government of-ficials also questioned the legitimacy of workingmen's political project and their intellectual capabilities. Perhaps the best example was the journalist, politician, and first director of Puerto Rico's Academy of History, Mariano Abril y Ostaló. As one of the Union Party's main ideologues, Abril y Ostaló penned his opinion on workingmen's political aspirations in his book *El socialismo moderno* (Modern socialism), published in 1911, four years before the creation of the Socialist Party.[6]

For Mariano Abril y Ostaló, obreros ilustrados had no idea what socialism meant and were incapable of understanding it because they lacked formal education. He mockingly argued, "The most prominent socialist leaders and agitators did not come from the working classes but from the BOURGEOISIE, and all of them came out of colleges and universities, like Turati, Ferri, Clemenceau, Milleanard, Berteaux, Briand, etc."[7] In Abril y Ostaló's opinion, the obreros ilustrados possessed only rustic libraries with a few libertarian newspapers from abroad, a clear reference to working-class centros. Thus, in his view, workingmen were incapable of understanding elaborate ideas, such as socialism. Even if some had read European socialist intellectuals, that did not matter because according to Abril y Ostaló, "reading is like eating, if the stomach is not prepared to receive it, it suffers from indigestion." With their "common phrases, coarse concepts, and crude attacks," he continued, "they are [only] contributing to the masses' ignorance."[8]

Abril y Ostaló believed that obreros ilustrados were not only ignorant but also mistaken because there was no such thing as a social problem in Puerto Rico. Socialists advocated for legislation that would ease workers' social problems—such as unsanitary housing conditions, low salaries, and malnutrition—but Abril y Ostaló flatly declared that such problems did not exist. Unlike European workers, who had factory jobs and lived in misery, in Puerto Rico there was no factory proletariat, and besides, "they rather heap their families in bad houses so they can have some extra money to have fun."[9] Workers' misery, if there was any, was their fault, according to Abril y Ostaló. Therefore, he condemned obreros ilustrados' audacity in attempting to create a class-based party, instead of participating in the island's traditional political parties.[10]

Governor Yager echoed Abril y Ostaló's contempt toward workingmen's political participation. He particularly distrusted Santiago Iglesias Pantín and the FLT in general. The governor went as far as trying to unsuccessfully encourage the creation of a government-sponsored labor federation to downplay the FLT's influence among the working classes.[11] In a letter to President Woodrow Wilson, the governor lamented: "It is most unfortunate that among the ameliorating agencies from the laboring masses of Porto Rico as a whole, it is not possible to give a prominent place to the Free Federation of Labor. . . . [T]his organization does not represent the agricultural workers at all, and at present it is really organized as a political party and seeks political rather than social aims."[12]

Not only was the FLT acting as a political party, but, according to him, its leaders were criminals. He accused them of "encouraging violence, disorder, and intimidation."[13] In September 1916, Governor Yager sent a letter to Frank McIntyre, chief of the Bureau of Insular Affairs. In it, he argued that labor leaders were acting without the consent of Samuel Gompers and the AFL, which did not approve of unions' political participation. He closed his letter to McIntyre asking for a favor: "You might have an opportunity to show this to Mr. Gompers as an illustration of how the Latin American politician performs his work."[14] But the AFL leader did not need a messenger. Gompers was already aware.

True to the turn of the century's global circulation of information, Gompers had learned about the Socialist Party's existence by reading the bilingual labor newspaper *Justicia* (Justice), not from official correspondence with the FLT's leadership.[15] "In the first instance, I desire to express considerable surprise," wrote Gompers to Santiago Iglesias Pantín on May 1916. "If any movement of such a character was contemplated, you as President of the Porto Rican Federation of Labor, should not have surprised me thereof." He reminded Iglesias, "The American labor movement is insistent that on any field of activity, whether economic or political, the sphere of its influence is not limited nor is it ceded to any political party bearing any name."[16]

Santiago Iglesias Pantín had opposed the creation of a political party and pushed the FLT to adopt the AFL's antielectoral policy in its 1910 congress. Yet Iglesias Pantín was also interested in controlling any labor-oriented effort in Puerto Rico. Iglesias Pantín attended the Socialist Party's inaugural convention in 1915 as a delegate and voiced his opinion but did not take a leadership role. In fact, he did not serve in any executive position within the party.[17] Nonetheless, Iglesias Pantín exerted great influence because all the Socialist Party members also belonged to the FLT, over which he presided. He was being cautious of not straining relations with the AFL.

When Iglesias Pantín received Gompers's dispatch, he immediately replied with a long letter explaining that the party was nothing new, a mere continuation of the one formed in 1899. It was a clever half-truth. The original party had been inactive since 1904 at the latest. Likewise, Santiago Iglesias

Pantín explained to Gompers, citing the AFL's twenty-sixth congress in Minneapolis, that the FLT did not violate the AFL's policy as they had members of all political orientations. Iglesias Pantín argued that Puerto Rico's political situation could not be compared to that of the United States. He asserted that Puerto Rican workers were under attack from all sides and that the patriotic Union Party controlled electoral politics and government offices and looked down on the labor movement's connection to the AFL. The only way to fight against these political efforts was in their own terrain. Two months after officially explaining his position to Gompers, Santiago Iglesias Pantín moved to consolidate his control over the Socialist Party leadership and expelled the members of the Arecibo branch that had laid the party's foundations.[18]

The FLT has often been historiographically interpreted as a colonial satellite of the AFL in Puerto Rico. While this relationship entailed the dominance of US-inspired trade unionism in Puerto Rico, the creation of the Socialist Party and the tensions behind it display the agency of the FLT organizers. As Iglesias Pantín's letter to Gompers noted, they were operating within the lived realities of Puerto Rico at the turn of the twentieth century. In a sense, the creation of the Socialist Party demonstrates how oftentimes Puerto Rican labor leaders used the AFL and its resources to advance their agendas and not the other way around.

The emergence of the Puerto Rican Socialist Party was not novel when compared to the long-standing histories of socialism in Latin America. The expansion of labor organizations throughout the region at the turn of the twentieth century gave way to the creation of several socialist parties in Argentina (1896), Uruguay (1910), and Paraguay (1914), to name a few examples. Later, the influence of Marxist ideas in the late 1920s and 1930s became fertile ground for the expansion, proliferation, and radicalization of socialist parties in the region.[19] While Puerto Rican workers had already created short-lived socialist labor parties since 1899, the establishment of the Socialist Party in 1915 and, more importantly, its electoral success after 1917—in the heat of the Russian Revolution and the anteroom of the US red scare—were unprecedented in the Hispanic Caribbean.

There had been collaboration between members of the FLT and workers that aspired to organize labor unions in the neighboring Dominican Republic since the turn of the twentieth century. For example, in January 1900, José Ferrer y Ferrer and Saturnino Dones participated in the creation of the Centro Propagador (Propaganda Center) of the Dominican Republic's Liga de Obreros y Artesanos (League of Workers and Artisans). Later, in 1917, Luisa Capetillo traveled there to sell books and propagate her ideas. While still unexplored by scholars, it seems that there were strong bonds of solidarity and collaboration between workers in both countries. The first Dominican Marxist centro opened its doors in the 1920s, but given the harsh conditions that radicals faced during Rafael Leónidas Trujillo's dictatorship, the first openly socialist party, the Democratic Revolutionary Dominican Party, was not established until the 1940s.[20]

In Cuba, the organized labor movement had multiple factions, from the conservatives and reformists to different schools of socialism and anarchism.[21] While these tensions had emerged in the late nineteenth century, they continued after the first US occupation (1898) and the creation of the Cuban Republic (1902). Given the precarious situation lived by most Cubans after the war of 1898, there was deep resentment toward the United States.[22] In fact, the AFL made Santiago Iglesias Pantín an organizer for both Cuba and Puerto Rico in 1902, but he succeeded in only the latter. When Luisa Capetillo defended the AFL's program in the Cuban newspaper El dependiente (The service worker), she was heavily attacked by anarchists and local members of the Industrial Workers of the World, a radical US-based labor federation that advocated industrial unionism in response to the AFL's trade unionism.[23] In that context, it was not until 1925—in the heat of student strikes and anti-imperialist mobilizations—that the Cuban Communist Party, later known as Popular Socialist Party, was born.[24]

In Puerto Rico, historians and social scientists have paid careful attention to how the Socialist Party was created, who constituted its electoral base, and how it was bureaucratized in the 1930s.[25] This chapter poses similar questions but through the lens of working-class knowledge production. It pays attention to the obreros ilustrados' longing to enter Puerto Rico's political spheres and how once they became legitimate politicians, they began to be distrusted by their rank and file. Nonetheless, the distance between obreros ilustrados and the laboring masses was nothing new; it had been crucial to the creation of the lettered barriada at the turn of the century. Rather, it was another consolidation produced by the transition from obreros ilustrados to "honorable" politicians. The Socialist Party and the FLT also sought to centralize the production of knowledge at a moment when workshop-educated working-class politicians began weaponizing historical knowledge to advance political agendas within the party.

The Socialist Party's Creation and Consolidation

Voters are sovereign if they have the power to create legislation and veto any measures they deem foolish and prejudicial.—LUZ Y VIDA, December 13, 1909

The 1914 elections renewed the labor movement's political aspirations. As was to be expected, the FLT immediately took notice. When the socialist-dominated municipal assembly of the northern town of Arecibo was to begin its term in January 1915, the FLT sent Manuel F. Rojas, a San Juan–based organizer, to act as the Insular Labor Party's general secretary. Rojas was a tailor from Vega Baja who had been arrested in 1899 on murder charges. After Governor Beekman Winthrop pardoned him on January 1, 1905, Rojas became a prominent labor leader, organizer, and ilustrado. He published various books theorizing about the island's social problems, historical development, and socialism in general. Throughout his life, Rojas occupied multiple positions within the labor movement, such as secretary for San Juan's Unión Obrera Central (Central Labor Union), later becoming the FLT's treasurer and general secretary.[26]

As sugarcane fields were blazing on February 24, 1915, Esteban Padilla, then president of the Insular Labor Party, called for organizers from across Puerto Rico to meet in the hill town of Cayey during the FLT's eighth congress to debate the possibility of creating a national party. On March 21, 1915, Padilla welcomed fifty-six male delegates to the Socialist Party's inaugural convention. He praised the FLT's work in the last decade and presented the labor federation as a "mother" to the Puerto Rican workingmen, whom he described as "weak," "disgraceful," and an "outcast." Afterward, the convention gave a vote of sympathy to Julio Aybar for his work on behalf of the laboring masses in the House of Delegates. Ignoring Ramón Romero Rosa and other working-class delegates elected in 1904, Manuel Rojas affirmed that Aybar was the country's first working-class delegate.[27]

Rojas took the stage and read his report as the party's general secretary. "Comrades," argued Rojas with bitter irony, "we cannot doubt that Puerto Rico is being governed with the ways and means used by slaveholding democrats in the South of the Great Republic of the United States."[28] Thus, it was time for "a positive revolution, a revolution of ideas" that must happen in the political and the economic spheres. Rojas continued, "Let's unite our party's destiny with the Great Socialist Party of the United States; let's give our party the latter's name; and let's affiliate to the cause sustained by socialists from around the globe."[29]

Affiliation with the US Socialist Party became the convention's most debated resolution. Some, like Cristino Domenech from Mayagüez, opposed it because it would complicate the collection of fees, and "besides," he argued, "most Puerto Rican workers do not want anything to do with Americans."[30] When it was time to vote for the party's creation, thirty delegates were in favor, six against, and four abstained; the Socialist Party of Puerto Rico was born. Although the party was to function separately from the FLT, it served as the federation's political arm in practice. Not only did the leadership of both institutions overlap, but the convention also voted to use "all of its influence and moral and financial support to propagate and defend workers on strike."[31]

The convention also declined to make any statement about the island's political status—but resolved to write a letter to President Wilson asking him to extend US citizenship and the protections granted by the US Constitution to Puerto Rico. The FLT's leadership and the AFL's president, Samuel Gompers, had been using all their contacts in Washington to extend US citizenship to Puerto Rico for years.[32] For Gompers this meant that US workers did not have to compete with their Puerto Rican counterparts. The FLT's leadership understood it as the possibility of attaining better living standards and legal protections. They also imagined this as a step toward annexation. Yet there is still much research to be done in relation to the rank and file's perceptions of these debates.[33]

The convention also voted to adopt the Socialist Party of America's bylaws as their own. The Puerto Rican Socialist Party's program was inherited from Arecibo's Insular Labor Party. It included the creation of a popular bank; the redistribution of lands; free education for children, including food, books, and clothing; the eight-hour workday; the abolition of child labor and women's night shifts; childbearing and breastfeeding time for working women; the creation of working-class neighborhoods; transformation of the penal system; absolute freedom of the press; abolition of the death penalty; and universal suffrage. Without any doubt, it was one of the most progressive political party programs in the history of Puerto Rico.[34]

As landowners and the political establishment accused the labor movement of setting fire to the sugarcane fields, the Socialist Party defiantly adopted the lighted *jacho* (torch) as their symbol. Labor leaders had used the jacho since their first incursions into the world of politics. It was the official symbol of both the Democratic Socialist Party (1899–1904) and the Insular Labor Party (1906–15). In an era when lampposts were rare, most peasants lit their way at night with a torch. Thus, the lighted jacho symbolized workingmen's enlightenment as they advanced through the darkness of ignorance, a notion deeply rooted in workers' desire to become civilized. As the Democratic Socialist Party had declared in 1900, "The torch of science is the emblem of our party."[35] While those behind the Socialist Party's creation sought to be treated and considered as legitimate politicians, the jacho also reminded the political establishment of workers' militancy and defiance. In other words, although the jacho could be interpreted as a symbol of progress and enlightenment through the ballot box, the spread of fires throughout the countryside gave it a completely different connotation in the minds of landowners and government officials.

Two year after the party's creation, in 1917, the US Congress approved the Jones Act. Samuel Gompers, who had advocated for it for years alongside Santiago Iglesias Pantín, was in the room when the act was signed.[36] It granted US citizenship and restructured the Puerto Rican government. While most of the fiscal and economic dispositions of the 1900 Foraker Act remained in place, the island's government would now use the US model of three branches of government. The judicial system was left intact, while the executive and legislative branches changed. The US president still appointed the governor, but some of his cabinet members now had to be approved by the newly installed Insular Senate. The legislative branch was divided into two bodies, the House of Representatives, composed of thirty-nine members, and the Insular Senate, composed of nineteen members. All legislators were to be elected through the popular vote. The next elections would take place on July 16, 1917, followed by elections in November 1920, and every four years after that.[37]

By then, the FLT's effort in organizing the agricultural proletariat had borne fruit. In 1915, 5,900 workers in 35 unions made up the federation. By 1917 the numbers had roughly tripled to 139 unions with a total of 16,000 members.[38] The Socialist Party used the FLT's unionized membership to collect the signatures needed to become an officially recognized party.[39] They also made sure to educate potential voters on how to cast their votes. Their political propaganda advised, "Keep an eye, voter, and make three crosses or lines below the TORCH, next to the PLOW, and next to the HOE." Since illiteracy was common among agricultural workingmen, the Socialist Party encouraged everyone to "be careful, learn how to vote, and teach your comrades."[40]

As the 1917 election results were coming in, the newspapers El tiempo (The time), edited by José Celso Barbosa from the Republican Party, and La democracia (The democracy), edited by Antonio Barceló from the Union Party, reported that Santiago Iglesias Pantín had lost his nomination for senator at large. Two days after the election, on July 18, 1917, *La democracia* reported, "After the clucking and boisterous socialist campaign, it turns out that Santiago Iglesias' followers have only won representatives in Naguabo, Ceíba, and Las Piedras, and all of this with help from their last-minute Komrade, the Republican leader Garset. . . . Even with the help of powerful bourgeois Komrades Iglesias and Aybar could not conquer their long-yearned seat in the senate and the house."[41] Meanwhile, the Socialist Party's headquarters in San Juan received telegrams and letters from different municipalities reporting irregularities in the voting booths, with missing or nontallied ballots.[42] Santiago Iglesias Pantín asked the Puerto Rico Executive Council to do a recount, which they denied, forcing the Socialist Party to go to court. The case made it all the way to the Puerto Rican Supreme Court in August 1917.[43] After the court deliberated in favor of Iglesias Pantín, the recount was done, and as the Socialists had warned, Iglesias Pantín's number of votes went up. He beat his contender, Santiago Veve from the Republican Party, by more than 1,324 votes. The latter accepted his defeat on September 11, 1917, making Santiago Iglesias part of the first-ever Insular Senate, a position he held for more than a decade.[44]

Despite the Socialist Party's moderate success in 1917, it was the 1920 elections that shook Puerto Rico's political establishment. The party obtained 59,140 out of the 249,431 island-wide votes. This translated into securing a seat in the Insular Senate and four seats in the House of Representatives. Yet there seemed to be a strong discrepancy between the growing number of Socialist voters in relation to unionized FLT members. In 1923, for example, the FLT had around 25,000 dues-paying members, less than half the number of votes the Socialist Party had accrued in the previous election. This discrepancy only grew as years went by. According to the labor historian Kenneth Lugo del Toro, this phenomenon "demonstrated the multiplying effect of votes coming from the labor movement's families, adherents, and sympathizers, as well as peripheral votes."[45] It seems that by the 1920s, however, obreros ilustrados had succeeded in creating a mass political movement and were not as effective in attracting workers to their unions.[46]

The Socialist leadership used their electoral momentum to cultivate amiable relations with the newly appointed Governor Emmet Montgomery Reily (1921–23). Because of that, the governor appointed dozens of self-educated workingmen to several key agencies, including the Bureau of Labor, the Department of Justice, and the Health Department. As the Socialist Party's electoral base increased throughout the 1920s—going from 24,468 votes in 1917 to 97,438 in 1932—the FLT began promoting a discourse of industrial peace, while the party sharply moved toward bureaucratization.[47] Although the Socialist Party's foundation represented the consolidation of a project that emerged in the turn-of-the-century lettered barriada, during the 1920s it became just another political institution increasingly detached from its working-class base. Some obreros ilustrados who came out of workshops and had dedicated their days to the organization of labor, and at times had possessed barely enough money to buy their essentials, were now powerful men in Puerto Rican politics.

The Socialists lacked the years of experience with the inner workings of political office that traditional parties had, but they excelled in other areas. Ever since the turn of the twentieth century, obreros ilustrados and labor leaders had refined their grassroots community organizing. They also had vast experience with producing knowledge and ideas through print media, labor rituals, and collective pedagogical efforts in the most precarious conditions. During the 1920s, the party now had the economic and organizational capability of spreading its ideas and organizers throughout Puerto Rico without difficulties. This came at a high cost for rank-and-file members because it also entailed the centralization of knowledge production and the suppression of any intellectual or political discourse not aligned with the Socialist Party's leadership.

The Allure of Bureaucratization

Monarchy is the government of a sole person. Aristocracy is the government of a minority. Democracy is the government of the majority.
—LUZ Y VIDA, December 13, 1909

In 1920, Santiago Iglesias Pantín gave an impassioned speech to the stockholders of the FLT's newspaper *Justicia*. He distinguished between obreros ilustrados and the "miserable masses from the countryside, factories, and workshops." Those who were fortunate enough to be lettered needed to enlighten those who were not. There had always been a handful of "intellectual workingmen" that had "served their duty as propagandists," and, according to Iglesias Pantín, they had to deal not only with persecution from the government and the police but also with the laboring masses' apathy.[48] To be sure, this approach was not new. It was the same paternalistic discourse obreros ilustrados had used to distance themselves from the laboring masses since the turn of the century. Nonetheless, they now had institutional power to enforce and centralize these ideas on a national scale.

Iglesias Pantín believed that obreros ilustrados were "noble and altruist," but their work had not been more successful because there was no thirst for knowledge among the poor laboring masses. According to him, it was obreros ilustrados' duty to teach them about "the millions of freed workingmen from the world's most civilized nations." That is, they needed to help the masses imagine themselves as part of the universal labor community. To do so, it was imperative for labor propagandists to cultivate the "unavoidable obligation to buy one or two newspapers a day, and it does not matter if they know how to read or not. If someone does not know how to read, their children or any other family member can read [the papers] to them. . . . [B]uying a newspaper should have the same importance to them as paying for any of life's urgent obligations."[49]

Yet Iglesias Pantín was not advocating for workers to read any labor newspaper. He lashed out against those small and independently run newspapers that circulated throughout Puerto Rico and had given life to the lettered barriada. To influence public opinion and to centralize what was said in the press, Iglesias Pantín wanted workers to read only newspapers affiliated with the FLT or the Socialist Party. This limited their options to Unión obrera and Justicia.[50] Throughout the 1920s, there were many conversations about the necessity of having only one official print organ that would effectively consolidate their opinions and silence any dissenting voices.[51]

The party also provided a centralized structure that allocated resources to promote events previously funded by local unions. Because of its mission as labor's political arm, the Socialist Party did not limit their political propaganda to electoral years but sought to constantly promote and spread their ideas. To do so, the party created a fund to cover all propaganda-related costs. Alfonso Torres, then the party's general secretary, argued that between the months of July 1923 and July 1924, those funds were used to recruit "412 men, either orators or writers," and to sponsor 447 public meetings, 342 conferences, and 2,935 local committee meetings and general assemblies. These impressive numbers could have been early twentieth-century obreros ilustrados' wildest dreams.[52]

In May 1924, six months before that year's elections, the party sponsored a national campaign called the Cruzada cívica de la victoria (Civic Crusade of Victory). It consisted of sending their most prestigious soapbox orators with a daily salary of three dollars to multiple towns and cities in Puerto Rico's eastern, western, and central districts.[53] This campaign was built on years of experience in grassroots labor organizing throughout the countryside, and it was spearheaded from San Juan. While the circulation of labor

FIGURE 4.1. The Socialist Party's leadership, 1924. Courtesy of Centro de Documentación Obrera Santiago Iglesias Pantín, University of Puerto Rico, Humacao.

orators affiliated to the FLT can be traced all the way back to the federation's origins in 1899, this practice was formally institutionalized in the 1909 Cruzada del Ideal (The Idea's Crusade). Organized from San Juan by the FLT and locally funded by unions throughout Puerto Rico, the Cruzada del Ideal consisted of a handful of obreros ilustrados in charge of attracting people to labor unions and spreading their socialist ideas. Luisa Capetillo was perhaps the only woman who participated in that crusade. She penned her memories as she traveled through villages, cities, and the countryside meeting other participating obreros ilustrados along the way.[54]

The aim of these public events had drastically changed from trying to boost union numbers to attracting votes. Yet Socialist leaders still framed their efforts as part of a global community. Throughout the 1920s, all the party's conventions opened with discourses about the progressive evolution of socialism in Europe and its expansion throughout the world, where they also proudly located themselves. In the Socialist Party's Sixth Convention of 1924 (figure 4.1), as delegates debated about the strategies used by their political enemies, Alfonso Torres defiantly asked: "Can a party that belongs to socialism, not only in Puerto Rico but from around the world, be destroyed?"[55]

All these party conventions also ended on the same note. They used the melody of "La Marseillaise" to sing their anthem, which had "revolutionary lyrics attuned with universal labor."[56] Much like the discourses articulated by obreros ilustrados at the turn of the century, the Socialist Party's conception of belonging to a universal labor community did not challenge the implicit hetero-patriarchal nature of those discourses. Workingwomen challenged that masculine ethos by demanding political participation.

PUERTO RICAN LABOR leaders were attentive to developments taking place in the US labor movement after World War I and the signing of the Treaty of Versailles. The treaty led to the creation of the International Labour Organization, and in October 1919, workingwomen from around the world gathered in Washington, DC, for the First International Congress of Workingwomen. Emulating their peers in Western countries, the completely male executive committee of the FLT called for the First Congress of Workingwomen of Puerto Rico to take place on November 30, 1919.[57]

Because of the short notice, the congress was postponed and took place on December 14 and 15 in the capital city of San Juan. For every fifty dues-paying members, each women's labor organization could send one delegate. The congress opened with sixty workingwomen delegates from all around Puerto Rico. Since the delegates were affiliated with the FLT, most of the congress's conversations, debates, and resolutions were around labor issues affecting women, but the congress was not limited to labor. They also demanded that the FLT incorporate workingwomen into their executive and legislative committees. This was approved by the workingwomen's congress but not ratified and put in practice by the labor federation.[58]

Workingwomen also understood the need for broader political representation. They cautiously followed the debates taking place in the United States about women's suffrage and demanded of Governor Yager, "If women in the United States earn the right to vote, Puerto Rican women should enjoy the same right to elect the representatives in our municipalities and the Insular Senate."[59] Literate women were allowed to vote in 1932, and that right was later extended to all women for the 1936 elections. It had been part of legislation passed by the Socialist and Republican Coalition.[60]

Workingwomen had been challenging the Socialist Party's masculine ethos in its conventions throughout the 1920s and 1930s.[61] One of the Socialist Party's most well-known leaders was the cigarmaker Prudencio Rivera Martínez. In 1913, he had openly expressed his contempt toward women in the workforce. "Since it is no longer feasible to completely stop the access of women to the [tobacco] industry, an easy and practical solution can be adopted by organizing them in their work centers, and, where possible, stop the growth of women in the cigar industry in Puerto Rico."[62] Unfortunately for Rivera Martínez, by the 1920s it was no longer feasible to completely stop the access of women into the Socialist Party either. Thus, in the party's 1924 convention, Rivera Martínez proposed a resolution to change the party's constitution. He wanted to change the number of regional vice presidents from nine to eighteen, so that workingwomen could occupy half of those positions. The resolution was approved, but as with the 1919 workingwomen's congress, it was not put in practice by the party's Territorial Executive Committee.[63]

Representation of workingwomen within the Socialist Party's highest spheres continued to be a topic of contention and debate in later conventions. When it was once again brought up in 1932, workingwomen were at the forefront of its discussion. In fact, some went as far as to challenge not only the party but also the movement's mythical leader, Santiago Iglesias Pantín. Arcadia Figueroa took a turn to speak and defiantly boasted, "I not only overcame my [liberal] husband, but I'd be willing to defeat Iglesias [Pantín], the maestro, if it is necessary."[64] After much discussion, the convention approved changing the party's constitution for the number of regional vice presidents from nine to twenty-seven, to have two men and one woman for each district. Workingwomen were allowed into the highest echelons of the party but not on an equal basis.[65] The convention and the party's Territorial Executive Committee approved the resolution this time, but male delegates in the following convention challenged it once again.

Arguing that twenty-seven vice presidents were too many, a group of male delegates presented a resolution in the 1936 party convention to abolish the constitutionally imposed gender quota. As had happened in the past, the topic produced a fiery debate. A workingwoman by the name of Arcadia Font sent a telegram to the convention asking labor delegates "not to make women's role [in the convention] solely decorative."[66] When it was time to debate the resolution, Antonio Arroyo, one of the party's founders, argued that although their constitution favored women's participation, "it was never true in practice [as] women have never had the opportunity to be represented in the Territorial Executive Committee because of our own egoism, which has always forced us to impose our will over women."[67] He was followed by Carmen Peña, who pointed her finger at those who presided over the convention: "While it is true that [the party's] Constitution grants us representation in our party's highest body, you, the men, have not allowed us to enjoy those rights."[68] The convention approved the motion to change the constitution's language. The clause that stated that there "needs to be one woman" in each regional vice presidency now read "at least one woman," giving way to the possibility of subverting male dominance within party structures.[69] Workingwomen's pressure succeeded, but only in 1936, the same year universal female suffrage was approved in Puerto Rico. Now their votes counted, and the party's leadership knew they would have an impact in the upcoming elections.

While the 1936 convention sided with workingwomen on an issue they had demanded for decades, it was not the only ongoing discussion within the party. Dissidence was brewing, and at times it was difficult to contain. The party used strategies of silencing and exclusion similar to those enacted in previous decades through the lettered barriada. Although the party did not officially advocate for statehood in its program, the majority of its leadership supported and worked for the annexation of Puerto Rico to the United States. Yet dissident voices pushed for independence on a local level. To contain those deviant opinions, the party went as far as expelling the Socialist mayor of Río Piedras because some believed he supported independence.[70] Communists, on the other hand, "became personas non-grata" as they built momentum in the early 1930s. In fact, while Santiago Iglesias Pantín had praised the Russian Revolution in 1919, throughout the 1920s and 1930s, there were no mentions of the Soviet Union in official party documents.[71]

But perhaps the most serious threat came from loyal rank-and-file Socialists who believed the party was deteriorating because of its bureaucratization. As early as 1923, Sandalio Alonso, one of the party's founders and longtime labor leader, warned that there was a growing layer of "socialist functionaries of a bureaucratic style" who had never set foot in a workshop or belonged to any union but had joined the party to "further their individual ambitions."[72] To counteract this trend, the party passed several resolutions forcing conventional delegates to be card-carrying union members for at least six months before each convention. Nonetheless, the number of delegates not from the ranks of the labor movement only increased with each passing election.

Rank-and-file Socialists protested overnight politicians and criticized how some longtime labor leaders had changed after arriving to political office. In 1920, Prudencio Rivera Martínez was appointed to the government's Labor Compensation Commission. His office received anywhere from 150 to 200 letters monthly. To alleviate some of the commission's work demands, he created a template letter to address all incoming inquiries. Since the commission was a government office, the letter was written using formal language. Many of those who contacted Rivera Martínez's office expected to be treated with the warm language of comradery and solidarity that was common among Socialists and union members. Some were upset to receive a letter in which they were addressed as "usted" (formal you) instead of "tú"; and they were called "Sir" instead of "Comrade." In the view of many rank-and-file Socialist workers, "after they [labor leaders] get into these positions, they forget what they were and start feeling like misters."[73]

It might be difficult to know if these Socialist leaders actually felt like misters. Nonetheless, these workers-turned-politicians were now treated as such by those who had scorned them in the past. Those who had started their careers as labor organizers and had received most of their education in workshops were now considered legitimate politicians. They also experienced upward mobility and amassed social capital. In 1923, for example, a prominent medical doctor and intellectual, Eugenio Fernández García, edited a massive bilingual book of 1,122 pages titled *El libro de Puerto Rico* (The book of Puerto Rico). The book's intention was, according to its editor, to consciously help "the development of a new civilization" and "prepare [Puerto Rico,] this young shoot of Latin-Anglo-Saxon civilization, the best possible surroundings for its highest development." Ultimately, the book was a "who's who" in the country's political, cultural, and civic life. From the fifty pictures included of some of the book's collaborators, the only phenotypically Black person was Joaquín Becerril, a member of the FLT and the Socialist Party.[74] Even though those labor organizations had silenced race from the historical narratives its cadre of intellectuals had crafted, they facilitated a Black workingman to be considered part of the (mostly white) world of letters and politics. Furthermore, as the Socialist Party consolidated its electoral power, some of its members were now invited to give lectures and speeches in several cultural and academic spaces.[75]

ON JANUARY 11, 1932, Juan Carreras, a teacher by trade and a Socialist Party leader, was invited to give the commencement speech to the first graduating class of the University of Puerto Rico's School of Arts and Trades. The program had been inaugurated in 1928 with much praise from organized labor's leadership.[76] It was highly gendered. Male students were offered programs on radio mechanics, cabinetmaking, and electricity, among others. Female students could get a degree in industrial sewing. According to Carreras, the school was "the first INTELLIGENT step toward industrializing our country."[77] But his commencement speech did not focus on industrialization. Instead, he talked at length about the Italian Renaissance and Western conceptions of civility.

Carreras opened his speech by stating how our modern times were changing the interactions between social classes. He argued, "The Kings of Holland now vote alongside their people. In the southern United States a statue of [chemist George Washington Carver], a Negro is unveiled. And one of the most powerful kings in the world, the Prince of Wales, married a plebeian woman."[78] He also presented the monarch Edward of Windsor as the embodiment of renaissance manhood in modern times because he possessed "human understanding," the only phrase used in English throughout Carreras's talk. "But, Edward of Windsor was born a king, some of you might say, and I answer that today any man can become one."[79] But to do so, working hard was not the only thing workingmen needed to do. Carreras believed they also needed to change their mindset because Puerto Rican workingmen suffered an inferiority complex. "In Puerto Rico, the tradesman, the carpenter, [and] the cabinetmaker, have come to dominate their profession, like Rousseau's *Emile*, through the pressure of blows and stumbles."[80]

It was precarity, not desire, that led workingmen to become tradesmen, Carreras argued. In fact, "life forced them to learn a trade when all they wanted was a profession," and although "there were no trade schools in those days, everyone wanted to be a señorito bien [a well-to-do mister]." He advised the three graduating students, professors, and the public to "say with pride, with a superiority complex, and with class vanity: 'My guild is the country's economic force.' That is true socialism."[81] The UPR's School of Arts and Trades had become a "School for the Forgotten Man," as he titled and finished his speech.

Juan Carreras was not the only Socialist Party leader to give invited lectures. Later that same year, on July 9, 1932, Prudencio Rivera Martínez was asked to give a keynote talk at the Rafael Cordero Casino in San Juan. Stemming from nineteenth-century artisanal traditions, casinos were spaces for workingmen and artisans to come together and socialize.[82] Rivera Martínez had been one of the Socialist Party's founders and a lifelong member of the FLT, where he helped organize cigarmakers across Puerto Rico. Rivera Martínez had been appointed as Puerto Rico's first commissioner of labor in 1931. Thus, the conference's promotion read, "Conference delivered by the Honorable Prudencio Rivera Martínez, Commissioner of Labor in P.R."[83] The lecture was intended to honor the life of Rafael Cordero Molina, a Black cigarmaker and teacher.[84]

Rivera Martínez opened his lecture by demonstrating his intellectual anxieties. After learning that Pedro Carlos Timothée would also be delivering a lecture that night, Rivera Martínez almost declined the invitation. Timo-thée was a Black lawyer, an award-winning author, and, like Rafael Cordero, a prominent educator. Not only had Timothée served the Puerto Rican leg-islature from 1902 to 1904, where he had pushed for the creation of high schools in Puerto Rico, but he was one of the founders of the Federación Regional de Trabajadores (FRT, Regional Federation of Workingmen), an organization he presided over until 1905. When the event honoring Cordero took place, Timothée was sixty-eight years old. He had lived long enough to befriend some of Puerto Rico's most esteemed nineteenth-century intel-lectuals, the likes of José Julián Acosta and Román Baldorioty de Castro.[85]

Both lectures were published in a pamphlet. While the picture of Pedro C. Timothée reproduced in its pages could be read as racially ambiguous to the gaze of contemporary historians, his actions demonstrated his race con-sciousness. When the Negro Society for Historical Research was created in New York by John Edward Bruce and the Afro–Puerto Rican intellectual Arturo Alfonso Schomburg, Timothée was its correspondent in Puerto Rico.[86] Thus, it should not come as a surprise that unlike the FLT, the FRT—which Timothée presided over in the early twentieth century—had a race-conscious discourse, as historian Ileana Rodríguez-Silva has noted.[87] The racial discourses and the tensions produced between these organizations and the labor movement as a whole might have been overlooked by histo-rians, and perhaps be inaccessible for researchers, because the FRT was not able to produce enduring archives (either material or ideational) as had the FLT and the Socialist Party, which actively silenced any reference to the com-peting labor federation and promoted a "raceless" class-based discourse to unify and attract the laboring masses.[88]

Resembling those books published within the lettered barriada at the turn of the century, Rivera Martínez's speech opened by warning his au-dience about his "little fostered intelligence."[89] Since biographical sources were scarce, he explained that his lecture focused on the historical context lived by Rafael Cordero Molina. Instead of centering the narrative on the European Renaissance as Juan Carrera had, Prudencio Rivera Martínez paid attention to race relations in nineteenth-century Puerto Rico and high-lighted the trade he shared with Cordero Molina: cigarmaking.

Rivera Martínez compared Cordero Molina's work with that of Black US educator Booker T. Washington. Unlike Washington, who had access to funds and led the Tuskegee Institute to expand tremendously, in 1810 Cordero Molina founded a small school in San Juan. Rivera Martínez then proceeded to explain the harsh laws implemented in Puerto Rico that severely monitored, repressed, and exploited Black people. He talked about the importance of tobacco production and the enlightenment of those in that trade. For example, he argued that Rafael Cordero Molina was the first cigarmaker "that gave honors and glories to our class, our trade, and our Island." That was no surprise because, after all, argued Rivera Martínez, those who accompanied the Cuban poet and revolutionary José Martí in creating a glorious independent Republic in Cuba were cigarmakers too.[90]

Rivera Martínez also used his speech to locate himself within the historical moment he lived in. Presenting the US occupation as a turning point in the country's historical development, he argued that because of the "Organic Laws Foraker and Jones, a considerable number of labor representatives and people of humble origins have marched through our Parliament."[91] He continued by listing all his fellow Socialists who had attained positions in the Insular Senate and the House of Representatives. Mentioning their names was intended to "demonstrate the representation we have obtained in the Parliament, which is this country's summit where popular will is expressed."[92] Finally, Rivera Martínez made a historical genealogy between Rafael Cordero Molina and himself. He argued, "The school of which Rafael Cordero was such a fervent follower, and the triumph of democracy, has made possible that a cigarmaker like Rafael Cordero has come to occupy a ministerial position in our country, the Department of Labor."[93]

It was precisely because workingmen now held political offices that they were invited to these spaces. For example, although Santiago Iglesias Pantín was self-educated and had never set foot in a university classroom during his formative years, he was invited to Georgetown University to chair and moderate debates between students from that institution and from the UPR in 1935 and 1936. Iglesias Pantín's replies to these invitations echoed Juan Carrera's thesis about workers' inferiority complex or perhaps his false modesty: "I accept your cordial invitation with pleasure, but with some difference, knowing full well my incapacity to deliver."[94] Santiago Iglesias Pantín was invited because he was an elected official, not because he was an intellectual.

Labor leaders' and Socialist Party members' entrance into these spaces was not clear-cut; they were porous processes. For example, although Rafael Alonso Torres had excelled in politics during the 1920s, when he was appointed to the UPR Board of Trustees in October 1933, he was fiercely attacked by students and his political opponents for lacking academic titles and for being culturally and intellectually unfit for the position. Students argued that his appointment would signal the death of Puerto Rican culture.[95] The student strike, however, was only one of several problems that the Socialist

Party faced in the 1930s. With increasing electoral power also came conversations as to where the party needed to be headed. This caused internal frictions that came to the fore in the party's 1932 convention.

The Political Uses of History

In most communities, your friends are outside and your enemies are inside.
—LUZ Y VIDA, August 30, 1909

As the Socialist Party's eighth convention was coming to an end in the evening of Wednesday, August 3, 1932, a major debate took place about the possibility of creating an electoral pact with the Republican Party in the upcoming elections. Known as the Coalición (Coalition), the pact was approved by the convention and ended up winning the 1932 and 1936 elections. As delegates took turns to speak in favor of or against the Coalición, however, they also showcased their intellectual capacities to downplay their contenders' opinions and positions. In the end, two conceptions of history clashed on the podium: history as poetics, and history as facts. These two conceptions of history were clearly aligned with the two different political projects that were being debated: one that justified an alliance with bourgeois politicians, and another that saw the pact as a lethal mistake and wanted to be absolved by history.

Bolívar Pagán (figure 4.2) was the president of the party's Comité del Pacto Libre Electoral (Committee for the Free Electoral Pact), in charge of studying the pros and cons of creating an alliance with Republicans in the coming elections. Pagán read a report to the convention about their findings and positions. As was expected, his report favored the alliance with the Republicans with hopes of conquering as many political offices as possible. To justify his position, Pagán used historical examples of socialist parties in Europe. Once again framing their project as global, Bolívar Pagán argued that to approve the pact would mean that they would follow socialist workingmen "in Italy, Belgium, England, France, Spain, and other countries that march in the vanguard of modern civilization."[96]

When Pagán finished reading the report, Isaac García, José A. Ríos, and Nelsón Silva, all of whom belonged to the same committee and were representative of the party's growing youth, proposed a dissident vote. They argued that the alliances the Socialist Party had created with bourgeois political parties in the 1920s had not given positive results. Furthermore, they feared that the party's ideas would degenerate because of those politicians

FIGURE 4.2. Santiago Iglesias Pantín (*third from left*) and Bolívar Pagán (*fourth from left*) in Washington, DC, ca. 1930. Author's personal collection.

that joined their ranks but did not care for the labor movement's best interests. Their words caused great commotion, and some joined their call.[97]

A decision needed to be reached before midnight. Twelve delegates equally divided into those in favor and those against took ten-minute turns to defend their positions. Many of those who were against the pact had been outspoken critics of past electoral alliances. For example, Florencio Cabello and Julio Aybar had sustained such views since the first proposed pact with the Republicans in 1920. Four years later, in 1924, Tadeo Rodríguez García even published *Ideales sociales* (Social ideals), a book in which he used history and socialist theory to argue against any alliance with bourgeois political parties.[98]

Julio Aybar, who was the first to take the podium, set the debate's intellectual tone. The longtime labor leader, politician, and editor of the newspaper *Unión obrera* argued that although Bolívar Pagán had used the history of remote European countries to justify the electoral pact, he did not believe such an approach was useful. "I believe in facts," reproached Aybar. For him, facts were palpable and verifiable things that happened in Puerto Rico. That is, he used a positivist logic based on lived experiences that distrusted textual narratives of those places he had not visited.[99]

Essentially, Aybar was not only against the pact itself but against the intellectual edifice that had been used to build the lettered barriada and the Socialist Party's political project. While delegate Lino Padrón Rivera defended the pact as part of a "worldwide working-class revolution," Aybar went against the notion of belonging to a universal labor community. Tadeo Rodríguez García echoed Aybar's position. He argued that the auditorium could be considered a university because of the brilliance of those who spoke in defense of the pact. Yet he was not interested in doing comparative studies with other countries but wanted the convention to focus on the "historical facts from Puerto Rico."[100]

Others decided to intellectually engage with the historical narratives presented in Pagán's report. Sixto Pacheco warned that in those European countries mentioned in the report, Socialists had been lured into positions of power, but their options had been limited once they attained governmental positions. In Europe, the upper classes had stopped persecuting workers in the street and allowed them to take their place in the world of politics, but the bourgeoisie maintained all the economic power and continued their abuses against the working classes. Ultimately, he warned against any pact that would make the working classes docile and dependent on those that exploit them.[101]

To yield light on this point, Pacheco gave the example of the rise to power of England's Labour Party. For Pacheco, the Labour Party had won seats in Parliament amid an economic crisis that eventually favored conservatives and capitalists. In the end, and paradoxically, the Labour Party ended up "securing the existence and reign of that country's aristocracy." While Pacheco's historical interpretation of these events can be heavily contested, it is important to note that he used such examples to debate with Bolívar Pagán in the realm of ideas. Contrary to Pacheco, Pagán represented a new generation of socialist cadres who came out of universities, not workshops. In fact, Pagán was a highly respected lawyer, and according to his 1961 obituary, published in the New York Times, he was "Puerto Rico's best-read man."[102]

For Isaac García, who opposed the pact, the debate had been plagued with "too much literature, too many beautiful passages from the history of the world, with special mentions of old Greece and Rome . . . superb discourses from a literary and poetic standpoint . . . they are homages to fantasy while reality has been orphaned from any humble attention."[103] García was referring to speeches like the one made by Victor Coll y Cuchi. The latter gave an impassionate discourse in which he talked at length about how the Roman emperor Constantine converted to Christianity. Coll y Cuchi used this example to argue that, just like Socialists and Republicans in Puerto Rico, "there are cases in history when two opposite poles have encountered themselves."[104]

And while those who favored the pact relied on the history of the Western world, those against it felt they were at a historical crossroads. Armando A. Miranda argued, "Tomorrow when the history of the Socialist Party is written and any reference is made to this night, August 3, 1932, it will be known as the Socialist Party's mournful night of Saint Bartholomew," a reference to the massacre of Huguenots committed by the Catholic Church in 1573. "Our responsibility is with the Socialist Party, with the people of Puerto Rico, and with history," affirmed Miranda.[105]

The fear of historical judgment was real. Florencio Cabello, in representation of the Socialist Section No. 74, also pondered on how these events would go down in history. His section had decided in assembly that "we will go wherever the Socialist Party goes but at least we will have the satisfaction of not having contributed to the Socialist Party's destruction . . . and when such destruction has been inevitably accomplished, we will simply say that our warning and alerting voices were heard here, but that it was our sacred duty to follow the party in the suicidal route that was laid out in this convention."[106] They were keenly aware of the importance of historical narratives and archival power. They knew that the convention's proceedings were being transcribed, and that they would lose the vote against the pact. Thus, Cabello's speech was a way of letting the record show that they had not gone down without a fight.

History was also used to perpetuate myths that carried enormous political power. Santiago Iglesias Pantín became a mythical figure in these debates. Coll y Cuchi, for example, argued that when Iglesias Pantín had arrived in Puerto Rico in 1897, he had brought the Socialist Party in his heart. Furthermore, Coll y Cuchi compared the arrival of Iglesias Pantín with the biblical story of Noah's Ark and said that he had brought to Puerto Rico a "new system, a new life, and a new era." Although Iglesias Pantín was physically present as the debate took place, some delegates spoke of him as a sacred unequivocal force. Antonio Arroyo argued that Iglesias Pantín supported the pact, and, thus, they all needed to follow him because he would not encourage anything that would destroy or dishonor the Socialist Party's principles. "Comrades," argued Arroyo, "I have the absolute faith in the men that lead our party, as they are the ones that gave me the ideas that I defend." Shortly after the 1932 convention and the electoral victories that followed, however, the party's leadership greatly changed.

In its growing interest in controlling the government, the Socialist Party received in its ranks professionals who sympathized with the party but not necessarily with the working class. The Socialist leadership hoped that these professionals would contribute the necessary expertise to deal with political matters on a governmental level.[107] Opposition began brewing within the party, and it led to factional splits and attacks throughout the 1930s. The first public blow Socialists suffered in the 1930s, however, did not come from within the party's ranks or from the world of labor. It was from the University of Puerto Rico, where students went on strike to protest Rafael Alonso Torres's appointment to the institution's board of trustees. As one workingman wrote in a letter to Alonso Torres, "we ceded our soul and weapon to our enemies: the strike."[108]

PUERTO RICAN LABOR leaders' interest in electoral politics did not begin with the Socialist Party's creation. They had experimented with different political formulas since the organized labor movement's early days. The party emerged from the FLT members' autonomous political excursion into partisan politics on a municipal level, with victories in the towns of Mayagüez and Arecibo in 1914. Likewise, the party was built on the obreros ilustrados' years of theorizing about the role of politics in their labor struggles. Ultimately, the Socialist Party was the lettered barriada's political project.

Shortly after its creation, the Socialist Party became an undeniable force within Puerto Rican politics. Yet the FLT struggled to keep their numbers while the party's electoral base increased. In the process, the party became highly bureaucratized, creating frictions within its rank and file. The party's leadership strategically used all their experiences in labor organizing and used the party structure to create a centralized national apparatus that also centralized working-class knowledge production. Furthermore, the party offered class mobility, respectability, and access to spaces that had been denied to the Socialist leadership in the past. Self-educated workingmen became senators, legislators, and participants in intellectual events in Puerto Rico and the United States.

While frictions were deepening within the party, obreros ilustrados used their conceptions of history to defend their political positions. In the labor movement's early days, workingmen considered tobacco workshops as their university classrooms. Now they envisioned their party's congressional debates the same way. The production of knowledge moved from the workshop to the political arena. While their political discussions had deep scholarly undertones, these workers-turned-politicians were not considered intellectuals. In other words, they were allowed into Puerto Rico's public sphere as respectable and legitimate politicians, not intellectuals.

CHAPTER 5. STRIKE AGAINST LABOR
The 1933 Student Mobilizations

On September 23, 1933, the US-appointed governor of Puerto Rico, Robert Hayes Gore, announced that he was going to pick a replacement for Mariano Abril y Ostaló, who was retiring from the UPR board of trustees. Abril y Ostaló had been a longtime enemy of organized labor, a Liberal, and a member of the Union Party prior to its extinction. Expectations were high as the names of Martha Roberts de Romeu and Rafael Alonso Torres circulated in the press as potential candidates. The former was highly respected in the world of medicine, while Alonso Torres was an autodidactic labor leader turned politician.[1] When it was announced that Governor Gore had appointed Alonso Torres, one of his political allies, students condemned it immediately. They argued that Alonso Torres was culturally and intellectually unfit to serve the university. Students and their supporters often compared him to an ox and made jokes about his lack of intellect. His appointment, students argued, would signal the death of their university and would render their diplomas worthless.

A week later, on September 27, 1933, UPR students met in assembly to discuss the possibility of creating a yearbook. But the meeting's original plan drastically changed. Students used the forum to protest Governor Gore's appointment of Alonso Torres, the interim president of both the FLT and the Socialist Party, as a member of the UPR board of trustees. After an intense debate, they approved a resolution stating that Alonso Torres was not culturally fit to execute the job because he lacked any intellectual merit or academic title. When the assembly came to an end, students organized an impromptu rally through San Juan to deliver the resolution to the governor.[2]

Five hundred students marched in silence as a symbol of mourning (figure 5.1). When students passed a statue of Román Baldorioty de Castro—a leading nineteenth-century autonomist politician and forebear of what later became the Liberal Party—they stopped and decorated it with black ribbons. They also put a sign that read: "Archimedes said 'Eureka!' and Alonso said moo!," a trope that became common during the strike to equate Alonso Torres with an animal. The students arrived in front of the governor's mansion and started chanting: "We want cultured men for our University."[3] A delegation of six students went inside the mansion, but Governor Gore did not receive them. Instead, his secretary delivered a message on his behalf: "I declare the matter of Alonso Torres finished. It will be sustained, and I absolutely do not want to further discuss this or any related matter."[4]

The following day, on September 28, students met again in assembly at Río Piedras's Victoria Theater to condemn the governor's actions. Because they believed that the governor lacked courtesy, students raised funds to hand him a copy of Manuel Antonio Carreño's *Manual de urbanidad* (Courtesy manual), Latin America's quintessential book on proper etiquette. Likewise, students reaffirmed their position against Alonso Torres and decided to march again toward the governor's mansion.[5] Three days later, students held a funeral procession through the streets of San Juan. They carried a coffin with the message "RIP culture." Alonso Torres, who was visiting the governor's mansion after an intense Socialist Party assembly that had rendered internal dissidence and divisions clear, saw the protest through the window. He later confessed to Santiago Iglesias Pantín in a letter, "Never in my life had I seen something like it. It was hard to realize that it was me who they wanted to destroy."[6] The following weeks, students started a protest movement that evolved into coordinated island-wide strikes against Rafael Alonso Torres. The strikes took place at the UPR's two existing campuses in Mayagüez and Río Piedras, as well as in several high schools. They all became part of a single struggle against Alonso Torres's appointment. Students received support from different social groups, including alumni, nationalists, and other radicals. Some agreed with students that Alonso Torres was intellectually unfit for the position, while others simply used the strike to advance their political careers.[7]

In 1933, multiple social actors—students, politicians, and the Socialist Party's rank and file, among others—imagined the strike from different perspectives. Its multiple meanings were negotiated through private correspondence,

FIGURE 5.1. Student protest in San Juan. Front cover of *El imparcial*, October 2, 1933. Courtesy of the Colección Puertorriqueña, University of Puerto Rico, Río Piedras.

print media, and public events. In the process, the strike became highly politicized by different factions that conceived it as something to be in favor of or against. Ultimately, the strike became a public relations nightmare for both the Socialist Party and Rafael Alonso Torres. Although self-educated obreros ilustrados like Alonso Torres had become legitimate political subjects through their participation in the Socialist Party, the strike and its media portrayal demonstrated that multiple social sectors did not consider people from working-class backgrounds as legitimate intellectuals.

This chapter focuses on Alonso Torres because his case is particularly telling. He was one of the most important obreros ilustrados of early twentieth-century Puerto Rico. Despite his humble origins and lack of formal education, Alonso Torres became a widely respected political figure in Puerto Rico and published in a variety of venues and on a wide range of topics. He was one of the creators of the working-class literary magazine *Luz y vida*, penned articles in *Puerto Rico ilustrado* (an illustrated magazine catered toward the island's cultural elite, published from 1910 to 1952), and wrote several books.[8] Alonso Torres worked really hard to establish himself as one of the labor movement's guiding intellectuals, only to be publicly neglected by thousands of people during the strike on the basis of not being precisely that, an intellectual.

BY THE 1930S THE PRESS was the embodiment of Puerto Rico's public sphere of opinion, where the lines of state discourse, politics, and public views often merged. Different social groups and actors used newspapers to express their thoughts about the strike. For example, although the Socialist Party did not officially advocate for the annexation of Puerto Rico to the United States, its leadership, including Alonso Torres, openly favored statehood. Thus, José Lanauze Rolón, who became one of the founders of the Communist Party in 1934, used the press to argue that Alonso Torres was a puppet of US imperialist ambitions. Lanauze also believed that the strike had revolutionary potential and that any true radical had an obligation to support it. For nationalists, like poet Fernando Torregrosa, who believed that culture was the ultimate battlefield, the strike represented a struggle against "yanki" ignorance, embodied in the figure of Alonso Torres. For high school students throughout the island, who held a national assembly and went on strike in solidarity with their university peers, and for the UPR's alumni, the strike was a fight to preserve the university's honor and prestige, which would be tainted by someone from a working-class background like Alonso Torres.[9]

Not everyone favored the strike, however. The letters published in the press or sent privately to Alonso Torres show how the Socialist Party's general membership understood his appointment as something to be defended at all costs. Furthermore, some intellectuals like Cayetano Coll y Cuhi used the press to support Alonso Torres's appointment and argued that it was a symbol of how the university was becoming a more modern and humane institution because it now included and represented the country's majority: the laboring masses. For others, the strike symbolized the entrance of Roosevelt's New Deal into the university.[10] In fact, on October 15, 1933—as the student strike was well on its way—the governor organized a massive event to endorse President Franklin D. Roosevelt's New Deal policies in Puerto Rico. The rally was led by a group of politicians from the recently formed Coalición, the electoral partnership between the Republican and the Socialist Party. Several marching bands, labor delegations, and carriages followed. As the parade made its way through San Juan's streets, US flags hung from balconies, and onlookers either joined or stared in awe at the massive crowd.[11]

The governor greeted the multitude and invited a delegation of politicians and journalists to join him in the balcony of the governor's mansion. Before the speakers addressed the rally, two telegrams were read out loud. The first was from President Roosevelt expressing his gratitude for the people of Puerto Rico's support for the New Deal. The other was from Santiago Iglesias Pantín, the Socialist Party's president and now the island's resident commissioner in Washington, congratulating the people and their legislators "for participating as US citizens in their duties and bearing the fruits of the National Rehabilitation and the New Deal."[12]

One of the speakers was Rafael Alonso Torres. He was introduced as a university trustee, and the crowd responded with lengthy applause and cheers. He gave a speech about the historical importance of the moment they were living in. According to Alonso Torres, the New Deal would go down in history as having economically rehabilitated the Puerto Rican masses, taking them out of misery. He also asked for the labor movement to fully cooperate with Governor Gore's administration to fight against reactionaries who worked against the masses' happiness under the US flag.[13] As he spoke, Alonso Torres could glance over the massive crowd and read some of their banners: "¡Viva el Nuevo Trato!" (Long live the New Deal), "Honor al gobierno de Gore!" (Honor to Gore's government), "¡Alonso es el Nuevo Trato aplicado a la Universidad!" (Alonso is the New Deal applied to the university), and "Alonso vale más que muchos titulados" (Alonso is worth more than many people with degrees).

THE UPR STUDENTS UNDERSTOOD their struggle as part of a broader moment of student activism throughout Latin America. In the press, in their correspondence, and in manifestos, Puerto Rican students often commented about student strikes in Argentina, Venezuela, and Cuba. Indeed, Puerto Rican students could draw from the region's recent histories of university activism. For example, in 1909, student representatives from Argentina, Brazil, Chile, Ecuador, Peru, Uruguay, Paraguay, and Bolivia came together for the International Congress of American Students in Montevideo. They shared experiences and debated about how to reform universities in their countries.[14]

In 1918, students in Córdoba, Argentina, organized a massive protest movement. After months of occupations, public demonstrations, and negotiations with government officials, students succeeded in securing a university reform that became the cornerstone for student demands in the region. They inspired student movements in Colombia (1922 and 1924), Peru (1923), and Venezuela (1928) and a second wave of student mobilizations in Argentina (1930), among others. The 1933 student strike at the UPR was part of that broader Latin American moment, although it has been mostly overlooked by historians, perhaps because of Puerto Rico's colonial condition. Unlike their Latin American counterparts, which had universities with centenary traditions, in Puerto Rico the UPR had opened its doors barely a few decades before.[15]

The UPR had been established in 1903 as a teachers' training college. In the following decades, it became the country's intellectual hub. By the 1920s it had a college of liberal arts, a school of law, and a department of Hispanic studies. When the strike broke out, the UPR was a cultural center in dialogue with literary and cultural currents in Latin America, Europe, and the United States. Perhaps unknowingly, the students who participated in the 1933 strike were pioneering a powerful protest tradition in Puerto Rico that expanded throughout the twentieth century and continues to this day.[16]

Alonso's Hell

A hypocrite does not deserve any consideration or respect.
—LUZ Y VIDA, August 30, 1909

In 1932, Franklin D. Roosevelt from the Democratic Party won the US presidential election and promised to jump-start the economy through his New Deal program. He appointed an old friend and retired businessman, Robert Hayes Gore, to be the new colonial governor of Puerto Rico. Gore arrived in July 1933 and hoped to reform the economy. In his inaugural speech, the new governor supported statehood, while also promoting the production and export of craftwork and the expansion of the Puerto Rican commercial sector; he also encouraged tourism through the promotion of crafts, afforestation, and the legalization of cockfights.[17]

Shortly after arriving, the governor created political alliances with the Coalición. Not only had they won the most recent elections, but they also supported statehood. When members of the Liberal Party approached the governor to ask for more representation in his government, their claims went ignored. Moreover, rumors circulated that he was going to ask for blank resignation letters without dates from everyone he appointed. That never materialized, but the suggestion was enough to generate great animosity in Puerto Rico's political establishment.[18]

The Liberal Party declared war on Gore. Luis Muñoz Marín—a Liberal senator who later became the first elected governor and the most important Puerto Rican statesman of the century—used his contacts and influence in Washington to discredit Gore. Another Liberal, Gustavo Jiménez Sicardó, coauthored a satirical political play titled *Gore's Hell*, which was staged in different theaters throughout the island. The Liberal Party also used their newspaper *La democracia* to viciously attack the governor. Furthermore, someone detonated a bomb in the governor's summer home, other explosives were found in the governor's mansion, and several anonymous threats were made to him and his family. The appointment of Rafael Alonso Torres sparked tensions that "would finally form the political hurricane that would destroy Gore's governorship beyond repair," as historian Gonzalo F. Córdova has noted.[19]

The student protest reached unprecedented levels for a university conflict in Puerto Rico. Within a week, hundreds of students met in assemblies and held several protests throughout the island. Students' opposition went unheeded, as Alonso Torres was to be sworn in to the trustee position on October 18. On that day, thousands of students met in Río Piedras's Victoria Theater. They approved a strike that would be called off only with Rafael Alonso Torres's resignation.[20] The UPR's chancellor, Carlos Chardón—who later became one of Puerto Rico's leading technocrats—and the institution's board of trustees responded by decreeing a two-week academic recess to find ways to solve the conflict. Alonso Torres's inauguration was postponed and eventually held in secret a week later.[21]

With each passing day, protests became stronger. High school students in different municipalities throughout the island also joined the movement by organizing assemblies, writing messages of solidarity, and arranging several school walkouts. While some schools had declared strikes, a group of representatives from several high schools met in a national assembly in the town of Caguas on November 5, 1933. They approved an unprecedented national high school strike in solidarity with their university peers if Alonso Torres did not resign over the weekend.[22]

The university students also created a strike committee, known as the General Directory. Its main objective was to travel through the island promoting the strike, raising funds, and addressing the media. Two members of the committee were César Andreu Iglesias and Arturo Morales Carrión. Iglesias eventually dropped out of the university because of his family's dire economic situation but later became one of the most important communist intellectuals in Puerto Rico. Morales Carrión pursued graduate studies at the University of Texas, where he got his MA in Latin American studies. He then went to Columbia University, where he obtained a PhD in history and government, and later occupied high-ranking positions under the guidance of Puerto Rican governor Luis Muñoz Marín and US president John F. Kennedy, eventually becoming the UPR's president (1973–77). Thus, for some of its leaders, the strike was an initial foray into politics, a field they subsequently excelled in.[23]

The media's fascination with what was happening in the university also played a significant role in the expansion of the strike. As historian Fernando Picó noted, "Its research community, its serious culture of learning, and its intellectual tradition took several decades and many sacrifices. . . . When the first traces of this being accomplished emerged towards the 1930s, the country responded by putting the university in a glass case."[24] In other words, the press documented with enthusiasm all the cultural events taking place within the university. Any time a foreign professor visited, when faculty published books, or whenever there was an important lecture, these accomplishments would be carefully reviewed in the press.

It was not surprising, then, that the press covered all strike-related events, at times dedicating multiple pages to editorials, developing stories, and unraveling events. Some newspapers did not limit their reporting to their pages. *El día* (The day), for example, which had offices in San Juan and Ponce, had big blackboards outside their offices. Whenever they received a telegram from strike-related events, they updated their boards with headlines. They often documented the commotion those headlines caused to crowds that gathered in front of their offices to read them.[25] Other newspapers, like *El imparcial* (The impartial), capitalized on the strike's popularity. On

October 30, 1933, it announced that it was going to assess people's opinion through a poll consisting of a simple question: "Do you feel that Mr. Alonso Torres is fit to exercise his role as a University of Puerto Rico trustee?" The only requirement for participating was knowing how to read and write because each vote required a signature. The survey was widely successful in documenting popular opinion about the strike (figure 5.2).

The day after *El imparcial* announced its survey, Rafael Alonso Torres threatened to sue the newspaper for libel.[26] Different local sections of the Socialist Party met to reaffirm their loyalty to Alonso Torres and to make sure their members would not participate in the poll.[27] Meanwhile, on the front cover of its November 3 edition, *El imparcial* reproduced pictures of long lines of people waiting to participate. Because of the influx of votes, the newspaper had to temporarily hire three secretaries. When the poll stopped after the strike's culmination, the results were 116 votes in favor and 3,166 against Alonso Torres's appointment.[28]

As the strike spread throughout the island, communist leader José Lanauze Rolón argued that it had been politicized by political parties.[29] As a member of the Coalición, Alonso Torres had publicly announced that he was going to crack down on Liberals within the university. A frequent joke from the era was that Alonso Torres was so excited when appointed that he vowed to make a priority changing the name of the bachelor of liberal arts degree to bachelor of coalitionist arts (bachillerato en artes coalicionistas).[30] Rumors also circulated that Governor Gore had ordered him to cut down spending in the university, and one of the people he wanted Alonso Torres to go against was Muna Lee, a poet and literature professor, then married to Luis Muñoz Marín.[31]

Muñoz Marín was an up-and-coming political powerhouse within the Liberal Party. He was the son of Luis Muñoz Rivera, one of the most important statesmen of late nineteenth- and early twentieth-century Puerto Rico. Like his father, Luis Muñoz Marín was a poet, journalist, and politician. He moved back and forth between Puerto Rico and the United States until finally settling in the island in 1931. A former member of the Socialist Party, Muñoz Marín was now the editor of *La democracia* and was elected as senator at large for the Liberal Party in the 1932 elections.[32]

Luis Muñoz Marín had to be careful with how he dealt with the strike. He was close with several key players in President Roosevelt's administration, specifically the president's wife, Eleanor Roosevelt. While he wanted to become a New Deal emissary in Puerto Rico, and eventually did, during the strike he was also weighing war against Governor Gore, who was an old

No se divulgarán los nombres de los votantes: envíenos su voto

UNA ENCUESTA DE "EL IMPARCIAL"

EL IMPARCIAL empieza desde hoy una encuesta que versando es de excepcional interés público encaminada a conocer el falla del país en el diversificado asunto de Alonso Torres. [...] preparado el Sr. Alonso Torres para ejercer el cargo de Síndico de la Universidad [...]

A fin de que la opinión inteligente de nuestro pueblo pueda manifestarse con pleno conocimiento de causa y exprese su pensamiento, [...]

1. Las condiciones que debe reunir los Síndicos de la Universidad.

2. Las funciones a desempeñar por los mismos.

Importantísimo la votación quedará cerrada el día 15 de noviembre a las doce [...] de la noche. Y el resultado definitivo de la encuesta se publicará en EL IMPARCIAL al día siguiente.

SECCIÓN 3.—El Gobierno de la Universidad de Puerto Rico [...]

¿Estima Ud. al Sr. Alonso capacitado para desempeñar el cargo de Síndico de la Universidad de Puerto Rico?

Haga una X dentro del cuadro.

Sí—

No—

ENVIE ESTE CUPON A LA DIRECCION DE ESTE DIARIO, BAJO SOBRE QUE DIGA "ENCUESTA ALONSO"

Tetuán 75,
San Juan, P: R.

NOMBRE _____

PROFESION U OCUPACION _____

RESIDENCIA _____

CIUDAD O PUEBLO _____

ESCRUTINIO CELEBRADO EN NOVIEMBRE 3, 1933

Votantes en la afirmativa (sí) 14

Votantes en la negativa (no) 634

Votos en blanco 4

Total votos en la afirmativa 100

Total votos en la negativa 1833

LA FE NOTARIAL.

Yo J. M. Toro Nazario, CERTIFICO: Que en mi carácter de notario público, y a requerimiento del Ledo. Antonio Ayuso Valdivieso, Director de EL IMPARCIAL, en el día de hoy y asistido por los señores Hermann Villalba y Lidia Cintrón, procedí a verificar el escrutinio de la Encuesta Alonso, abriendo seiscientos cincuenta y dos sobres dirigidos a EL IMPARCIAL, contando los votos emitidos hasta hoy, los que arrojaron el siguiente resultado:

AFIRMATIVAMENTE	14
NEGATIVAMENTE	634
EN BLANCO	4
TOTAL	652

Dada bajo mi firma y sello en San Juan, Puerto Rico, hoy día 3 de noviembre de 1933.

J. M. TORO NAZARIO.
Notario Público.

FIGURE 5.2. Poll about Rafael Alonso Torres in *El imparcial*. The question reads: "Do you feel that Mr. Alonso is capable of performing the position of a University of Puerto Rico trustee?" *El imparcial*, November 4, 1933. Courtesy of the Colección Puertorriqueña, University of Puerto Rico, Río Piedras.

friend of President Roosevelt. Likewise, Antonio Barceló, then president of the Liberal Party, was a former political enemy and now acquaintance of Alonso Torres and did not want to get involved in public accusations against the labor leader. Thus, they used the Liberal Party's newspaper *La democracia* to discredit both Alonso Torres and Gore.[33]

Years later, Luis Muñoz Marín confessed that he had played a significant but silent role in the strike's development. He recalled meeting on several occasions with both student leaders and UPR's chancellor, Carlos E. Chardón. Because of the political climate, these meetings were secret. They met at midnight near the university, in the basement of the home of one of the student leaders, in what is now known as the Santa Rita neighborhood. There, they discussed media strategies. Chardón and Muñoz Marín helped students write and phrase their demands, to be published in *El mundo* (The world) the following day. Then, they collectively wrote Chardón's answer to the students. Finally, they did the same with editorials signed by Muñoz Marín in which he acted as mediator. If these meetings did in fact take place, as Muñoz Marín later argued, they were a testament to the partisan political nature of some of the strike's participants.[34]

AFTER SANTIAGO IGLESIAS PANTÍN left Puerto Rico in 1925 to work in the Pan-American Federation of Labor and later, in 1932, to serve as resident commissioner, a silent power struggle had developed within the party. Bolívar Pagán—Iglesias Pantín's son-in-law—and Rafael Alonso Torres competed for the party's control. Muñoz Marín later argued that the idea of appointing Alonso Torres to the trustee position came from Pagán. Pagán, who was a lawyer and a publicly renowned intellectual, thought that the university community would never accept Alonso Torres for the position and wanted him to be publicly shamed. In fact, in 1938 a group of labor leaders drafted a document explaining the twenty-two ways in which Pagán had acted against the Socialist Party's best interests. In the document, they directly accused Pagán of silently orchestrating the UPR strike against Alonso Torres. While it might be impossible to confirm such assertions, Alonso Torres was indeed portrayed in the media and by the student movement as uncultured and uncivilized because of his working-class background.[35]

Students discursively framed the strike as a struggle to defend the university as a space of honor. As one student argued in one of their many assemblies, if Alonso Torres became a trustee, their diplomas would be stained with dishonor. One recurring symbol in students' protests was mourning. On more than one occasion students in San Juan and Mayagüez carried a coffin symbolizing the death of culture. Some of the banners they carried during the protest read, "Culture has died," "Universitat non et pessebrum" (The university is not a manger), and "We are not attacking a political leader, we are defending culture."[36] While using a discourse centered on honor and the need to save the university, these strikes were political mobilizations.

Through editorials, cartoons, and letters, newspapers became open forums where the strike was imagined and discussed. Various newspapers circulated throughout the island in 1933. Some were openly affiliated to political parties, such as *La democracia* (Liberal Party), *El día* (Republican Union Party), and *Unión obrera* (Socialist Party). Others were satirical, such as *El diluvio* (The flood), *El flote* (The float), and *Pica* (Itching powder). Lastly, *La correspondencia* and *El mundo* took pride in being unbiased, although the veracity of this was also questionable at times.[37]

Because of its satirical nature, *El diluvio* criticized all political parties, while at times demonstrating sympathy toward communists and other radicals. Weeks before Gore took office, and months before the strike, the newspaper had already established its position toward the incoming governor (figure 5.3). On the front cover of its May 13 edition, it published a cartoon of Gore dressed as a Roman emperor—he later became known as Caligula—and three people kneeling before him; each one represented the island's main political parties. The title read, "The usual comedy," and the subtitle added, "Allah's eternal servants at the newest proconsul's feet."[38] Thus, when the strike took place, its editors criticized the Liberal Party for using *La democracia* to politicize students' struggle. They also accused Liberals of using worn-out tactics that jeopardized the duel being fought by students, who represented "the moral nucleus of Puerto Rican society, who have awakened feelings of dignity in our cultured nation."[39] Ultimately, *El diluvio* portrayed students as an intellectual vanguard that fought against the danger of having "the ignorant masses occupy positions of power" within the island's polity.[40]

Although *El diluvio*'s editors were critical of the Liberal Party, their opinions of Alonso Torres and the Socialists were far from cordial. "There's nothing more painful than the spectacle of our country in the past elections when they glorified and gave power to a party like the Socialist, scamming workers' illusions, brokers of strikes and proletarian rights."[41] The editors portrayed Alonso Torres as belonging to a group of "ignorant caudillos, prowlers of benefits with their political shortcuts and [personal] gains." *El diluvio*'s editors argued that Alonso Torres was part of a new caste: the

FIGURE 5.3. Cartoon mocking Governor Gore and other political parties in *El diluvio*, May 13, 1933. Courtesy of the Colección Puertorriqueña, University of Puerto Rico, Río Piedras.

Socialist tyranny. These new Socialists fought against students with the same passion they had fought with in the past when they struggled against employers.[42]

La democracia was unsurprisingly the most critical newspaper of Alonso Torres. On September 27 it published a protest letter sent to the president of the university's alumni association. The letter argued that the university should be led by people who had excelled in the arts, not experts in corralling the votes of the illiterate masses.[43] *La democracia* published articles against Alonso Torres almost daily. They ridiculed him as lacking the most basic knowledge in grammar, law, and literature. Similarly, they reproduced a dehumanizing discourse that equated him to an animal. On multiple occasions, they published articles arguing that "saying that Alonso Torres had any intellect was like saying that an ox could write verses."[44]

Trying to shape public opinion, Alonso Torres decided to publish an article to help establish his intellectual credibility. "La misión del perro en el mundo" (The dog's mission in the world), as the article was titled, was published in the newspaper *El mundo* in its Sunday, October 1, edition. In private, Alonso Torres referred to it as his doctoral dissertation.[45] When the newspaper's editor read the article, he sent it back because it needed substantial revisions. Alonso Torres bitterly replied, "Take the article and publish it without changing a word. If you make any alteration, it's better for you to return it to me." *El mundo* published the article without alterations or revisions.[46]

Signing as a UPR trustee, Alonso Torres opened the article with enthusiasm: "I dedicate this article to those that believe that academic titles are the only basis for human knowledge, I must warn that I neither possess one nor want to, because I have others of greater value, which I have acquired through the noble struggle for existence." He stated that man was born out of clay and was a complex being. The dog, argued Alonso Torres, had been his loyal friend throughout time. He also talked about the adaptability of dogs and cited authors such as Francisco de Asís, Charles Darwin, and Victor Hugo. Analyzing the role of dogs in different regions of the world, Alonso Torres tried to showcase his understanding of different cultures from around the globe. Yet as the editor had noted, the article was plagued with errors. Perhaps the most noticeable was calling dogs felines. His enemies capitalized on it immediately.[47]

Two days later, Victor Gutierrez Franqui, who would later become Puerto Rico's attorney general under the governorship of Luis Muñoz Marín, and prominent Liberal lawyer Manuel Rodríguez Ramos published a satirical piece in *El mundo*. It was titled "The feline dogs versus the canine cats." The article used the same analogies Alonso Torres had employed (the annoyance of dogs' barks, their loyalty, and their uses in different parts of the world) but from a dog's perspective. "You have slandered me, human brothers. Who has told you that there are transatlantic ships in the Siberian steppes? Who has informed you about the poles' high temperatures? You have slandered me."[48] Afterward, Alonso Torres became a laughingstock in Puerto Rico's intellectual community. As communist leader José Lanauze Rolón argued, "Alonso, miserable author of the offspring about dogs and human destinies, is an ignorant with airs of litterateur and deserves all the ridicule and burden he suffers nowadays."[49]

But not everyone was against Alonso Torres. For many labor leaders and everyday members of the Socialist Party, his appointment symbolized the entrance of the working masses into the ivory tower, a space that had been historically denied to them. Newspapers like *Unión obrera* and *El mundo* published dozens of letters and telegrams from Socialists throughout the island. Others penned their opinions in correspondence with Alonso Torres and other Socialist Party leaders. These letters and telegrams serve as an archive of feelings and demonstrate the wide-ranging significance his appointment had for countless Puerto Rican workers. Many argued that Alonso Torres gave representation in the university to more than one hundred thousand Socialist voters.[50] Lino Padrón Rivera, a Socialist leader and longtime labor organizer, wrote a telegram to Alonso Torres, accusing students, Liberals, and reactionary intellectuals of turning the university into a center to conspire against democracy. As historian Luis Ángel Ferrao has noted, Puerto Rican elites in the 1930s were tied together by a series of socially visible traits: "the urban nature of the group, [they were also] cultured, predominantly white, and, in many cases, from direct Hispanic heritage."[51] Thus, Padrón Rivera argued that those on strike despised and denied the children of workers entrance into the university and aspired to uphold their class and racial privileges.[52]

Rank-and-file Socialists imagined Alonso Torres as the self-made man that came out of the workshop to conquer the manly world of politics.[53] Thus, honor was also a recurring theme in their correspondence. Short telegrams that read "Alonso's appointment is a staple of honor for Puerto Rico" or "Alonso's appointment gives honor to those who deserve it" were not uncommon.[54] A flyer distributed among Socialist circles argued, "Shame is what the working people, the honorable people, and the sensible and conscious people" felt toward striking students.[55]

Meanwhile, tensions increased in the last weeks of October and the first days of November as the university-mandated recess was coming to an end without any solution in sight. Many Socialists sent letters to Alonso Torres arguing in his favor and against his resignation.[56] Octavio Freytes, a lawyer from the Coalición, was perhaps one of the most vocal critics against his resignation. "Do not quit, Don Rafael, even if the campus gets stained with blood" was the first line from a letter he sent to Alonso Torres. Freytes also appealed to Alonso's manhood and honor as the main reasons to keep his post at the university. "Be virile and brave, maintain that civic gesture the Coalición trusted in you. . . . Be a man, be a macho, and [you will be] a hero." Referring to the critiques made against Alonso Torres as ignorant, Freytes closed his letter by arguing, "If they are full of Ortega y Gassett, we have the [Coalición's] tricolor flag and the New Deal's democracy. Palante (Forward) and palante (forward), even if blood is spilled."[57]

Some Socialists portrayed students as ignorant and just following orders from the Coalición's political adversaries. Labor leader Prudencio Rivera Martínez argued that three things permeated the strike: classism, partisan politics, and imitation. Indeed, Rivera Martínez believed that students were imitating their peers in other countries, but they had failed to understand that students in Cuba or Mexico were fighting for different things and in distinctive sociohistorical contexts. He was referring to the student movements that developed in different parts of Latin America in the first three decades of the twentieth century.[58]

Historian Renate Marsiske identifies these Latin American movements as part of the "reform generation," when students sought to transform not only their universities but also their societies. Nonetheless, each movement had its unique qualities. As Marsiske notes, "The reform movements in Argentina and later in Mexico were university-centered . . . in Peru and Cuba, student movements were tied to their leaders . . . and the political development of their countries."[59] In fact, in Peru and Cuba, the student movements were crucial in the creation and development of radical political parties like the Alianza Popular Revolucionaria Americana (APRA; American Popular Revolutionary Alliance) and the Cuban Communist Party.[60]

For Rivera Martínez, however, the students leading the Puerto Rican strike were not genuinely interested in defending the university's honor or prestige but were instead looking for fame and celebrity status. He concluded: "I publicly consign my protest to what I consider an insult by the so-called university youth toward the representation of Puerto Rico's working classes in the university's Board of Trustees." Unlike the cases in

Cuba and Mexico cited by Rivera Martínez, the nascent Puerto Rican student movement led the strike and called for greater autonomy but without proposing to transform Puerto Rican society. In the process, the strike also became a battleground for traditional political parties.[61]

During the last weeks of October, many labor unions and local sections of the Socialist Party held assemblies and meetings to discuss the political situation. Most Socialist sections approved resolutions in support of Governor Gore's administration and Alonso Torres's appointment.[62] Some party members complained that the Socialist Party had not acted in a virile manner in response to Alonso Torres's situation and that it needed to create a national propaganda campaign.[63] Their opinions did not go unheard. The Coalición organized the Loyalty Crusade in hopes to counter the media attack on their party. Speakers would travel throughout the island defending Alonso Torres and the Coalición while handing out caps, T-shirts, and other gifts.[64] Unfortunately for Alonso Torres, these efforts came too late.

The Final Countdown

After all, we shall see worst things because it is innate for humans to fall today so they can stand tomorrow. —LUZ Y VIDA, December 13, 1909

On Sunday, November 5, 1933, an atmosphere of uncertainty reigned throughout the country. In less than twenty-four hours the academic recess decreed by Chancellor Chardón would come to an end without any solution to the conflict in sight. In the eastern town of Caguas, high school students held their national assembly and ratified their solidarity with university students. Although some high schools had decreed stoppages or short-term strikes, the national assembly approved an indefinite strike pending Alonso Torres's resignation.[65] In Mayagüez, students at the UPR Agricultural College ratified the strike and said they would not go back to classes the following day.[66] In Río Piedras, a parents' assembly took place in the town's Victoria Theater and culminated with a resolution to support striking students.[67]

Panic reigned in the governor's mansion as telegrams and phone calls were received with rumors that blood would be spilled on Monday morning.[68] The governor feared that the strike would spread through not only high schools but also elementary schools.[69] Later that Sunday night, more than eight thousand people gathered in Río Piedras's public plaza to attend a public meeting organized by students. Their message was clear; they would rather have the university closed than have Alonso Torres as a trustee.[70] Their meeting ended at 2 AM, and instead of heading home, students marched toward the university gates to prevent anyone from entering the following morning. While tensions were high, an aura of celebration spread; rumors about Alonso Torres's imminent resignation started to circulate.[71]

Those in favor of the university strike were not the only ones active that Sunday. The Socialist Party's executive committee held an all-day emergency meeting to discuss the situation. Members of the Coalición and even Governor Gore had urged President Roosevelt and the secretary of war, George Dern, to appoint a new commissioner of education, because they considered the current one responsible for the strike.[72] Their claims went unheard.[73]

The public image of the Coalición and, most importantly, of the Socialist Party had suffered a great deal. Not only was Rafael Alonso Torres publicly ridiculed, but growing tensions within the party were giving way to factions and dissident groups that openly challenged the leadership's authority. Moreover, the FLT, which Alonso Torres also presided over, suffered significant setbacks. They had negotiated a collective bargaining agreement with sugar barons without consulting their membership. This caused the latter to go against the FLT's leadership in a series of massive strikes in the sugarcane sector in 1933 and 1934.[74]

The Socialist Party's meeting started early on Sunday morning. During the lunch break Governor Gore summoned the Socialists Prudencio Rivera Martínez and Pedro L. Sosa to his mansion, which was a stone's throw away from FLT headquarters. Governor Gore had been ill in past days; he was pale and weak. The governor talked about how the situation was affecting his family and his health, and how he feared the worst if the strike continued.[75] He suggested two possible solutions to the strike. The first was to dissolve the university's board of trustees, giving absolute power to Chancellor Chardón and the education commissioner. Both Rivera Martínez and Sosa immediately rejected the proposal because it would favor the Liberals, which they vehemently opposed. The second proposal consisted of Alonso Torres's resignation, solving the conflict once and for all. If Alonso Torres did not quit on his own, the governor was going to ask for his resignation anyway.[76]

Later that afternoon, Rivera Martínez delivered the governor's proposals to the party's executive committee and said he would stand behind any resolution they agreed on. Nonetheless, he remarked that if Alonso Torres did not resign, the Socialist Party had to be ready to go to war against the governor, which would inevitably favor the Liberals. After hours of debate and deliberations, Rafael Alonso Torres agreed to quit his position as a university trustee, under one condition. Alonso Torres wanted the Socialist Party to officially resign from any future appointment or representation in the university's board of trustees. Against the party's advice, Alonso Torres declared war on the university as an institution. Before the meeting was adjourned, a committee composed of Prudencio Rivera Martínez, Pedro Sosa, and Juan Carreras was appointed the task of revising the resolution and delivering it to both the media and the governor. Newspapers waited for it and did not print their next day's edition until early dawn hours.[77]

On Monday, November 6, the newspaper *El mundo* published the resolution approved by the Socialist Party's executive committee. Thus, before the committee arrived at the governor's mansion to deliver Alonso Torres's resignation, Gore had already read it in the press. Likewise, Santiago Iglesias Pantín, who was in Washington, sent a letter to Alonso Torres telling him that he was following the events but was surprised to read about his resignation in the press. Iglesias Pantín affirmed, "Naturally, I was startled by the news at first, but after meditating for a while I was happy with the decision although I do not know the details yet."[78]

The resolution that was approved by the executive committee and was now circulating in the media had a fiery tone. It called on Socialists throughout the island to organize protests and any other action that could help in the struggle against "reactionaries." It also declared that the Socialist Party declined any future appointment to the board of trustees, and if any individual accepted such a position, they were acting outside the party and were to be expelled. That determination had been opposed by members of the executive committee and made the governor uncomfortable, as he told the commission that handed him Alonso Torres's resignation.[79] A few days later, the governor left with his family to get treatment in the United States for his kidney problems; he never came back. Governor Gore officially resigned on January 8, 1934.[80]

Following his resignation from UPR's board of trustees, Alonso Torres received various letters of support from Socialists throughout the island. "At first I considered your resignation as cowardice," wrote Agustín Alonso, a Socialist from the eastern town of Río Grande, "but after studying the situation and its depth I have concluded that it is a noble and altruist action, I congratulate you and sincerely have your back."[81] Altruism and the noble dimension of his actions were common themes throughout the letters of support Alonso Torres received. "Unlike the reactionaries at the university," wrote Olivia vda. de Braschi, "Alonso or the 'Socialist Party's' resignation from that trustship (I do not know if that is properly spelled [she recalled]), has been a glorious act. . . . I congratulate Alonso and the 'Socialist Party' from the bottom of my heart for your Christian-like actions, they are more spiritual in their feelings than those artificially educated because education today lacks a culture of feelings."[82]

But not all Socialists celebrated Alonso Torres's resignation. Francisca Barrios and her daughter Acracia sent a scorching letter expressing their dissatisfaction with Alonso Torres and the Socialist Party's decision. Both women came from a family of well-known radicals from the northern town of Bayamón. Francisca was a school principal and was married to longtime labor leader, agitator, and cigarmaker Ramón Barrios. Acracia, who was twenty-two at the time they wrote the letter, was the oldest of five children. Her name, which meant "lack of order," was a subtle tribute to her parents' anarchist ideology at the time of her birth.[83] The letter, signed by Francisca and Acracia, started by offering an apology for any annoyance that it might cause. Nonetheless, they felt entitled to write to "V. H." (Spanish acronym for "your honor") "on behalf of the two votes we deposited in the ballot box to support the representation of the working class in any institution that the working class has a right to be represented."[84]

Francisca and Acracia recognized that they did not know him personally, but they knew of him and his actions through the press. Newspapers apparently gave some workers a sense of social proximity with labor leaders. Casting their votes justified their intervention in the Socialist Party's affairs, which Francisca and Acracia understood as the political representation of the working classes. "We burned with rebelliousness after learning about your resignation at a critical moment to your position as a trustee of the wrongly called University." It did not matter if it was Alonso Torres or any other labor leader, but resigning such a position "has directly hurt our personality as respectable workingmen as we handed them our weapons in the height of the struggle, without consulting the movements that indirectly support you."[85]

Another workingman, Francisco Govas, developed a similar argument to that of Francisca and Acracia. He argued that although Alonso Torres did not have an academic title, it did not matter because "experience is life's knowledge." Nonetheless, he heavily criticized how the Socialist Party handled the strike. For Govas, the results were the fault of the organized labor movement. "The battle in which the reaction's plutocratic interests were imposed took place because we allowed our enemies to choose a favorable space and we handed them our alma [soul]: the arma [weapon] of the strike." According to Govas, the Socialist Party and the FLT should have responded with a general strike in every industry.[86] The voices of people like Francisca and Acracia Barrios and Francisco Govas demonstrate a deep resentment toward labor leaders and their growing disconnection with the party's membership.

IN THE MONTHS following the strike, there were calls of treason, expulsions, and factional splits within the Socialist Party. The political project that a cluster of urban skilled workingmen had built for three decades was starting to fall apart, and the UPR student strike became a watershed moment. It was the first in a series of events that would eventually turn the Socialist Party from a powerful force into an almost insignificant player in the island's political sphere. After the student strike, a series of wildcat strikes against the FLT spread throughout the countryside in 1933 and 1934. Meanwhile, a dissident group that called itself Afirmación Socialista (Socialist Affirmation) emerged from within the Socialist Party and promoted Puerto Rico's independence and the resignation of Alonso Torres. Afirmación Socialista also advocated the creation of a new labor federation and unsuccessfully ran in the 1936 elections as a separate political entity. Although Afirmación Socialista lasted only two years, its impact was long-lasting.[87] Furthermore, during a series of dockworker strikes in 1938, new labor unions as well as other international federations, like the Congress of Industrial Organizations (CIO), arrived in Puerto Rico and fractured the FLT's hegemonic power over the organized labor movement.[88]

As the student strike had demonstrated, a large segment of the university population—including students, faculty, and administration—distrusted workers and considered them culturally and intellectually unfit. Two years after the strike, in 1935, the university created a partnership with the Department of Labor to create an educational program for workers. It was a short-term program for a degree in "teacher in workers' education" from the university.[89] Not much is known about this partnership, but one thing is sure: workers were allowed into the university as consumers of knowledge, but as the strike demonstrated, they were not considered legitimate producers of it. In fact, the 1930s was an important turning point for the country's intellectual elite. They went from articulating their literary and aesthetic projects in cafés, private residences, and literary magazines toward using the university and a renovated Ateneo Puertorriqueño as the locus of the country's intellectual power. Scholars like Antonio S. Pedreira, Tomás Blanco, and

Antonio S. Beleval began setting the foundations of Puerto Rico's literary establishment, while also redefining and reimagining the nation. As had happened at the turn of the twentieth century, workingmen were not part of such conversations. In fact, Rafael Alonso Torres was excluded from the UPR precisely when these processes began to take place.[90]

The strike also proved fatal for Rafael Alonso Torres's political career. He went from having eleven official positions within the FLT, the Socialist Party, and Puerto Rico's House of Representatives to having none three years after the strike. As Alonso Torres became ill, dissidents within the party pushed him to resign and, in his absence during the 1936 party convention, went against the resolution he had developed during the strike. Hundreds of delegates unanimously voted that "the Socialist Party should claim adequate representation" in the UPR. To do so, they approved a resolution that nulled "any previous agreement adopted by our party." The days of Rafael Alonso Torres's control over the party's direction were gone. Perhaps the strike became a chronicle of a death foretold; it anticipated the inevitable demise of the Socialist Party, the FLT, and the lettered barriada, but no one tried to stop it.[91] Thus, as internal party frictions began to deepen, as a generational relay began to take place, and as their hegemonic power over organized labor was effectively challenged, it was imperative for those that had built the lettered barriada and the Socialist Party to craft and bequeath a set of historical narratives centering themselves and the organizations over which they presided.

Obreros ilustrados had built an intellectual community.

They had built a party.

They had become public figures.

Now, it was time to consolidate labor's ideational archive.

CHAPTER 6. **MINOR THEFT**

Consolidating the Barriada's Ideational Archive

Fifteen years before the student strike, in 1918, Antonio R. Barceló, then president of the Senate and leader of the Union Party, accused labor organizers Rafael Alonso Torres and Jesús M. Balsac of stealing official Senate documents. He was referring to a series of private letters published in the working-class newspapers *Unión obrera* and *El baluarte* (The stronghold). In the letters, Barceló corresponded with various people about the possibility of creating a labor federation to diminish the FLT's sphere of influence. In possession of a court-ordered search warrant, on August 23, 1918, the police raided the FLT's headquarters in San Juan. Joined by the Senate's stenograph, police officers flipped and tossed over documents while searching through desks and cabinets. Rafael Alonso Torres, famously known for his hot temper, cursed and complained as he waited for the FLT's lawyer, Abraham Peña, to arrive at the scene.[1]

Peña's loyalty to the FLT was unquestioned. He was a Black lawyer from Mayagüez who resided in San Juan. Peña had joined the labor federation in its early days, along with his now-deceased wife, Paca Escabí. Upon arrival, Peña asked to read the court order. After carefully reading the warrant, he ordered the police to stop; it was plagued with errors, making the search illegal. For example, the warrant was for the American Federation of Labor. Their headquarters were in Washington, not San Juan, as Peña mockingly told the officers. Similarly, the warrant did not specify which documents they were looking for, giving officers impunity to take whatever they wanted. As tensions escalated, Rafael Alonso Torres opened a file cabinet, took copies of the notorious letters, and handed them to the police.[2]

Rafael Alonso Torres was cited to court and charged with "minor theft." Socialists used the press to condemn Barceló, the unionists, and the government's politically motivated repression and intimidation. The following day, solidarity mítines were reported in almost all of Puerto Rico's towns and municipalities. In Puerta de Tierra, for example, more than three thousand Socialists came together and agreed to send a telegram to Washington in protest.[3] But demonstrations were not limited to public plazas. Alonso Torres compiled all correspondence, newspaper clippings, and court documents related to the incident and published a book tauntingly titled *Hurto menor* (Minor theft). But, if the incident had been well documented in the press, what was the purpose of publishing a book? Was the publication of such a book a stance against newspaper's ephemerality or were these the first steps toward the consolidation of labor's ideational archive?

According to Alonso Torres, he published *Hurto menor* "in case any curious researcher decides to unravel this [court] process' foundations, which constitutes, like other events, the history of the Puerto Rican labor movement, in which we have the honor of participating, and . . . there's nothing better than to leave a brief story that can guide them and their research."[4] As Alonso Torres's trial progressed, it became clear that Barceló's letters were not stolen from the Senate, but that an anonymous source had given them to Santiago Iglesias Pantín in Washington. Since he did not have a use for them there, Iglesias Pantín sent them—as *Hurto menor* emphatically recalled in bold letters—"to the ARCHIVE AND HISTORY OF THE COUNTRY'S LABOR MOVEMENT."[5]

But *Hurto Menor* was not the first book of its kind published by labor leaders. The publication of edited volumes documenting specific historical events was not uncommon; it was part of the lettered barriada's broader print tradition since the turn of the twentieth century. When labor leaders were unlawfully charged and imprisoned, or when mítines were violently suppressed, obreros ilustrados compiled books with all related documents.[6] It was a way of spreading information to workers throughout the island and abroad. It also preserved the movement's histories. Indeed, edited collections became mobile archives.

Hurto menor hit the streets in 1919. The following decade, the Socialist Party turned into a force to be reckoned with, consolidating the lettered barriada's political project. Meanwhile, it became increasingly important for labor leaders not only to document events through edited volumes, but also to create their own historical narratives and interpretations. Three of the island's most important labor leaders—all of them founding members of both the FLT and the Socialist Party—published a series of books framed as memoirs, opinions, and historical accounts. These were Santiago Iglesias Pantín's *Luchas emancipadoras* (Emancipatory struggles, 1929), José Ferrer y Ferrer's *Los ideales del siglo XX* (The ideals of the twentieth century, 1932), and Rafael Alonso Torres's *Cuarenta años de lucha proletaria* (Forty years of proletarian struggle, 1939). While they wrote each book with a different perspective and style, all of them shared the logic of crafting a historical narrative of the movement centered on its authors and the institutions over which they presided. To be sure, there had been dozens of working-class books published before, but because of their chronological breadth and impact in later labor historiography, these three books became foundational texts; together, they became the consolidation of labor's ideational archive.[7]

But why was there a desire to publish these books at that specific historical moment? Like most early twentieth-century *obreros ilustrados*, these three authors, Iglesias Pantín, Ferrer y Ferrer, and Alonso Torres, had received most of their education in workshops and working-class centros. While they lacked formal school instruction, they had participated in popular educational projects that allowed them to articulate political ideas and to develop their own historical narratives. Meanwhile, a generational relay started to take place among the FLT and the Socialist Party's leadership. The new generation of labor leaders that emerged in the late 1920s and throughout the 1930s—exemplified in the likes of Lino Padrón Rivera, Bolívar Pagán, and Francisco Colón Gordiany—entered the movement from vastly different social positions. Most were university-trained professionals; for example, Padrón Rivera studied agriculture, while Pagán and Colón Gordiany both practiced law.[8]

There was a clear turnover in the social and educational upbringing of these new cadres of working-class intellectuals. The first generation of working-class thinkers—the *obreros ilustrados* we have followed throughout the pages of this book—went from the workshop to their unions, and only then to the political tribune. The newer generation, which can be identified as "working-class intellectuals," came out of universities, to their professional jobs, to the political tribune, and only later, if ever, to workers' unions. In other words, their social upbringing had been different from those who were educated in workshops and who oftentimes received formal instruction only in working-class centros and makeshift night schools.

Besides the generational relay that threatened obreros ilustrados' power within labor institutions, there were a series of internal splits caused by groups of workers that did not feel represented by the labor movement's leadership in the 1930s. While the FLT had dominated the world of unions, being the leading labor federation in the island since the turn of the century, new organizations and independent unions challenged its hegemonic control over the movement. Other working-class parties, including the Communist Party (1934), the Popular Democratic Party (1938), and the Pure Labor Party (1939), also challenged or appropriated certain aspects of the Socialist Party's political project.[9]

These frictions took place at an institutional level but were also personally felt by these obreros ilustrados. Some Socialists accused Santiago Iglesias Pantín of abandoning the labor movement after he left Puerto Rico in 1924 to work with the Pan-American Federation of Labor and later in 1932 when elected as the island's resident commissioner in Washington. Others argued that if he had stayed in Puerto Rico, most frictions would have been avoided. Nonetheless, members of the FLT and the Socialist Party still referred to Iglesias Pantín as the "maestro" and "creator of the labor movement," a myth that eventually became history. Not all labor leaders were as lucky. After being active for three decades in the labor movement, Ferrer y Ferrer was expelled from the Socialist Party, while Alonso Torres was forced to step down from the party's leadership in 1936.[10] Leaving their historical accounts, thus, became a highly political act. If they could not be absolved in the present, history could do so in the future. Such was the power of dominating the production of history, or so they believed. Like those obreros ilustrados at the beginning of the century who used print media to become journalists, poets, and litterateurs, through the publication of their books, these workers-turned-politicians now imagined themselves as historians at a moment when the discipline of history was being consolidated in Puerto Rico.

Five years after the publication of Iglesias Pantín's *Luchas emancipadoras*, in 1934, a group of intellectuals under the leadership of the writer and lawyer Vicente Geigel Polanco created the Academy of History at the Ateneo Puertorriqueño. Its first director was Mariano Abril y Ostaló, the same person who had mocked Puerto Rican workingmen for trying to enter the political sphere in 1911, and whom Rafael Alonso Torres was unsuccessfully appointed to succeed as a university trustee in 1933. During the 1930s, the Ateneo Puertorriqueño underwent a revival as one of the premier cultural and intellectual hubs in Puerto Rico. This was tied to a broader cultural shift from the country's intellectual elites' concentration in cafés, *tertulías* (social gatherings), and private soirees toward the consolidation of the UPR and the Ateneo Puertorriqueño as the bastions of what would be considered legitimate cultural production.[11]

It was also a moment when the intellectual elite began using history to trace the coordinates of what it meant to be Puerto Rican. One of the most important publications of the time was *Índice* (Index), a monthly magazine that served as Puerto Rico's cultural compass.[12] Its editor, Antonio S. Pedreira, a professor of Hispanic studies at UPR, became the country's leading intellectual. Pedreira's book *Insularismo* (Insularism), published in 1934, and physician Tomás Blanco's *Prontuario histórico de Puerto Rico* (Puerto Rico's historical record), published in 1935, became the blueprints for the formation of an imagined "Puerto Rican essence."[13] Most of these thinkers were writing from an Hispanista (Hispanic-centric) tradition that understood the US occupation as detrimental toward the creation of a homogenous national identity.[14] The three obreros ilustrados that I study in this chapter operated outside those precepts. In fact, they supported the annexation of Puerto Rico to the United States. It is no surprise, then, that when Iglesias Pantín's *Luchas emancipadoras* was reviewed in *Índice*, its editors could not hide their contempt. While they acknowledged the book's importance in "exhuming some events from oblivion," they also noted that "these events seem transmuted rather than generated by our own environment, as if they responded to an imported ideology and not to the one forged by the working classes of this island."[15] As the following pages demonstrate, their assessment was not completely inaccurate.

The 1930s also became a transitional moment for the professionalization of history. In the mid-1920s, Rafael W. Ramírez de Arellano was appointed as the UPR's first professor of history.[16] This signaled a shift in how historical knowledge was going to be produced in the following decades. Before, the production of history had been an intellectual pursuit of professionals (lawyers, physicians, and journalists), as exemplified by who can be considered Puerto Rico's first historians: José Julián Acosta (journalist), Salvador Brau (journalist), Cayetano Coll y Toste (physician), and Mariano Abril y Ostaló (journalist), among others.[17] Ramírez de Arellano continued with the nineteenth-century tradition of publishing edited collections rooted in a positivist understanding of history as empirical knowledge extracted from primary sources.[18] This theoretical orientation changed in the following decade with the rise of the Popular Democratic Party, which radically transformed the university and gave way to the creation of the

UPR's Department of History in 1941.[19] Nonetheless, it is in tune with that nineteenth-century positivist tradition that obreros ilustrados began writing their own historical narratives. As one review of Iglesias Pantín's book published in a Cuban socialist newspaper read, "As a source for consultation for the future history of socialism in America, the book *Luchas emancipadoras* will have a truly insurmountable value."[20] These books, then, were imagined as blueprints for future historians to write a "real" history of the laboring masses—that is, to reproduce the historical narratives obreros ilustrados crafted as the laboring masses' self-assigned interlocutors.

In the process, these books also archived the authors' desires and anxieties. To unearth them, we must not only pay attention to content but also understand these books as the product of specific temporal and spatial moments in their authors' political careers. As essayist Alejandro Chacoff argued about Argentinian writer Ricardo Piglia's work, "Making history, it turns out, is a little like making sense of a novel. There is a voice to be heard, hidden patterns, and repetitions."[21] This chapter seeks to tease out those voices, hidden patterns, and repetitions within the barriada's ideational archive. To do so, I follow Ricardo Piglia's dictum and "read between the lines, as though there was always something to decipher," which "is in itself a political act."[22]

Crafting a Historical Genealogy: *Luchas emancipadoras*

It is better to say the truth, no matter what it takes, than let it transpire and mystify with lies or hypocrisy.—LUZ Y VIDA, August 30, 1909

Santiago Iglesias Pantín's entrance into the world of letters can be traced all the way back to a newspaper article from 1892. He then resided in Cuba but published in *El corsario* (The corsair), an anarchist publication from his hometown of La Coruña, Spain.[23] In Puerto Rico, he became an active member of the lettered barriada, penning articles in various newspapers, publishing books, and even acting in working-class theatrical plays.[24] Iglesias Pantín arrived in Puerto Rico as a carpenter by trade, but he excelled not in his wood skills but in social networking. As early as 1901 he had made acquaintances in the United States that went from befriending leaders like the Socialist Daniel DeLeon and the AFL's president Samuel Gompers to meeting and corresponding with the presidents of the United States. These contacts led to the FLT's incorporation under the AFL's umbrella. On October 14, 1901, Iglesias Pantín officially became the AFL's general organizer for both Puerto Rico and Cuba, thus abandoning the workshop for the rest of his life and starting his long journey to become a statesman.[25] That was the journey he sought to document in his book *Luchas emancipadoras: Crónicas de Puerto Rico* (Emancipatory struggles: Chronicles of Puerto Rico).

Iglesias Pantín's book was published in 1929, when he started his second term as senator at large. It was an impressive 388-page book divided into thirty-six chapters. Through its pages, Iglesias Pantín crafted the labor movement's first comprehensive history. He did so by centering the narrative on himself and the FLT. The book's introduction set the narrative in La Coruña, where Iglesias Pantín spent his first days, and it then covered his time in Havana, Cuba, where he came of age. Iglesias Pantín advised readers that his time in Cuba would be the topic of a future volume, which he never got to publish.[26] While *Luchas emancipadoras* aspired to present the first ten years of the twentieth century, the book documented his arrival to Puerto Rico in 1896 until 1905, dedicating only one chapter to events that happened from that year until 1910. In the last chapter, Iglesias Pantín broke away from the book's narrative arc to summarize debates regarding Puerto Rico's political status from the US occupation in 1898 until 1917, when Puerto Ricans were granted US citizenship through the Jones Act.

The book's original title, *Crónicas de Puerto Rico* (Chronicles of Puerto Rico), which eventually became its subtitle, presents another way of understanding the book. Centering the narrative on his experiences, Iglesias Pantín meant to offer a written record of past labor struggles that had been ignored by official histories until then. In tune with the theory of history developed by obreros ilustrados—undoubtedly influenced by contemporaneous professional historians' understanding of the past as fixed and reachable through official documents—*Luchas emancipadoras* constantly used and reproduced historical sources in the text. For example, there are chapters that consist only of cited legal documents, newspaper clippings, or correspondence.

If Santiago Iglesias Pantín and his contemporaries understood the role of historians as making the past accessible to the public, then it is important to ask who was *Luchas emancipadoras*'s intended audience. At the beginning of the book Iglesias Pantín addressed two vastly different group of readers. First, he wanted "the intellectual and working-class youth, from workshops and factories, from the countryside and offices, to familiarize themselves with past struggles."[27] While the events he covered in the book had been mostly ignored by contemporaneous professional historians,

Iglesias Pantín believed that they were the foundations of the country's civic life. In other words, he attempted to create a historical genealogy of the labor movement's advancements until the book's publication. If workers enjoyed any rights or benefits, it was, according to Iglesias Pantín, the product of the work done by labor organizations he had presided over.

But since Iglesias Pantín could not establish the labor movement's historical genealogy by himself, he turned his attention to the second group of desired readers: historians. Echoing the aspirations of edited collections like *Hurto menor*, he asked historians to use *Luchas emancipadoras* to create an objective history of the labor movement. In this sense, Iglesias Pantín imagined the book's historical contribution as twofold. It was a narrative created by the movement's undisputable leader but was also a primary source. Recognizing the book's multiple aspirations, Iglesias Pantín considered it a chronicle, an autobiography, and narrations all at once. It was historians who, in the words of Iglesias Pantín, needed to document "the formative period of many fighters in the proletarian's preliminary struggles for civilization and justice, in which thousands of working peasants were liberated."[28] *Luchas emancipadoras*, then, was a history not of the working classes but of those who, according to its author, liberated the working peasants, created orators, and granted the masses rights that were until then unthinkable. It was a history of the movement's leaders, all of whom were, according to the author, influenced by him.

From the book's first pages, Iglesias Pantín differentiates between labor leaders and the rest. To center the narrative on himself, Iglesias Pantín employed two different discursive strategies. The first one was explicit. He used more than a dozen "I" statements throughout *Luchas emancipadoras*, specifically when recounting important historical events. For example, after describing a scuffle with the editors of *Ensayo obrero*, which he helped found, Iglesias Pantín argued, "They [Romero Rosa, José Ferrer y Ferrer, Fernando Acosta, and Eduardo Conde] were not efficient organizers and their ideas were not clearly established in relation to . . . trade-unionism and socialism."[29] Thus, as he mentioned twice in the book, "orators had to be 'fabricated.'" All those orators that were fabricated and mobilized in the movement's early days "were stimulated and induced by me."[30]

Likewise, when Iglesias Pantín narrated the events that took place during a series of agricultural strikes in 1905, he wrote: "The FLT was the organizer of these first coordinated grand movements of agricultural workingmen. . . . *I was in charge of the organization and direction of these great strikes* that shook the country."[31] But these strikes were the product of the unacknowledged effort of local, often nonunionized organizers. Agricultural workingmen went on strike in the thousands without consulting the FLT, which arrived at the scene after the strike was well underway. Furthermore, although the FLT did ultimately support the 1905 strikes, agricultural workingmen did not join the labor federation led by Iglesias Pantín afterward. In fact, the number of agricultural workingmen unionized plummeted to an all-time low in the following years.[32]

The other discursive strategy used by Iglesias Pantín to center *Luchas emancipadoras*'s narrative on himself was nonexplicit. He narrated events claiming he was presenting an objective historical reality but always suggesting that he influenced them. Perhaps one of the most striking was his account of how Puerto Rico's military government ended. After the invasion of 1898, the United States set up a military government to overlook Puerto Rico's administrative and political affairs. It lasted until May 1, 1900, when the Foraker Act was inaugurated, which established a somewhat democratic government and made the island's inhabitants Puerto Rican citizens, something that changed in 1917.

To explain the end of the military government (1898–1900) in Puerto Rico, Santiago Iglesias Pantín described a trip he made with Eduardo Conde to the Socialist Labor Party's national convention in Rochester, New York, in 1900. According to Iglesias Pantín, it was after he gave a series of speeches in New York that public opinion in the United States started to condemn Puerto Rico's military government. After the convention, both labor leaders stayed in New York and gave several public speeches about the situation workers faced in Puerto Rico. On March 8, 1900, for example, Iglesias Pantín addressed a large crowd at an event in Cooper Union. Parts of Iglesias Pantín's speech were reproduced in various news outlets, including the *Worker*, the *New York Tribune*, and the *New York Sun*, among others. In *Luchas emancipadoras* Iglesias Pantín argued that public "opinion in the Nation agreed almost unanimously that [Puerto Rico's] military government should be abolished."[33] He cited an article published in the *Journal of Commerce* about a meeting President McKinley had held with various senators about the situation of Puerto Rico. According to Iglesias Pantín, the statesmen agreed with what the *New York Sun* had published. In other words, they agreed with his speech and, thus, the presidential meeting sought to "lessen the existing burden among the producers of Puerto Rico."[34] Although the 1900 Foraker Act that ended the US military government was already being discussed in Congress and would be approved a few weeks later, on April 12, 1900, Iglesias Pantín suggested that the articles published in the press documenting his speeches in New York ultimately influenced public opinion and, thus, forced the US president to end Puerto Rico's military government.

Understanding the political climate when the book came out also allows another reading of some of Iglesias Pantín's arguments. He published *Luchas emancipadoras* a year after the 1928 elections. The Alianza Puertorriqueña (Puerto Rican Alliance)—composed of the Union Party and dissident members from the Republican Party—crushed the electoral pact between Socialists and Republicans through the ballot box, greatly demoralizing the Socialist leadership. According to Bolívar Pagán, it was Iglesias Pantín who continued to encourage the party's leadership to organize its rank and file for the next election cycle.[35]

Through his book, Iglesias Pantín used historical narratives to attack his political opponents. For example, he argued that Rosendo Matienzo Cintrón, the Puerto Rican lawyer and politician who cofounded the Union Party, had been greatly influenced by him. While it may seem like one of the book's simple historical details, it was, nonetheless, a politically charged statement. Since the Union Party had been the Alianza Puertorriqueña's forerunner, Santiago Iglesias Pantín ultimately projected himself as the inspiration behind the creation of his opponent's party. Using history to argue that he led the movement for the proletarian masses' regeneration might have been not only the product of his ego but perhaps a discursive trope to attract voters in the following 1932 elections. A few months before the elections, Ferrer y Ferrer published *Los ideales del siglo XX*.

A Mythology of Radicalism: *Los ideales del siglo XX*

Work is the great engine that gives life and moves the gears of science, industry, and the arts.—LUZ Y VIDA, February 15, 1910

Contrary to the weighty tone of *Luchas emancipadoras*, the format and aesthetics of Ferrer y Ferrer's book resembled the political pamphlets that circulated in the lettered barriada at the beginning of the century (figure 6.1). Printing technologies had advanced by the 1930s, and the production of books was vastly refined. Some now had colorful artwork and elegant hard covers, but that was not the case for Ferrer y Ferrer's book. It had a simple front page, with the title in bold and a small picture of an open book in the center. It also included glossy black-and-white photos of some of the labor movement's most famous leaders, including, of course, Santiago Iglesias Pantín and Rafael Alonso Torres.

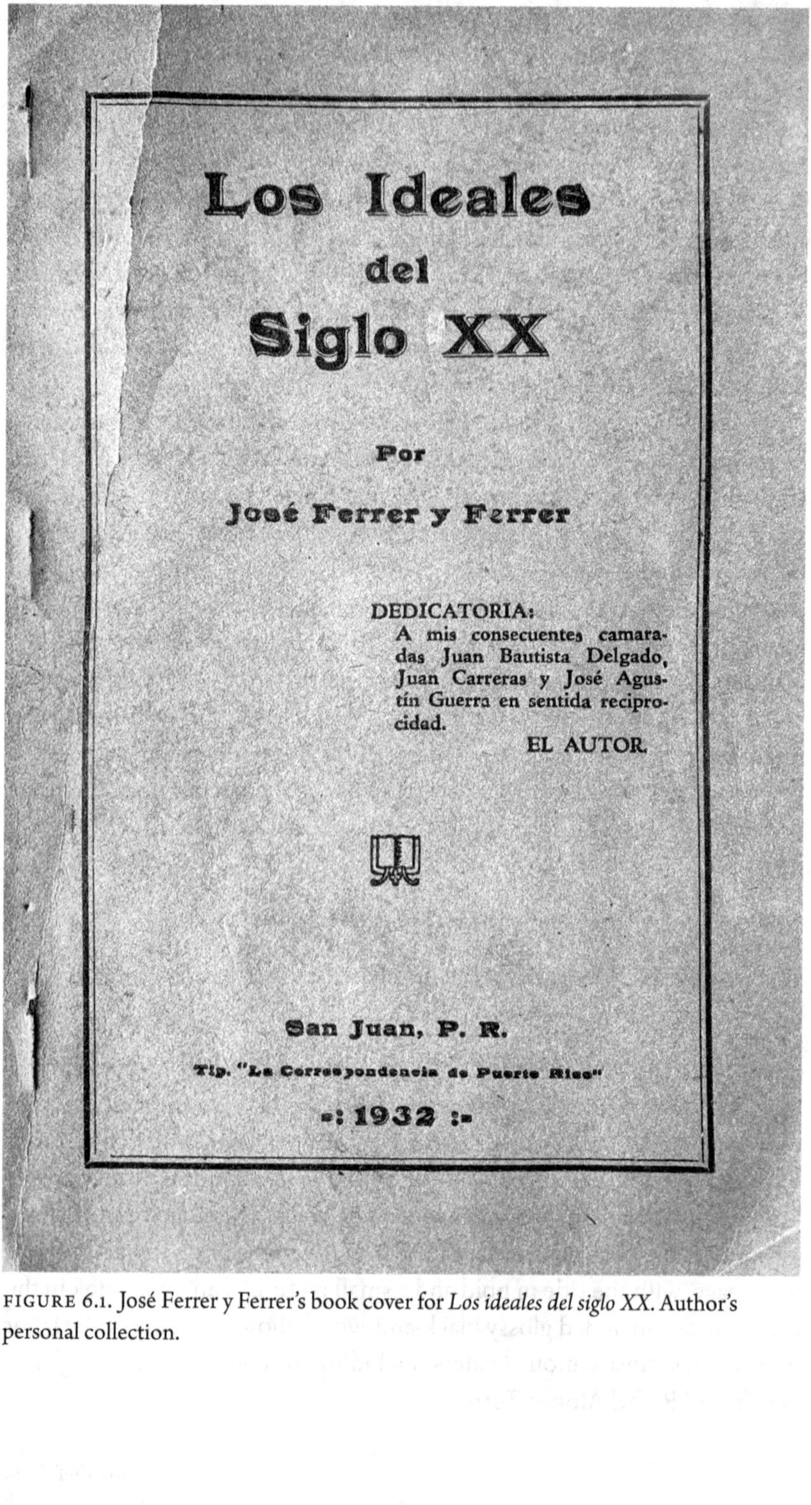

Los Ideales
del
Siglo XX

Por

José Ferrer y Ferrer

DEDICATORIA:
A mis consecuentes camara-
das Juan Bautista Delgado,
Juan Carreras y José Agustín Guerra en sentida recipro-
cidad.

EL AUTOR.

San Juan, P. R.

Tip. "La Correspondencia de Puerto Rico"

-: 1932 :-

FIGURE 6.1. José Ferrer y Ferrer's book cover for *Los ideales del siglo XX*. Author's personal collection.

Los ideales del siglo XX was a 134-page pamphlet divided into sixteen chapters. Unlike the books by Iglesias Pantín and Alonso Torres, it was neither autobiography nor history, but instead it mixed historical examples and philosophical analyses to explain the development of socialism in Puerto Rico and abroad. Some chapters, like "El hombre" (The man), offered abstract theoretical interventions about the role of humans in society, while others presented insights into the history of socialism in Mexico, Europe, and the Soviet Union. These were complemented with political commentaries and historical interpretations of socialism's origins in Puerto Rico and how multiple schools of radical thought found a space within the Socialist Party.

The book also demonstrated the anxiety of producing intellectual work without having an academic degree. Ferrer y Ferrer rhetorically asked, "Is it required for a workingman to worthily represent his class in the Parliament to be a philosopher of poor blood, to possess and enjoy the monopoly of critical and historical research, usurping the prestige of those heroes from workshops, factories, and fields?"[36] Citing the works of the Russian anarchist philosopher Piotr Kropotkin, Ferrer y Ferrer argued that class prejudices had violently separated intellectual and manual labor. "Since men of science feel contempt towards manual labor," noted Ferrer y Ferrer, "they have elevated their contempt to theory."[37] That was precisely what Ferrer y Ferrer wanted to reconcile in the pages of *Los ideales*: manual and intellectual labor. After all, his life was the clearest example of someone who merged both; he was a workshop-educated Black workingman who eventually became one of the movement's most prominent thinkers.

The pen was not his only forte. Ferrer y Ferrer collaborated in the creation of several social study centers in San Juan and in the eastern town of Caguas. He also organized various speaking tours throughout Puerto Rico in hopes of attracting workers to the FLT's ranks. Unlike Santiago Iglesias Pantín, Ferrer y Ferrer's name is mostly unknown nowadays. Nonetheless, he was one of the most esteemed and well-known labor leaders of his times. In the prologue of Valentín Castrillo's book *Mis experiencias a través de 50 años* (My experience through 50 years), one of Ferrer y Ferrer's disciples, Juan S. Marcano, wrote in 1952: "Whoever has known Valentín Castrillo [knows that] he is made of the same real wood as Cropoquín, Malatesta, Malato, Sebastían Faure, Anselmo Lorenzo, and the *maestro* José Ferrer y Ferrer."[38] For Marcano, Ferrer y Ferrer was part of the international canon of radical thinkers that had greatly influenced the lettered barriada. Ferrer y Ferrer's book, *Los ideales del siglo XX*, published in 1932, opted to do precisely that: to locate

Puerto Rican Socialists and the Socialist Party within a global genealogy of radicalism.

Ferrer y Ferrer's book's title, *Los ideales del siglo XX*, is a tribute to the Catalan anarchist intellectual Adrián del Valle, who in 1900 published a short book called *El ideal del siglo XX* (The twentieth-century ideal) under the pseudonym of Palmiro de Lidia. Both books demonstrated a shared teleological notion of moving toward progress. "Without a doubt," wrote Ferrer y Ferrer, "progress is caused by a permanent, rational revolution, and its effects are the transformation of society. Humanity constantly moves towards purification."[39] These authors reproduced the notion, quite in vogue at the turn of the century, that the masses' transformation and regeneration could happen only if they studied and absorbed rational ideas.[40]

While explaining the meaning of socialism and how it had developed, Ferrer y Ferrer identified a canon of radical thinkers that had influenced Puerto Rican workers since the turn of the twentieth century. He dedicated several pages to explaining the theories of Piotr Kropotkin, Jean Grave, Pierre-Joseph Proudhon, and José Rizal; except for Rizal, all were anarchist intellectuals. He argued, "Contemporary Sociology, which takes shape in modern civilization[,] now offers more humane and intelligent things to thinking men."[41] Using the example of Jean Grave, Ferrer y Ferrer once again tackled the topic of producing knowledge without academic degrees. He wrote that Grave was "a workingman that was elevated to great intellectual potential. Those whose spirit have been formed listening to meritless professors; those that look over the shoulder at those that have never set foot in an academic classroom; those that have learned what they know in explanations and books of wise men at the service of the dominant classes and ideas, will not comprehend how a shoemaker could write universally famed books."[42] At times the text feels as if Ferrer y Ferrer were talking about himself, rather than about other intellectuals. Creating this canon was not simply a mechanism to legitimize his intellectual production in the eyes of the country's cultural elite or a way to channel his anxieties. Taking into consideration the historical moment when the book came out also allows another interpretation.

Los ideales del siglo XX was published months before the 1932 elections. Ferrer y Ferrer, age seventy-one when the book came out, was respected by his comrades not only for being one of the oldest labor leaders still active but also because of his unquestionable socialist trajectory in the movement. Unlike Santiago Iglesias Pantín or Rafael Alonso Torres, Ferrer y Ferrer did not use his book to address a broader audience but intended to reach the Socialist Party's rank and file. Even though there were multiple schools of thought within socialism, he argued that the party's ideal was rooted in an emancipatory doctrine based in social justice: "We cannot hide the fact (which would be infantile cowardice) that the ideology of these doctrines . . . have in us the sincerest admirers." Nonetheless, he continued, "There should not emerge from the core of our ideological collectivity groups that promote Machiavelli's thoughtless maxim, announcing morbid seeds of disaffection to our cause."[43] His critique was not one-sided and could be read as a direct attack on the party's leadership.

After making a list of all the prominent members within the party, Ferrer y Ferrer added, "Without a doubt, because of the relationships established with other opinion groups, the socialist camp has been invaded by certain rowdy [bullanguero] spirit, typical of ideal-less revolutionaries with large sleeves [*manga ancha*, a term used to describe a swindler]."[44] Perhaps the Coalition and the political associations with the Republican Party introduced such germs into the Socialist Party. If so, Ferrer y Ferrer believed, it was not the fault of the rank and file but of the leadership. The book often criticized political enemies, both Nationalists and Liberals, because they had disseminated the politics of "I am in charge" (*yo lo mando*). Still, he added, "We need to extinguish the traditional and corrupt politics of 'I am in charge' in our neighbor's house, but we also need to clean ours of the authoritarianism that is starting to emerge."[45]

Tensions existed inside the party because of hierarchies among its members, argued Ferrer y Ferrer. For him, good Socialists were those who propagated *el ideal* (the idea) from soapboxes or newspaper pages, as well as those anonymous leaders who did the same privately in their homes, public plazas, cafés, or tertulias. He argued that other Socialists who were mostly ignored constituted the heart of the party, the ones who carried flags, helped carry the soapboxes, and, after the electoral cycle ended, went back to their workshops or the fields. "I have often internally rebelled when I see the ways many of those [invisible workers] were treated by some comrades in high positions who have forgotten the fraternal link that unites us."[46] In this hierarchy, Ferrer y Ferrer identified with those at the bottom. "We are the ones that cultivate the fields," he wrote.[47] Although he had experienced upward class mobility—to the point of having a live-in maid in his house, as the 1940 census demonstrates—Ferrer y Ferrer used the pages of his pamphlet to join the ignored, the invisible.[48] At the beginning of the twentieth century, obreros ilustrados sought to distance themselves from the laboring masses through print media. Ferrer y Ferrer aspired to do the opposite in his book. He was repositioning himself as undeniably *del pueblo* (from the populace).

The tensions described by Ferrer y Ferrer in his book materialized in a series of splits and fractions within the party and the FLT. A year after Ferrer y Ferrer's book was published, in 1933, wildcat strikes that challenged the legitimacy of the FLT spread throughout the island. In October of that year, the unprecedented university strike against Rafael Alonso Torres was a major public relations blow for the party. Meanwhile, the dissident group known as Afirmación Socialista (Socialist Affirmation) was created in 1934. Although the group dissolved in 1936, it drew thousands of people to their mítines in the meantime. In the sugarcane fields, workers declared strikes, created alliances with the Nationalist Party, and went against the Socialist leadership.[49]

The Socialist Party expelled all the Afirmación Socialista members. Drawing from the lettered barriada's print tradition of compiling edited collections, the old labor leader and Afirmación Socialista member Tadeo Rodríguez García published *Brevario histórico* (Historical breviary). It was an edited volume with documents related to their expulsion. In its first page, Tadeo Rodríguez writes, "No one has more authority or would be more fit to write the premise of these series of monographs that give to posterity, in golden pages under the title *Brevario histórico*, than the old and enlightened leader José Ferrer y Ferrer." They proceeded to cite parts of *Los ideales del siglo XX*, which they called his magnum opus. While Ferrer y Ferrer was not part of Afirmación Socialista and might not have even agreed with them, his words had echoed in the ears of those Socialists who felt betrayed by their leaders.

Power struggles were high in the party's leadership, and after the 1936 elections, Bolívar Pagán made sure to get anyone he perceived as an adversary out of his way. For example, Ferrer y Ferrer was expelled from the party he had helped build. While not much information is known about Ferrer y Ferrer's exclusion, the same is not true of Rafael Alonso Torres's removal. That same year, in 1936, Alonso Torres stepped down from his leadership positions within the Socialist Party and the FLT, dedicating his last years to writing a comprehensive history of the labor movement that would serve as his apologia.

An Apologetic History: *Cuarenta años de lucha proletaria*

Oh! Virtue is a shield through which writers cover themselves from human events.
—LUZ Y VIDA, February 15, 1910

In late October 1933, the Socialist Party's executive committee called an emergency meeting to assess tensions within its ranks. During the meeting, conflict materialized in screams and accusations among the party's leadership. José Ferrer y Ferrer took a turn to speak and accused some of the party's leaders of betraying the socialist ideals he had explained and defended in his book *Los ideales del siglo XX*. Ferrer y Ferrer left the meeting in tears. In Alonso Torres's correspondence with Iglesias Pantín, he argued that some of the Socialists' political appointments as senators or legislators had gone to their heads. He also believed that the debate was not about preserving the rights workers had conquered in the field of politics but about destroying personas for individual gains. Beyond the political situation, another unspoken layer was identified by Alonso Torres. "Thus," he wrote, "*it will soon become a crime to have [our] history*."[50] In his mind, it became imperative to write a historical narrative of the movement along with his participation in it.

Some of Alonso Torres's critics accused him of being addicted to power because by 1936, he held at least eleven executive positions within the Socialist Party and the FLT.[51] That same year, his health deteriorated, and he decided to abandon the party. Three months after the 1936 party convention, and while the Coalición was celebrating another electoral victory in November, Alonso Torres was hospitalized. Meanwhile, the FLT's executive committee met and decided it was time to elect a person to relieve him as head of the labor federation. Weakened and without any official obligations, Rafael Alonso Torres kept visiting the FLT's headquarters, not as an active member, but as a historian. He would be seen reading old documents and compiling materials for a book that he imagined as the most comprehensive history of the movement during the last forty years. He finished the book in 1938 and died the following year without ever seeing it published.[52]

Envisioned as a history book, *Cuarenta años de lucha proletaria* was written for the newer generation of labor activists emerging in the 1930s. For example, Nicolas Nogueras Rivera, who took over Alonso Torres's position in the FLT and was left the task of editing *Cuarenta años*, wrote, "It seems that he [Alonso Torres] was convinced of the fatal outcome that awaited him, and wanted to leave the organized labor movement and its leadership a work that not only served as an authorized historical source, but also as inspiration for current and future generations to faithfully continue the work of social redemption set forward by the Federación Libre."[53] Given the historical moment in which Alonso Torres wrote the book—shortly after abruptly stepping down from leadership positions within the labor movement—it can also be read as a last attempt to defend his name and honor. It was also probably imagined as undeniable proof that he was, in fact, "a man of letters."

FIGURE 6.2. Rafael Alonso Torres's book cover for *Cuarenta años de lucha proletaria*. Courtesy of the University of Connecticut's Archives and Special Collections.

Alonso Torres began *Cuarenta años de lucha proletaria* (figure 6.2) with the history of the Spanish empire during the nineteenth century to describe the conditions that led his family to migrate to Puerto Rico. Thus, from its first pages, Alonso Torres set the tone for the rest of his book; it was history through an autobiographical lens that located the author as part of the events described. Using this approach of narrating events through the lens of his own experiences, Rafael Alonso Torres created a larger and more far-reaching historical narrative than Iglesias Pantín did, yet both books shared the same logic of crafting historical narratives from within the lettered barriada. Alonso Torres's book became the labor movement's second comprehensive history book following Santiago Iglesias Pantíns' *Luchas emancipadoras*.

The book's 397 pages were divided into two sections; the first two hundred pages were dedicated to events that happened during Spanish colonialism, while the second part began with the US occupation, which the author called "the change of sovereignty." The first section was divided into eight different chapters and touched upon a wide range of topics not limited to Puerto Rican history. For example, in chapter 4, he described how those who governed the island did so with an iron fist. The chapter ended with a summary of the Paris Commune and its influence on the development of labor ideas on a global scale.

While in his book Santiago Iglesias Pantín ignored any previous labor organizations before his arrival to Puerto Rico in 1896 and argued that orators had to be created, Rafael Alonso Torres described the vibrant labor culture that started to emerge from the 1870s onward; that is, Rafael Alonso Torres did not use the chronological arc developed by Iglesias Pantín in *Luchas emancipadoras*. Instead, Alonso Torres traced the genealogy of the modern labor movement to the nineteenth century's historical developments. For example, using his own experience in typographic workshops, he explained the intellectual activities that took place both within and outside workplaces. Alonso Torres wrote about the wine-fueled intellectual debates among "enlightened printers," the occupation of public spaces to present makeshift theatrical plays, and how revolutionary literature "freely circulated and served as the basis for an advanced consciousness against the established order."[54]

While the events he described took place in San Juan and other urban centers in Puerto Rico, most workingmen's only aspiration, argued Alonso Torres, "was to use their free time for pleasure and enjoyment," not politics. In the meantime, a cluster of self-educated workingmen, who eventually became the lettered barriada's architects, started to study European socialist ideas. He described how they discussed the works of Karl Marx, Friedrich Engels, and Mikhail Bakunin, while also studying the histories of the International Workingmen's Association, along with the ideological rivalries that emerged from those congresses. In sum, Rafael Alonso Torres used *Cuarenta años de lucha proletaria* to locate the genesis of the Puerto Rican labor movement within the circulation of socialist ideas coming from Europe. He carefully detailed how these ideas arrived in the form of newspapers and books via dockworkers who smuggled them into San Juan.[55]

The second part of the book, which was divided into six chapters, began with the US occupation and the emergence of labor unions. After describing the historical events that led to the FLT's creation and the arrival of the AFL in Puerto Rico, Alonso Torres's book went from a chronological narrative to theme-focused chapters. At times the text read as a list of sources rather than as a history book. For example, he dedicated a full chapter to making an inventory of every FLT congress, along with data on the number of unionized workers and the most important agreements reached. Likewise, Alonso Torres reproduced a previously published short history of the Puerto Rican labor press during the first three decades of the twentieth century, while devoting another chapter to the most important labor struggles before 1905.[56] The book's last chapter offered an insight into the author's worldviews as he analyzed the labor movement's trajectory until his present day.

Rafael Alonso Torres was not a founding member of either Federación Regional or the FLT, but he did participate in the creation of Puerto Rico's first social study center. "When undertaking the task of revising and analyzing the social and economic work realized in Puerto Rico for more than a third of a century," wrote Alonso Torres, "we feel obligated to emphasize in its just value, the influence exerted over the study and presentation of [socialist] ideas, the first Social Study Group that represented a column of support for the social push that has led to the progress attained in the political, social, and humane transformation of these past 39 years."[57] If progress came from the study of socialist (i.e., European) ideas, then he had been one of the first to promote them. Like Iglesias Pantín, he was centering the narrative, albeit subtly, on himself.

In his book, Rafael Alonso Torres divided his experiences as a member of the organized labor movement into three periods. The first took place during the Spanish colonial regime, in which, although radical ideas were often suppressed, "the diffusion of the principles and doctrines of social and humane enlargement began." The second period started with the emergence of labor organizations, like the FLT, while the third consisted of the enlargement, expansion, and consolidation of those institutions.[58] Curiously enough, the Socialist Party entered the book's narrative only in its last twenty-five pages.

Alonso Torres stressed the importance of the labor movement's origins and particularities because its development significantly differed from those in "the Old Continent and even in the New World." The Puerto Rican labor movement did not come out of university classrooms or emerge from a highly industrialized society. It was not the product of "intellectual diplomacy," but instead, argued Alonso Torres, it came out of workshops.[59] Although this can be understood as a simple historical observation, framing the book's content in the context of Alonso Torres's departure from the party allows another reading.

As the Socialist Party was getting ready for the 1936 elections, delegates assembled on August 15 in the eastern town of Caguas for the Socialist Party's Ninth Convention. Before it started, a telegram from Alonso Torres, who missed such an important event for the first time, was read out loud. In it, he explained that his delicate health condition did not allow him to attend the convention. He continued, "I ratify my firm decision of not being a candidate for either the Territorial Committee or the Insular Parliament's presidency." After having helped to found the Socialist Party in 1915 and serving sixteen years in Puerto Rico's House of Representatives, he was stepping down.[60]

Alonso Torres's announcement was anything but surprising. For the past four years, he had been in the public eye fighting other labor leaders over the Socialist Party's control and against rank-and-file members of the FLT who publicly called for his resignation.[61] Although he did not go into details, perhaps for the sake of peacekeeping, these tensions were accentuated in his message. "The last four years have shown me that the Socialist Party has been nourished by many good, intelligent men. But, at the same time, it has received some of the most disloyal, audacious, and insincere [people] who will create great difficulties in the future to the cause we have been fighting for during the past 36 years." After reading the telegram, the convention honored Alonso Torres with a standing ovation. A motion to send a telegram in solidarity and asking him not to abandon the labor movement was approved unanimously. But although unspoken, his delicate health condition was not the only thing that kept him away from the labor organizations he had helped create.[62]

Since at least 1932, there had been a power struggle between Rafael Alonso Torres and Bolívar Pagán over the party's leadership. After the Coalition between the Republican and Socialist Party won that year's elections, some Socialists considered the electoral alliance detrimental to their party's ideals. Furthermore, some of the party's leaders complained that the most important government posts and positions were unequally divided, favoring the Republicans. Thus, a group of longtime labor leaders who had enjoyed public recognition and support, such as Epifanio Fiz Jiménez and Bolívar Ochart, used the press to express their discontent with the Socialist Party's leadership. Bolívar Pagán, who would come to be the Socialist Party's undisputed leader after Santiago Iglesias Pantín's death later in 1939, supported the dissenters. In confidential correspondence with Iglesias Pantín in 1933, Alonso Torres wrote, "There are two fires: one inside and one outside." He was referring to dissidence within the party led by Bolívar Pagán, and to the strike situation, with UPR students and their allies protesting Governor Gore's appointment of Rafael Alonso Torres to the university's board of trustees.[63]

In *Cuarenta años de lucha proletaria*, Rafael Alonso Torres does not mention the fierce opposition he faced within the FLT and the Socialist Party during the 1930s or the UPR student strike. But taking such events into consideration allows us to comprehend his emphasis on the "nonintellectual" (i.e., nonacademic) origins of the socialist movement in Puerto Rico. Alonso Torres argued, "Diplomatic intellectualism, formed in the classroom or university podium, always felt more comfortable and protected by serving corporate capitalist interests, despotism, and serfdom."[64] Thus, it was important for him to state that "the first spark that ripped through the shadows and shook the Puerto Rican proletarian consciousness, and that inspired the longing for the dignity and enlargement of work, was the product of the non-political intellectualism [*intelectualismo no-diplomático*] formed in the workshop, the factory, and the field."[65]

Writing a history book might have been Alonso Torres's way to secure his place in labor's annals, but he might have also had a desire to become a legitimate producer of knowledge. Although he wrote outside academic circles, perhaps Alonso Torres wanted to demonstrate that he had nothing to envy them. He too could produce a lengthy scholarly book. Alonso Torres did not live to see his work published, but one of his deepest desires came true: the book became an important contribution to the lettered barriada's ideational archive, and alongside Iglesias Pantín's book, it set the foundation for later historical narratives about both the FLT and the Socialist Party.[66]

First as Myth, Then as History: Haunting the Archive

The labor movement's annals document all the great things that have been remarkably achieved.—LUZ Y VIDA, December 30, 1909

Two major absences haunted the pages of these books: gender and race. At a moment when women entered the labor market and became active participants in unions, they were nonetheless silenced from obreros ilustrados' intellectual production and were rendered invisible in labor's archives. But as litterateur Arundhati Roy has argued, "There is no such thing as the 'voiceless.' There are only the deliberately silenced, or the preferably unheard."[67] Through these silences, these books were crucial in discursively consolidating the labor movement's patriarchal ethos.

In *Luchas emancipadoras*'s nearly four hundred pages, there are only five mentions of women. The first woman to appear in the narrative was a comrade who visited Iglesias Pantín when he was fleeing from justice in 1898 but whose identity is kept anonymous in the text.[68] The next woman to enter the narrative was his wife, Justa Bocanegra. When explaining the persecution labor leaders faced at the turn of the twentieth century, Iglesias Pantín narrated the time he was arrested in the town of Aguadilla in 1902. He then cited a newspaper article from *La democracia* that briefly mentioned, "Don Santiago Iglesias, organizer for the American Federation of Labor, got married [in Aguadilla] to the señorita Justa Bocanegra."[69] Although they spent a life together, raising three sons and eight daughters, his wife entered the text to explain an event, not as a historical subject. Other workingwomen appear in *Luchas emancipadoras*—Concha Torres, Paca Escabí, and Carmen Rosario—but only in lists of names mentioned when describing events, such as public meetings or the FLT's national conventions. None of the women were part of Iglesias Pantín's analysis or his narrative; they were mere details to what he considered to be important events. Similarly, women appeared in Rafael Alonso Torres's *Cuarenta años de lucha proletaria* and José Ferrer y Ferrer's *Los ideales del siglo XX* only as wives and mothers.

Another strategic silence was related to race. Since the FLT's early days, its leaders opted for a raceless rhetoric to unite its rank and file through a discourse anchored in class. Ever since its 1899 constitution, the FLT constructed the notion of an ideal worker as raceless and male. In fact, labor leaders and obreros ilustrados excluded race from their discursive repertoire of propaganda. For the FLT's leadership, who shared their ideas through the publication of books and newspapers, or through public speeches, the language of class was more effective to deal with colonial authorities and the upper classes.[70] The absence of race in these three books, and subsequently in the archive they produced, can be understood as a consolidation of these silences, not as a beginning.

The structure of archives, argued philosopher of history Ethan Kleinberg, are spectral a priori because they are neither visible nor invisible.[71] There are ideas, persons, or events that could be absent from historical narratives but that inform them, ghosts from the past that linger in the present. For example, the ghost that haunted José Ferrer y Ferrer's *Los ideales del siglo XX* was race. While the book did not have a single chapter or section specifically dedicated to the topic of race, Ferrer y Ferrer's positionality as a Black man permeated his analysis throughout the book. "Following the course of historical processes," wrote Ferrer y Ferrer, "it would be impossible to narrate all of the infamies committed by white terror."[72] Ferrer y Ferrer explained that "white" was the color of the reaction in the Russian Revolution and used it as an analogy for the capitalist system as a whole. He believed not only that capitalism had established class-based exploitation, but that it also depended on, and perpetuated, racial oppression. For example, he dedicated several pages to explaining how the French Revolution had made an impact in debates about the abolition of chattel slavery. The abolition of "that disgusting business" was, according to Ferrer y Ferrer, "a requisite for social equality and a chapter of glory that enlightens universal history."[73] Whether in France during the revolution or in his contemporary Puerto Rico, he acknowledged that racism and ideas of racial superiority were linked to the expansion of capitalism.[74]

But not every book was haunted by race. As previously mentioned, Rafael Alonso Torres dedicated the first two hundred pages of *Cuarenta años de lucha proletaria* to Puerto Rico's history within the Spanish empire. Nonetheless, race, slavery, and the incorporation of formerly enslaved people into the labor market after abolition in 1873 were completely absent from his narrative. But why omit such a central part of the workforce and the social relations he navigated in San Juan? It seems implausible that Rafael Alonso Torres did not interact with Black workingmen. According to an 1899 report commissioned by the United States government, which was also reproduced in Santiago Iglesias Pantín's *Luchas emancipadoras*, "colored men . . . seem to monopolize the [artisan] trades, at least in the capital."[75]

All these books also shared a temporal understanding of the labor movement's historical development, in which the arrival of Santiago Iglesias Pantín and the foundation of the Socialist Party were turning points. This, of course, was nothing new. They were part of the print tradition of those affiliated with the FLT or the Socialist Party. The first short biography of Santiago Iglesias Pantín was published in 1901 by Ramón Romero Rosa and jump-started the myth of Iglesias Pantín as the "creator of the labor movement."[76] Romero Rosa's biography of Iglesias Pantín began in 1896, ignoring all the labor and artisan organizations and publications that had flourished in Puerto Rico since the 1870s. "Santiago Iglesias emerged from the penumbra we were wrapped in to start his good teachings," Romero Rosa stated.[77] And like that, the biography created a temporal break—the "before and after" of Iglesias Pantín's arrival to Puerto Rico. After the publication of this biography, the "creator" myth was repeated by FLT members in public demonstrations, labor congresses, books, newspapers, and leaflets. For example, the Socialist Party became colloquially known as the "party created by Iglesias," even though he had fiercely opposed its creation at first. Thus, by the time the three books under analysis were published, the myth was well articulated. As with the silencing of race and gender, these books marked not the beginning but the consolidation of the "creator" myth.

A DOCUMENT PUBLISHED in 1938 by the FLT read: "In the exercise of civic and political rights, and in the development of practices of citizenship, the Puerto Rican workingman has nothing to envy any other workingman in the world for, on the contrary, it is more advanced than many civilized nations, all thanks to the Federación Libre."[78] Nine years before that document, Santiago Iglesias Pantín had used his book to present himself as the creator of the movement as well as the node that connected Puerto Rican workers with the global cartography of socialist and modern ideas. Ferrer y Ferrer made a similar argument about the Socialist Party as the locus of modernization for Puerto Rican workers, while Rafael Alonso Torres understood workers' self-educational projects as the genesis of the masses' regeneration.

That was precisely what these books and the archive they produced perpetuated: the idea that Puerto Rican workers (always male and raceless) had become civilized, and that everything they enjoyed had been because of the socialist program promoted by obreros ilustrados and the Socialist Party. In the decades that followed the publication of these books, the Socialist Party's leadership employed this discourse to garner votes as other political and intellectual communities emerged and as the recently formed Popular Democratic Party shook and redefined Puerto Rican politics. Restating Karl Marx's famous phrase, "first as tragedy, then as farce," it is safe to say that labor's ideational archive produced a series of genealogies, ideas, and omissions, *first as myths, then as history*.

Those who met in February 1897 to talk about the possibility of publishing the newspaper *Ensayo obrero* perhaps never imagined the repercussions that meeting would have in Puerto Rican society. Building on a broader working-class print tradition that stemmed from the late nineteenth century, obreros ilustrados used books and newspapers, pedagogical projects, and public events to craft protean identities as workers, politicians, and global subjects, all at once. They planted the seeds for the creation of a militant labor movement that went from a few scattered unions in urban centers to setting the base for a political project that would bring self-educated workingmen into spaces of power, such as the Insular Senate and the House of Representatives. On his deathbed, Rafael Alonso Torres—one of the lettered barriada's main architects—affirmed with pride all the identities he had carefully crafted throughout four decades.

After 1936, Alonso Torres became critically ill, dedicating his time to the writing of his book *Cuarenta años de lucha proletaria*. In 1938, he was admitted to the Díaz García Clinic, known today as the Pavía Hospital in Santurce, Puerto Rico, where he spent his last days. Serving in the country's legislature for twenty-two years had earned Alonso Torres many political adversaries. Manuel González was one of them. González was a millionaire who owned, among other things, the Condado Vanderbilt Hotel, San Vicente Sugar Central in Vega Baja, and large amounts of land in Puerto Rico's southern district.[1]

Prudencio Rivera Martínez, who was a founding member of the Socialist Party and became the first commissioner of labor in Puerto Rico, recalled receiving a visit from Manuel González to talk about Alonso Torres's frail health. González believed that Alonso Torres could not die because the country needed more men like him. In confidence, he recalled how as a legislator, Alonso Torres had vetoed many of his projects and tax exemptions because he considered González an "exploiter" and a "reactionary." Nonetheless, González argued, "Alonso Torres is a righteous man and I do not know anybody else like him in Puerto Rico, neither within the labor movement nor outside of it . . . a man of such spirit needs to be saved even if he is not a friend of mine."[2] According to González, Alonso Torres needed a trip to Spain, France, or wherever he wanted. He offered to pay for him to take "a long trip to rest for however long, bringing along his doctors, his nurses, his family, and spending everything he needs to spend without a limit [and with] an absolute blank card."[3] González's offer stemmed from a nineteenth-century oligarchic tradition of visiting Europe as a rite of passage in the formation of any wealthy individual.[4] He also sustained that visiting those foreign lands, attending the French Comedic Theatre, and drinking from Munich's water would surely help recover his health.[5]

Alonso Torres, like many other early twentieth-century obreros ilustrados, had been intellectually formed through Eurocentric conceptions of the world. The global subjectivities these workingmen crafted were rooted in the logic and desire of becoming part of Western civilization. Alonso Torres had carefully read and discussed with his comrades the works of Élisée Reclus, Charles Darwin, and Émile Zola. He had also scolded nonunionized workingmen for not wanting to become civilized like their working-class peers in the world's "advanced nations." Yet most of Puerto Rico's obreros ilustrados visited Europe only through the realm of letters, print media, and their imagination.

The trip that Manuel González offered never materialized. González was wary of making the offer himself, so he left it to Prudencio Rivera Martínez to do so. But Rivera Martínez, who had been a lifelong friend of Alonso Torres, knew he would never agree to it. Thus, he never made the offer. Alonso Torres passed away in February 1939. It is very possible that he died without ever setting foot outside Puerto Rico and the United States. Nonetheless, Alonso Torres lived his life thinking of himself as a global subject. Such was the power of the lettered barriada. Furthermore, Alonso Torres died trying to write a book that would serve as his intellectual apologia and would establish his intellectual legitimacy. The same year he died, a series of events provided symbolic rupture for the project that had begun at the turn of the century.

Another death became a turning point in the lettered barriada's history and development. On December 5, 1939, Santiago Iglesias Pantín passed away after contracting malaria on a trip to Mexico and Cuba, where he had tried to revive the Pan-American Federation of Labor.[6] By the time of his death, the myth of Iglesias Pantín as "the creator of the labor movement" was well articulated and had accrued political currency. For example, as delegates entered the doors of the Campo Alegre Theatre in Caguas to attend the 1936 Socialist Party convention, they found a giant picture of Santiago Iglesias Pantín as the stage's backdrop. Next to Iglesias Pantín were pictures of Eugenio Sánchez López and Juan Vidal, considered to be the labor movement's first martyrs. Although Iglesias Pantín was still alive and physically present in the convention, the party consciously fostered a cult of personality, a cult celebrating "the creator myth."[7]

While Iglesias Pantín served as resident commissioner in Washington, the Socialist Party and the FLT's leadership still revered him as the infallible "maestro" back in Puerto Rico. The leadership of both labor organizations consulted him and asked for guidance as they suffered tremendous internal tensions. For example, in 1936, sixteen prominent Socialists, most of whom were founding members of the Socialist Party, sent a lengthy report to Iglesias Pantín about the twenty-two ways in which Bolívar Pagán had acted against the party's will, persecuted comrades, and abused his position of power. Iglesias Pantín called for an Extraordinary Assembly to address the party's situation. It took place on August 20, 1939, and ended with the expulsion of several members, including Prudencio Rivera Martínez.[8]

When addressing the Extraordinary Assembly, Victor Coll y Cuchi argued, "This is not a fight between Prudencio and Bolívar, it's a struggle between light and darkness. Prudencio was in the light but he now joins the darkness. He will become a rat tail with bubonic plague when he could have been a lion's head."[9] When Iglesias Pantín passed away later that year, these existing divisions deepened. Rivera Martínez created the short-lived Pure Labor Party while also consolidating his control over the FLT and later rejoined the Socialist Party. Bolívar Pagán, who was Iglesias Pantín's son-in-law, continued to preside over the Socialist Party and was elected to the position of resident commissioner in 1940.[10]

But internal struggles that had led to these fractions were not the only thing that severely weakened the labor organizations built at the beginning of the twentieth century. They were also challenged by the arrival of new international federations to Puerto Rico, like the Congress of Industrial Organizations in 1938, the formation of independent unions not affiliated

FIGURE E.1. Socialist Party founding members with Luis Muñoz Marín, 1956. Courtesy of the Colección de Fotos del Periódico *El Mundo*, University of Puerto Rico, Río Piedras.

with traditional labor federations, the rise of new labor federations like the Confederación General de Trabajadores (General Confederation of Workingmen), and the growth of the Nationalist and Communist parties.[11] The biggest setback faced by the Socialist Party in the 1940s was the rise of the Popular Democratic Party (PPD). Luis Muñoz Marín, a former member of the Socialist Party, led the PPD.

Longtime members like Epifanio Fiz Jiménez and Blas Oliveras left the Socialist Party because they were discontent with Bolívar Pagán's leadership. In fact, Oliveras put it succinctly, "True socialists buried with great pain the old party of Santiago Iglesias, deceased by the lust and apostasy combined with the sinister forces of the furious reaction. Nonetheless, we live to see its resurrection and glory in another party that is not called socialist, but like the Phoenix bird has risen from its ashes, triumphant and magnificent, before the stupefied eyes of the enemies of the bread, of the land, and the liberty of the Puerto Rican people."[12] Oliveras's word choice was not coincidental; the PPD slogan was "land, bread, and liberty."[13]

When Luis Muñoz Marín (figure E.1) was running to become the first elected governor of Puerto Rico in 1948, he went against Martín Travieso, a lawyer from Mayagüez. The now severely weakened Socialist Party sponsored

Travieso, but not every Socialist rallied behind him. For example, Fernando López, a Socialist candidate for mayor in the eastern town of Fajardo, argued that any vote for Travieso was a vote against the maxims of our "maestro and leader, Santiago Iglesias Pantín." The town of Fajardo, known as Puerto Rico's "red city," had been an important political enclave for the Socialists. They won every municipal election from 1917 until 1944, when the PPD broke the Socialist hegemony to establish its own.[14] López also believed that the Socialist Party had been invaded by the privileged, like Travieso and Pagán, who were both lawyers. Thus, López concluded, "the Popular Democratic Party is the only defender of the poor and humble classes."[15]

Ultimately, when the lettered barriada's pillars collapsed as the FLT and the Socialist Party's sphere of influence declined, its intellectual and political legacy continued. Not only was there an exodus of members from the Socialist Party to the PPD, but the cultural apparatus that Muñoz Marín created also appropriated and resignified some of the lettered barriada's key myths and discourses. Iglesias Pantín's "creator myth" set the foundations for another political trope: the "disciple myth."

In the 1940s and 1950s, the PPD redefined the Puerto Rican nation. "During this epoch," as literary scholar Catherine Marsh Kennerly has argued, "Puerto Rico partook for the first time in what could be compared to the foundational moments of Latin American republics. It [the PPD] constructed a beginning that generated its own myths."[16] A similar process, albeit on a much smaller scale, had taken place within the lettered barriada with the consolidation of labor's ideational archive in the 1930s. When the obreros ilustrados created an archive to imagine the origins of the labor organizations they presided over, they did not aim to reconfigure the nation. Even if they had wanted to shape the archive of puertorriqueñidad, the Socialist Party—which had attained electoral success only through political alliances that ended up dividing its rank and file—did not have a cultural apparatus capable of doing so. Furthermore, internal struggles within the Socialist Party made it impossible to create a cohesive discourse.

The PPD was created in 1938 and immediately took advantage of the Socialist Party's internal situation to attract more people into its ranks. In Muñoz Marín's memoirs, he located the genesis of his political career in his involvement with the Socialist Party (figure E.2).[17] The young Muñoz Marín was so devoted to socialist ideas that he toured all of Puerto Rico with the Socialist Party in its 1920 electoral campaign, as well as briefly serving as Santiago Iglesias Pantín's secretary. Muñoz Marín also organized a

FIGURE E.2. Prudencio Rivera Martínez, David Dubinsky (president of the International Ladies' Garment Workers' Union), and Luis Muñoz Marín break ground for the union-sponsored Santiago Iglesias Pantín Housing Complex, 1957. Courtesy of the Colección de Fotos del Periódico *El Mundo*, University of Puerto Rico, Río Piedras.

socialist newspaper, *Espártaco* (Spartacus), along with a social study center, which resembled those that had mushroomed throughout early twentieth-century Puerto Rico. Named Escuela Espartaco de Ciencia Social (Spartacus School of Social Science), and located in Santurce's 18th Street, the centro was free and open to anyone who wished "to learn, and to explore." It also had a "Proletarian Bookstore." The books sold, according to its organizers, were "written for working men and women, and people interested in the international proletarian movement" and "interpret[ed] History and Social Sciences from the standpoint of the Working Classes."[18]

The PPD's leadership understood the importance of dominating the means of intellectual and cultural production to consolidate its power. After 1948, Luis Muñoz Marín sponsored a wide range of cultural and intellectual institutions aimed at reconfiguring and dominating the archive of puertorriqueñidad. These included but were not limited to the División de Educación de la Comunidad (DiVedCo; Division for the Community's Education), formed in 1949, and the Puerto Rican Institute of Culture in 1955.[19] Luis Muñoz Marín named the PPD's cultural project the Serenity Operation. It was envisioned as the intellectual counterpart for the industrialization project known as Operation Bootstraps.[20] Through its cultural apparatus, the PPD sought to create a sense of belonging to the Puerto Rican nation and an understanding of its place in the world, without altering the political status of the island.[21] The creation of the Puerto Rican Commonwealth in 1952 consolidated that project. Symbolically, workers and a whitened image of the *jíbaro* (peasant) were at the forefront of that nation-building cultural project.[22]

Without a doubt, DiVedCo was one of the most important cultural organizations created by the PPD. It was a pedagogical project aimed at educating communities through the use of films, books, and posters. DiVedCo produced more than one hundred films (including feature movies, short musicals, news, and documentaries), more than forty books and pamphlets, posters, and murals.[23] Audiovisual materials were a vital component of the project because of Puerto Rico's widespread illiteracy. In sum, DiVedCo promoted the newly imagined nation's democratic values while also serving as a massive literacy program.[24]

DiVedCo's books were called *Libros para el pueblo* (Books for the people). Each one covered a specific topic, including, for example, hygiene, history, and popular tradition. One of them was *Lucha obrera* (Workers' struggle). Like most of DiVedCo's books, it was edited and written by one of the country's leading intellectuals, René Marqués. *Lucha obrera* also included artwork by famed artists like Isabel Bernal, Antonio Maldonado, and Rafael Tufiño, among others (figure E.3). Its seventy-one pages contained nineteen short articles that went from the history of slavery and socialism in Europe to poems by Pablo Neruda and Fernán Silva Valdés. It read like any of the books or pamphlets that circulated in Puerto Rico's early twentieth-century lettered barriada. One of its chapters told the story of how the Puerto Rican labor movement came to be: through the intervention of Santiago Iglesias Pantín. While the book acknowledged that workers had organized mutual aid societies and other associations in the nineteenth century, it suggested that because of Santiago Iglesias Pantín, workers assembled their first labor unions and the Socialist Party. "Without a doubt," read the book, "Santiago Iglesias Pantín's most important contribution to Puerto Rican labor was precisely his eagerness to guide and educate the laboring masses."[25] After describing how Iglesias Pantín used every means

LIBROS PARA EL PUEBLO NÚM. 15

FIGURE E.3. Front cover of René Marqués's *Lucha obrera*. Author's personal collection.

available to advance his ideas, the book argued, "One of his disciples will come to use the same tactics when undertaking a campaign of political guidance many years later. That disciple was Luis Muñoz Marín."[26]

Later in the book, Marqués argued, "The Popular Party received in its platform socialist ideas and advanced actions for social reform. Its president, Luis Muñoz Marín, had battled next to Santiago Iglesias in the Socialist Party."[27] Furthermore, the book argued that after taking power, "the Popular Party approved laws that had been ideas of the old Socialist Party, but that could have never been put into practice."[28] The PPD, similar to what former Socialist Blas Oliveras had stated, was revolutionary because it "had a social justice program fundamentally identical to the old socialist program."[29] *Lucha obrera* was crucial in spreading those ideas far and wide across Puerto Rico.

But the lettered barriada's influence was not limited to the world of culture. In 1950, the government of Puerto Rico, led by Luis Muñoz Marín, called for a constitutional assembly after the US Congress approved the Puerto Rico Federal Relations Law, known as Law 600. Wary of the constitution being interpreted as that of a single party, Muñoz Marín invited minority parties to join the process. The PPD had seventy delegates, while the Statehood Party had fourteen, and the Socialist Party had only seven. The Independence Party abstained. The document approved by the constitutional assembly included a Bill of Rights that made it one of the most progressive constitutions ever written. The US Congress vetoed its Bill of Rights, which contained many amendments proposed by the Socialists and that had been heavily contested in the constitutional debates. As legal scholar Jorge M. Farinacci Fernós has argued, if the Socialist Party had not participated, "the result would have been a Constitution less protective of workers' rights."[30]

The constitution came into effect with the commonwealth on July 25, 1952. Even though the Socialist Party was on its dying breath, its members could argue that because of their participation in the constitutional assembly, their decades-old demands, most of them emerging from the turn of the century's lettered barriada, had been elevated to constitutional rank. In 1954, the Socialist Party, then led by Lino Padrón Rivera, met in assembly one last time to dissolve itself. As had the Communist Party ten years earlier, in its last assembly, the Socialist Party advised all its members to join the PPD.[31] The Moroccan rooster—as Bolívar Pagán had described the PPD in a 1941 radio speech—won the battle once and for all.[32] To the comfort of Socialist leadership, they believed that the PPD owed its success to the fact that it had appropriated the Socialist Party's social justice program and because its leader, Luis Muñoz Marín, was a disciple of the mythical creator: Santiago Iglesias Pantín.

Final Thought

Puerto Rican scholars began to deconstruct some of the lettered barriada's myths and silences from the 1970s onward. Yet labor's ideational archive still operates with great transhistorical power. It still dictates some of the questions historians and social scientists pose and shapes the limits of our historical imagination; lack of sources only adds more power to it. Perhaps that is why I have finished this book without finding any traces of my family members: the scabs, the nonunionized, and the self-educated peasants. In turn, this book has mapped a genealogy of an intellectual community created by a handful of individuals who sought to speak on behalf of the *others*. Early twentieth-century obreros ilustrados succeeded in shaping political debates, influencing Puerto Rico's national mythology, and, ultimately, affecting how we conceive the past. Most importantly, those who became the laboring masses' self-assigned interlocutors were able to fulfill their desires of moving from the lettered barriada to the lettered city.

The rest stayed behind.

The rest

remain

unnamed.

INTRODUCTION

1. *El combate* was sold for one cent in three different locations throughout Arecibo, and all were *cafetines*: Nemesio Morales's in the plazuela del mercado; Antero López's at Santa María Street, No. 2; and Don José Bonet's (father), located in La Puntilla. See *El combate*, December 19, 1910, 4.

2. Two phrases could be read in *El combate*'s masthead: "Labor Omnia Vincit," which was conveniently translated into Spanish as "El trabajo todo vence," and "Instrucción y Trabajo son las ruedas delanteras del Carro del Progreso que nos conducirá á la Libertad y a la Dicha" (Education and Labor are the front wheels of Progress's vehicle, and they will guide us toward Freedom and Happiness). See *El combate*, December 2, 1910.

3. Luis Guillermo Marín, Sebastián Siragusa de la Huerga, and Esteban Padilla edited the paper. See Limón de Arce, *Arecibo histórico*, 475, 486–87; Meléndez-Badillo, *Voces libertarias*, 124–25; and Pedreira, *El periodismo en Puerto Rico*, 418.

4. Limón de Arce, *Arecibo histórico*, 487.

5. According to historian Antonio S. Pedreira, around five hundred newspaper titles were published from 1898 to 1912, and dozens were labor oriented; see Pedreira, *El periodismo en Puerto Rico*, 363; and Meléndez-Badillo, *Voces libertarias*, 93, 110–28.

6. Burton, *Archive Stories*, 3.

7. García-Peña, *Borders of Dominicanidad*, 12.

8. Foucault, *Archeology of Knowledge*, 129.

9. That is still the case even with recent historiographical interventions. See Sanabria, *Puerto Rican Labor History*; and Rivera Caballero, *De lobos y corderos*.

10. Meléndez-Badillo, "Mateo and Juana."

11. Trouillot, *Silencing the Past*, 99.

12. "Convención de tipógrafos," *Obrero libre*, June 14, 1903, 3.

13. A. J. González, "Apuntes para la historia del movimiento sindical"; Carreras, *Santiago Iglesias Pantín*; Senior, *Santiago Iglesias: Apóstol*.

14. See Lebrón, "Creación, control y disputas"; Castro Arroyo, "De Salvador Brau a la 'novísima historia'"; and Matos Rodríguez, "New Currents in Puerto Rican History."

15. Barcia, *Capas populares y modernidad en Cuba*.

16. See Rama, *La ciudad letrada*. For the English translation, see Rama, *Lettered City*.

17. Rama, *Lettered City*, 113.

18. Ward, *La anarquía inmanentista*; Etcheverri, *Rafael Barrett*.

19. For other examples of Black artisans, see Hoffnung-Garskoff, "To Abolish the Law of Castes."

20. Rama, *Lettered City*, 119.

21. Meléndez-Badillo, "Radical Genealogies"; Sueiro Seoane, "Anarquismo e independentismo cubano"; Geli, "Los anarquistas en el gabinete antropométrico."

22. Meléndez-Badillo, "Labor History's Transnational Turn."

23. Some examples include Baerga, "A la organización"; Findlay, *Imposing Decency*, 135–66; and Rodríguez-Silva, "Racial Silencing."

24. See Rodríguez-Silva, *Silencing Race*.

25. Godreau, *Scripts of Blackness*; Godreau, "Slippery Semantics"; Godreau, "Changing Space, Making Race"; Findlay, "Slipping and Sliding"; Arlene Torres, "La gran familia puertorriqueña"; Meléndez-Badillo, "Mateo and Juana."

26. Díaz-Quiñones, "Cultura, memoria y diáspora."

27. Some examples include del Moral, *Negotiating Empire*; Briggs, *Reproducing Empire*; and Levy, *Puerto Ricans in the Empire*.

28. I have published pieces about Puerto Rico's possible decolonial and anticolonial futures, the queering of protest, and radicalism in the contemporary moment. See Santiago-Ortiz and Meléndez-Badillo, "Puerto Rico's Multiple Solidarities"; Meléndez-Badillo, "Commemorating May Day in Puerto Rico"; and Santiago-Ortiz and Meléndez-Badillo, "La Calle Fortaleza."

29. Silén, *Apuntes para la historia*, 85.

30. Rancière, *Philosopher and His Poor*, xi.

31. I have explored these tensions in Meléndez-Badillo, "Party of Ex-convicts."

32. Known as the *giro decolonial* (decolonial turn), a wealth of knowledge production has explored the coloniality of power, a concept originally developed by the Peruvian sociologist Aníbal Quijano. See Walsh and Mignolo, *On Decoloniality*. For more recent interventions from an Afro-Caribbean perspective, see Lebrón Ortiz, *Filosofía del cimarronaje*.

33. García, *Historia crítica, historia sin coartadas*, 69.

34. Quintero Rivera, *Patricios y plebeyos*, 195–98.

35. Álvarez Curbelo, *Un país del porvenir*, 213–316; Rodríguez-Silva, *Silencing Race*, 27–58; García, *Historia bajo sospecha*, 27–54.

36. Alamo-Pastrana, *Seams of Empire*; Llorens, *Imaging the Great Puerto Rican Family*; Arlene Torres, "La gran familia puertorriqueña."

37. For an example of how these processes of former slaves becoming proletarianized unraveled in the town of Guayama, see Luis A. Figueroa, *Sugar, Slavery, and Freedom*, 175–200.

38. Of those unemployed, 283,677 (84.2 percent) were women. Cited in Dietz, *Historia económica de Puerto Rico*, 149.

39. Romeral, *Musarañas*, 13.

40. Tirado Avilés, "Ramón Romero Rosa," 5–6.

41. Cited in Silén, *Apuntes para la historia*, 57–58.

42. Negrón Portillo, *Las turbas republicanas*, 82.

43. Silén, *Apuntes para la historia*, 57.

44. Acosta Lespier, *Una historia olvidada*, 22.

45. Ayala and Bernabe, *Puerto Rico in the American Century*, 62.

46. For the transformation of cigarmakers after the entrance of US capitalism, see Quintero Rivera, "Socialista y tabaquero"; and Baldrich, "Gender and the Decomposition."

47. Acosta Lespier, *Biografía de los alcaldes*, 8; Negrón Portillo, *Las turbas republicanas*.

48. For the myth, see García, *Historia crítica, historia sin coartadas*, 69–70. For Romero Rosa's expulsion, see Tirado Avilés, "Ramón Romero Rosa," 17.

49. For the strike, see Córdova Iturregui, *Ante la frontera del infierno*; Meléndez-Badillo, "Imagining Resistance"; and Rodríguez Vera, *Los fantoches del obrerismo*.

50. For a history of the Partido Obrero Insular, see Colón González, "¡Trabajadores al poder!"

51. I. Picó, *La mujer y la política puertorriqueña*, 30; Barceló Miller, *La lucha por el sufragio femenino*, 67–68.

52. Partido Socialista, *Actuaciones de la primera convención territorial celebrada*, 36.

53. See *Justicia: Órgano de la Federación Libre*, November 3, 1919, 8, 13; December 1, 1919, 5; December 22, 3, 19; January 19, 1920, 4, 18; March 1, 1920, 13–14; March 8, 1920, 9; and March 15, 1920, 10.

54. García and Quintero Rivera, *Desafío y solidaridad*, 82.

55. For other factors, see Álvarez Curbelo, "Un discurso ideológico olvidado."

56. Ayala and Bernabe, *Puerto Rico in the American Century*, 47.

57. Ayala and Bernabe, *Puerto Rico in the American Century*, 79.

58. See Álvarez Curbelo and Raffucci, *Frente a la torre*.

59. See Llorens, *Imaging the Great Puerto Rican Family*; and Rodríguez Castro, "Tradición y modernidad."

60. See E. Amador, "Women Ask Relief for Puerto Ricans."

61. Hall, *Cultural Studies 1983*, 37.

62. See Silvestrini, *Los trabajadores puertorriqueños*. From Taller de Formación Política, see *¡Huelga en la caña!*, *La cuestión nacional*, and *No estamos pidiendo el cielo*. See also Guadalupe de Jesús, *Sindicalismo y lucha política*; Rivera Caballero, *De lobos y corderos*; and Sanabria, *Puerto Rican Labor History*.

63. Ahmed, *Archaeology of Babel*, 3.

64. Conner, *Dreyfus Affair*, 120.

65. Meléndez-Badillo, "Imagining Resistance," 44.

66. Meléndez-Badillo, "Imagining Resistance," 44.

67. Lori L. Tharps, "The Case for Black with a Capital B," *New York Times*, November 18, 2014.

CHAPTER ONE. WORDS AS BRICKS AND PAGES AS MORTAR

1. A similar description of the city's night sounds was used by Torres de Solón in his short story "La balada," published in the workers' literary magazine *Luz y vida*, January 20, 1910, 9–10. Santiago Iglesias Pantín also remembered, "Not many people walked through those dark streets after nine at night. Pedestrians' steps echoed over the sidewalk slate, like a hollow grave. The gas and oil lighting were defective, so the shadows of the night gave the city an almost gloomy appearance." Iglesias Pantín, *Luchas emancipadoras*, 1:35.

2. While sources agree on the whereabouts and the attendance of the meeting, some disagree on when it took place. Sources also mention "5 San José St," but there was no such number, which leads me to believe it was "55 San José St." See Federación Libre de los Trabajadores de Puerto Rico, *Reporte de procedimientos*, 45; Romeral, *Santiago Iglesias*, 6; Valencia, "Raíces del movimiento obrero puertorriqueño"; Iglesias Pantín, *Luchas emancipadoras*, 1:40; and Alonso Torres, *Cuarenta años de lucha proletaria*, 104.

3. For the term "the alternate capital," see Quintero Rivera, *Ponce*. For *El artesano*, see Meléndez-Badillo, *Voces libertarias*, 93.

4. Pedreira, *El periodismo*, 30.

5. García, "Las primeras actividades."

6. "Artesanos: Unión! Unión!," *El artesano*, January 11, 1874, 1–2.

7. "Correspondencia 'El artesano,'" *El artesano*, January 25, 1874, 3.

8. Trouillot, *Silencing the Past*, 23.

9. For *Ensayo obrero*, see Meléndez-Badillo, "Orígenes del 1ro de Mayo en Puerto Rico."; for May Day celebrations, see Gutiérrez, *Los orígenes libertarios del Primero de Mayo*; Goyens, "Introduction," 4; and "Lo que ocurre" and "Era de esperarse," *El productor* (Havana, Cuba) May 11, 1890, 1–2.

10. Cohn, *Underground Passages*.

11. *1ro de maio: Organo de propaganda socialista no Brasil* (Federal Capital, Brazil), May 1, 1898.

12. See Foucault, *Lectures on the Will to Know*, 213; and Foucault, *Archeology of Knowledge*, 15n2.

13. As Benjamin wrote of the Soviet press in the 1920s, in this period in Puerto Rico, "work itself has its turn to speak." Benjamin, "The Author as Producer," in *Walter Benjamin*, 225.

14. See Pedreira, *El periodismo*. For the *Aguinaldo puertorriqueño*, see Álvarez Curbelo, *Un país del porvenir*, 230.

15. Print laws were compiled and revised in 1880. See *Ley de imprenta para la isla de Puerto Rico*. Unions, nonetheless, were banned. See García Leduc, *Apuntes para una historia breve de Puerto Rico*, 250–53.

16. Some of the lectures and conferences given at the Ateneo Puertorriqueño are reproduced in Coll y Toste, *Boletín histórico de Puerto Rico*.

17. I am using the term "ciudad letrada" (lettered city) in reference to Ángel Rama's book by the same name. It refers to the cultural worlds that emerge in urban centers and intellectually organize those physical spaces through letters, be they laws, literature, maps, or the press. See Rama, *La ciudad letrada*.

18. Nazario Velasco, *Historia de los derrotados*.

19. For the social, military, and political context, see Figueroa, *Breve historia de Puerto Rico*, 2:181–260; also see Dávila Santiago, *El derribo de las murallas*, 23; and Quintero Rivera, *Patricios y plebeyos*.

20. Brennan, "Latin American Labor History."

21. Alexander, *History of Organized Labor in Brazil*, 5–20; Bilhão, "Impresa e educação operária."

22. Álvarez Curbelo, *Un país del porvenir*.

23. For the modernizing eagerness, see Álvarez Curbelo, *Un país del porvenir*, chapter 4. For an analysis of the centrality of labor in nineteenth-century liberal discourses, see Rodríguez-Silva, *Silencing Race*, 89. For artisans in the public sphere, see Hoffnung-Garskof, "To Abolish the Law of Castes."

24. García, *Primeros fermentos*.

25. See "Sobre propaganda del ideario anarquista," Ultramar, 5143, exp. 21, Archivo Histórico Nacional de España, Madrid, Spain. For the assassination of Cánovas del Castillo, see Fernández, *La sangre de Santa Agueda*.

26. "¿Anarquistas . . . ? ¡No!," *Ensayo obrero*, April 10, 1898, 1–2.

27. D' Gualfiricio, "Los obreros puertorriqueños," *Ensayo obrero*, December 19, 1897, 2.

28. Rodolfo López Soto, "Redención del obrero," *Ensayo obrero*, September 30, 1897, 1.

29. Rodríguez-Silva, "Abolition, Race, and the Politics of Gratitude," 656.

30. Findlay, *Imposing Decency*, 7.

31. Guridy, *Forging Diaspora*, 25.

32. Ferrer y Ferrer, "Horas de placer," *Ensayo obrero*, December 19, 1897, 3.

33. *El obrero*, November 10, 1889, 2.

34. Rodríguez Vera, *Los fantoches del obrerismo*, 6. Historian Gervasio García later formally developed this thesis in García, *Historia crítica, historia sin coartadas*, 67.

35. According to Kenneth Lugo del Toro, immediately after the Federación Libre joined the AFL, they established "a weekly network of reports on both organizations." Lugo del Toro, *Nacimiento y auge*, 30.

36. "Luisa Capetillo," *Justicia*, April 17, 1922, 3.

37. US War Department, *Report on the Census of Porto Rico, 1899*, 73.

38. Silvestrini, "La mujer puertorriqueña"; Baerga, "'A la organización'"; Baerga, "Exclusion and Resistance."

39. Valle Ferrer, *Luisa Capetillo: Historia*.

40. Alonso Torres, *Cuarenta años de lucha proletaria*, 67.

41. Fiz Jiménez, *Bayamón y su gente*, 124.

42. Alonso Torres, *Cuarenta años de lucha proletaria*, 60.

43. Alonso Torres, *Cuarenta años de lucha proletaria*, 66; Tirado Avilés, "Ramón Romero Rosa," 5.

44. Pratt, *Imperial Eyes*, 7.

45. Alonso Torres, *Cuarenta años de lucha proletaria*, 35–39, 65–70.

46. See Meléndez-Badillo, *Voces libertarias*, 72. For a broader history of lectores, see Tinarejo, *El lector*. For printers in Latin America, see Abad de Santillan and Alba, *Historia del movimiento*; and Zeltsman, "Defining Responsibility."

47. R. del Romeral, "Diálogo," *Ensayo obrero*, March 6, 1898, 2.

48. "Mirando al porvenir," *Ensayo obrero*, February 6, 1898, 1.

49. The writer used the initials E. C. M. and probably was Eduardo Conde Mañón, a painter, writer, and socialist from San Juan. E. C. M., "La mano de hierro," *Ensayo obrero*, February 6, 1898.

50. Mariano Abril served in the Puerto Rican Senate for many years and was the first president of the Puerto Rican Academy of History from 1931 until his death in 1935. See Silva, *Mariano Abril y Ostaló*.

51. Abril y Ostaló, *El socialismo moderno*, 7. "Coryphaei" is the plural of the Greek word "coryphaeus" and in the text refers to a leader of a party but originally referred to the director of a drama in Ancient Greece.

52. Rabachol, "¿Por qué no sómos politicos? I," *La miseria*, March 8, 1901.

53. Rabachol, "¿Por qué no somos politicos? II," *La miseria*, March 9, 1901.

54. Ramos, *Amor y anarquía*, 34.

55. Balsac and Valle, *Revolución*, 46.

56. Gómez Acosta, "Prólogo," n.p.

57. Editorial, "Crónicas," *Ensayo obrero*, January 30, 1898, 1. They also argued they had the capability of producing a lengthier newspaper than the *New York Herald*. See *Ensayo obrero*, September 30, 1897.

58. See "Pro-Julio Aybar," *El combate*, December 19, 1910, 1–2; and "Solidaridad," *El combate*, December 20, 1910, 3. Other newspapers would always side with journalists charged with libel. See "Noticias," *La voz del obrero*, September 3, 1903.

59. "Noticias," *Luz y vida*, January 20, 1910.

60. *Luz y vida*, February 15, 1910, 6.

61. Back cover, *Luz y vida*, December 13, 1909.

62. Eileen J. Suárez Findlay has called this a "sophisticated brega." She coined the word "brega" from cultural theorist Arcadio Díaz Quiñones. Findlay, *We Are Left without a Father Here*, 152.

63. Alfonso Torres, *Solidaridad*, 39.

64. As philosopher Judith Butler has argued, "'media' is not just reporting who the people claim to be. . . . It does not simply assist that definition or make it possible, it is the stuff of self-constitution, the site of hegemonic struggle over 'who we are.'" See Butler, *Notes towards a Performative Theory of Assembly*, 20.

65. The newspapers were *La miseria* (1901), *El pan del pobre* (The poor's bread, 1901), *El porvenir obrero* (The worker's future, 1902), *Hijo del pueblo* (Son of the people, 1903), *La humanidad libre* (Free humanity, 1904), *Voz humana* (Human voice, 1906), *Adelante* (Forward, 1907), *Yo acuso* (I accuse, 1918), and *Avante* (Forward, n.d.). See Lugo del Toro, *Nacimiento y auge*, 32–33; Shaffer, *Black Flag Boricuas*, 31; Meléndez-Badillo,

"Imagining Resistance"; Silén, *Apuntes para la historia*, 28–29; Alonso Torres, *Cuarenta años de lucha proletaria*, 328–29; Ramos, *Amor y anarquía*, 75–86; and Federación Libre de los Trabajadores de Puerto Rico, *Procedimientos del Sexto Congreso*.

66. Struthers, *World in a City*, 52.

67. See *Ensayo obrero*, September 30, 1897; *La miseria*, March 21, 1901; *La voz del obrero*, September 3, 1903; and *Luz y vida*, August 8, 1909.

68. *El porvenir social*, December 12, 1898.

69. See "Balance," *Ensayo obrero*, March 13, 1898, 3; and *El eco del torcedor*, November 7, 1908, 1.

70. Tirado Avilés, "Cigar Workers," 195–96.

71. "El proceso," *El eco del torcedor*, November 7, 1908, 2.

72. "Es una necesidad la imprenta" and "Notas," *El eco del torcedor*, November 7, 1909, 1, 3.

73. "No había muerto," *El eco del torcedor*, January 9, 1910, 1–2.

74. Pedro Moreno y Díaz, in 1910 Census: Bayamón, Puerto Rico, roll T624-1760, p. 19B, Enumeration District 0032, FHL microfilm 1375773, National Archives and Records Administration (NARA), Washington, DC.

75. "La prensa, Crespo Molina y la Comisión," *El eco del torcedor*, January 9, 1910, 1–2.

76. Latiguillo, "Lo que aconseja un sano criterio," *El combate*, December 6, 1910, 1–2.

77. See A. Hernández, *Políticas imperiales sobre la educación*; and del Moral, *Negotiating Empire*.

78. "Bases para formar elementos," *El centinela*, November 28, 1909, 1–2, and December 15, 1909, 1–2.

79. For example, *El combate* had a section titled "Socialist Thoughts," where they would commonly cite Vandervelde, Eugenio Fournière, Carlos Kautoky [sic], Liebknecht, and Kreuxtalko. See *El combate*, December 3, 1910, 4.

80. Acabá de Franco, "Retamos," *El combate*, December 6, 1910, 2–3.

81. See *La miseria*, April 10, 1901, 1.

82. See, for example, the front cover of Padilla, *O perecer o unirse*; and Alfonso Torres, *Solidaridad*. In both books, their authors explained in the front cover how the funds collected from their sale were going to be used for the publication of newspapers and buying a printing press.

83. Her comments were part of a broader critique of the workers' movement in Cuba and Tampa because they slandered Capetillo for her stance and practice of free love. See Luisa Capetillo, "Una entrevista interesante," *¡Tierra!*, February 19, 1914, 2.

84. Rabasa, *Book in Movement*, 13.

85. See Romeral, *Musarañas*.

86. Alfonso Torres, *Solidaridad*.

87. Alfonso Torres, "Dedicatoria," in *Solidaridad*, n.p.

88. Alfonso Torres, *Solidaridad*, 8–9.

89. D. M. Williams, "Society in Revolt or Under Analysis?," 6.

90. See Quintero Rivera, "La ideología populista."

91. Alfonso Torres, *Solidaridad*, 6.

92. Alfonso Torres, *Solidaridad*, 13.

93. Alfonso Torres, *Solidaridad*, 20.

94. Carmelo Honoré, in 1910 US Census: Candelaria, Mayaguez, Puerto Rico, roll T624-1771, p. 26A, Enumeration District 0427, FHL microfilm 1375784, NARA. Carmelo Honoré, in 1920 US Census, Santurce, San Juan, Puerto Rico, roll T625-2070, p. 35A, Enumeration District 19, NARA. Interestingly, while the early twentieth-century census records identify him as an English-speaking mulatto, his death record identifies him as racially white. It seems that class mobility also allowed him racial fluidity. See Carmelo Honoré, death certificate, *Puerto Rico, Civil Registrations, 1885–2001*, online database based on Registro Civil, 1836–2001, digital images, Departamento de Salud de Puerto Rico, San Juan.

95. Arroyo Cordero, *Cabezas*, 3.

96. Arroyo Cordero, *Cabezas*, 4.

97. Arroyo Cordero, *Cabezas*, iii.

98. Arroyo Cordero, *Cabezas*, iv–v.

99. Arroyo Cordero, *Cabezas*, 11.

100. Arroyo Cordero, *Cabezas*, 14, 18–19.

101. Arroyo Cordero, *Cabezas*, 20.

102. Arroyo Cordero, *Cabezas*, 18.

103. See Sarmiento, *Civilización i barbarie*. Arroyo could also draw influence from Puerto Rican naturalists like Manuel Zeno Gandía, José Elías Levis Bernal, and Ramón Juliá Marín.

104. Dávila Santiago, *Teatro obrero*, 106.

105. Dávila Santiago, *Teatro obrero*, 106.

106. Balsac and Valle, *Revolución*, 17. By 1910, Balsac was the general secretary of Mayagüez's Unión Obrera Central; in 1903, Santiago Valle was the president of the Unión de Tipógrafos. See Balsac, *Unión y fuerza;* and Directorio, *Obrero libre*, June 14, 1903, 4.

107. Balsac and Valle, "Prologue," in *Revolución*, n.p.

108. "Información," *Obrero libre*, June 14, 1903, 3.

109. Libraries and centros have a history that dates to the late nineteenth-century mutual aid societies and casinos. The Casino del Centro Hispáno de Mayagüez had a bookshelf of national and international books allowed by the authorities. See Casino del Centro Hispáno de Mayagüez, *Reglamento*.

110. Esteban Rivera and Gabino Moczó, "Iniciativa," *Ensayo obrero*, March 6, 1898, 4.

111. Ferrer y Ferrer, *Los ideales del siglo XX*, 38–39. Ferrer y Ferrer argued this happened in 1897, a year before the Federación Regional was founded. But Romero Rosa argued it took place in 1898. See Dávila Santiago, *El derribo de las murallas*, 78n75.

112. In the first decade of the twentieth century, there were also at least two radical book distributors, Germinal and La Reforma Social. See Meléndez-Badillo, *Voces libertarias*, 103–4.

113. Compañía Editora de Justicia, *Informe annual de Justicia*, 5.

114. Dávila Santiago, *El derribo de las murallas*.

115. Acabá de Franco, "Retamas: Deberes para la causa II," *El combate*, December 17, 1910, 1–2.

116. Acabá de Franco, "Retamas," 1–2.

117. "Noticias de Arecibo," *La correspondencia de Puerto Rico*, December 3, 1906, 4.

118. Meléndez-Badillo, "Radical Genealogies."

119. Domínguez Rubio, "Un intinerario por los proyectos editoriales," 24.

120. Suriano, *Paradoxes of Utopia*, 13–42.

121. Casanovas, *Bread or Bullets!*, 151–52, cited in Fernández, "Los precursores del 1ro de Mayo en Cuba."

122. "Notas y noticias," *El productor* (Havana, Cuba), October 6, 1887, 4.

123. See Dávila Santiago, *Teatro obrero*, 9–29; and Alonso Torres, *Cuarenta años de lucha proletaria*, 97.

124. "Club Ideas Nuevas," *Luz y vida*, February 15, 1910, 1.

125. "Club Ideas Nuevas," *Luz y vida*, February 15, 1910, 1.

126. "Club Ideas Nuevas," *Luz y vida*, February 15, 1910, 10.

127. "Club Ideas Nuevas," *Luz y vida*, February 15, 1910, 2–3.

128. Fiz Jiménez, *Bayamón y su gente*, 127–28.

CHAPTER TWO. THE WORKSHOP IS OUR HOMELAND

1. See Meléndez-Badillo, "Anarchist Imaginary."

2. Guillermo Delgado López to Max Nettlau, December 29, 1906, file 2327, Max Nettlau Papers, International Institute of Social History, Amsterdam.

3. "Papel recibido," *Luz y vida*, January 20, 1910, 10.

4. Seigel, *Uneven Encounters*, 3; Putnam, *Radical Moves*.

5. Allen, *First Annual Report*, 401–5.

6. Allen, *First Annual Report*, 401–5. For a historical overview of the Puerto Rican police, see Martínez, *Presencia de la policía*.

7. Letter to Graham L. Rice, Esq., Commissioner of Immigration, May 28, 1908, *Immigration and Naturalization Records, 1880–1930, Part 6: The Suppression of Radicals*, reel 1, NARA.

8. Meléndez-Badillo, *Voces libertarias*, 177.

9. Duany, *Blurred Borders*, 48–49.

10. For Luisa Capetillo, see Valle Ferrer, *Luisa Capetillo: Historia*; Peña Jordán, "Luisa Capetillo"; and González Morales, "Luisa Capetillo y Luisa Galvão," 107. For Ferrer and Dones, see Alejandro Paulino R., "Historia de las ideas socialistas en la República Dominicana," *Historia dominicana*, May 18, 2008, http://historiadominicana.blogspot.com /2008_05_01_archive.html. For cigarmaker migration, see Andreu Iglesias, *Memorias de Bernardo Vega*.

11. "Compañeros de la redacción de El productor, ¡Salud!," *El productor* (Havana, Cuba), 5 April, 1888, 2; Fernández, *Cuban Anarchism*.

12. Cores Trasmonte, "La actividad política," 63–67.

13. "Celebración del día 1ro de Mayo de 1900," box 99, Junghamns Collection, Archivo General de Puerto Rico (AGPR), San Juan, Puerto Rico.

14. "Celebración del día 1ro de Mayo de 1900."

15. Conde, *Acusación y protesta*, 6.

16. Negrón Portillo, *Las turbas republicanas*, 124–58.

17. For the participation of Conde and Iglesias Pantín, see "La delegación obrera socialista en Nueva York," single leaflet, 1900, microfilm, Puerto Rican Labor Press, Homer Babbidge Library, University of Connecticut, Storrs. For the situation among US socialists, see Hillquit, *History of Socialism in the United States*, 193–300.

18. Santiago Iglesias to Samuel Gompers, October 14, 1901, L3-C2, CDOSIP.

19. Sanabria, *Puerto Rican Labor History*, 97–128.

20. Iglesias to Gompers, October 14, 1901.

21. For recent debates around the AFL's political orientation, see Cobble et al., "Up for Debate," 61–116; and Greene, *Pure and Simple Politics*.

22. "Cost of attendance," L4-C14, Fondo SIP, CDOSIP.

23. See "Report del Pte. Gompers sobre Pto-Rico en la Convención de la American Federation of Labor," *Unión obrera*, November 27, 1904, 2; "Puerto Rico en los E.U.," *Unión obrera*, November 24, 1906, 3; and "Report provisional," *Unión obrera*, December 2, 1906, 2.

24. "Proceedings of the American Federation of Labor," University of Pennsylvania Online Books Page, accessed October 3, 2016, http://onlinebooks.library.upenn.edu /webbin/serial?id=aflannual.

25. According to Italian communist theorist Antonio Gramsci, "organic intellectuals" were those who gave a social group (or class) "homogeneity and an awareness of its own function not only in the economic but also in the social and political fields." See Gramsci, *Selections from the Prison Notebooks*, 3–23.

26. Balsac, *Unión y fuerza*, 9.

27. The competition took place during the Second Regular Assembly of Puerto Rico's Tobacco Unions. See Balsac, *Unión y fuerza*, 58.

28. Balsac, *Unión y fuerza*, 13–17.

29. Balsac, *Unión y fuerza*, 19–22.

30. Balsac, *Unión y fuerza*, 25–26

31. Alonso Torres, *Cuarenta años de lucha proletaria*, 263.

32. Samuel Gompers to Santiago Iglesias Pantín, July 11, 1907, L8-C33, Fondo SIP, CDOSIP.

33. Gompers to Iglesias Pantín, July 11, 1907.

34. Iglesias Pantín, *¿Quiénes sómos?*, 80.

35. Iglesias Pantín, *¿Quiénes sómos?*, 80.

36. Iglesias Pantín, *¿Quiénes sómos?*, 78–79.

37. For workers' interactions with the Spanish Civil Guard, see "Entrevista al Sr. Mateo Pérez Sancuno," file 8301, Historia Oral del Movimiento Obrero CGT, Centro de Investigacion e Historia Oral (CIHO), Universidad Interamericana de Puerto Rico, San Juan.

38. Alonso Torres, *Cuarenta años de lucha proletaria*, 109. It is impossible to verify the veracity of the details as, for example, Alonso Torres argued that Madrid's *La revista blanca* was inside the package, yet it was first published in 1898, a year after the events described. Nonetheless, his account offers a window into the shipment of radical press to Puerto Rico.

39. Shaffer, "Havana Hub," 47.

40. For anarchist networks in the Caribbean, see Shaffer, *Anarchists of the Caribbean*.

41. Caguas went from a village to officially becoming a city in 1894. See Bunker, *Caguas*, 28. While there was an urban migration from the countryside—in part due to the investment of foreign capital—Rosa E. Carrasquillo documents how most Caguas citizens lived in the countryside. In 1899 Caguas had a population of 19,857 people and

27.45 percent (5,450) lived in the city. In 1910 the population increased to 27,169, yet still only 38.11 percent (10,354) were urban dwellers. See Carrasquillo, *Our Landless Patria*, 8–9.

42. Baldrich, *Sembraron la no siembra*, 40; Dietz, *Historia económica de Puerto Rico*, 135.

43. J. D. Hernández, *Nuevas fuentes*, 99–100.

44. See Quintero Rivera, "Socialist and Cigarmaker"; and Baldrich, prologue to *Voces libertarias*.

45. Vega Santos, "Correspondencia, Puerto Rico," *¡Tierra!*, June 24 1905, 3.

46. "De administración," *Voz humana*, September 2, 1906, 4.

47. Grupo editor de Solidaridad, "Proposición," *Voz humana*, September 30, 1906, 2–3.

48. J. Guillermo Osorio, "Aviso," *Voz humana*, October 22, 1906, 4.

49. Communiqué by *Grupo Solidaridad*, "A los compañeros," file 3409, Max Nettlau Papers, International Institute of Social History, Amsterdam.

50. Dávila Santiago, *El derribo de las murallas*, 145–54.

51. See Plaza, *Futuro*; and Gómez, *Arte y rebeldía*.

52. Meléndez-Badillo, *Voces libertarias*, 113.

53. Dávila Santiago, *El derribo de las murallas*, 183; Plaza, *Futuro*, 3.

54. Women's names do not appear listed as part of the centro's committees or in any list of supporters printed in the pages of *Voz humana*. See *Voz humana*, September 2, September 30, and October 22, 1906.

55. For a few examples, see *¡Tierra!*, May 20, 1905, 2–3; August 26, 1905, 2–3; September 2, 1905, 2; November 25, 1905, 3; June 2, 1906, 3; and June 30, 1906. See also *Cultura obrera*, December 14, 1912, 2; February 22, 1913, 2; July 12, 1913; and September 4, 1915.

56. See Adams, "Possibilities of Anarchist History," 45.

57. Meléndez-Badillo, "Los ecos del silencio." For Nettlau's collection, see Margreet Schrevel, "Max Nettlau (1865–1944)," International Institute of Social History, accessed August 21, 2016, http://www.iisg.nl/collections/nettlau/.

58. For weather conditions, see US Department of Agriculture, *Report for August 1909*, 59–63. For San Ciriaco, see Cáldera Ortiz, *Historia de los ciclones y huracanes tropicales*, 107–12.

59. Declaration of Detective Felipe Maldonado, file 121-13, Record Group (RG) 350, Bureau of Insular Affairs, NARA.

60. "Noticias," *Luz y vida*, August 30, 1909, 10.

61. Declaration of Detective Felipe Maldonado.

62. Declaration of Detective Felipe Maldonado.

63. Declaration of Corporal Torres Quintero, file 121113, RG 350, Bureau of Insular Affairs, NARA.

64. See Ullman, *Tragic Week*.

65. Tussel Gómez, *Antonio Maura*.

66. Secretary of War to the Chief of the Bureau of Insular Affairs, September 14, 1909, file 121-12, RG 350, Bureau of Insular Affairs, NARA.

67. Governor Colton to the Chief of the Bureau of Insular Affairs, file 121-12, RG 350, Bureau of Insular Affairs, NARA.

68. Declaration of Corporal Torres Quintero, Insular Police, September 14, 1909, file 121-12, RG 350, Bureau of Insular Affairs, NARA.

69. For Coll y Cuchi's memoirs, see *Historias que parecen cuento*, 197. For the contempt of casino members toward labor leaders, see Alonso Torres, *Cuarenta años de lucha proletaria*, xvii. For the detective's declarations, see Declaration of Detective Felipe Maldonado.

70. Coll y Cuchi, *Historias que parecen cuento*, 197.

71. Cappelletti, *Francisco Ferrer*, 117.

72. Bilhão, "Impresa e eduçacão operária," 180.

73. Bray and Haworth, *Anarchist Education and the Modern School*, 244–56.

74. "Por Ferrer," *Voz Humana*, September 30, 1906, 1.

75. Alonso Torres, "Epilogue," in *Cuarenta años de lucha proletaria*, ix.

76. Alonso Torres, "Epilogue," in *Cuarenta años de lucha proletaria*, xii.

77. For Bayamón, see Fiz Jiménez, *Bayamón y su gente*, 128. For Arecibo, "Las últimas cartas del Martir Francisco Ferrer," *El combate*, December 3, 1910, 1. The anarchist meeting is documented in detail in Dávila Santiago, *El derribo de las murallas*, 171.

78. "¡Gloria al 1ro de Mayo!," box 99, Junghmans Collection, AGPR.

79. Balsac, *Unión y fuerza*, 40.

80. Romeral, *Entre broma y en serio*, 18.

81. See Romeral, *Musarañas*, 32.

82. Romeral, *Musarañas*.

83. Rodríguez-Silva, *Silencing Race*.

84. Ramón Romero Rosa, "A los negros puertorriqueños," reproduced in Ramos Perea, *Literatura puertorriqueña negra*, 471.

85. Eduardo Conde, "A niño Ramón Rivera," reproduced in Ramos Perea, *Literatura puertorriqueña negra*, 469.

86. Eduardo Conde Mañon, in 1920 US Census: San Cristobal, San Juan, Puerto Rico, roll T625-2069, p. 5A, Enumeration District 2, FHL microfilm 1375773, NARA; Ramos Perea, *Literatura puertorriqueña negra*.

87. Conde, "A niño Ramón Rivera," 469.

88. Romero Rosa, "A los negros puertorriqueños," 471.

89. Dávila Santiago, *El derribo de las murallas*, 168; Meléndez-Badillo, *Voces libertarias*, 55, 93–95; Alonso Torres, *Cuarenta años de lucha proletaria*, 338.

90. Enrique Plaza, "De Puerto Rico: Juan Vilar, el joven libertario puertorriqueño," *Cultura obrera*, May 22, 1915, 2.

91. José Ferrer y Ferrer, "Juan Vilar, ha fallecido," *Justicia*, May 15, 1915, 2.

92. See "Un libro de Juan Vilar," *Unión obrera*, August 17, 1911, 2; and Dávila Santiago, *El derribo de las murallas*, 181–92. On the back cover of *Paginas libres*, two additional books are mentioned: *Regionalismo científico* and *Ética social*.

93. Vilar, *Páginas libres*.

94. See "El suceso de Caguas: Una fiera humana," *La democracia*, March 11, 1911, 3.

95. Cited in Dávila Santiago, *El derribo de las murallas*, 203. The Federación Libre's executive committee met on March 23 to articulate an official institutional stance. In it, they asked for the immediate release of all prisoners except for Ventura Grillo, who had committed "an execrable crime." See *La democracia*, March 23, 24, and 25, 1911; and *El tiempo*, March 27, 1911.

96. See Dávila Santiago, *El derribo de las murallas*, 181–92; Meléndez-Badillo, *Voces libertarias*, 172–78; and Shaffer, *Black Flag Boricuas*, 84–91.

97. Vilar was set free a month after the socialist lawyer Rafael López Landrón presented a habeas corpus appeal. A few weeks later, the District Court of Humacao sentenced Vilar to two years in prison because of two articles published in *Voz humana*. He served his sentence in the prison's infirmary. See Dávila Santiago, *El derribo de las murallas*, 204–9.

98. Shaffer, *Black Flag Boricuas*, xvi; Meléndez-Badillo, *Voces libertarias*, 172–77.

99. For Juan Vilar's public letters to Santiago Iglesias Pantín, see Juan Vilar, "Cartas abiertas a Santiago Iglesias," in *Unión obrera*, June 1, 1910, 2; June 7, 1910, 1; June 8, 1910, 1; and June 9, 1910, 2.

100. Pedro Rosa, "Los sucesos de Caguas," *Unión obrera*, August 17, 1911, 1.

101. Luisa Capetillo, "Inicuo atropello: El Centro de Estudios Sociales, de Caguas, clausurado. Brutalidades del fiscal y de la policía," *¡Tierra!*, April 15, 1911, 3–4.

102. Luisa Capetillo, "Inicuo atropello."

103. Plaza, "De Puerto Rico: Juan Vilar," 2.

104. González Prada, *Páginas libres*.

105. Cappelletti, *Francisco Ferrer*, 25.

106. Vilar, *Páginas libres*, 70.

107. Vilar, *Páginas libres*, 53, 66–67.

108. Vilar, *Páginas libres*, 84–85.

109. Vilar, *Páginas libres*, 79, 94.

110. Findlay, *Imposing Decency*, 136.

111. Vilar, *Páginas libres*, 91.

112. For a broader overview of racial democracy discourses in Latin America, see Alberto and Hoffnung-Garskof, "'Racial Democracy' and Racial Inclusion."

113. Diego Vázquez, "Dos líneas," in Vilar, *Páginas libres*, 7. In 1934 a group of anarchists from New York created a group called Juan Vilar, and their newspaper was titled *Páginas libres*. There are no surviving copies, perhaps because of the group's ephemeral existence.

114. Márcano, *Páginas rojas*, 51–52.

115. See Baerga, "A la organización, a uniros."

116. Godreau, "Slippery Semantics," 8.

117. For more information about Mateo Pérez Sanjurjo, see Meléndez-Badillo, "Mateo and Juana."

118. "Entrevista al Sr. Mateo Pérez Sanjurjo," file 8301, pp. 2–3, Historia Oral del Movimiento Obrero CGT, CIHO.

119. "Entrevista al Sr. Mateo Pérez Sanjurjo," CIHO, 12.

120. Romero Rosa wrote, "When I was elected as Delegate of the House of Representatives, instead of inquiring about what I should do in favor the working people, many workers just looked at my shoes, my clothing, and my hat as if they wanted to ask: is this a Delegate?" Romeral, *Entre broma y vera*, 62.

121. "Entrevista al Sr. Mateo Pérez Sanjurjo," CIHO, 12–13.

122. For black internationalism, see Putnam, *Radical Moves*; Stevens, *Red International and Black Caribbean*; Giovannetti-Torres, *Black British Migrants in Cuba*; Blain, *Set the*

World on Fire; Guridy, *Forging Diaspora*; Valdés, *Diasporic Blackness*. For *antillanismo*, see Gaztambide Geigel, "La geopolítica del antillanismo." One of the main ideologues of antillanismo was Eugenio María de Hostos; he participated in labor-related events during the first May Day celebrations in Puerto Rico on 1899. See "1ro de Mayo en la isla," *El porvenir social*, May 6, 1899.

123. Farmer, *Remaking Black Power*, 22.

124. See, for example, Román, "Scandalous Race"; and Cruz Rosa, "El Panafricanismo."

CHAPTER THREE. **IN THE MARGINS OF THE MARGIN**

1. Medina Báez, *Juana Colón*, 196.

2. Hernández et al., *Juana Colón*, 6; Rogler, *Comerío*, 44.

3. See López Rojas, *Historiar la muerte*, 54–55.

4. See López Rojas, *Historiar la muerte*, 55. For a description of funeral processions in early twentieth-century Comerío, see Rogler, *Comerío*, 35.

5. The Socialist Party was dissolved on August 1, 1954, and its members were ordered to join the Popular Democratic Party (PPD). See Pagán, *Historia de los partidos políticos puertorriqueños*, 2:346–48.

6. Hernández et al., *Juana Colón*, 13.

7. Torres Rosario, *Juana Colón*, 125.

8. Torres Rosario, *Juana Colón*, 126.

9. Cited in Torres Rosario, *Juana Colón*, 124.

10. Fiz Jiménez, *Comerío y su gente* and *Bayamón y su gente*.

11. Trouillot, *Silencing the Past*, 53.

12. James C. Scott, *Hidden Transcripts*, 4.

13. Foucault, *Power/Knowledge*, 82.

14. Cited in Shaffer, *Black Flag Boricuas*, 110.

15. See "Suscripción," *Ensayo obrero*, March 6, 1898, 4; Marcelina Vázquez to *Ensayo obrero*, March 13, 1898, 4; and "Suscripción," *Ensayo obrero*, March 27, 1898, 4.

16. "Congreso Internacional Feminista," *El porvenir social*, July 27, 1899, 2–3.

17. For the male rhetoric of working-class discourse, see Findlay, "Slavery, Sexuality, and the Early Labor Movement, 1900–1917," in *Imposing Decency*, 110–34.

18. See Josefa G. de Maldonado, "Manifiesto obrero: A mis compañeras," *El pan del pobre*, August 31, 1901, 1.

19. See R. D. de Otero, "Labor funesta," *El pan del pobre*, September 7, 1901, 1. For the use of the male noun "compañero," see Baerga, "A la organización, a uniros."

20. Francisca Escabí y Montalvo, in *Puerto Rico, Civil Registrations, 1885–2001*, online database based on *Registro Civil, 1836–2001*, digital images, Departamento de Salud de Puerto Rico, San Juan.

21. See Federación Libre de los Trabajadores de Puerto Rico, *Report de procedimientos del tercer congreso*; and Federación Libre de los Trabajadores de Puerto Rico, *Procedimientos del Sexto Congreso*.

22. Merino Falú, "El gremio de lavanderas de Puerta de Tierra."

23. Merino Falú, *Raza, género y clase social*, 125–44.

24. Curiously, in the Federación Libre's 1905 congress, Santiago Iglesias Pantín also appears to be representing the same union. See Federación Libre de los Trabajadores de Puerto Rico, *Report de procedimientos del tercer congreso*, 2.

25. Escabí, "Nuestra misión," 37–39.

26. Escabí, "Nuestra misión," 37–39.

27. For the strike and the decision to change the date, see Meléndez-Badillo, "Imagining Resistance," 33–81.

28. Yamila Azize identified three other women as part of Mayagüez's early twentieth-century labor organizing community: Evangelista Segarra, Adela Mejías, and Emilia Bell. See Azize, *La mujer en la lucha*, 60n18.

29. See Federación Libre de los Trabajadores de Puerto Rico, *Report de procedimientos del tercer congreso*.

30. Paca Escabí, "La ola avanza," *¡Tierra!*, October 7, 1905, 2.

31. Escabí, "La ola avanza," 2.

32. "Defunciones de 1908–1911, Mayagüez," Francisca Escabí y Monsanto, June 6, 1909, in *Puerto Rico, Civil Registrations, 1885–2001*. Although she signed as Francisca Escabí y Peña, the death certificate uses her full birth name.

33. Valle Ferrer, *Luisa Capetillo: Historia de una mujer proscrita*, 39–58.

34. Valle Ferrer, *Luisa Capetillo: Historia de una mujer proscrita*, 39–58.

35. Quoted in Ramos, *Amor y anarquía*, 18.

36. Valle Ferrer, *Luisa Capetillo, Pioneer*.

37. For the 1905 strike, see Córdova Iturregui, *Ante la frontera del infierno*. For Capetilo as a lectora, see Valle Ferrer, "Luisa Capetillo," 6. For the broader practice of lectores, see Tinarejo, *El Lector*.

38. Fiz Jiménez, *Bayamón y su gente*, 124–25.

39. Capetillo, *Ensayos libertarios*.

40. Ramos, *Amor y anarquía*, 32, 75–87.

41. "Notas diversas," *¡Tierra!*, March 12, 1910, 4.

42. Valle Ferrer, *Luisa Capetillo, Pioneer*, 45–59.

43. Capetillo, *Nation of Women*, 143.

44. For other obreros ilustrados who advocated free love, see Meléndez-Badillo, *Voces libertarias*, 150–51.

45. Peña Jordán, "Luisa Capetillo: Estratégica y transversal."

46. For more on her travels, see Valle Ferrer, "Luisa Capetillo," 6–7.

47. Bacci and Fernández Cordero, "Feroces de lengua y pluma"; Guzzo, *Libertarias en América del Sur*; Guzzo, "Luisa Capetillo y Salvadora Medina Onrubia de Botana."

48. Lomas, "Transborder Discourse," 54. For the Moncelanos' travels, see Paredes Goicochea, "Los orígenes del anarquismo en Colombia," 401; Flores Magón, "Rafael Romero Palacios (Concluye)"; and Flores Magón, "¡Despechados!"

49. Luisa Capetillo, "La revolución por la mujer libre," *¡Tierra!*, November 23, 1912, 3.

50. "Noticias," *Luz y vida*, September 30, 1909, 10.

51. "Ecos y notas," *El tipógrafo*, April 16, 1911, 3.

52. Valle Ferrer, *Luisa Capetillo, Pioneer*, 51–52.

53. Valle Ferrer, *Luisa Capetillo, Pioneer*, 52.

54. Peña Jordan, "Luisa Capetillo: Estratégica y transversal," 3–4.

55. Peña Jordan, "Luisa Capetillo." Although Capetillo wore men's clothing, she also condemned homosexuality.

56. Ramos, *Amor y anarquía*, 12–13.

57. Rivera-Giusti, "Gender, Labor, and Working-Class Activism," 161–66.

58. Partido Socialista de América, *Actuaciones de la primera convención territorial celebrada*, 36.

59. Cited in Azize, *La mujer en la lucha*, 70.

60. Estado Libre Asociado de Puerto Rico, Junta de Planificación, *Municipio de Comerío*, 9.

61. Torres Rosario, *Juana Colón*, 33–34.

62. Medina Báez, *Juana Colón*, 29.

63. Marino Faliú, *Raza, género y clase social*, 123. The 1899 census also identifies women, albeit on a much smaller scale, as laborers, merchants, hat and cap makers, teachers, planters, hucksters, and peddlers. US War Department, *Report on the Census of Porto Rico, 1899*.

64. US War Department, *Report on the Census of Porto Rico, 1899*, 93–96.

65. See Quintero Rivera, "Socialist and Cigarmaker."

66. Baldrich, "Gender and the Decomposition," 106.

67. Baldrich, "Gender and the Decomposition," 105.

68. For how she is remembered, see the subtitle of one of her biographies: Torres Rosario, *Juana Colón: Combatiente en el tabacal puertorriqueño*.

69. Torres Rosario, *Juana Colón*, 146.

70. Quintero Rivera and Milagros González, *La otra cara de la historia*, 40–43.

71. For the familial division of labor in nineteenth-century Puerto Rican coffee production, see Fernando Picó, "La mano de obra en la pequeña y mediana producción," in *Amargo café*, 85–96.

72. Picó, *Amargo café*, 44.

73. One of her neighbors provided information about the scuffle, cited in Torres Rosario, *Juana Colón*, 38.

74. On work periods, see Silvestrini, "La mujer puertorriqueña," 77. On other trades, see Medina Báez, *Juana Colón*, 119.

75. Torres Rosario, *Juana Colón*, 101–2; Medina Báez, *Juana Colón*, 69–70.

76. Cited in Torres Rosario, *Juana Colón*, 106–9.

77. See Silvestrini, "La política de salud"; Briggs, *Reproducing Empire*; Trujillo-Pagán, *Modern Colonization by Medical Intervention*; and J. Amador, *Medicine and Nation Building in the Americas*.

78. Torres Rosario, *Juana Colón*, 108.

79. Romeral, *Musarañas*, 29.

80. The PRATC was a proxy of the US-based American Tobacco Company (ATC) and run by local executives. These corporations sought to monopolize cigar manufacturing, and in 1902 they also created the Porto Rico Tobacco Leaf Company (PRTLC), so they could also invest in the farming, buying, and selling of tobacco. See Baldrich, *Sembraron*

la no siembra, 41–42. For information of how these corporations evolved, see Levy, *Puerto Ricans in the Empire*.

81. Bird Carmona, *Parejeros y desafiantes*, 65–86.

82. "Estamos en línea de combate," propaganda leaflet, 1917, *Periódicos obreros puerto-rriqueños*, microfilm, Colección Puertorriqueña, Biblioteca José M. Lázaro, University of Puerto Rico (UPR).

83. Cuerpo Consultivo Conjunto Distrito de Puerto Rico, "Proclama de paz."

84. Cuerpo Consultivo Conjunto Distrito de Puerto Rico, "Proclama de paz," 8.

85. See L. Toro, president of the PRATC, "Historia de la huelga de los tabaqueros de la Porto Rico American Tobacco Company," leaflet, 1919, microfilm, Colección Puertorriqueña, Biblioteca General, UPR; Cuerpo Consultivo Conjunto de las Uniones de Tabaqueros, "La huelga del Trust del Tabaco"; and Comité Central de Resistencia, "¡Última hora!," single-page leaflet, box 100, Particular Collections: Junghamns Collections, AGPR.

86. Cited in Torres Rosario, *Juana Colón*, 77–78.

87. For an overview of female work in tobacco factories, see José Artemio Torres, dir., *Luchando por la vida: Las despalilladoras de Tabaco y su mundo* (San Juan: Aliento Cinematográfico, 1984), DVD.

88. Torres Rosario, *Juana Colón*, 76–94.

89. Medina Báez, *Juana Colón*, 97.

90. Medina Báez, *Juana Colón*, 98.

91. See "Sangrienta masacre en Bayamón," *La correspondencia de Puerto Rico*, March 11, 1911, 1; and "Crimen en Bayamón," *La democracia*, March 11, 1911, 1.

92. "¡Siempre socialistas!," *La federación obrera*, January 21, 1899, 4.

93. Medina Báez, *Juana Colón*, 116–17, 138.

94. Santiago, *Comerío*, 107.

95. Santiago, *Comerío*, 97.

96. Santiago, *Comerío*, 99.

97. Torres Rosario, *Juana Colón*, 119.

98. Fiz Jiménez, *Comerío y su gente*; Fiz Jiménez, *Bayamón y su gente*.

99. Four years after Juana Colón passed away, in 1971, a new Puerto Rican Socialist Party was established. Internal conflicts shrank the party, and it officially disbanded in 1993. See Agosto, *Lustro de gloria*; Mattos Cintrón, *Puerta sin casa*; Mattos Cintrón, *Breve historia*; and Meléndez, *El fracaso del proyecto PSP*.

100. Mari V. de González, "El pueblo habla de Juana Colón."

101. Mari V. de González, "El pueblo habla de Juana Colón," 10–11.

CHAPTER FOUR. **BECOMING POLITICIANS**

1. Pedreira, *El periodismo*, 453.

2. There were at least 335 recorded strikes from 1915 to 1920. See Baldrich, *La huelga como instrumento*. For the history of the Partido Obrero Insular, see Partido Socialista, *Actuaciones de la primera convención regular celebrada en la ciudad de Cayey durante los días 21 y 22 de marzo de 1915*, pp. 7–12, L15-C6, Fondo SIP, CDOSIP.

3. See, for example, McGreevey, *Borderline Citizens*, 106–10.

4. "A ras de tierra," *La fuerza pública*, March 21, 1916, 1–2.

5. "A ras de tierra," 1–2.

6. Silva, *Mariano Abril y Ostaló*.

7. Abril y Ostaló, *El socialismo moderno*, 36–37.

8. Abril y Ostaló, *El socialismo moderno*, 8.

9. Abril y Ostaló, *El socialismo moderno*, 52.

10. Abril y Ostaló, *El socialismo moderno*, 37–38. For more on Mariano Abril y Ostaló's politics, see Negrón Portillo, "Puerto Rico."

11. Historians have yet to explore this organization. See Alonso Torres, *Hurto menor*, 11–12.

12. Governor Arthur Yager to President Woodrow Wilson, n.d., 1916, L16-C46, Fondo SIP, CDOSIP.

13. Cited in Ramos, *Amor y anarquía*, 37. See also Alonso Torres, *Hurto menor*, 5.

14. Governor Arthur Yager to the Chief of the Bureau of Insular Affairs, September 12, 1916, L16-C6, Fondo SIP, CDOSIP.

15. Samuel Gompers to Santiago Iglesias Pantín, May 19, 1916, L16-C50, Fondo SIP, CDOSIP.

16. Gompers to Iglesias Pantín, May 19, 1916.

17. Partido Socialista Puertorriqueño, *Actuaciones de la primera convención regular*, 54.

18. Gompers to Iglesias Pantín, May 19, 1916. A fiery conversation developed between Iglesias Pantín and Esteban Padilla through correspondence. None of the members of the Arecibo branch attended the Socialist Party's second congress in San Juan, when Epifanio Fiz Jimenez was elected president and Iglesias Pantín nominated for resident commissioner. See Esteban Padilla to Santiago Iglesias Pantín, May 24, 1916, L16-C24, Fondo SIP, CDOSIP; message from the newly elected mayor of Arecibo, January 1916, L16-C29, CDOSIP; Esteban Padilla to Santiago Iglesias Pantín, February 22, 1916, L16-C24, CDOSIP; Alonso Torres, *Cuarenta años de lucha proletaria*, 373; and Quintero Rivera, "El Partido Socialista," 71.

19. Alcántara Saez, *El origen de los partidos políticos*, 19.

20. For Ferrer and Osorio, see Alejandro Paulino R., "Historia de las ideas socialistas en la República Dominicana," *Historia dominicana*, May 18, 2008, http://historiadominicana.blogspot.com/2008_05_01_archive.html. For Capetillo, see González Morales, "Luisa Capetillo y Luisa Galvão," 107. For the history of socialism in the Dominican Republic, see Cassá, *Movimiento obrero y lucha socialista*.

21. Casanovas, *Bread or Bullets!*

22. Pérez, *Lords of the Mountain*.

23. Luisa Capetillo, "Dolor y miseria," *El dependiente: Periódico sindicalista* (Havana, Cuba), January 24, 1914, 2–3; M. Sastre, "A Luisa Capetillo y demás yervas que les venga el saco," *El dependiente: Periódico sindicalista* (Havana, Cuba), March 25, 1914, 3.

24. Rojas Blaquier, *El primer Partido Comunista de Cuba*.

25. Silvestrini, *Los trabajadores puertorriqueños*; Rivera Caballero, *De lobos y corderos*; Quintero Rivera, "El Partido Socialista."

26. Sanabria, *Ricardo Campos*, 38; "Acta de antecedente penales de Manuel Francisco Rojas," September 11, 1916, L16-C33, Fondo SIP, CDOSIP. Manuel F. Rojas's books

included *Cuatro siglos de ignorancia; Estudios sociales o frutos del sistema;* and *Hablan las víctimas.*

27. Partido Socialista Puertorriqueño, *Actuaciones de la primera convención regular,* 5–13, 19.

28. Partido Socialista Puertorriqueño, *Actuaciones de la primera convención regular,* 18.

29. Partido Socialista Puertorriqueño, *Actuaciones de la primera convención regular,* 22–23, 33.

30. Partido Socialista Puertorriqueño, *Actuaciones de la primera convención regular,* 41.

31. Partido Socialista Puertorriqueño, *Actuaciones de la primera convención regular,* 50.

32. Sanabria, *Puerto Rican Labor History,* 108.

33. Burnett and Marshall, *Foreign in a Domestic Sense;* Erman, *Almost Citizens;* Mc-Greevey, *Borderline Citizens.*

34. Partido Socialista, *Programa y constitución territorial del Partido Socialista,* 7–11.

35. "Partido Democrático Socialista de los Estados Unidos de América: Territorio de Puerto Rico-Comité Ejecutivo," Puerto Rican Collection Microfilms, 1900, Biblioteca José M. Lázaro, UPR, Río Piedras.

36. Fors, "Jones Act for Puerto Rico," 288.

37. Pagán, *Historia de los partidos puertorriqueños,* 1:179.

38. Alonso Torres, *Cuarenta años de lucha proletaria,* 263.

39. Quintero Rivera, "El Partido Socialista," 63.

40. Manuel F. Rojas, "Programa del Partido Socialista: Al pueblo de Puerto Rico," single-page leaflet, 1917, Puerto Rican Collection, Biblioteca José M. Lárazo, UPR, Río Piedras.

41. *La democracia,* July 18, 1917.

42. For copies of the telegrams, see "Apuntes de las elecciones de 1917," in L18-C1, Fondo SIP, CDOSIP.

43. See "Apelación al Tribunal Supremo, Santiago Iglesias vs El Consejo Ejecutivo de Puerto Rico," L17-C43, CDOSIP.

44. Dr. Santiago Veve to Antonio Barceló, published in *La democracia,* September 11, 1911. After the Socialist Party joined the Republican Party in the creation of the Coalición in 1932, Dr. Veve became an important socialist ally.

45. Lugo del Toro, *Nacimiento y auge,* 54.

46. Alonso Torres, *Cuarenta años de lucha proletaria,* 263.

47. "Actas de la Quinta Convención del Partido Socialista celebrada en la ciudad de Ponce, durante los días 29, 39 y 31 de julio del año 1923," in *Partido Socialista Ejecutivo Territorial, San Juan, P.R., Actas de jul. 1923 a dic. 1926,* p. 22, Fondo SIP, CDOSIP.

48. Compañía Editora de Justicia, *Informe anual,* 6–7.

49. Compañía Editora de Justicia, *Informe anual,* 7.

50. Compañía Editora de Justicia, *Informe anual,* 8.

51. See *Partido Socialista Ejecutivo Territorial.*

52. "Sexta Convención del Partido Socialista celebrada en el Teatro Municipal de San Juan, los días 13 y 14 de julio de 1924," in *Partido Socialista Ejecutivo Territorial,* 237–49.

53. "Sesion del día 25 de septiembre de 1924 del Comité Ejecutivo Territorial," in *Partido Socialista Ejecutivo,* 302.

54. Ramos, *Amor y anarquía,* 78; Shaffer, *Black Flag Boricuas,* 69–70; García and Quintero Rivera, *Desafío y solidaridad,* 59.

55. "Sexta Convención del Partido Socialista," 248–49.

56. "Actas de la Quinta Convención del Partido Socialista," 150.

57. Santiago Iglesias Pantín and Rafael Alonso Torres, "Primer Congreso de Trabajadoras de Puerto Rico," *Justicia*, November 3, 1919, 8, 13.

58. "El Congreso de Trabajadoras y el Gobernador Yager," *Justicia*, December 22, 1919, 3, 19; "Primer Congreso de Trabajadoras de Pto. Rico," *Justicia*, March 1, 1920, 13–14.

59. "El Congreso de Trabajadoras y el Gobernador Yager," 19.

60. Ayala and Bernabe, *Puerto Rico in the American Century*, 69.

61. See Barceló Miller, *La lucha por el sufragio femenino*.

62. Quoted in Baldrich, "Gender and the Decomposition," 106.

63. "Sexta Convención del Partido Socialista," 268–69.

64. "Actuaciones de la Octava Convención del Partido Socialista de Puerto Rico: Agosto 1932," 107–8, Fondo SIP, CDOSIP.

65. "Actuaciones de la Octava Convención," 107–8.

66. "Actuaciones, procedimientos, resoluciones, acuerdos y prácticas de la Novena Convención Ordinaria del Partido Socialista, celebrada en la ciudad de Caguas durante los días 14, 15, 16 y 17 de agosto de 1936," vol. 1, pp. 120–21, Fondo SIP, CDOSIP.

67. "Novena Convención Ordinaria del Partido Socialista," 323.

68. "Novena Convención Ordinaria del Partido Socialista," 324.

69. "Novena Convención Ordinaria del Partido Socialista," 326–28.

70. "Actuaciones de la Octava Convención," 38, 69–72, 120.

71. For anticommunist rhetoric, see Blas Oliveras's speech in favor of the electoral pact in "Actuaciones de la Octava Convención," 194–203.

72. Cited in Ayala and Bernabe, *Puerto Rico in the American Century*, 65.

73. "Actas de la Quinta Convención del Partido Socialista," 34–37.

74. Fernández Garcia, *El libro de Puerto Rico*, n.p. The book included articles about the Socialist Party by Santiago Iglesias Pantín (208–14) and the Federación Libre by Prudencio Rivera Martínez (898–902).

75. Fernández García, *El libro de Puerto Rico*.

76. This is a topic that is yet to be fully explored by historians; see "Labor and the PRRA," L95, Fondo SIP, CDOSIP; and "Special Papers on Puerto Rico," box 22, Brooke Russell Astor Reading Room for Rare Books and Manuscripts, Rose Pesotta Papers, New York Public Library (NYPL).

77. Carreras, *Escuelas para el hombre olvidado*, 17.

78. Carreras, *Escuelas para el hombre olvidado*, 4.

79. Carreras, *Escuelas para el hombre olvidado*, 12.

80. Carreras, *Escuelas para el hombre olvidado*, 15–16.

81. Carreras, *Escuelas para el hombre olvidado*, 18.

82. See Dávila Santiago, "Algunas consideraciones."

83. Rivera Martínez, *Conferencia dictada*.

84. For the liberals' appropriation of the figure of Rafael Cordero, see Findlay, *Imposing Decency*, 77–79; and Hoffnung-Garskof, "Abolish the Law of Castes," 336.

85. Díaz de Román, "Pedro C. Timothée Morales."

86. For the affiliation to the Negro Society for Historical Research, see Sinnette, *Arthur Alfonso Schomburg*, 41–42. For more on Schomburg, see Hoffnung-Garskof, "Migrations of Arturo Schomburg"; and Valdés, *Diasporic Blackness*.

87. Rodríguez-Silva, "Racial Silencing."

88. Meléndez-Badillo, "Mateo and Juana."

89. Rivera Martínez, *Conferencia dictada*, 5–6.

90. Rivera Martínez, *Conferencia dictada*, 7–13. For the intersections of race and the revolutionary politics of the Hispanic Caribbean, see Hoffnung-Garskof, *Racial Migrations*.

91. Rivera Martínez, *Conferencia dictada*, 14.

92. Rivera Martínez, *Conferencia dictada*, 15.

93. Rivera Martínez, *Conferencia dictada*, 15.

94. Correspondence between Mr. H. G. Roberts and Santiago Iglesias Pantín, March 20 and 26, 1936, L96, Fondo SIP, CDOSIP.

95. "Asamblea de Estudiantes," *El mundo*, September 28, 1933, 1, 8, 13.

96. "Actuaciones de la Octava Convención," 141.

97. "Actuaciones de la Octava Convención," 152.

98. For Florencio Cabello and Julio Aybar's position, see Rivera Caballero, *De lobos y corderos*; and Rodríguez García, *Ideales sociales*.

99. "Actuaciones de la Octava Convención," 157–59.

100. "Actuaciones de la Octava Convención," 157, 169, 179.

101. "Actuaciones de la Octava Convención," 164–66.

102. For Sixto Pachecho, "Actuaciones de la Octava Convención," 164. For Bolívar Pagán's obituary, see "Bolívar Pagán, 61, Puerto Rican Aide," *New York Times*, February 10, 1961, 24.

103. "Actuaciones de la Octava Convención," 187.

104. "Actuaciones de la Octava Convención," 184–85.

105. "Actuaciones de la Octava Convención," 180.

106. "Actuaciones de la Octava Convención," 176–77.

107. Silvestrini, *Los trabajadores y el Partido Socialista*, 24.

108. Francisco Govas to Rafael Alonso Torres, November 11, 1933, Colección Prudencio Rivera Martínez, CDOSIP.

CHAPTER FIVE. **STRIKE AGAINST LABOR**

1. "Síndico de la universidad: Ha sido nombrado Rafael Alonso Torres," *El mundo*, September 23, 1933, 1.

2. See "Asamblea de Estudiantes," *El mundo*, September 28, 1933, 1, 8, 13.

3. "Al grito de 'Queremos hombres cultos para nuestra universidad,'" *El día*, September 28, 1933, 1.

4. "Los ocurrido ayer tarde en Fortaleza," *El mundo*, September 29, 1933, 1, 6.

5. The manual was originally published in 1865, but it is still in print.

6. Rafael Alonso Torres to Santiago Iglesias Pantín, October 29, 1933, L72, Fondo SIP, CDOSIP.

7. For the assembly and the march, see "Estudiantes universitario vendrán hoy a Fortaleza," *El mundo*, September 30, 1933, 1, 4; and *El imparcial*, October 2, 1933, front page.

8. Unedited biographical sketch of Rafael Alonso Torres by Prudencio Rivera Martínez, Prudencio Rivera Martínez Collection, CDOSIP; W. D. López, "Rafael Alonso Torres," *Unión obera*, October 19, 1933, 2; October 21, 1933, 1–2, 4; and October 21, 1933, 1.

9. See Dr. José Lanauze Rolón, "Los comunistas y la huelga universitaria," *El imparcial* November 1, 1933, 15; "La huelga universitaria: Es política. Es rebeldía. Es la guerra civil," *El día*, November 4, 1933, 1, 8; "El porvenir de la huelga: Rumores y verdades," *El día*, November 2, 1933, 1, 8; and "Viva la huelga," *El día*, October 25, 1933, 1, 8. For Torregrosa, see "Los nacionalistas debemos estar al lado del movimiento universitario," *El imparcial*, October 28, 1933, 6. For the high school student movement, see "La asamblea de Estudiantes de Escuelas Superiores de Puerto Rico . . . acordó ir a la huelga si se decretaba un paro en nuestra universidad," *El día*, November 6, 1933, 4. For alumni, see "Los descontentos de la Asamblea de Graduados Universitarios," *El día*, October 30, 1933.

10. Both *El mundo* and *Unión obrera* published various letters in solidarity with Alonso Torres from throughout the island. Also see Alonso Torres's correspondence in Prudencio Rivera Martínez's Collection, CDOSIP. For Coll y Cuchi's defense, see his article "Estudiantes, obreros y soldados," *El imparcial*, October 2, 1933, 1, 16. For banners in support of Alonso as a New Deal emissary, see "San Juan presenció ayer un gran desfile en ocasión de la parada del Nuevo Trato," *El mundo*, October 16, 1933, 1.

11. See "San Juan presenció ayer un gran desfile," *El mundo*, October 16, 1933, 1.

12. Rafael Alonso Torres to Santiago Iglesias Pantín, October 16, 1933, L72, Fondo SIP, CDOSIP.

13. "Nuevo Trato," *Unión obrera*, October 17, 1933, 2.

14. Puiggrós, *La educación popular en América Latina*, 145n180. Another congress took place in Mexico City in 1921; see Moraga Valle, "Reforma desde el sur, revolución desde el norte."

15. Boren, *Student Resistance*, 70–77.

16. Fernando Picó, Pabón, and Rivera, *Las vallas rotas*; Rodríguez Graciani, *¿Rebelión o protesta?*; Nieves Falcón, García Rodríguez, and Ojeda Reyes, *Puerto Rico*; Laguarta Ramírez, "Struggling to Learn, Learning to Struggle"; Everhart, "Everything but the Funnel Cake." Aura Jirau Arroyo is working on a dissertation tentatively titled "Campus, Conflict, and Island Transformations: The People of the UPR–Río Piedras, 1952–1981," at the University of Pittsburgh.

17. Silvestrini, *El partido socialista*, 41.

18. Córdova, *Resident Commissioner*, 286–89.

19. Córdova, *Resident Commissioner*, 288.

20. "Los estudiantes han acordado ir a huelga," *El imparcial*, October 19, 1933, 1.

21. Rafael Alonso Torres to Carlos Chardón, October 16, 1933, L72, Fondo SIP, CDOSIP; José Padín to Santiago Iglesias Pantín, October 26, 1933, L72, Fondo SIP, CDOSIP.

22. "La Asamblea de Estudiantes de Escuelas Superiores de Puerto Rico," *El día*, November 6, 1933, 4.

23. "El directorio de protesta contra el nombramiento de don Rafael Alonso Torres para síndico de nuestra Alma Mater," 1933, Centro de Documentación Histórica Arturo Morales Carrión, Universidad Interamericana de San German, http://dspace.cai.sg .inter.edu/xmlui/handle/123456789/15100; Fromm, *César Andreu Iglesias*; Eric Pace, "Dr. Arturo Morales Carrión, 75, Top Aide in Kennedy State Dpt.," Obituaries, *New York Times*, June 30, 1989.

24. Fernando Picó, "La universidad imaginada."

25. See *El día*, September 28, 1933, 1.

26. Rafael Alonso Torres to Santiago Iglesias Pantín, October 30, 1933, L72, Fondo SIP, CDOSIP.

27. Isabel González de Benitez, Secretary of the Socialist Party's Santurce Section, to Rafael Alonso Torres, November 3, 1933, Colección Prudencio Rivera Martínez, CDOSIP.

28. *El imparcial*, November 6, 1933, 24.

29. José Lanauze Rolón, "La huelga universitaria: Es política. Es rebeldía. Es la guerra civil," *El día*, November 4, 1933, 1, 8.

30. Bird Piñero, *Don Luis Muñoz Marín*, 36.

31. He informed Santiago Iglesias Pantín but asked for confidentiality. See Alonso Torres to Iglesias Pantín, October 16, 1933.

32. See Benítez Rexach, *Vida y obra de Luis Münoz Marín*.

33. Bird Piñero, *Don Luis Muñoz Marín*, 36–39.

34. Bird Piñero, *Don Luis Muñoz Marín*, 36–39.

35. For Bolivar Pagán and Rafael Alonso Torres's power struggles, see the letters the latter sent to Santiago Iglesias Pantín, located in L72, Fondo SIP, CDOSIP. For rumors of Bolivar Pagán framing Alonso Torres, see Bird Piñero, *Don Luis Muñoz Marín*, 36–39. For the 1939 document, see "Exposición que someten los representantes obreros y socialistas de Puerto Rico reunidos en sesión el 3 de julio de 1938 al Hon. Santiago Iglesias, Presidente del Partido Socialista de Puerto Rico," folder 133, box 3, section 13, Blas Oliveras Collection, Fundación Luis Muñoz Marín, San Juan, Puerto Rico.

36. "Mitin en Ponce," *El día*, November 1, 1933, 1, 4.

37. See Pedreira, *El periodismo en Puerto Rico*.

38. *El diluvio*, May 18, 1933, front cover.

39. "En el pórtico: Reprobable actitud de 'La Democracia,'" *El diluvio*, October 30, 1933, 1–2.

40. "En el pórtico: Reprobable."

41. "En el portico: El odio del obrero manual al obrero del pensamiento," *El diluvio*, November 18, 1933, 1–2.

42. "En el portico," *El diluvio*, November 4, 1933, 1–3.

43. Gabriel Soler Cátala, "El señor Alonso Torres fue siempre enemigo de nuestra universidad," *La democracia*, September 27, 1933, 1, 4.

44. For example, see *La democracia*, October 3, 1933, 4.

45. T. Maldonado, *Ese fue mi maestro*, 131.

46. T. Maldonado, *Ese fue mi maestro*, 131.

47. Rafael Alonso Torres, Síndico de la Universidad de Puerto Rico, "La misión del perro en el mundo," *El mundo*, October 1, 1933, 3, 11.

48. Victor Gutierrez Franqui and Manuel Rodríguez Ramos, "Los perros felinos versus los gatos caninos," *El mundo*, October 3, 1933, 2.

49. José Lanauze Rolón, "Viva la huelga," *El día*, October 25, 1933, n.p.

50. See the telegrams published in *El mundo*, September 30, 1933, 4.

51. Ferrao, "Nacionalismo, hispanismo y elite intelectual," 40.

52. Telegram from Lino Padrón Rivera to Rafael Alonso Torres, November 13, 1933, Prudencio Rivera Martínez Collection, CDOSIP.

53. W. D. López, "Rafael Alonso Torres," *Unión obera*, October 19, 1933, 2; October 21, 1933, 1–2, 4.

54. "Contra la protesta de los estudiantes universitarios," *El mundo*, October 2, 1933, 1, 3.

55. Single-page leaflet, Prudencio Rivera Martínez Collection, CDOSIP.

56. Most of these letters were published in the press, specifically in *El mundo* and *Unión obrera*. Personal correspondence can be found in L72, Fondo SIP, and Prudencio Rivera Martínez Collection, CDOSIP.

57. Octavio Freytes to Rafael Alonso Torres, October 28, 1933, Prudencio Rivera Martínez Collection, CDOSIP.

58. Prudencio Rivera Martínez, "Opiniones de Prudencio Rivera Martínez desde Washington," *Unión obrera*, November 2, 1933, 1, 2, 4.

59. Marsiske, "Los estudiantes de la reforma universitaria en América Latina," 22.

60. García Bryce, *Haya de la Torre*; Lambe, "Hope and Despair: The Fight for a New Cuba," in *No Barrier Can Contain It*, 23–53.

61. Prudencio Rivera Martínez, "Opiniones de Prudencio Rivera Martínez desde Washington," *Unión obrera*, November 2, 1933, 1, 2, 4.

62. See, for example, "Resolución de la Asamblea Conjunta de Miembros de la Asamblea Municipal, Junsta Administrativa, Comités Políticos de los Partidos Unión Republicana y Socialista y Empleados Municipales," November 1, 1933; letters from the United Brotherhood of Carpenters and Joiners of Puerto Rico, October 14, 1933; Blas Oliveras, Mayor of Ponce, to Rafael Alonso Torres, October 28, 1933, all in Prudencio Rivera Martínez Collection, CDOSIP.

63. Anselmo Vidal to Rafael Alonso Torres, October 31, 1933, Prudencio Rivera Martínez Collection, CDOSIP.

64. Leonor Rodríguez and José Serrano to Rafael Alonso Torres, October 28, 1933, Prudencio Rivera Martínez Collection, CDOSIP.

65. "La Asamblea de Estudiantes de Escuelas Superiores de Puerto Rico," *El día*, November 6, 1933, 4.

66. M. del Toro Peralta, "Los universitarios en Mayagüez," *El día*, November 6, 1933, 8.

67. "La Asamblea de Padres Universitarios se ratificó ayer en su respaldo al movimiento huelgario," *El imparcial*, November 6, 1933, 4.

68. Prudencio Martínez Rivera to Santiago Iglesias Pantín, November 8, 1933, L74, Fondo SIP, CDOSIP.

69. Martínez Rivera to Iglesias Pantín, November 8, 1933.

70. "La universidad permanece cerrada," *El día*, November 6, 1933, 5.

71. See the front page of *El imparcial*, November 6, 1933.

72. Rafael Alonso Torres to Santiago Iglesias Pantín, December 5, 1933, L72, Fondo SIP, CDOSIP.

73. Córdova, *Resident Commissioner*, 290–93.

74. Silvestrini, *El partido socialista*; Taller de Formación Política, *¡Huelga en la caña!*

75. Martínez Rivera to Iglesias Pantín, November 8, 1933.

76. Martínez Rivera to Iglesias Pantín, November 8, 1933.

77. Martínez Rivera to Iglesias Pantín, November 8, 1933.

78. Santiago Iglesias Pantín to Rafael Alonso Torres, November 8, 1933, L72, Fondo SIP, CDOSIP.

79. Martínez Rivera to Iglesias Pantín, November 8, 1933.

80. Córdova, *Resident Commissioner*, 298.

81. Agustín Alonso to Rafael Alonso Torres, November 7, 1933, Colección Prudencio Rivera Martínez, CDOSIP.

82. Olivia vda. de Braschi to Prudencio Rivera Martínez, November 12, 1933, Colección Prudencio Rivera Martínez, CDOSIP.

83. Ramón Barrios eventually moved away from anarchism and became a marshal, for which he was severely criticized by his US anarchist comrades. See Emil Olay to Rose Pesotta, August 31, 1934, box 1, Correspondence, Rose Pesotta Papers, NYPL. For the Barrios family's composition, see 1930 US Census: Bayamón, Puerto Rico, roll 2642, p. 21B, Enumeration District 0002, image 752.0, FHL microfilm 2342376, NARA.

84. Francisca and Acracia Barrios to Rafael Alonso Torres, November 6, 1933, Prudencio Rivera Martínez Collection, CDOSIP.

85. Francisca and Acracia Barrios to Alonso Torres, November 6, 1933.

86. Francisco Govas to Rafael Alonso Torres, November 11, 1933, Prudencio Rivera Martínez Collection, CDOSIP.

87. Silvestrini, *Los trabajadores puertorriqueños*, 77–80; García and Quintero Rivera, *Desafío y solidaridad*, 107; Lugo del Toro, *Nacimimento y auge*, 110–12; Rivera Caballero, *De lobos y corderos*, 168.

88. Taller de Formación Política, *La cuestión nacional*, *¡Huelga en la caña!*, and *No estamos pidiendo el cielo*.

89. This program remains to be fully explored by historians. See Medina Báez, *Teresa Angleró Sepúlveda*, 195–211; and newspaper clippings, box 22, Special Papers on Puerto Rico, Rose Pesotta Papers, NYPL.

90. Rodríguez Castro, "Tradición y modernidad"; Díaz-Quiñones, "Recordando el futuro imaginario"; Rodríguez Beruff, "Antonio S. Pedreira"; Díaz-Quiñones, "Tomas Blanco (1896–1975): La reinvención de la tradición," in *Sobre los principios*, 377–442.

91. Partido Socialista, *Actuaciones, procedimientos, resoluciones*, 186–88.

CHAPTER SIX. **MINOR THEFT**

1. Alonso Torres, *Hurto menor*, 13–18.

2. Alonso Torres, *Hurto menor*, 13–18.

3. Alonso Torres, *Hurto menor*, 18–36.

4. Alonso Torres, *Hurto menor*, 3.

5. Alonso Torres, *Hurto menor*, 36.

6. For example, see Federación Libre de Ponce, *Crímenes policíacos*; Balsac, *Apuntes históricos*; Aybar, *Labor parlamentaria*; and Ochart, *La noche del 12 de marzo*.

7. Burton, *Archive Stories*, 3. For more interpretations about the fluid nature of archives, see Arondekar, *For the Record*; Burton, *Dwelling in the Archive*; and Cvetkovich, *Archive of Feelings*.

8. For Padrón Rivera, see Padrón Martínez, *Biografía y obra de Lino Padrón Rivera*. For Bólivar Pagán and Colón Gordiany, see Lugo del Toro, *Nacimiento y auge*.

9. Silvestrini, *Los trabajadores puertorriqueños*; Rivera Caballero, *De lobos y corderos*.

10. These tensions are summarized in Fiz Jiménez, *El racket en el capitolio*.

11. Rodríguez Castro, "Tradición y modernidad." For a contemporary approach to these elites, see Villanueva, Cobián, and Rodríguez, "San Juan, the Fragile City."

12. Díaz-Quiñones, "Recordando el future imaginario"; Rodríguez Beruff, "Antonio S. Pedreira."

13. Díaz-Quiñones, *Sobre los principios*, 329.

14. Ferrao, "Nacionalismo, hispanismo y elite intelectual." This has been studied and problematized by various scholars. For example, see Flores, *Insularismo e ideología burguesa*; and Rodríguez Castro, "Tradición y modernidad."

15. "Libros de hoy," *Índice* 1, no. 12 (March 13, 1930), in *Índice: Mensuario de historia, literatura y ciencia*, 197.

16. Scarano, "La historia heredada," 45. For the teaching of history, see Silvestrini, "Los libros de texto de historia de Puerto Rico."

17. For the first historians, see Scarano, "La historia heredada"; and Castro Arroyo, "De Salvador Brau."

18. Scarano, "La historia heredada."

19. Scarano, "La historia heredada"; Castro Arroyo, "El Centro de Investigaciones Históricas"; Díaz-Quiñones, *La memoria rota*; Quintero Rivera, "La ideología populista"; Méndez, "Las ciencias sociales."

20. "Notas bibliográficas: Luchas emancipadoras por Santiago Iglesias," *Acción socialista* (Havana, Cuba), February 10, 1935, 6.

21. Alejandro Chacoff, "Ricardo Piglia's Prescient Conspiracies," *New Yorker*, August 15, 2017.

22. Chacoff, "Ricardo Piglia's Prescient Conspiracies."

23. Iglesias Pantín, *Luchas emancipadoras:*, 29. Also see "Desde La Habana," *El corsario*, March 26, 1893.

24. See Dávila Santiago, *Teatro obrero en Puerto Rico*.

25. See Córdova, *Resident Commissioner*.

26. Iglesias Pantín, *Luchas emancipadoras*, 1:33. The page numbers I am using are from the second edition of the book. Both texts are identical except for a prologue written by Bolívar Pagán and the elimination of advertisements in the second edition.

27. Iglesias Pantín, *Luchas emancipadoras*, 1:11.

28. Iglesias Pantín, *Luchas emancipadoras*, 1:11.

29. Iglesias Pantín, *Luchas emancipadoras*, 1:57–58.

30. Iglesias Pantín, *Luchas emancipadoras*, 1:63, 1:94

31. Iglesias Pantín, *Luchas emancipadoras*, 1:333; emphasis added.

32. Meléndez-Badillo, "Imagining Resistance," 33–81.

33. Iglesias Pantín, *Luchas emancipadoras*, 1:151.

34. Iglesias Pantín, *Luchas emancipadoras*, 1:151.

35. See Pagán, *Discurso pronunciado*.

36. Ferrer y Ferrer, *Los ideales del siglo XX*, 28. Original quotation: "¿Es acaso, que para representar dignamente a su clase, en el Parlamento, necesita el obrero ser filósofo, de sangre pura, poseer y gozar el monopolio de las investigaciones críticas e históricas, ursurpando el presitigio de heroes del taller, fábricas y campos?"

37. Ferrer y Ferrer, *Los ideales del siglo XX*, 30.

38. Castrillo, *Mis experiencias*, 2.

39. Ferrer y Ferrer, *Los ideales del siglo XX*, 19.

40. See Dana M. Williams, "Society in Revolt."

41. Ferrer y Ferrer, *Los ideales del siglo XX*, 31.

42. Ferrer y Ferrer, *Los ideales del siglo XX*, 56.

43. Ferrer y Ferrer, *Los ideales del siglo XX*, 20.

44. Ferrer y Ferrer, *Los ideales del siglo XX*, 51.

45. Ferrer y Ferrer, *Los ideales del siglo XX*, 74.

46. Ferrer y Ferrer, *Los ideales del siglo XX*, 73.

47. Ferrer y Ferrer, *Los ideales del siglo XX*, 81.

48. Departamento de Comercio, Oficina del Censo, *Censo décimosexto de los Estados Unidos, 1940: Población de Puerto Rico*, San Juan Municipality, Santurce Neighborhood.

49. Silvestrini, *El partido socialista*; Taller de Formación Política, *La cuestión nacional*.

50. Rafael Alonso Torres to Santiago Iglesias Pantín, October 29, 1933, L72, Fondo SIP, CDOSIP; emphasis added.

51. Rodríguez García, *Brevario histórico*, 11–12.

52. Alonso Torres, *Cuarenta años de lucha proletaria*, 9–10.

53. Alonso Torres, *Cuarenta años de lucha proletaria*, 9–10.

54. Alonso Torres, *Cuarenta años de lucha proletaria*, 39, 65, 66–68.

55. Alonso Torres, *Cuarenta años de lucha proletaria*, 108–9.

56. The chapter was originally titled "Procedimientos del Sexto Congreso Obrero de la Federación Libre de los Trabajadores de Puerto Rico." It was also reproduced, without acknowledgment, in Compañía Editora de Justicia, *Informe anual de la Compañía Editora de Justicia*.

57. Alonso Torres, *Cuarenta años de lucha proletaria*, 343.

58. Alonso Torres, *Cuarenta años de lucha proletaria*, 344–45.

59. Alonso Torres, *Cuarenta años de lucha proletaria*, 346.

60. Partido Socialista, *Actuaciones, procedimientos, resoluciones*, 122.

61. Silvestrini, *El partido socialista*; Rivera Caballero, *De lobos y corderos*.

62. Partido Socialista, *Novena convención*, 122.

63. Alonso Torres to Iglesias Pantín, October 29, 1933.

64. Alonso Torres, *Cuarenta años de lucha proletaria*, 347.

65. Alonso Torres, *Cuarenta años de lucha proletaria*, 346.

66. For example, in a recently published book, Alonso Torres is identified as "one of our first labor historians." Toledo, *Luisa Acevedo Zambrana*, 22.

67. Arundhati Roy, "Peace and the New Corporate Liberation Theology," the 2004 Sydney Peace Prize Lecture, November 4, 2004, http://sydney.edu.au/news/84.html?newsstoryid=279.

68. Iglesias Pantín, *Luchas emancipadoras*, 1:68.

69. Iglesias Pantín, *Luchas emancipadoras*, 1:293.

70. Rodríguez-Silva, *Silencing Race*, 7–8.

71. Kleinberg, *Haunting History*, 10.

72. Ferrer y Ferrer, *Los ideales del siglo XX*, 65.

73. Ferrer y Ferrer, *Los ideales del siglo XX*, 99–102.

74. Ferrer y Ferrer, *Los ideales del siglo XX*, 26–27, 65, 106.

75. Iglesias Pantín, *Luchas emancipadoras*, 105; Carroll, Report on Porto Rico, 1899, 51.

76. Romeral, *Santiago Iglesias.*

77. Romeral, *Santiago Iglesias,* 7.

78. Federación Libre de los Trabajadores de Puerto Rico, *Día del Trabajo,* 4.

EPILOGUE

1. Prudencio Rivera Martínez, "Rasgo de filantropía inusitado," Prudencio Rivera Martínez Collection, CDOSIP.

2. Rivera Martínez, "Rasgo de filantropía inusitado."

3. Rivera Martínez, "Rasgo de filantropía inusitado."

4. Rivera Martínez, "Rasgo de filantropía inusitado."

5. Caballero Wangüemert, *El Caribe en la encrucijada,* 14–15.

6. Rivera Martínez, "Rasgo de filantropía inusitado."

7. "Actuaciones, procedimientos, resoluciones, acuerdos y prácticas de la Novena Convención Ordinaria del Partido Socialista, celebrada en la ciudad de Caguas durante los días 14, 15, 16 y 17 de agosto de 1936," vol. 1, p. 3, Fondo SIP, CDOSIP.

8. "Exposición que someten los representantes obreros y socialistas de Puerto Rico reunidos en sesión el 3 de julio de 1938 al Hon. Santiago Iglesias, Presidente del Partido Socialista de Puerto Rico," folder 133, box 3, section 13, Blas Oliveras Collection, Luis Muñoz Marín Foundation, San Juan, Puerto Rico.

9. "Convención Extaordinaria del Partido Socialista, San Juan, Puerto Rico, Agosto 20, 1939," p. 38, Fondo SIP, CDOSIP.

10. For more information about the Pure Labor Party, see folders 268–76, box 10, Blas Oliveras Collection, Luis Muñoz Marín Foundation, San Juan, Puerto Rico.

11. Jiménez, "Puerto Rico under the Colonial Gaze."

12. Blas Oliveras, prologue to Fiz Jiménez, *El racket en el capitolio,* 17.

13. This was also the slogan of the Puerto Rican Communist Party. See Pujals, "De un pájaro last tres alas," 280.

14. Rivera Colón, *Fajardo,* 25–26.

15. "Fernando López, Candidato a alcalde socialista en Fajardo: Reprocha a la mogolla y no respalda a Martín Travieso para gobernador," document 6, folder 1776, subseries 6, section 4, Luis Muñoz Marín Collection, Luis Muñoz Marín Foundation, San Juan, Puerto Rico.

16. Marsh Kennerly, *Negociaciones culturales,* 19.

17. Muñoz Marín, *Memoria,* 89. See also Rosario Natal, *La juventud de Luis Muñoz Marín*; and Benítez Rexach, *Vida y obra de Luis Muñoz Marín.*

18. Ad in *Espartaco* 1, no. 2 (April 1921): n.p.

19. Marsh Kennerly, *Negociaciones culturales,* 21.

20. See Esterrich, "The Momentous 1950s: Bootstrapping Puerto Rican Culture," part 1 in *Concrete and Countryside,* 3–68.

21. According to Sanabria, "Muñoz Marín continued to propound Santiago Iglesias's idea that the political status of Puerto Rico was not an issue. Instead, like Santiago Iglesias, [he] argued that it was more important to address the immediate economic and social

needs of the population." See Sanabria, *Puerto Rican Labor History*, 6; and Cruz Santos, *Afirmando la nación*.

22. Díaz-Quiñones, *La memoria rota*, 20. See also Guerra, *Popular Expression and National Identity*; and Scarano, "Jíbaro Masquerade."

23. Marsh Kennerly, *Negociaciones culturales*, 133.

24. Marsh Kennerly, *Negociaciones culturales*. See also Vélez Rivera, *Las ilustraciones*.

25. Marqués, *Lucha obrera*, 43.

26. Marqués, *Lucha obrera*, 44.

27. Marqués, *Lucha obrera*, 45.

28. Marqués, *Lucha obrera*, 45.

29. Marqués, *Lucha obrera*, 17.

30. Farinacci Fernós, *La constitución obrera de Puerto Rico*, 218.

31. Pagán, *Historia de los partidos políticos*, 2:347.

32. Bolívar Pagán's speech was reproduced in *Discurso pronunciado*, 32.

ARCHIVES, LIBRARIES, AND INSTITUTIONS

Archivo General de Puerto Rico (AGPR), San Juan, Puerto Rico
Archivo Histórico Nacional de España, Madrid, Spain
Archivo Municipal de Caguas, Puerto Rico
Biblioteca José M. Lázaro, Universidad de Puerto Rico (UPR), Río Piedras
Brooke Russell Astor Reading Room for Rare Books and Manuscripts, Rose Pesotta
    Papers, New York Public Library (NYPL)
Centro: Center for Puerto Rican Studies, City University of New York
Centro de Documentación Obrera Santiago Iglesias Pantín, Universidad de Puerto
    Rico, Humacao
Centro de Investigación e Historia Oral (CIHO), Universidad Interamericana de Puerto Rico
Centro de Investigaciones Históricas, Universidad de Puerto Rico, Río Piedras
Fundación Anselmo Lorenzo, Madrid, Spain
Fundación Luis Muñoz Marín, San Juan
Homer Babbidge Library, University of Connecticut, Storrs
International Institute of Social History, Amsterdam, Netherlands
Thomas J. Dodd Research Center, the University of Connecticut, Storrs
US National Archives and Records Administration, Washington, DC

NEWSPAPERS

El abayarde rojo, 2011
Acción socialista (Havana, Cuba), 1935
Alma popular, 1924
El artesano, 1874

El boletín mercantil, 1904
Campaña obrera, 1906
El centinela, 1909
Chispa, 1937
Claridad, 1972, 1981, 1989, 2009
Cogito Ergo Sum (San Francisco), 1908
El combate, 1910
El comunista, 1920–21
Conciencia libre, 1909–10
Conciencia popular, 1919
La correspondencia de Puerto Rico, 1906, 1911
El corsario (Coruña, Spain), 1891–96
Cultura obrera (New York), 1912–15
La democracia, 1909–11, 1917, 1933
El dependiente (Havana, Cuba), 1914
El día, 1933
El diluvio, 1933
El eco del torcedor, 1908–10
Eco proletario, 1892
Ensayo obrero, 1897, 1898
Espartaco, 1921
La federación libre, 1902
La federación obrera, 1899
El florete, 1933
La fuerza pública, 1916
El heraldo del trabajo, 1878–80
La huelga, 1911
El imparcial, 1933
J'accuse, 1933
Justicia, 1914–26
Luz y vida, 1909, 1910
La miseria, 1901–2
El mundo, 1933, 1936
New York Times, 1961, 1989, 2014
La obrera, 1899
El obrero, 1889
Obrero libre, 1903
El pan del pobre, 1901
Pica Pica, 1933
El Porvenir social, 1898–99
1ro de maio (Capital Federal, Brazil), 1898
El Productor (Havana, Cuba), 1887–98
El Prospecto, 1894
Puerto Rico ilustrado, 1910–21
Puerto Rico Workingmen's Journal, 1905, 1910–11

Regeneración (Mexico City), 1914–15
Revista obrera, 1893
La sotana, 1912
El Tiempo, 1911
¡Tierra! (Havana, Cuba), 1902–15
El tipógrafo, 1911
El trabuco, 1901
Unión obrera, 1902–20, 1933
El vigilante, 1911
La Voz del obrero, 1903, 1919
Voz humana, 1906
Yo acuso, 1918

OTHER SOURCES

Abad de Santillan, Diego, and Victor Alba. *Historia del movimiento obrero en América Latina*. Mexico City: Libreros Mexicanos Unidos, 1964.

Abril y Ostaló, Mariano. *El socialismo moderno*. San Juan: Tipografía La Primavera, 1911.

Acevedo González, Andino. *¡Qué tiempos aquellos!* Río Piedras: Editorial de la Universidad de Puerto Rico, 1989.

Acosta-Belén, Edna, ed. *La mujer en la sociedad puertorriqueña*. Río Piedras: Ediciones Huracán, 1980.

Acosta-Belén, Edna, and Elia Hidalgo Christensen, eds. *The Puerto Rican Woman*. New York: Praeger, 1979.

Acosta Lespier, Ivonne. *Biografía de los alcaldes*. San Juan: Asamblea Municipal de San Juan, 2000.

Acosta Lespier, Ivonne. *Una historia olvidada: Un siglo en la asamblea municipal de San Juan*. San Juan: Asamblea Municipal de San Juan, 2000.

Adams, Matthew S. "The Possibilities of Anarchist History: Rethinking the Canon and Writing History." *Anarchist Developments in Cultural Studies* 3, no. 1 (2013): 33–63.

Agosto, Ángel M. *Lustro de gloria: Cinco años que estremecieron el siglo*. 3rd ed. Río Grande: La Casa Editora de Puerto Rico, 2014.

Ahmed, Siraj. *Archaeology of Babel: The Colonial Foundation of the Humanities*. Stanford, CA: Stanford University Press, 2018.

Alamo-Pastrana, Carlos. *Seams of Empire: Race and Radicalism in Puerto Rico and the United States*. Gainesville: University Press of Florida, 2016.

Alberto, Paulina L., and Jesse Hoffnung-Garskof. "'Racial Democracy' and Racial Inclusion: Hemispheric Histories." In *Afro-Latin American Studies: An Introduction*, edited by Alejandro de la Fuente and George Reid Andrews, 264–318. Cambridge: Cambridge University Press, 2018.

Alcántara Saez, Manuel. *El origen de los partidos políticos en América Latina*. Barcelona: Institut de Ciènces Polítiques I Socials, 2001.

Alexander, Robert J. *A History of Organized Labor in Brazil*. Westport, CT: Praeger, 2003.

Allen, Charles H. *First Annual Report of Charles H. Allen, Governor of Porto Rico Covering the Period from May 1, 1900, to May 1, 1901.* Washington, DC: Government Printing Office, 1901.

Alonso Torres, Rafael. *Cuarenta años de lucha proletaria.* San Juan: Imprenta Baldrich, 1939.

Alonso Torres, Rafael. *Hurto menor: El célebre caso de allanamiento de morada contra la Federación Libre y el proceso de hurto menor contra el Secretario General de la institución.* San Juan: privately printed, 1919.

Altagracia Espada, Carlos D. *La utopia del territorio perfectamente gobernado: Miedo y poder en la época de Miguel de la Torre, Puerto Rico, 1822–1837.* [Puerto Rico?]: privately printed, 2013.

Álvarez Curbelo, Silvia. "Un discurso ideológico olvidado: Los agricultores puertorriqueños (1924–1928)." *Op. Cit.: Revista del Centro de Investigaciones Históricas*, no. 2 (1986): 141–60.

Álvarez Curbelo, Silvia. *Un país del porvenir: El afán de modernidad en Puerto Rico, siglo XIX.* San Juan: Ediciones Callejón, 2001.

Álvarez Curbelo, Silvia, and Carmen Raffucci, eds. *Frente a la torre: Ensayos del centenario de la Universidad de Puerto Rico, 1903–2003.* Río Piedras: Editorial de la Universidad de Puerto Rico, 2005.

Álvarez Curbelo, Silvia, and María Elena Rodríguez Castro, eds. *Del nacionalismo al populismo: Cultura y política en Puerto Rico.* Río Piedras: Decanato de Estudios Graduados e Investigación, UPR, and Ediciones Huracán, 1993.

Alverio Ramos, Zulmarie. *La gran ausente: La maestra Celestina Cordero Molina.* Hato Rey: Editorial EDP University, 2017.

Amador, Emma. "'Women Ask Relief for Puerto Ricans': Territorial Citizenship, the Social Security Act, and Puerto Rican Communities, 1933–1939." *Labor: Studies in Working-Class History of the Americas* 13, no. 3–4 (December 2016): 105–30.

Amador, José. *Medicine and Nation Building in the Americas: 1890–1940.* Nashville, TN: Vanderbilt University Press, 2015.

Ames, Azel. *Labor Conditions in Puerto Rico.* Washington, DC: Government Publishing Office, 1901.

Anderson, Robert W. *Party Politics in Puerto Rico.* Stanford, CA: Stanford University Press, 1965.

Andreu Iglesias, César, ed. *Memorias de Bernardo Vega: Contribución a la historia de la comunidad puertorriqueña en Nueva York.* Río Piedras: Ediciones Huracán, 1994.

Aparicio, Juan Ricardo, and Mario Blaser. "The 'Lettered City' and the Insurrection of Subjugated Knowledges in Latin America." *Anthropological Quarterly* 81, no. 1 (Winter 2008): 59–94.

Arondekar, Anjali. *For the Record: On Sexuality and the Colonial Archive in India.* Durham, NC: Duke University Press, 2009.

Arroyo Cordero, Américo. *Cabezas: Novela de escuela naturalista.* Mayagüez: Imprenta de Fernández and Roig, 1904.

Arroyo Cordero, Américo. *Escalinata social.* Mayagüez: Tipografía Aurora, 1908.

Avrich, Paul. *The Modern School Movement: Anarchism and Education in the United States.* Oakland, CA: AK Press, 2006.

Ayala, César, and Rafael Bernabe. *Puerto Rico in the American Century: A History since 1898.* Chapel Hill: University of North Carolina Press, 2009.

Aybar, Julio. *Labor parlamentaria del delegado a la Cámara Insular de Puerto Rico: El absentismo*. Puerta de Tierra: Imprenta Unión Obrera, 1916.

Azize, Yamila. *La mujer en la lucha*. 2nd ed. San Juan: Editorial Cultural, 1985.

Azize, Yamila. *Luchas de la mujer en Puerto Rico, 1898-1919*. [San Juan]: Litografía Metropolitana, 1979.

Bacci, Claudia, and Laura Fernández Cordero. "Feroces de la lengua y pluma: Sobre algunas escrituras de mujeres anarquistas." *Políticas de la memoria* 6–7 (Summer 2006–7): 190–95.

Baerga, María del Carmen. "'A la organización, a uniros como un solo hombre!': La Federación Libre de Trabajadores y el mundo masculino del trabajo." In *100 años de sindicalismo puertorriqueño: Memorias del congreso internacional del centenario del sindicalismo organizado en Puerto Rico, 1898–1998*, edited by Erick Pérez Velasco, 143. Humacao: Universidad de Puerto Rico, Humacao, 2007.

Baerga, María del Carmen. "'A la organización: A uniros como un solo hombre . . .': La Federación Libre de Trabajadores y el mundo masculino del trabajo." *Op. Cit. : Revista del Centro de Investigaciones Históricas*, no. 11 (1999):219–52.

Baerga, María del Carmen. "Exclusion and Resistance: Household, Gender, and Work in the Needlework Industry in Puerto Rico, 1914–1940." PhD diss., State University of New York, 1996.

Baldrich, Juan José. "Class and the State: The Origins of Populism in Puerto Rico, 1934–1952." PhD diss., Yale University, 1981.

Baldrich, Juan José. "Gender and the Decomposition of the Cigar-Making Craft in Puerto Rico." In *Puerto Rican Women's History: New Perspectives*, edited by Felix V. Matos Rodríguez and Linda C. Delgado, 105–25. Armonk, NY: M. R. Sharpe, 1998.

Baldrich, Juan José. "Género y la descomposición del oficio de tabaquero en Puerto Rico, 1899–1934." In *Cayey: Miradas históricas*, 12–42. Cayey: Instituto de Investigaciones Interdisciplinarias, 2009.

Baldrich, Juan José. *La huelga como instrumento de lucha obrera, 1915–1942*. Río Piedras: Departamento de Sociología y Antropología, Universidad de Puerto Rico, 2012.

Baldrich, Juan José. Prologue to *Voces libertarias: Los orígenes del anarquismo en Puerto Rico*, by Jorell Meléndez-Badillo. Lajas: Editorial Akelarre and Centro de Estudios e Investigación del Suroeste de Puerto Rico, 2015.

Baldrich, Juan José. *Sembraron la no siembra: Los cosecheros de Tabaco puertorriqueños frente a las corporaciones tabacaleras, 1920–1934*. Río Piedras: Ediciones Huracán, 1988.

Balsac, Jesús María. *Apuntes históricos*. Mayagüez: Imprenta Montalvo, 1906.

Balsac, Jesús María. *Unión y fuerza*. Mayagüez: Tipografía Gente Nueva, 1910.

Balsac, Jesús María, and Santiago Valle. *Revolución*. Mayagüez: Imprenta La Bruja, 1900.

Barceló Miller, María de Fátima. *La lucha por el sufragio femenino en Puerto Rico, 1896–1935*. Río Piedras: Centro de Investigaciones Sociales, University of Puerto Rico, and Ediciones Huracán, 2006.

Barcia, María del Carmen. *Capas populares y modernidad en Cuba, 1878–1930*. Havana: Fundación Fernando Ortiz, 2005.

Bayrón Toro, Fernando. *Elecciones y partidos políticos de Puerto Rico, 1809–2000*. Mayagüez: Editorial Isla, 2003.

Belaval, Emilio. *Los cuentos de la universidad*. San Juan: Editorial de Autores Puerto-rriqueños, 1935.

Belaval, Emilio. *Los problemas de la cultura puertorriqueña*. Río Piedras: Editorial Cultural, 1977.

Benítez Rexach, Jesús. *Vida y obra de Luis Muñoz Marín*. Río Piedras: Editorial Edil, 1989.

Benjamin, Walter. "The Author as Producer." In *Walter Benjamin: Reflections, Essays, Aphorisms, Autobiographical Writings*, edited by Peter Demetz, 223–25. New York: Schocken, 2007.

Bernabe, Rafael. *La maldición de Pedreira: Aspectos de la crítica romántico-cultural de la modernidad en Puerto Rico*. Río Piedras: Ediciones Huracán, 2002.

Bernabe, Rafael. *Respuestas al colonialismo en la política puertorriqueña, 1899–1929*. Río Piedras: Ediciones Huracán and Decanato de Estudios Graduados e Investigación de Universidad de Puerto Rico, 1996.

Bilhão, Isabel. "Impresa e educação operária: Análise da difusão do ensino racionalista em jornais anarquistas braileiros (1900–1920)." *Edução Unisinos* 20, no. 2 (May–August 2016): 176–84.

Bird Carmona, Aturo. *A lima y machete: La huelga cañera de 1915 y la fundación del Partido Socialista*. Río Piedras: Ediciones Huracán, 2001.

Bird Carmona, Aturo. *Parejeros y desafiantes: La huelga cañera de 1915 y el Partido Socialista*. Río Piedras: Ediciones Huracán, 2008.

Bird Piñero, Enrique. *Don Luis Muñoz Marín: El poder de la excelencia*. San Juan: Fundación Luis Muñoz Marín, 1991.

Blain, Keisha L. *Set the World on Fire: Black Nationalist Women and the Global Struggle for Freedom*. Philadelphia: University of Pennsylvania Press, 2018.

Blanco, Tomás. *El prejuicio racial en Puerto Rico*. San Juan: Editorial Biblioteca de Autores Puertorriqueños, 1942.

Blanco, Tomás. *Prontuario histórico de Puerto Rico*. Río Piedras: Ediciones Huracán, 1981.

Boren, Mark Edelman. *Student Resistance: A History of the Unruly Subject*. New York: Routledge, 2001.

Brás Feliciano, Dianne. "El cartel politico como instrument de lucha: La aportación del Taller Bija y el Taller El Seco a la experiencia política del Movimiento Pro Independencia-Partido Socialista Puertorriqueño (MPI-PSP), 1959–1985." PhD diss., Centro de Estudios Avanzados de Puerto Rico y el Caribe, 2018.

Bray, Mark, and Robert H. Haworth. *Anarchist Education and the Modern School: A Francisco Ferrer Reader*. Oakland, CA: PM Press, 2018.

Brennan, James P. "Latin American Labor History." In *The Oxford Handbook on Latin American History*, edited by José C. Moya, 342–66. Oxford: Oxford University Press, 2010.

Briggs, Laura. *Reproducing Empire: Race, Sex, Science, and US Imperialism in Puerto Rico*. Berkeley: University of California Press, 2002.

Bronfman, Alejandra. *Measures of Equality: Social Science, Citizenship, and Race in Cuba, 1902–1940*. Chapel Hill: University of North Carolina Press, 2004.

Bunker, Oscar L. *Caguas: Notas para su historia*. San Juan: Comité Historia de los Pueblos, 1983.

Burke, Peter. *Formas de hacer historia*. Madrid: Alianza Editorial, 2009.

Burke, Peter. *What Is the History of Knowledge?* Cambridge, UK: Polity Press, 2016.

Burnett, Christina Duffy, and Burke Marshall, eds. *Foreign in a Domestic Sense: Puerto Rico, American Expansion, and the Constitution.* Durham, NC: Duke University Press, 2001.

Burton, Antoinette, ed. *Archive Stories: Facts, Fictions, and the Writing of History.* Durham, NC: Duke University Press, 2005.

Burton, Antoinette. *Dwelling in the Archive: Women Writing House, Home, and History in Late Colonial India.* Oxford: Oxford University Press, 2003.

Butler, Judith. *Notes towards a Performative Theory of Assembly.* Cambridge, MA: Harvard University Press, 2015.

Caballero Wangüemert, María. *El Caribe en la encrucijada: La narrativa puertorriqueña.* Madrid: Iberoamericana Editorial Vervuert, 2016.

Cáldera Ortiz, Luis. *Historia de los ciclones y huracanes tropicales en Puerto Rico.* Lajas: Editorial Akelarre, 2014.

Campos, Ricardo. *Apuntes sobre la expression cultural obrera en Puerto Rico.* San Juan: CEREP, 1973.

Capetillo, Luisa. *Ensayos libertarios.* Arecibo: Tipografía Real Hermanos, 1907.

Capetillo, Luisa. *Influencias de las ideas modernas.* San Juan: Tipografía Negrón Flores, 1916.

Capetillo, Luisa. *La humanidad en el futuro.* San Juan: Biblioteca Roja, 1910.

Capetillo, Luisa. *Mi opinión sobre las libertades, derechos y deberes de la mujer como compañera, madre y ser independiente.* San Juan: Biblioteca Roja, 1910.

Capetillo, Luisa. *A Nation of Women: An Early Feminist Speaks Out = Mi opinión sobre las libertades, derechos y deberes de la mujer.* Edited and introduction by Félix V. Matos Rodríguez. Translated by Alan West. Houston: Arte Público Press, 2004.

Cappelletti, Ángel. *Francisco Ferrer y la pedagogía libertaria.* Tenerife: Tierra de Fuego, 2010.

Carnegie, Charles V. *Postnationalism Prefigured: Caribbean Borderlands.* New Brunswick, NJ: Rutgers University Press, 2002.

Carrasquillo, Rosa E. *Our Landless Patria: Marginal Citizenship and Race in Caguas, Puerto Rico, 1880–1910.* Lincoln: University of Nebraska Press, 2006.

Carreras, Juan. *Escuelas para el hombre olvidado.* San Juan: Imprenta Venezuela, 1932.

Carreras, Juan. *Santiago Iglesias Pantín: Su vida, su obra, su pensamiento.* San Juan: Editorial Club de la Prensa, 1967.

Carroll, Henry K. *Report on Porto Rico, 1899.* San Juan: Fundación Puertorriqueña de las Humanidades, 2005.

Casa Juana Colón. *El caso Karina y los derechos civiles.* Comerío: Casa Juana Colón, 2016.

Casanovas, Joan. *Bread or Bullets! Urban Labor and Spanish Colonialism in Cuba, 1850–1898.* Pittsburgh, PA: University of Pittsburgh Press, 1998.

Casanovas, Joan. *¡O Pan, O Plomo!: Los trabajadores urbanos y el colonialismo español en Cuba, 1850–1898.* Madrid: Siglo XXI, 2000.

Casino del Centro Hispáno de Mayagüez. *Reglamento.* Mayagüez: Imprenta de Arecco Hijo, 1884.

Cassá, Roberto. *Movimiento obrero y lucha socialista en la República Dominicana: Desde los orígenes hasta 1960.* Santo Domingo: Fundación Cultural Dominicana, 1990.

Castrillo, Valentín. *Mis experiencias a través de cincuenta años.* Caguas: Imprenta La Mariposa, 1952.

Castro Arroyo, María de los Ángeles. "De Salvador Brau a la 'novísima' historia: Un replanteamiento y una crítica." *Op. Cit.: Revista del Centro de Investigaciones Históricas,* no. 4 (1988): 9–25.

Castro Arroyo, María de los Ángeles. "El Centro de Investigaciones Históricas: Breve historia de un proceso (1946–1986)." *Op. Cit.: Revista del Centro de Investigaciones Históricas* no. 2 (1986): 9–25.

Castro-Gómez, Santiago, and Ramón Grosfoguel, eds. *El giro decolonial: Reflexiones para una diversidad epistémica más allá del capitalismo global.* Bogotá: Siglo Hombre Editores, 2007.

Centeno Añeses, Carmen. *Modernidad y resistencia: Literatura obrera en Puerto Rico (1898–1910).* San Juan: Centro de Estudios Avanzados de Puerto Rico y el Caribe and Ediciones Callejón, 2005.

Chartier, Roger. *The Author's Hand and the Printer's Mind.* Translated by Lydia G. Cochrane. Cambridge, MA: Polity Press, 2014.

Chomsky, Aviva, and Aldo Lauria-Santiago, eds. *Identity and Struggle at the Margins of the Nation-State: The Laboring Peoples of Central America and the Hispanic Caribbean.* Durham, NC: Duke University Press, 1998.

Cobble, Dorothy Sue, Melvin Dubofsky, Andrew Wender Cohen, Donna T. Haverty-Stacke, and Julie Greene. "Up for Debate: The Fall and Rise of Samuel Gompers." *Labor* 10, no. 4 (Winter 2013): 61–116.

Cobos, Amparo Sánchez. *Sembrando ideales. Anarquistas españoles en Cuba.* Madrid: CSIC Ediciones, 2008.

Cohn, Jesse. *Underground Passages: Anarchist Resistance Culture, 1848–2016.* Oakland, CA: AK Press, 2015.

Coll y Cuchi, Cayetano. *Historias que parecen cuento.* Río Piedras: UPRX, 1972.

Coll y Toste, Cayetano. *Boletín histórico de Puerto Rico.* 15 vols. San Juan: Ateneo Puertorriqueño y LEA, 2004.

Colón González, José. "¡Trabajadores al poder! Orígen y desarrollo del Partido Obrero de Arecibo, 1910–1914." In *Puerto Rico y el Caribe: Momentos históricos,* edited by José Carlos Arroyo Muñoz, 91–120. Río Piedras: Editorial de la Universidad Interamericana de Puerto Rico, 2019.

Colón Rivera, Jorge, Felix Córdova Iturregui, and José Cordova Iturregui. *El proyecto de explotación minera en Puerto Rico, 1962–1968: Nacimiento de la conciencia ambiental.* Río Piedras: Ediciones Huracán, 2014.

Colorado, A. J., and Jorge Font Saldaña. *Una entrevista con Bolívar Pagán.* San Juan: privately printed, 1937.

Compañía Editora de Justicia. *Informe anual de la compañía editora de Justicia.* San Juan: Tipografía Compañía Editora de Justicia, 1920.

Conde, Eduardo. *Acusación y protesta.* Puerta de Tierra: Imprenta Unión Obrera, 1919.

Conner, Tom. *The Dreyfus Affair and the Rise of the French Public Intellectual.* Jefferson, NC: McFarland, 2014.

Córdova, Gonzalo F. *Resident Commissioner Santiago Iglesias and His Times.* Río Piedras: Editorial de la Universidad de Puerto Rico, 1993.

Córdova, Gonzalo F. *Santiago Iglesias, creador del movimiento obrero en Puerto Rico.* Río Piedras: Editorial Universitaria, 1980.

Córdova, Gonzalo F. "Santiago Iglesias, Creator of the Labor Movement in Puerto Rico." Master's thesis, Georgetown University, 1964.

Córdova Iturregui, Félix. *Ante la frontera del infierno: El impacto social de las huelgas azucareras y portuarias de 1905.* Río Piedras: Ediciones Huracán, 2007.

Cores Trasmote, Baldomero. "La actividad política de Santiago Iglesias Pantín." *Cuadernos de Estudios Gallegos* 105 (1992): 63–82.

Cortés Zavala, María Teresa. *Los hombres de la nación: Itinerarios del progreso económico y el desarrollo intelectual, Puerto Rico en el siglo XIX.* Morelia: Coordinación de la Investigación Científica, 2013.

Cruz, Venancio. *Fragmentos.* San Juan: Tipografía Listín Mercantil, 1903.

Cruz, Venancio. *Hacia el porvenir.* San Juan: Tipografía La República Española, 1906.

Cruz Pérez, Ángel Luis. "Proceso histórico de la expulsión de los padres Dominicos de la parroquia de Comerío." *El salto: Revista histórico-social de Comerío* 2, no. 2 (January–June, 1995): 17–27.

Cruz Rosa, Paul. "El Panafricanismo y la Asociación Universal de Desarrollo Negro en Puerto Rico, 1920–22." In *En pié de lucha: Nuevas investigaciones históricas puertorriqueñas,* edited by Evelyn Vélez Rodríguez and Carmelo Campos Cruz, 27–62. Ponce: Mariana Editores, 2019.

Cruz Santos, Martín. *Afirmando la nación: Políticas culturales em Puerto Rico, 1949–1968.* San Juan: Ediciones Callejón, 2014.

Cuerpo Consultivo Conjunto de las Uniones de Tabaqueros, Distrito de Puerto Rico. "La huelga del Trust del Tabaco: Manifiesto de información." *Boletín Oficial* 2, no. 1 (January 22, 1919).

Cuerpo Consultivo Conjunto Distrito de Puerto Rico. "Proclama de paz: De vuelta al trabajo." *Boletín oficial* 1, no. 3 (December 27, 1917): 1–8.

Cvetkovich, Ann. *An Archive of Feelings: Trauma, Sexuality, and Lesbian Public Cultures.* Durham, NC: Duke University Press, 2003.

Darnton, Robert. *The Great Cat Massacre and Other Episodes in French Cultural History.* New York: Vintage, 1984.

Dávila, Jerry. *Diplomas of Whiteness: Race and Social Policy in Brazil, 1917–1945.* Durham, NC: Duke University Press, 2003.

Dávila Santiago, Rubén. "Algunas consideraciones sobre las primeras organizaciones obreras y la conciencia de clase." *Revista de Ciencias Sociales* 22, no. 3–4 (September–December 1980): 300–327.

Dávila Santiago, Rubén. *El derribo de las murallas: Orígenes intelectuales del socialismo en Puerto Rico.* Río Piedras: Editorial Cultural, 1988.

Dávila Santiago, Rubén. *Teatro obrero en Puerto Rico, 1900–1920.* Río Piedras: Editorial Edil, 1985.

De la Fuente, Alejandro. "The New Afro-Cuban Cultural Movement and the Debate on Race in Contemporary Cuba." *Journal of Latin American Studies* 40, no. 4 (November 2008): 697–720.

De la Fuente, Alejandro, and George Reid Andres, eds. *Afro-Latin American Studies: An Introduction.* Cambridge: Cambridge University Press, 2019.

del Moral, Solsiree. *Negotiating Empire: The Cultural Politics of Schools in Puerto Rico, 1898–1952.* Madison: University of Wisconsin Press, 2013.

Departamento del Trabajo. *Discursos pronunciados en la celebración del Día del Trabajo.* San Juan: Oficina de Compras, División de Imprenta, 1943.

Departamento del Trabajo. *Informes sobre las condiciones generales de la industria de trenes y lavado.* San Juan: Negociado de Materiales, Imprenta y Transporte, 1935.

Derrida, Jacques. *Archive Fever: A Freudian Impression.* Translated by Eric Prenowitz. Chicago: University of Chicago Press, 1995.

Díaz, Manuel D. "Puerto Rican Labor Movement, an Historical Movement." Master's thesis, Clark University, 1943.

Díaz de Román, Haydée. "Pedro C. Timothée Morales: Su vida y obra educativa." Master's thesis, University of Puerto Rico, 1966.

Díaz-Quiñones, Arcadio. "Cultura, memoria y diáspora." *Nueva Sociedad* 116 (November–December 1991): 153–58.

Díaz-Quiñones, Arcadio. *El arte de bregar: Ensayos.* San Juan: Ediciones Callejón, 2000.

Díaz-Quiñones, Arcadio. *La memoria rota.* Río Piedras: Ediciones Huracán, 1993.

Díaz-Quiñones, Arcadio. "Recordando el futuro imaginario: La escritura histórica en la década del treinta." *Sin nombre* 14, no. 3 (1984): 16–35.

Díaz-Quiñones, Arcadio. *Sobre los principios: Los intelectuales caribeños y la tradición.* Quilmes: Universidad Nacional de Quilmes Editorial, 2006.

Dieppa, Ángel María. *El porvenir de la sociedad humana.* San Juan: Tipografía El Eco, 1915.

Dietz, James L. *Historia económica de Puerto Rico.* Río Piedras: Ediciones Huracán, 1989.

Dillon, Irene M. "Problems of Labor in Puerto Rico." Master's thesis, Columbia University, 1949.

Domínguez Rubio, Lucas. "Un itinerario por los proyectos editoriales del anarquismo en Argentina: Cambios, maniobras y permanencias." *Izquierdas* 33 (May 2017): 21–41.

Draper, Susana. *Mexico 1968: Constellations of Freedom and Democracy.* Durham, NC: Duke University Press, 2018.

Duany, Jorge. *Blurred Borders: Transnational Migration between the Hispanic Caribbean and the United States.* Chapel Hill: University of North Carolina Press, 2011.

Duprey Salgado, Nelsón R. *Independentista popular: Las causas de Vicente Geigel Polanco.* San Juan: privately printed, 2005.

Duprey Salgado, Nelson R., Mayi Marrero, and José Sánchez. Eds. *Lluvias borrascosas: El PIP, el MPI-PSP y el debate dentro del independentismo electoral puertorriqueño durante la Guerra Fría, 1964–1992.* Ponce: Mariana Editores, 2019.

Erman, Sam. *Almost Citizens: Puerto Rico, the US Constitution, and Empire.* Cambridge: Cambridge University Press, 2019.

Escabí, Paca. "Nuestra misión." In *Páginas del obrero: Colección de artículos escritos para comemorar el Primero de Mayo*, by Unión de Tipográfos, no. 422. Mayagüez: Imprenta La Protesta, 1904.

Estado Libre Asociado de Puerto Rico, Junta de Planificación. *Municipio de Comerío: Memoria suplementaria al mapa de límites del municipio y sus barrios.* San Juan: Junta de Planificación, 1955.

Esterrich, Carmelo. *Concrete and Countryside: The Urban and Rural in 1950s Puerto Rican Culture.* Pittsburgh, PA: University of Pittsburgh Press, 2018.

Etcheverri, Catriel. *Rafael Barrett: Una leyenda anarquista*. Buenos Aires: Capital Industrial, 2007.

Everhart, Katherine. "Everything but the Funnel Cake: Creative Protest and the University of Puerto Rico Student Occupation of 2010." PhD diss., Vanderbilt University, 2015.

Farinacci Fernós, Jorge M. *La constitución obrera de Puerto Rico: El Partido Socialista y la Convención Constituyente*. Río Piedras: Ediciones Huracán, 2015.

Farmer, Ashley D. *Remaking Black Power: How Black Women Transformed an Era*. Chapel Hill: University of North Carolina Press, 2017.

Federación Libre de los Trabajadores de Puerto Rico. *Constitución de la Unión de Despalilladoras, No. 12, 439*. Puerta de Tierra: Federación Libre Press, 1916.

Federación Libre de los Trabajadores de Puerto Rico. *Constitución y programa*. San Juan: Tipografía Compañía Editora de Justicia, 1920.

Federación Libre de los Trabajadores de Puerto Rico. *Crímenes policiacos, 16 de abril de 1905*. Ponce: Tipografía de M. López, 1905.

Federación Libre de los Trabajadores de Puerto Rico. *Día del Trabajo, Septiembre 5 de 1938: Manifiesto que dirige el Consejo Ejecutivo de la Institución a todas las organizaicones afiliadas y a los trabajadores de Puerto Rico*. San Juan: privately printed, 1938.

Federación Libre de los Trabajadores de Puerto Rico. *Informe de procedimientos del Tercer Congreso*. Mayagüez: Imprenta Unión Obrera, 1905.

Federación Libre de los Trabajadores de Puerto Rico. *Procedimientos del Sexto Congreso*. San Juan: Tipografía M. Burillo, 1910.

Federación Libre de los Trabajadores de Puerto Rico. *Programa*. San Juan: Press of the San Juan News, 1903.

Federación Libre de los Trabajadores de Puerto Rico. *Reporte de procedimientos del tercer congreso de la Federación Libre de los Trabajadores afiliada a la American Federation of Labor, celebrado en Mayagüez del 18 al 25 de junio*. Mayagüez: Imprenta Unión Obrera, 1905.

Federación Libre de los Trabajadores de Puerto Rico. *The Tyranny of the House of Delegates of Porto Rico*. Washington, DC: Government Printing Office, 1913.

Federación Libre de Ponce. *Crímenes policíacos, 16 de abril de 1905*. Ponce: Tipografía de M. López, 1905.

Federación Puertorriqueña del Trabajo. *Declaración de principios, programa y constitución*. San Juan: privately printed, 1940.

Fernández, Frank. *Cuban Anarchism: The History of a Movement*. Tucson, AZ: See Sharp Press, 2001.

Fernández, Frank. *El anarquismo en Cuba*. Madrid: Fundacion de Estudios Libertarios Anselmo Lorenzo, 2000.

Fernández, Frank. *La sangre de Santa Agueda: Angiolillo, Betances y Cánovas. Análisis de un magnicidio y sus consecuencias históricas*. Miami: Ediciones Universal, 1994.

Fernández, Frank. "Los precursores del 1ro de Mayo en Cuba: La primera jornada, La Habana 1890." In *Los orígenes libertarios del Primero de Mayo: De Chicago a América Latina, 1886–1930*, edited by José Antonio Gutiérrez, 75. Santiago, Chile: Editorial Quimantú, 2010.

Fernández Calderón, Alejandro Leonardo. *Páginas en conflicto: Debate racial en la prensa cubana (1912–1930)*. Havana: Editorial UH, 2014.

Fernández García, E. *El libro de Puerto Rico: The Book of Porto Rico*. San Juan: El Libro Azul, 1923.

Ferrao, Luis Ángel. "Nacionalismo, hispanismo y elite intelectual en el Puerto Rico de la década de 1930." In *Del nacionalismo al populismo: Cultura y política en Puerto Rico*, edited by Silvia Álvarez-Curbelo and María Elena Rodríguez Castro, 37–60. Río Piedras: Ediciones Huracán, 1993.

Ferrer, Ada. "History and the Idea of Hispanic Caribbean Studies." *Small Axe* 20, no. 3 (November 2016): 49–64.

Ferrer y Ferrer, José. *Los ideales del siglo XX*. San Juan: Tip. La Correspondencia de Puerto Rico, 1932.

Figueroa, Loida. *Breve historia de Puerto Rico*. 2 vols. Río Piedras: Editorial Edil, 1983.

Figueroa, Luis A. *Sugar, Slavery, and Freedom in Nineteenth-Century Puerto Rico*. Río Piedras: University of Puerto Rico Press, 2005.

Figueroa Díaz, Wilfredo. *El movimiento estadista en Puerto Rico: Pasado, presente y future*. San Juan: Editorial Cultural, 1979.

Findlay, Eileen J. Suárez. *Imposing Decency: The Politics of Sexuality and Race in Puerto Rico, 1870–1920*. Durham, NC: Duke University Press, 1999.

Findlay, Eileen J. Suárez. "Slipping and Sliding: The Many Meanings of Race in Life Histories of New York Puerto Rican Return Migrants in San Juan." *Centro Journal* 24, no. 1 (Spring 2012): 20–43.

Findlay, Eileen J. Suárez. *We Are Left without a Father Here: Masculinity, Domesticity, and Migration in Postwar Puerto Rico*. Durham, NC: Duke University Press, 2014.

Fink, Leon. *Workers across the Americas: The Transnational Turn in Labor History*. Oxford: Oxford University Press, 2011.

Fiorucci, Flavia. *Intelectuales y peronismo, 1944–1955*. Buenos Aires: Editorial Biblos, 2011.

Fiz Jiménez, Epifanio. *Bayamón y su gente*. Barcelona: Ediciones Rumbos, 1960.

Fiz Jiménez, Epifanio. *Comerío y su gente*. Barcelona: Ediciones Rumbos, 1957.

Fiz Jiménez, Epifanio. *El racket en el capitolio (Gobierno de la Coalición Republico-Socialista, años 1932–1940)*. San Juan: Editorial Esther, 1944.

Fiz Jiménez, Epifanio. *Informe y comentarios sobre la huelga agrícola de Humacao*. Humacao: Tipografía Conciencia Popular, 1919.

Flores, Juan. *Insularismo e ideologia burguesa: Nueva lectura de A.S. Pedreira*. Río Piedras: Ediciones Huracán, 1979.

Flores Magón, Ricardo. "¡Despechados!" *Regeneración*, no. 205 (March 6, 1915). Archivo Digital de Ricardo Flores Magón. http://archivomagon.net/obras-completas/art-periodisticos-1900-1918/1915/1915-03/.

Flores Magón, Ricardo. "Rafael Romero Palacios (Concluye)." *Regeneración*, no. 182 (March 28, 1914), footnote 1. Archivo Digital de Ricardo Flores Magón. http://archivomagon.net/obras-completas/art-periodisticos-1900-1918/1914/1914-40.

Fors, Bonnie D. "The Jones Act for Puerto Rico." PhD diss., Loyola University of Chicago, 1975.

Foucault, Michel. *The Archeology of Knowledge and the Discourse of Language*. Translated by Sheridan Smith. New York: Pantheon, 1972.

Foucault, Michel. *Lectures on the Will to Know: Lectures at the Collége de France, 1970–1971.* New York: Picador, 2014.

Foucault, Michel. *Power/Knowledge: Selected Interviews and Other Writings, 1972–1977.* Translated by Colin Gordon, Leo Marshall, John Mepham, and Kate Soper. New York: Pantheon, 1980.

Fransworth-Alvear, Ann. *Dulcinea in the Factory: Myths, Morals, Men, and Women in Colombia's Industrial Experiment, 1905–1960.* Durham, NC: Duke University Press, 2000.

Freire, João. *Freedom Fighters: Anarchist Intellectuals, Workers, and Soldiers in Portugal's History.* Translated by Maria Fernanda Noronha da Costa e Sousa. Montreal: Black Rose, 2001.

Fritsch, Kelly, Clare O'Connor, and A. K. Thompson. *Keywords for Radicals: The Contested Vocabulary of Late-Capitalist Struggle.* Oakland: AK Press, 2016.

Fromm, Georg H. *César Andreu Iglesias: Una aproximación a su vida y obra.* Río Piedras: Ediciones Huracán, 1977.

Fuentes, Marissa. *Dispossessed Lives: Enslaved Women, Violence, and the Archive.* Philadelphia: University of Pennsylvania Press, 2016.

Galvin, Miles. *The Organized Labor Movement in Puerto Rico.* Cranbury, NJ: Associated University Presses, 1979.

García, Gervasio L. *Historia bajo sospecha.* Río Piedras: Publicaciones Gaviota, 2015.

García, Gervasio L. *Historia crítica, historia sin coartadas: Algunos problemas de la historia de Puerto Rico.* Río Piedras: Ediciones Huracán, 1985.

García, Gervasio L. "José Julio Henna Pérez: Tema del traidor y el héroe (O los bordes detentados a principios de siglo)." *Op. Cit.: Revista del Centro de Investigaciones Históricas,* no. 11 (1999): 73–108.

García, Gervasio L. "Las primeras actividades de los honrados hijos del trabajo: 1873–1898." *Op. Cit.: Revista del Centro de Investigaciones Históricas,* no. 5 (1990): 217–27.

García, Gervasio L. *Primeros fermentos de organización obrera en Puerto Rico.* Río Piedras: CEREP, 1985.

García, Gervasio L., and Ángel G. Quintero Rivera. *Desafío y solidaridad: Breve historia del movimiento obrero puertorriqueño.* Río Piedras: Ediciones Huracán, 1982.

García Bryce, Iñigo. *Haya de la Torre and the Pursuit of Power in Twentieth-Century Peru and Latin America.* Chapel Hill: University of North Carolina Press, 2018.

García Leduc, José Manuel. *Apuntes para una historia breve de Puerto Rico: Desde la prehistoria hasta 1898.* San Juan: Isla Negra Editores, 2002.

García Muñoz, Humberto. *Sugar and Power in the Caribbean: The South Porto Rico Sugar Company in Puerto Rico and the Dominican Republic, 1900–1921.* Río Piedras: Editorial Universidad de Puerto Rico, 2010.

García-Peña, Lorgia. *The Borders of Dominicanidad: Race, Nations, and Archives of Contradictions.* Durham, NC: Duke University Press, 2016.

Gaztambide Geigel, Antonio. "La geopolítica del antillanismo en el Caribe de fines de siglo XIX." *Ciencia y sociedad* 29, no. 4 (October–December 2004): 570–615.

Gaztambide Geigel, Antonio, and Silvia Álvarez Curbelo, eds. *Historias vivas: Historiografía puertorriqueña contemporánea.* San Juan: Asociación Puertorriqueña de Historiadores and Editorial Postdata, 1996.

Geigel Polanco, Vicente. *El despertar de un pueblo.* San Juan: Biblioteca de Autores Puertorriqueños, 1942.

Geli, Patricio. "Los anarquistas en el gabinete antropométrico: Anarquismo y criminología en la sociedad argentina de los 900." *Entrepasados* 2 (1992): 7–24.

Giovannetti-Torres, Jorge. *Black British Migrants in Cuba: Race, Labor, and Empire in the Twentieth-Century Caribbean, 1898–1948*. Cambridge: Cambridge University Press, 2018.

Giovannetti-Torres, Jorge. "The Elusive Organization of 'Identity': Race, Religion, and Empire among Caribbean Migrants in Cuba." *Small Axe* 10, no. 1 (2006): 1–27.

Godreau, Isar. "Changing Space, Making Race: Distance, Nostalgia, and the Folklorization of Blackness in Puerto Rico." *Identities: Global Studies in Cultura and Power* 9, no. 3 (2002): 281–304.

Godreau, Isar. *Scripts of Blackness: Race, Cultural Nationalism, and US Colonialism in Puerto Rico*. Urbana: University of Illinois Press, 2015.

Godreau, Isar. "Slippery Semantics: Race Talk and Everyday Uses of Racial Terminology in Puerto Rico." *Centro Journal* 20, no. 2 (Fall 2008): 5–33.

Gómez, Magdaleno. *Arte y rebeldía*. Caguas: Tipografía Vida Libre, 1920.

Gómez Acosta, Fernando. "Prólogo." In *Fragmentos*, by Venancio Cruz, n.p. San Juan: Tipografía del Listín Mercantil, 1903.

Gompers, Samuel. *Justicia para Puerto Rico*. San Juan: Federación Libre, 1904.

González, Antonio J. "Apuntes para la historia del movimiento sindical en Puerto Rico, 1896–1941." *Revista de Ciencias Sociales* 1, no. 3 (1957): 444–68.

González, Maria V. de. "El pueblo habla de Juana Colón." In *Juana Colón: La Juana de Arco comerieña*, edited by Daniela Hernández, Ramón Luis Aponte, Papo Vázquez, Wilfredo López, and Padre Alfonso, 8–11. Comerío: Secretaría de Prensa y Propaganda del Partido Socialista Puertorriqueño, 1972.

González Morales, Zuleima. "Luisa Capetillo y Luisa Galvão—Voces de la Transición: Negociación y Reconstrucción de la Condición Femenina." PhD diss., University of Arizona, 2015.

González Prada, Manuel. *Páginas libres*. Paris: Tip. de Paul Dupont, 1894.

Goyens, Tom. Introduction to *Storm in My Heart: Memories from the Widow of Johann Most*, by Helen Minken, 1–20. Edited by Tom Goyens. Translated by Alisa Braun. Oakland, CA: AK Press, 2015.

Gramsci, Antonio. *Selections from the Prison Notebooks*. Edited by Quintin Hoare and Geoffrey Nowell Smith. New York: International Publishers, 2008.

Greene, Julie. *Pure and Simple Politics: The American Federation of Labor and Political Activism, 1881–1917*. Cambridge: Cambridge University Press, 1998.

Guadalupe de Jesús, Raúl. *Sindicalismo y lucha política: Apuntes históricos sobre el movimiento obrero puertorriqueño*. Río Piedras: Editorial Tiempo Nuevo, 2009.

Guerra, Lilian. *Popular Expression and National Identity in Puerto Rico: The Struggle of Self, Community, and Nation*. Gainesville: University Press of Florida, 1998.

Guerra de Colón, María Luisa. "Trayectoria, acción y desenvolvimiento del movimiento obrero en Puerto Rico." Master's thesis, University of Puerto Rico, 1963.

Guridy, Frank Andre. *Forging Diaspora: Afro-Cubans and African Americans in a World of Empire and Jim Crow*. Chapel Hill: University of North Carolina Press, 2010.

Gutiérrez, José Antonio, ed. *Los orígenes libertarios del Primero de Mayo: De Chicago a América Latina, 1886–1930*. Santiago, Chile: Editorial Quimantú, 2010.

Guzzo, Cristina. *Libertarias en América del Sur: De la A a la Z.* Buenos Aires: Libros de Anarres, 2014.

Guzzo, Cristina. "Luisa Capetillo y Salvadora Medina Onrubia de Botana: Dos íconos anarquistas. Una comparación." *Alpha* 20 (December 2004): 165–80.

Hall, Stuart. *Cultural Studies 1983: A Theoretical History.* Edited by Jennifer Daryl Slack and Lawrence Grossberg. Durham, NC: Duke University Press, 2016.

Hernández, Axel. *Políticas imperiales sobre la educación de Puerto Rico, 1800–1920.* Lajas: Editorial Akelarre, 2015.

Hernández, Daniela, Ramón Luis Aponte, Papo Vázquez, Wilfredo López, and Padre Alfonso, eds. *Juana Colón: La Juana de Arco comerieña.* Comerío: Secretaría de Prensa y Propaganda del Partido Socialista Puertorriqueño, 1972.

Hérnandez, Jesús Manuel. *Nilita Vientós Gastón y la legitimación de las disidencias políticas bajo su presidencia en el Ateneo Puertorriqueño, 1946–1961.* San Juan: Disonante, 2018.

Hernández, Juan David. *Nuevas fuentes para la historia de Caguas.* Caguas: Municipio Autónomo de Caguas, 2014.

Hillquit, Morris. *History of Socialism in the United States.* New York: Funk and Wagnalls, 1910.

Hoffnung-Garskof, Jesse. "The Migrations of Arturo Schomburg: On Being Antillano, Negro, and Puerto Rican in New York, 1891–1938." *Journal of American Ethnic History* 21, no. 1 (Fall 2001): 3–49.

Hoffnung-Garskof, Jesse. *Racial Migrations: New York City and the Revolutionary Politics of the Spanish Caribbean.* Princeton, NJ: Princeton University Press, 2019.

Hoffnung-Garskof, Jesse. "To Abolish the Law of Castes: Merit, Manhood, and the Problem of Colour in the Puerto Rican Liberal Movement, 1873–92." *Social History* 36, no. 3 (August 2011): 312–42.

Iglesias Pantín, Santiago. *Brillante discurso parlamanetario contra el Bill Campbell.* Humacao: Tipografía Conciencia Popular, 1922.

Iglesias Pantín, Santiago, ed. *Gobierno propio, ¿Para quién?* San Juan: Imprenta Federación Libre, 1907.

Iglesias Pantín, Santiago. "La cuestión social en el mundo." In *Almanaque de Puerto Rico, 1911,* 235–38. San Juan: M. Burillo, 1910.

Iglesias Pantín, Santiago. *Luchas emancipadoras.* Vol. 1, San Juan: Imprenta Cantero Fernández, 1929; vol. 2, San Juan: Imprenta Venezuela, 1962.

Iglesias Pantín, Santiago. "Partido Socialista." In *El libro de Puerto Rico,* edited by E. Fernández García, 208–15. San Juan: El Libro Azul de Puerto Rico, 1923.

Iglesias Pantín, Santiago. *¿Quiénes sómos? Organizaciones obreras.* San Juan: Puerto Rico Progress, 1914.

Índice: Mensuario de historia, literatura y ciencia (23 de abril de 1929 a 28 de julio de 1931). Facsimile ed. Río Piedras: Editorial Universitaria, 1979.

Jelin, Elizabeth. *Repression and the Labors of Memory.* Translated by Judy Rein and Marcial Godoy-Anativa. Minneapolis: University of Minnesota Press, 2003.

Jiménez, Mónica A. "Puerto Rico under the Colonial Gaze: Oppression, Resistance, and the Myth of the Nationalist Enemy." *Latino Studies* 18, no. 1 (January 2020): 27–44.

Joseph, Gilbert M., and Daniel Nugent, eds. *Everyday Forms of State Formation: Revolution and the Negotiation of Rule in Modern Mexico*. Durham, NC: Duke University Press, 1994.

Joseph, Gilbert M., Catherine C. LeGrand, and Ricardo D. Salvatore, eds. *Close Encounters of Empire: Writing the Cultural History of U.S.-Latin American Relations*. Durham, NC: Duke University Press, 1998.

Joyce, Patrick. *Visions of the People: Industrial England and the Question of Class, 1848–1914*. Cambridge: Cambridge University Press, 1991.

Kleinberg, Ethan. *Haunting History: For a Deconstructive Approach to the Past*. Stanford, CA: Stanford University Press, 2017.

Laguarta Ramírez, José A. "Struggling to Learn, Learning to Struggle: Strategy and Structure in the 2010–11 University of Puerto Rico Student Strike." PhD diss., Graduate Center, City University of New York, 2016.

Lambe, Ariel Mae. *No Barrier Can Contain It: Cuban Anti-Fascism and the Spanish Civil War*. Chapel Hill: University of North Carolina Press, 2019.

Lanauze Rolón, José A. *El mal de muchos hijos*. Ponce: Imprenta La Tribuna, 1928.

Lanauze Rolón, José A. *Por los caminos de la violencia: La idea comunista*. Ponce: Casa Editorial América, 1932.

Lebrón, Rodney. "Creación, control y disputas: Los debates sobre la significación del concepto de historiografía puertorriqueña." Master's thesis, University of Puerto Rico, Río Piedras, 2018.

Lebrón Ortiz, Pedro. *Filosofía del cimarronaje*. Mayagüez: Editora Educación Emergente, 2020.

Levis Bernard, José Elías. *El estercolero*. Ponce: Imprenta de M. López, 1936.

Levy, Teresita. *Puerto Ricans in the Empire: Tobacco Growers and US Colonialism*. New Brunswick, NJ: Rutgers University Press, 2015.

Ley de imprenta para la isla de Puerto Rico: Aprobada por S.M. el 27 de agosto de 1880. San Juan: Imprenta de José González Font, 1882.

Limón de Arce, José. *Arecibo histórico*. 1938. Arecibo: Ok Printing, 2007.

Limón de Arce, José. *Redención*. San Juan: Tipografía El Alba, 1906.

Limón de Arce, José. *Siempre adelante*. Arecibo: privately printed, 1904.

Llorens, Hilda. *Imaging the Great Puerto Rican Family: Framing Nation, Race, and Gender during the American Century*. Lanham, MD: Lexington Books, 2014.

Lomas, Clara. "Transborder Discourse: The Articulation of Gender in the Borderlands in the Early Twentieth Century." *Frontiers: A Journal of Women Studies* 24, no. 2–3 (2003): 51–74.

López, Juan José. *Voces libertarias*. San Juan: Tipografía La Bomba, 1910.

López Landrón, Rafael. "Los ideales socialistas." In *Gobierno propio, ¿Para quién?*, edited by Santiago Iglesias Pantín, 69–165. San Juan: Imprenta Federación Libre, 1907.

López Rojas, Luis Alfredo. *Historiar la muerte, 1508–1920*. San Juan: Isla Negra Editores, 2006.

Lozano, Rafael. *Relampagueos (Historia de una huelga)*. Ponce: Imprenta El Día, 1918.

Lugo del Toro, Kenneth. *Nacimiento y auge de la Confederación General de Trabajadores, 1940–1945*. San Juan: Editorial de la Universidad Interamericana de Puerto Rico, 2013.

Maldonado, José. *El hombre y el derecho*. Humacao: Tipografía La Oriental, n.d.

Maldonado, Teofilo. *Ese fue mi maestro: José Coll Vidal*. San Juan: La Primavera, 1960.

Manalansan, Martin F., IV. "The 'Stuff' of Archives: Mess, Migration, and Queer Lives." *Radical History Review* 120 (2014): 94–107.

Manoff, Marlene. "Theories of the Archive from Across the Disciplines." *portal: Libraries and the Academy* 4, no. 1 (2004): 9–25.

Márcano, Juan S. *Páginas rojas.* Humacao: Tipografía Conciencia Popular, 1919.

Marino Faliú, Aixa. *Raza, género y clase social: El discrimen contra las mujeres afropuertorriqueñas.* San Juan: Oficina de la Procuraduría de la Mujer, 2004.

Marqués, René. *Lucha obrera: Libros para el pueblo, núm. 15.* San Juan: Departamento de Instrucción Pública, n.d.

Marsh Kennerly, Catherine. *Negociaciones culturales: Los intelectuales y el proyecto pedagógico del estado muñocista.* San Juan: Ediciones Callejón, 2009.

Marsiske, Renate. "Los estudiantes de la reforma universitaria en América Latina: ¿Una generación?" In *Movimientos estudiantiles en la historia de América Latina,* vol. 4, edited by Renate Marsiske, 21–36. Mexico City: UNAM, Instituto de Investigaciones sobre la Universidad y la Educación, 2015.

Martínez, José. *Presencia de la policía en la historia de Puerto Rico, 1898–1995.* San Juan: J. E. Martínez Valentín, 1995.

Matos Rodríguez, Félix V. "New Currents in Puerto Rican History: Legacy, Continuity, and Challenges on the 'Nueva Historia.'" *Latin American Research Review* 32, no. 3 (1997): 193–208.

Matos Rodríguez, Félix V. *Women and Urban Change in San Juan Puerto Rico, 1820–1868.* Gainesville: University Press of Florida, 1999.

Matos Rodríguez, Félix V., and Linda C. Delgado, eds. *Puerto Rican Women's History: New Perspectives.* Armonk, NY: M. E. Sharpe, 1998.

Mattos Cintrón, Wilfredo. *Breve historia del Partido Socialista Puertorriqueño.* San Juan: Partido Socialista Puertorriqueño, 1979.

Mattos Cintrón, Wilfredo. *Puerta sin casa: Crisis del PSP y encrucijada de la izquierda.* San Juan: Ediciones La Sierra, 1984.

Mayes, April. *The Mulatto Republic: Class, Race, and Dominican National Identity.* Gainesville: University Press of Florida, 2014.

Mayo Santana, Raúl, Annette B. Ramírez de Arellano, and José G. Riguau-Pérez, eds. *A Sojourn in Tropical Medicine: Francis O'Connor's Diary of a Porto Rican Trip, 1927.* Río Piedras: Editorial de la Universidad de Puerto Rico, 2008.

McGreevey, Robert C. *Borderline Citizens: The United States, Puerto Rico, and the Politics of Colonial Migration.* Ithaca, NY: Cornell University Press, 2018.

Medina Báez, Bianca M. *Juana Colón y la lucha de la mujer obrera.* San Juan: Ediciones Huracán, 2013.

Medina Báez, Bianca M. *Teresa Angleró Sepúlveda: Primera organizadora de las trabajadoras de la industria de la aguja en Puerto Rico.* San Juan: Publicaciones Gaviota, 2019.

Mejías, Félix. *Condiciones de vida de las clases jornaleras de Puerto Rico.* Río Piedras: Junta Editora de la Universidad de Puerto Rico, 1946.

Mejías, Félix. "Conditions of Labor in Puerto Rico." Master's thesis, New York University, 1944.

Meléndez, Hector. *El fracaso del proyecto PSP de la pequeña burguesía.* San Juan: Editorial Edil, 1984.

Meléndez-Badillo, Jorell A. "Radical Genealogies: The Beginnings of Anarchism in Nineteenth-Century Latin America: Havana and Buenos Aires, 1860–1890." In *Routledge Companion to Nineteenth-Century Latin America*, edited by Agnes Lugo-Ortiz and Graciela Montaldo. New York: Routledge, forthcoming.

Meléndez-Badillo, Jorell A. "The Anarchist Imaginary: Max Nettlau and Latin America." In *Writing Revolution: Hispanic Anarchist Print Culture and the United States, 1868–2015*, edited by Montse Feu and Chris Castañeda, 177–93. Urbana: University of Illinois Press, 2019.

Meléndez-Badillo, Jorell A. "Commemorating May Day in Puerto Rico." NACLA: *Report on the Americas* 51, no. 3 (September 2019): 301–5.

Meléndez-Badillo, Jorell A. "Imagining Resistance: Organizing the Puerto Rican Southern Agricultural Strike of 1905." *Caribbean Studies* 43, no. 2 (July-December 2015): 33–81.

Meléndez-Badillo, Jorell A. "Labor History's Transnational Turn: Rethinking Latin American and Caribbean Migrant Workers." *Latin American Perspectives* 42, no. 4 (July 2015): 117–22.

Meléndez-Badillo, Jorell A. "Los ecos del silencio: Dimensiones globales y aspiraciones locales del periódico *Voz humana*." *La brecha* 2, no. 2 (Fall 2016): 23–27.

Meléndez-Badillo, Jorell A. "Mateo and Juana: Racial Silencing, Epistemic Violence, and Counterarchives in Puerto Rican Labor History." *International Labor and Working-Class History* 96 (Fall 2019): 103–21.

Meléndez-Badillo, Jorell A. "Orígenes del 1ro de Mayo en Puerto Rico." *Claridad: El periódico de la nación puertorriqueña* no. 3,082 (April 26–May 2, 2012): 26–29.

Meléndez-Badillo, Jorell A. "A Party of Ex-convicts: Bolívar Ochart, Incarceration, and the Socialist Party in Early Twentieth-Century Puerto Rico." *Hispanic American Historical Review* 101, no. 1 (February 2021): 73–99.

Meléndez-Badillo, Jorell A. *Voces libertarias: Los orígenes del anarquismo en Puerto Rico.* 3rd ed. Lajas: Editorial Akelarre and Centro de Estudios e Investigación del Suroeste de Puerto Rico, 2015.

Méndez, José Luis. "Las ciencias sociales y la política en Puerto Rico." *Revista de Ciencias Sociales* 17 (2007): 40–57.

Merino Falú, Aixa. "El gremio de lavanderas de Puerta de Tierra." In *Historias vivas: Historiografía puertorriqueña contemporánea*, edited by Antonio Gaztambide Geigel and Silvia Álvarez Curbelo, 74–79. San Juan: Asociación Puertorriqueña de Historiadores and Editorial Postdata, 1996.

Merino Falú, Aixa. *Raza, género y clase social: El discrimen contra las mujeres afropuertorriqueñas.* San Juan: Oficina de la Procuradora de la Mujer, 2004.

Mintz, Sindey. *Taso, trabajador de la caña.* Río Piedras: Ediciones Huracán, 1988.

Moraga Valle, Fabio. "Reforma desde el sur, revolución desde el norte: El Primer Congreso Internacional de Estudiantes de 1921." *Estudios de historia moderna y contempoánea de México* 47 (January–June 2014): 155–95.

Moya, José C. *The Oxford Handbook on Latin American History.* Oxford: Oxford University Press, 2010.

Muñoz Marín, Luis. *Función del movimiento obrero en la democracia puertorriqueña.* Santurce: privately printed, 1957.

Muñoz Marín, Luis. *Memoria: Autobiografía pública, 1898–1940.* San Juan: Universidad Interamericana, 1982.

Nazario Velasco, Rubén. *Historia de los derrotados: Americanización y romanticismo en Puerto Rico, 1898–1917.* San Juan: Ediciones Laberinto, 2019.

Negrón-Montaner, Frances, and Ramón Grosfoguel, eds. *Puerto Rican Jam: Essays on Culture and Politics.* Minneapolis: University of Minnesota Press, 1997.

Negrón Portillo, Mariano. *Las turbas republicanas, 1900–1904.* Río Piedras: Ediciones Huracán, 1990.

Negrón Portillo, Mariano. "Puerto Rico: Surviving Colonialism and Nationalism." In *Puerto Rican Jam: Essays on Culture and Politics,* edited by Frances Negrón-Montaner and Ramón Grosfoguel, 48. Minneapolis: University of Minnesota Press, 1997.

Nguyen, Mimi Thi. "Minor Threats." *Radical History Review* 122 (2015): 11–24.

Nieves Falcón, Luis, Pablo García Rodríguez, and Félix Ojeda Reyes. *Puerto Rico: Grito y mordaza.* Río Piedras: Ediciones Librería Internacional, 1971.

Nolla Acosta, Juan José. *Elecciones en Puerto Rico.* Vol 1. Ponce: privately printed, 2013.

Ochart, Bolívar. *La noche del 12 de marzo.* Humacao: Imprenta Conciencia Popular, 1919.

Ochart, Bolívar. *Mis dos años de prisión.* San Juan: Cantero Fernández, 1919.

Oliveras, Blas, and Críspulo Oliveras. "Síntesis histórica del movimiento obrero en Yauco." In *Álbum histórico de Yauco,* edited by Francisco Lluch Negroni, 141–50. Valencia: Editorial Guerri, 1960.

Ortiz Santini, Francisco. "La ilusión rota: Balzac vs. People of Porto Rico—Orígen y desarrollo del último de los Casos Insulares." PhD diss., Centro de Estudios Avanzados de Puerto Rico y el Caribe, 2007.

Osten, Sarah. *The Mexican Revolution's Wake: The Making of a Political System, 1920–1929.* Cambridge: Cambridge University Press, 2018.

Padilla, Esteban. *O perecer o unirse.* Mayagüez: Imprenta Unión, 1905.

Padrón Martínez, Lino. *Biografía y obra de Lino Padrón Rivera.* Vega Baja: privately printed, 1972.

Padro Quiles, José. *Luchas obreras y datos históricos del Pepinio sesenta años atrás.* San Sebastían: privately printed, 1950.

Pagán, Bolívar. *Conmemoración del Primero de Mayo.* San Juan: privately printed, 1938.

Pagán, Bolívar. *Discurso pronunciado por Bolívar Pagán en el Club de la Sección de Socialista del Barrio Obrero de Santurce, Día del Trabajo y Día de Santiago Iglesias, primero de septiembre de 1941.* San Juan: privately printed, 1941.

Pagán, Bolívar. *Discurso: Significación del día del trabajo.* San Juan: Imprenta Varona, 1937.

Pagán, Bolívar. *Discursos: El gobierno fascista que oprime a Puerto Rico. Análisis de la legislación del Partido "Popular."* San Juan: privately printed, 1943.

Pagán, Bolívar. *Handbook for Puerto Rico.* Washington, DC: Office of the Resident Commissioner, n.d.

Pagán, Bolívar. *Historia de los partidos políticos puertorriqueños, 1898–1956.* 2 vols. San Juan: Librería Campos, 1972.

Pagán, Bolívar. *Informe del representante del Partido Socialista en la junta insular de elecciones ante la 7ma convención regular del Partido Socialista celebrada en Arecibo, 1928.* San Juan: privately printed, 1928.

Pagán, Bolívar. *Todo el poder a los trabajadores.* San Juan: privately printed, 1945.

Paralitici, Ché. *Historia de la lucha por la independencia de Puerto Rico: Una lucha por la soberania y la igualdad social bajo el dominio estadounidense.* San Juan: Publicaciones Gaviota, 2017.

Paredes Goicochea, Diego. "Los orígenes del anarquismo en Colombia y su relación con el liberalismo." *Tabula Rasa* 27 (July–December 2017): 391–407.

Partido Socialista de América. *Actuaciones de la primera convención territorial celebrada los días 21 y 22 de marzo de 1915 en la ciudad de Cayey, P.R. en cuya fecha se fundó la rama de estado en Puerto Rico.* Bayamón: Tipografía El Progreso, 1915.

Partido Socialista. *Actas del partido, 1923–1926.* San Juan: privately printed, n.d.

Partido Socialista. *Actas del partido, 1943, 1944, 1948.* San Juan: privately printed, n.d.

Partido Socialista. *Actuaciones de la primera convención regular.* Bayamón: Tipografía El Progreso, 1915.

Partido Socialista. *Actuaciones, procedimientos, resoluciones, acuerdos y practices de la Novena Convención del Partido Socialista celebrada en la ciudad de Caguas durante los días 14, 15, 16 y 17 de agosto de 1936.* San Juan: privately printed, 1936.

Partido Socialista. *Constitución aprobada en 1924 y enmendada en 1928.* San Juan: Tipografía Real Hermanos, 1930.

Partido Socialista. *Convención extraordinaria del Partido Socialista, 1939.* San Juan: privately printed, 1939.

Partido Socialista. *Novena convención.* San Juan: privately printed, 1936.

Partido Socialista. *Programa Constitución.* Puerta de Tierra: Tipografía Unión Obrera, 1919.

Partido Socialista. *Programa y constitución.* Santurce: Santurce Printing, 1924.

Partido Socialista. *Programa y constitución territorial del Partido Socialista, 1917.* San Juan: Tipografía Boletín Mercantil, 1917.

Partido Socialista. *Programa y constitución territorial y actuaciones.* San Juan: Tipografía Justicia, 1919.

Partido Socialista. *Reglamento del Comité Central de las Secciones Socialistas.* San Juan: privately printed, 1934.

Partsch, Jaime. *Jesus T. Piñero: El exiliado en su patria.* Río Piedras: Ediciones Huracán, 2006.

Pedreira, Antonio S. *El periodismo en Puerto Rico.* Río Piedras: Editorial Edil, 1969.

Pedreira, Antonio S. *Un hombre del pueblo: José Celso Barbosa.* San Juan: Imprenta Venezuela, 1937.

Peña Jordán, Teresa. "Luisa Capetillo: Estratégica y transversal." Paper presented at Annual Meeting of the Latin American Studies Association, San Juan, Puerto Rico, May 30, 2015.

Peña Jordán, Teresa. "Luisa Capetillo y los límites del efecto travestí." *Ajiaco: Revista literaria* 4 (Fall 2004): 55–70.

Pérez, Louis A., Jr. *Lords of the Mountain: Social Banditry and Peasant Protest in Cuba, 1878–1918.* Pittsburgh, PA: University of Pittsburgh Press, 1989.

Pérez Soler, Ángel. *Del movimiento pro independencia al Partido Socialista Puertorriqueño: La transición de la lucha nacionalista a la lucha de los trabajadores, 1959–1971.* San Juan: Publicaciones Gaviota, 2018.

Pérez Velasco, Erick J. *Bibliografía sobre el movimiento obrero puertorriqueño, 1873–1940*. Santurce: Centro de Investigaciones Académicas, Universidad del Sagrado Corazón, 1992.

Pérez Velasco, Erick J. "La condición obrera en Puerto Rico, 1898–1920." *Plural* 3, no. 1–2 (January–December 1984): 157–70.

Pérez Velasco, Erick J. *100 años de sindicalismo puertorriqueño: Memorias del congreso internacional del centenario del sindicalismo organizado en Puerto Rico, 1898–1998*. Humacao: Centro de Documentación Obrera Santiago Iglesias Pantín, 2006.

Pérez Velasco, Erick J. "Los orígenes del Primero de Mayo en Puerto Rico: Notas y documentos." *Suplemento En Rojo, Claridad*, April 28–May 4, 1989, 25.

Pessota, Rosa. *Bread upon the Waters*. New York: Dodd, Mead, 1945.

Piccato, Pablo. "Public Sphere in Latin America: A Map of the Historiography." *Social History* 35, no. 2 (2010): 165–92.

Picó, Fernando. *Amargo café: Los pequeños y medianos caficultores de Utuado en la segunda mitad del siglo XIX*. Río Piedras: Ediciones Huracán, 1981.

Picó, Fernando. *Historia general de Puerto Rico*. Río Piedras: Ediciones Huracán, 1990.

Picó, Fernando. "La universidad imaginada." In *Frente a la torre: Ensayos del centenario de la Universidad de Puerto Rico, 1903–2003*, 6–7. Río Piedras: Editorial de Universidad de Puerto Rico, 2005.

Picó, Fernando, ed. *Luis Muñoz Marín: Imágenes de la memoria*. San Juan: Fundación Luis Muñoz Marín, 2008.

Picó, Fernando, Milton Pabón, and Roberto Alejandro Rivera. *Las vallas rotas*. Río Piedras: Ediciones Huracán, 1982.

Picó, Isabel. *La mujer y la política puertorriqueña: Informe técnico a la Fundación Nacional de las Ciencias*. Río Piedras: Centro de Investigaciones Sociales, University of Puerto Rico, 1983.

Picó, Isabel. "Los estudiantes universitarios y el proceso político puertorriqueño, 1903–1948." PhD diss., Harvard University, 1974.

Piz Diez, Naila. "La reforma universitaria peronista y el movimiento estudiantil reformista: Actores, conflicto y visiones opuestas (1943–1955)." *Los trabajos y días* 4, no. 3 (2012): 41–63.

Plaza, Enrique. *Futuro*. San Juan: Tipografía El Lápiz Rojos, 1920.

Pratt, Mary Louise. *Imperial Eyes: Travel Writing and Transculturation*. New York: Routledge, 2008.

Puiggrós, Adriana. *La educación popular en América Latina: Orígenes, polémicas y perspectivas*. Buenos Aires: Colihue, 2016.

Pujals, Sandra. "Bolchquivismo isleño: Rusia y la Tercera en los imaginarios revolucionarios puertorriqueños, 1919–1936." *Historia crítica* 64 (April–June 2017): 61–80.

Pujals, Sandra. "De un pájaro las tres alas: El Buró del Caribe de la Comintern, Cuba y el radicalismo comunista en Puerto Rico, 1931–1936." *Op. Cit.: Revista del Centro de Investigaciones Históricas*, no. 21 (2012–13): 255–83.

Pujals, Sandra. "¿Una perla en el Caribe Soviético?: Puerto Rico en los archivos de la Komintern en Moscú, 1921–1943." *Op. Cit.: Revista del Centro de Investigaciones Históricas*, no. 17 (2006–7): 117–57.

Putnam, Lara. *Radical Moves: Caribbean Migrants and the Politics of Race in the Jazz Age.* Chapel Hill: University of North Carolina Press, 2013.

Quiñones Pérez, Gustavo Adolfo. *Sofocracia: El imaginario nacional de los intelectuales puertorriqueños, 1920–1940.* San Juan: Ediciones Puerto, 2016.

Quintero Rivera, Ángel. "El Partido Socialista y la lucha política triangular de las primeras décadas bajo la dominación norteamericana." *Revista de Ciencias Sociales* 19, no. 1 (1975): 49–100.

Quintero Rivera, Ángel. "La ideología populista y la institucionalización universitaria de las ciencias sociales." In *Del nacionalismo al populismo: Cultura y política en Puerto Rico,* edited by Silvia Álvarez-Curbelo and María Elena Rodríguez Castro, 107–46. Río Piedras: Ediciones Huracán, 1993.

Quintero Rivera, Ángel. *Lucha obrera en Puerto Rico.* Río Piedras: CEREP, 1971.

Quintero Rivera, Ángel. *Patricios y plebeyos: Burgueses, hacendados, artesanos y obreros. Las relaciones de clase en el Puerto Rico de cambio de siglo.* Río Piedras: Ediciones Huracán, 1988.

Quintero Rivera, Ángel. *Ponce: La capital alterna. Sociología de la sociedad civil y la cultura urbana en la historia de la relación entre clase, "raza" y nación en Puerto Rico.* Ponce: Ponceños de Verdad y Centro de Investigaciones Sociales de la Universidad de Puerto Rico, 2003.

Quintero Rivera, Ángel. "Socialist and Cigarmaker: Artisans' Proletarianization in the Making of the Puerto Rican Working Class." *Latin American Perspectives* 10, no. 2–3 (Spring–Summer, 1983): 19–38.

Quintero Rivera, Ángel. "Socialista y tabaquero: La proletarización de los artesanos." *Sin Nombre* 8, no. 4 (1978): 100–37.

Quintero Rivera, Ángel, José Luis González, Ricardo Campos, and Juan Flores. *Puerto Rico: Identidad nacional y clases sociales—Coloquio de Princeton.* 2nd ed. Río Piedras: Ediciones Huracán, 1981.

Quintero Rivera, Ángel, and Lydia Milagros González. *La otra cara de la historia: La historia de Puerto Rico desde su cara obrera, 1800–1925.* Río Piedras: CEREP, 1984.

Rabasa, Magalí. *The Book in Movement: Autonomous and the Lettered City Underground.* Pittsburgh, PA: University of Pittsburgh Press, 2019.

Raffuci, Carmen I., Silvia Álvarez Curbelo, and Fernando Picó. *Senado de Puerto Rico, 1917–1992: Ensayos de historia institucional.* San Juan: Senado de Puerto Rico, 1992.

Rama, Ángel. *La ciudad letrada.* Hanover, NH: Ediciones del Norte, 1984.

Rama, Ángel. *The Lettered City.* Translated by John Charles Chasteen. Durham, NC: Duke University Press, 1996.

Ramírez, Dixa. *Colonial Phantoms: Belonging and Refusal in the Dominican Americas, from the 19th Century to the Present.* New York: New York University Press, 2018.

Ramos, Julio, ed. *Amor y anarquía: Los escritos de Luisa Capetillo.* Río Piedras: Ediciones Huracán, 1992.

Ramos de Santiago, Carmen. *El gobierno de Puerto Rico.* Río Piedras: Editorial de la Universidad de Puerto Rico, 1989.

Ramos Méndez, Mario. *Posesión del ayer: La nacionalidad cultural en la estadidad.* San Juan: Isla Negra Editores, 2007.

Ramos Perea, Roberto, ed. *Literatura puertorriqueña negra del siglo XIX escrita por negros*. San Juan: Publicaciones Gaviota, 2011.

Rancière, Jacques. *The Philosopher and His Poor*. Edited by Andrew Parker. Durham, NC: Duke University Press, 2004.

Rancière, Jacques. *Proletarian Nights: The Workers' Dream in Nineteenth-Century France*. 2nd ed. Translated by Donald Reid. London: Verso, 2012.

Rancière, Jacques. *Staging the People: The Proletarian and His Double*. Translated by David Fernbach. London: Verso, 2011.

Rivas, Nicolás F. *Política del Partido Republicano Puertorriqueña y perfiles de jóvenes obreros republicanos*. San Juan: Tipo. L Ferreras, 1903.

Rivera, Antonio, and Arturo Morales Carrión. *La enseñanza de la historia en Puerto Rico*. Mexico City: Instituto Panamericano de Geografía e Historia, 1953.

Rivera Caballero, José R. *De lobos y corderos: Afirmación Socialista y la disidencia interna del Partido Socialista de Puerto Rico, 1915–1934*. San Juan: ED RAW, 2015.

Rivera Colón, Nilsa. *Fajardo: Notas para su historia*. San Juan: privately printed, 1983.

Rivera-Giusti, Ivette Marie. "Gender, Labor, and Working-Class Activism in the PR Tobacco Industry, 1898–1924." PhD diss., State University of New York at Binghamton, 1998.

Rivera Martínez, Prudencio. *Conferencia dictada por el Hon. Prudencio Rivera Martínez, Comisionado del Trabajo de P.R. y el Discurso Pronunciado por el Ilustre Profesor Lcdo. Pedro C. Timothée en Homenaje a Rafael Cordero Molina*. San Juan: La Voz del Obrero, 1932.

Rivera Martínez, Prudencio. "Federación Libre de los Trabajadores de Puerto Rico." In *El libro de Puerto Rico*, edited by E. Fernández García, 898–902. San Juan: El Libro Azul, 1923.

Rivera Quintero, Marcia. "The Development of Capitalism in Puerto Rico and the Incorporation of Women into the Labor Force." In *The Puerto Rican Woman*, edited by Edna Acosta Belén y Elia Hidalgo Christensen. New York: Praeger, 1979.

Rivera-Rideau, Petra R. "From Carolina to Loíza: Race, Place, and Puerto Rican Racial Democracy." *Identities: Global Studies in Culture and Power* 20, no. 5 (2013): 616–32.

Rodríguez Arvelo, V. A. "José Elías Levis Bernard: Su vida y su obra." Master's thesis, University of Puerto Rico, 1964.

Rodríguez Beruff, Jorge. "Antonio S. Pedreira, la universidad y el proyecto populista." *Revista de Administración Pública* 18, no. 2 (March 1986): 5–20.

Rodríguez Castro, María Elena. "Tradición y modernidad: El intelectual puertorriqueña ante la década del treinta." *Op. Cit: Revista del Centro de Investigaciones Históricas*, no. 3 (1987): 45–65.

Rodríguez García, Tadeo. *Brevario histórico*. San Juan: privately printed, 1936.

Rodríguez García, Tadeo. *Ideales sociales*. Caguas: Tip. R. Morel Campos, 1924.

Rodríguez Graciani, David. *¿Rebelión o protesta? La lucha estudiantil en Puerto Rico*. Río Piedras: Ediciones Puerto, 1972.

Rodríguez-Silva, Ileana M. "Abolition, Race, and the Politics of Gratitude in Late Nineteenth-Century Puerto Rico." *Hispanic American Historical Review* 93, no. 4 (2013): 621–57.

Rodríguez-Silva, Ileana M. "Racial Silencing and the Organizing of Puerto Rican Labor." In *Silencing Race: Disentangling Blackness, Colonialism, and National Identities in Puerto Rico*, 159–86. New York: Palgrave Macmillan, 2012.

Rodríguez-Silva, Ileana M. *Silencing Race: Disentangling Blackness, Colonialism, and National Identities in Puerto Rico*. New York: Palgrave Macmillan, 2012.

Rodríguez Vázquez, José Juan. *El sueño que no cesa: La nación deseada en el debate intelectual y político puertorriqueño, 1920–1940*. San Juan: Ediciones Callejón, 2004.

Rodríguez Vera, Andrés. *El triunfo de la apostasía*. San Juan: Tipografía La Democracia, 1930.

Rodríguez Vera, Andrés. "La Federación Puertorriqueña del Trabajo." In *El libro de Puerto Rico*, edited by E. Fernández García, 902–4. San Juan: El Libro Azul, 1923.

Rodríguez Vera, Andrés. *Los fantoches del obrerismo o el fracaso de una institución*. San Juan: Tipografía Negrón Flores, 1915.

Rogler, Charles C. *Comerío: A Study of a Puerto Rican Town*. Lawrence: University of Kansas, 1940.

Rojas, Manuel F. *Cuatro siglos de ignorancia y servidumbre*. San Juan: Imprenta La Primavera, 1914.

Rojas, Manuel F. *Estudios sociales o frutos del sistema*. San Juan: Federación Libre, 1918.

Rojas, Manuel F. *Hablan las víctimas de las expediciones de trabajadores a Estados Unidos*. San Juan: privately printed, 1919.

Rojas Blaquier, Angelina. *El primer Partido Comunista de Cuba: Sus tácticas y estrategias, 1925–1935*. Santiago de Cuba: Editorial Oriente, 2005.

Román, Reinaldo L. *Governing Spirits: Religion, Miracles, and Spectacles in Cuba and Puerto Rico, 1898–1956*. Chapel Hill: University of North Carolina Press, 2007.

Román, Reinaldo L. "Scandalous Race: Garveyism, the Bomba, and the Discourse of Blackness in 1920s Puerto Rico." *Caribbean Studies* 31, no. 1 (January–June, 2003): 213–59.

Romeral, R. del [Ramón Romero Rosa]. *Catecismo socialista*. San Juan: Imprenta Labrador, 1905.

Romeral, R. del [Ramón Romero Rosa]. *¡El 16 de abril de 1905! Lucha entre capital y trabajo*. San Juan: Unión Tipográfica, 1905.

Romeral, R. del [Ramón Romero Rosa]. *Entre broma y vera*. San Juan: Tipografía La República Españnla, 1906.

Romeral, R. del [Ramón Romero Rosa]. *La cuestión social y Puerto Rico*. San Juan: privately printed, 1904.

Romeral, R. del [Ramón Romero Rosa]. *La emancipación del obrero*. Mayagüez: Imprenta La Bruja, 1903.

Romeral, R. del [Ramón Romero Rosa]. *Musarañas: Opúsculo sobre ciertas preocupaciones y costumbres que son un estorbo á los trabajadores puertorriqueños para la compenetración de los reinvidicadores ideales del obrerismo universal*. San Juan: Tipografía El Carnaval, 1904.

Romeral, R. del [Ramón Romero Rosa]. *Santiago Iglesias: Su biografía en el movimiento obrero de Puerto Rico*. San Juan: Tipografía de L. Carreras, 1901.

Rosario Natal, Carmelo. *La juventud de Luis Muñoz Marín: Vida y pensamiento, 1898–1932*. San Juan: Editorial Edil, 1989.

Sáez Corales, Juan. *25 años de lucha, mi respuesta a la persecusión*. San Juan: Gauthier Multigraph, 1955.

Sanabria, Carlos. *Puerto Rican Labor History: Revolutionary Ideals and Reformist Politics, 1898–1934*. Lanham, MD: Lexington, 2018.

Sanabria, Carlos, ed. *Ricardo Campos, 1946–2012: En memoria*. San Juan: Editorial El Antillano/Escuela Manuel Francisco Rojas, 2013.

Sanabria, Carlos. "Samuel Gompers and the American Federation of Labor in Puerto Rico," *Centro Journal* 17, no. 1 (Spring 2005): 140–61.

Sánchez Korrol, Virginia E. *From Colonia to Community: The History of Puerto Ricans in New York City*. Berkeley: University of California Press, 1994.

Sánchez López, Eugenio. "Un loco revolucionario." In *Almanaque de Puerto Rico, 1911*, 299–302. San Juan: M. Burillo, 1910.

San Miguel, Pedro. "Fernando Picó y la nueva historia puertorriqueña: Una reflexión intempestiva." *Caribbean Studies Journal* 45, no. 1–2 (January–December 2017): 216–41.

Santiago, William Fred. *Comerío: Cacique Comerío*. Cupey: Santiago, 2008.

Santiago-Ortiz, Aurora, and Jorell Meléndez-Badillo. "La Calle Fortaleza in Puerto Rico's Primavera de Verano." Decolonial Geographies of Puerto Rico's 2019 Protests, an online forum edited by Marisol LeBrón and Joaquín Villanueva. *Society and Space Journal*, February 25, 2020. https://www.societyandspace.org/articles/la-calle -fortaleza-in-puerto-ricos-primavera-de-verano.

Santiago-Ortiz, Aurora, and Jorell Meléndez-Badillo. "Puerto Rico's Multiple Solidarities: Emergent Landscapes and the Geographies of Protest." *The Abusable Past, Radical History Review*, July 22, 2019. https://www.radicalhistoryreview.org /abusablepast/?p=3152.

Santiago Valles, Kelvin. *Subject People and Colonial Discourses: Economic Transformations and Social Disorders in Puerto Rico, 1898–1947*. Albany, NY: SUNY Press, 1994.

Sarmiento, Domingo F. *Civilización i barbarie: Vida de Juan Facundo Quiroga*. Santiago: Imprenta del Progreso, 1845.

Scarano, Francisco. "The *Jíbaro* Masquerade and the Subaltern Politics of Creole Identity Formation in Puerto Rico, 1745–1823." *American Historical Review* 101, no. 5 (December 1996): 1398–1431.

Scarano, Francisco. "La historia heredada: Cauces y corrientes de la historiografía puertorriqueña, 1880–1970." *Exégis* 6, no. 17 (1993): 40–52.

Scott, James C. *Hidden Transcripts: Domination and the Arts of Resistance*. New Haven, CT: Yale University Press, 1990.

Scott, Joan W. *Gender and the Politics of History*. New York: Columbia University Press, 1999.

Seigel, Micol. *Uneven Encounters: Making Race and Nation in Brazil and the United States*. Durham, NC: Duke University Press, 2009.

Senior, Clarence Ollson. *Santiago Iglesias: Apóstol de los trabajadores*. Hato Rey: Editorial de la Universidad Interamericana, 1972.

Senior, Clarence Ollson. *Santiago Iglesias: Labor Crusader*. Hato Rey: Editorial de la Universidad Interamericana, 1972.

Shaffer, Kirwin R. *Anarchism and Countercultural Politics in Early Twentieth-Century Cuba*. Gainesville: University Press of Florida, 2005.

Shaffer, Kirwin R. *Anarchists of the Caribbean: Countercultural Politics and Transnational Networks in the Age of US Expansion.* Cambridge: Cambridge University Press, 2020.

Shaffer, Kirwin R. *Black Flag Boricuas: Anarchism, Antiauthoritarianism, and the Left in Puerto Rico, 1897–1921.* Urbana: University of Illinois Press, 2013.

Shaffer, Kirwin R. "Havana Hub: Cuban Anarchism, Radical Media and the Trans-Caribbean Anarchist Network, 1902–1915." *Caribbean Studies* 37, no. 2 (July–December 2009): 45–81.

Silén, Juan Ángel. *Apuntes para la historia del movimiento obrero puertorriqueño.* Río Piedras: Publicaciones Gaviota, 2001.

Silva, Ana Margarita. *Mariano Abril y Ostaló: Su vida y obra, 1861–1935.* San Juan: Editorial Club de la Prensa, 1969.

Silvestrini, Blanca G. "La mujer puertorriqueña y el movimiento obrero en la década de 1930." In *La mujer en la sociedad puertorriqueña,* edited by Edna Acosta-Belén, 67–90. Río Piedras: Ediciones Huracán, 1980.

Silvestrini, Blanca G. "La política de salud de los Estados Unidos en Puerto Rico, 1898–1913: Consecuencias de la americanización." In *Politics, Society, and Culture in the Caribbean,* edited by Blanca G. Silvestrini, 69–83. San Juan: Editorial de la Universidad de Puerto Rico, 1983.

Silvestrini, Blanca G. "Los libros de texto de historia de Puerto Rico y el contexto caribeño." *Cuadernos de la Facultad de Humanidades, Universidad de Puerto Rico, Recinto de Río Piedras,* no. 12 (1984): 49–66.

Silvestrini, Blanca G. *Los trabajadores puertorriqueños y el Partido Socialista, 1932–1940.* Río Piedras: Editorial de la UPR, 1979.

Silvestrini, Blanca G. "Perspectiva de los estudios históricos en Puerto Rico en la década de los setenta." *Cuadernos de la Facultad de Humanidades, Universidad de Puerto Rico, Recinto de Río Piedras,* no. 10 (1983): 27–54.

Silvestrini, Blanca G., ed. *Politics, Society, and Culture in the Caribbean.* San Juan: University of Puerto Rico Press, 1983.

Silvestrini, Blanca G. *Violencia y criminalidad en Puerto Rico, 1898–1973: Apuntes para un estudio de historia social.* Río Piedras: Editorial de la Universidad de Puerto Rico, 1980.

Sinnette, Elinor Des Verney. *Arthur Alfonso Schomburg, Black Bibliophile and Collector: A Biography.* Detroit: New York Public Library and Wayne State University Press, 1989.

Stern, Steve J. *Battling for Hearts and Minds: Memory Struggles in Pinochet's Chile, 1973–1988.* Durham, NC: Duke University Press, 2006.

Stevens, Margaret. *Red International and Black Caribbean: Communists in New York City, Mexico, and the West Indies, 1919–1939.* London: Pluto Press, 2017.

Stoler, Ann Laura. *Along the Archival Grain: Epistemic Anxieties and Colonial Common Sense.* Princeton, NJ: Princeton University Press, 2009.

Struthers, David M. *The World in a City: Multiethnic Radicalism in Early Twentieth-Century Los Angeles.* Urbana: University of Illinois Press, 2019.

Sueiro Seoane, Susana. "Anarquismo e independentismo cubano: Las figuras olvidadas de Enrique Roig, Enrique Creci y Pedro Esteve." *Espacio, tiempo y forma* 30 (2018): 97–120.

Suriano, Juan. *Paradoxes of Utopia: Anarchist Culture and Politics in Buenos Aires, 1890–1910.* Oakland, CA: AK Press, 2010.

Taller Benéfico de Artesanos de Ponce. *Reglamento*. Ponce: Tipografía el Vapor, 1888.

Taller de Formación Política. *¡Huelga en la caña! 1933–1934*. Río Piedras: Ediciones Huracán, 1982.

Taller de Formación Política. *La cuestión nacional: El Partido Nacionalista y el movimiento obrero puertorriqueño. Aspectos de las luchas ecónomicas y políticas de 1930–1940*. Río Piedras: Ediciones Huracán, 1982.

Taller de Formación Política. *No estamos pidiendo el cielo: Huelga portuaria de 1938*. Río Piedras: Ediciones Huracán, 1988.

Tinarejo, Aracelis. *El lector: A History of the Cigar Factory Reader*. Austin: University of Texas Press, 2010.

Tirado Avilés, Amilcar. "Cigar Workers and the History of the Labor Movement in Puerto Rico, 1890–1920." PhD diss., City University of New York, 2012.

Tirado Avilés, Amilcar. "Ramón Romero Rosa: Su participación en las luchas obreras, 1896–1906." *Caribe* 2, no. 2–3 (1980–1981): 3–26.

Todd, Roberto H. *Desfile de gobernadores de Puerto Rico, 1898–1943*. Madrid: Ediciones Iberoamericanas, 1966.

Toledo, Evaristo M. *Luisa Acevedo Zambrana: Toda una vida dedicada a los trabajadores*. San Juan: Ediciones SITUM, 2017.

Torregrosa, José Luis. *Historia de la radio en Puerto Rico*. San Juan: privately printed, 1992.

Torres, Alfonso. *Espíritu de clase*. San Juan: Imprenta Federación Libre, 1917.

Torres, Alfonso. *Solidaridad*. San Juan: Unión Tipográfica, 1905.

Torres, Arlene. "La gran familia puertorriqueña 'ej prieta de beldá' (The Great Puerto Rican Family Is Really Black)." In *Blackness in Latin America and the Caribbean*, vol. 2, edited by Arlene Torres and Norman E. Whitten Jr., 285–306. Bloomington: Indiana University Press, 1998.

Torres Rosario, Wilson. *Juana Colón: Combatiente en el tabacal puertorriqueño*. Comerío: privately printed, 2011.

Toth, Charles W. "Samuel Gompers, el comunismo y la Federación Panamericana del Trabajo." *Revista de Ciencias Sociales* 17, no. 1 (1973): 95–191.

Trouillot, Michel-Rolph. *Silencing the Past: Power and the Production of History*. Boston: Beacon, 1995.

Trujillo-Pagán, Nicole. *Modern Colonization by Medical Intervention*. Leiden: Brill, 2013.

Tussel Gómez, Javier. *Antonio Maura: Una biografía política*. Madrid: Alianza Editorial, 1994.

Ullman, Joan Connelly. *The Tragic Week: A Study of Anticlericalism in Spain, 1875–1912*. Cambridge, MA: Harvard University Press, 1965.

Unión de Tipográfos, Núm. 422. *Páginas del obrero: Colección de artículos escritos para comemorar el Primero de Mayo*. Mayagüez: Imprenta La Protesta, 1904.

Uniones de Tabaqueros de Puerto Rico. *Actuaciones de la segunda y tercera asambleas de las uniones de tabaqueros de Puerto Rico*. San Juan: Porto Rico Progress, 1914.

Uniones de Tabaqueros de Puerto Rico. *Libro de actuaciones de la primera asamblea regular*. San Juan: Tipografía Real Hermanos, 1910.

US Department of Agriculture. *Report for August 1909: Porto Rico Section of the Climatological Service of the Weather Bureau*. Richmond, VA: Weather Bureau Office, 1909.

US War Department, Porto Rico Census Office. *Report on the Census of Porto Rico, 1899.* Washington, DC: Government Printing Office, 1900.

Valdés, Vanessa. *Diasporic Blackness: The Life and Times of Arturo Alfonso Schomburg.* Albany: State University of New York Press, 2017.

Valencia, Samuel E. de la Rosa. "Raíces del movimiento obrero puertorriqueño." Unpublished manuscript, Centro de Documentación Obrera Santiago Iglesias Pantín, Humacao, Universidad de Puerto Rico, 1977.

Valle Ferrer, Norma. "Luisa Capetillo (1879–1922), una herejía en la sociedad puertorriqueña." *Caribe* 4–5, no. 5–6 (1983–84): 3–36.

Valle Ferrer, Norma. *Luisa Capetillo: Historia de una mujer proscrita.* Río Piedras: Editorial Cultural, 1900.

Valle Ferrer, Norma. *Luisa Capetillo: Obra competa, "Mi patria es la libertad."* San Juan: Departamento del Trabajo y Recursos Humanos and the Proyecto de Estudios de las Mujeres, Universidad de Puerto Rico, Cayey, 2008.

Valle Ferrer, Norma. *Luisa Capetillo, Pioneer Puerto Rican Feminist.* Translated by Gloria Waldman-Schwartz. New York: Peter Lang, 2006.

Vargas Canales, Margarita. *Del batey al papel mojado: Campesinos cañeros y vida cotidiana en Puerto Rico.* Mexico City: Universidad Nacional Autónoma de México, 2011.

Vargas Rodríguez, Pedro. *La esclavitud blanca o el imperio de la burocracia.* Guánica: Tipografía Brisas del Caribe, 1918.

Vélez Rivera, Marcos A. *Las ilustraciones de los Libros para el Pueblo de la División de Educación de la Comunidad y la modernización de Puerto Rico, 1949–1964.* Carolina: Ediciones UNE, 2016.

Vilar, Juan. *Páginas libres.* San Juan: Editorial Antillana, 1914.

Villanueva, Joaquín, Martín Cobián, and Félix Rodríguez. "San Juan, the Fragile City: Finance Capital, Class, and the Making of Puerto Rico's Economic Crisis." *Antipode* 50, no. 5 (November 2018): 1415–37.

Villaronga, Gabriel. *Toward a Discourse of Consent: Mass Mobilization and Colonial Politics in Puerto Rico, 1932–1948.* Westport, CT: Praeger, 2004.

Vosloo, R. "Archiving Otherwise: Some Remarks on Memory and Historical Responsibility." *Studia Historiae Ecclesiasticae* 31, no. 2 (October 2005): 379–99.

Walsh, Catherine E., and Walter D. Mignolo. *On Decoloniality: Concepts, Analytics, Praxis.* Durham, NC: Duke University Press, 2018.

Ward, Thomas. *La anarquía inmanentista de Manuel González Prada.* New York: Peter Lang, 1998.

Weyl, Walter. *Labor Conditions in Porto Rico.* Washington, DC: Government Printing Office, 1905.

Williams, Dana M. "A Society in Revolt or Under Analysis? Investigating the Dialogue between Nineteenth-Century Anarchists and Sociologists." In *Without Borders or Limits: An Interdisciplinary Approach to Anarchist Studies,* edited by Jorell A. Meléndez-Badillo and Nathan Jun, 3–36. Newcastle upon Tyne: Cambridge Scholars, 2013.

Williams, Daryle. *Culture Wars in Brazil: The First Vargas Regime, 1930–1945.* Durham, NC: Duke University Press, 2001.

Williams, Raymond. *Keywords: A Vocabulary of Culture and Society.* New York: Oxford University Press, 1976.

Woodcock, George. *Peter Kropotkin: From Prince to Rebel*. Montreal: Black Rose, 1990.

Zeltsman, Corinna. "Defining Responsibility: Printers, Politics, and the Law in Early Republican Mexico City." *Hispanic American Historical Review* 98, no. 2 (May 2018): 189–222.

Zimmer, Kenyon. *Immigrants against the State: Yiddish and Italian Anarchism in America*. Urbana: University of Illinois Press, 2015.

Page numbers in italics refer to figures.

New Deal, 17, 138
newspapers: audiences for, 28–29, 118–19; funding and material support for, 28–29, 40–41, 65; international circulation of, 54–66, 181; labor's self-fashioning and, 5–6, 18, 27–29, 39–40; masses' relation(s) to, 18, 28–29, 31–32, 35–36, 163, 167; pedagogical uses of, 41–42; as Puerto Rican public sphere, 137–38, 141–47; repression of, 74–75; women writers and, 85–86; workingmen's production of, 1–3, 25–29, 180. *See also specific newspapers*
New York Call (newspaper), 74
New York Sun (newspaper)), 164
New York Tribune (newspaper), 164
night schools, 3, 49, 66
Nogueras Rivera, Nicolas, 171
"Nuestra misión" (Escabí), 87–88
nueva historia, 7

obreras ilustradas, 84–85
Obrero libre (newspaper), 48
obreros ilustrados: archives created by, 3–4, 10, 157–61, 171–76; books and, 42–48; bureaucratization and, 117–28; *centros* and, 3, 28–29, 48–53, 73–76, 174, 198n109, 201n54; cigarmakers and, 13–14; colonial systems and, 10–11; cultural projects of, 12–13; definition of, 21; elite aspirations of, 21–22, 32, 35–38, 53, 75–76, 109–10, 113, 127, 129, 131–33, 137–38, 144–48, 150–55, 167–70, 175–76; Eurocentrism and, 18–20, 30, 38–39, 47, 51–58, 65, 80, 110, 128–30, 173–74, 181; gender and, 4–5, 9, 34, 47, 71, 97–98, 176–79; government appointments of, 117–18; Gramsci on, 200n25; international identifications of, 5, 9, 54–81, 120, 128–29, 181; the masses' relation to, 18, 28–32, 35–36, 163, 167–70; oratory of, 39–40, 42, 67, 124–26; party politics and, 7–8, 14, 17–19, 30–31, 36, 42–43; paternalistic tendencies of, 31–39, 77, 85–89, 97–98, 109, 118; racialization of, 4–5, 9, 32–33, 72, 176–79; rational education and, 69–81; self-definition and, 1–3, 25–29, 33; student rejections of, 134–39; women activists and, 85–89, 106–7. *See also* FLT (Federación Libre de Trabajadores); Socialist Party; *specific books and newspapers*
Ochart, Bolívar, 175

Oliveras, Blas, 183, 187
Once de marzo (*centro*), 49–50
Operation Bootstraps, 186
O perecer o unirse (Padilla), 197n82
organic intellectuals, 200n25
Organic Law of 1900. *See* Foraker Act
Osorio, José Guillermo, 65
Otero, R. D. de, 86

Pacheco, Sixto, 130
Padilla, Esteban, 1–3, 15, 109, 114, 208n18
Padilla, José Gualberto, 32
Padrón Rivera, Lino, 130, 148, 158
Pagán, Bolívar, 128–29, 129, 129–30, 144, 158, 165, 170, 175, 182–83, 188
Páginas del obrero (essay collection), 87
Páginas libres (Vilar), 76–78
Páginas rojas (Márcano), 78
Palés Matos, Luis, 17
Palmer Plaza, 70
pamphlets, 8, 165. *See also* newspapers
Pan-American Federation of Labor, 144, 159, 182
Paraguay, 7, 112, 139
Paris Commune, 173
Partido Obrero Insular, 2, 15, 79, 109, 114–15
Partido Obrero Socialista (in Puerto Rico), 58
Partido Popular Democrático, 17, 159–61, 179, 183–84, 186–88
Partido Socialista Puertorriqueño, 103
Pedreira, Antonio, 17, 154–55, 160, 191n5
Peña, Abraham, 156
Peña, Carmen, 122
Peña Jordán, Teresa, 94
Pérez Sanjurjo, Mateo, 79–81, 108–9
Perón, Margarita, 89
Peru, 7, 139
Pica (newspaper), 145
Picó, Fernando, 141
Piglia, Ricardo, 161
planchadoras, 82–87, 89–90, 96
Plaza, Enrique, 65
Plaza Baldorioty, 67–69
Pluma roja (newspaper), 93
police officers, 108–9
Ponce, 26–27, 41, 59, 71
Popular Democratic Party. *See* Partido Popular Democrático
Porto Alegre, 69

positivism, 160
Post, Regis, 56, 68
PRATC (Puerto Rican American Tobacco Company), 99, 206n80
Pratt, Mary Louise, 35
PRERA (Puerto Rican Emergency Relief Administration), 17
primary sources, 163. See also historiography; ideational archives
1ro de Maio (newspaper), 28
Primero de mayo (Gori), 70
printers, 34–35
Printers' Union No. 422, 87
print media. See newspapers
Prontuario histórico de Puerto Rico (Blanco), 160
Proudhon, Pierre-Joseph, 38, 168
PRRA (Puerto Rican Reconstruction Administration), 17
PRTLC (Porto Rico Leaf Tobacco Company), 64, 99–100, 206n80
PSOE (Partido Obrero Socialista Español), 58
Puerta de Tierra, 20, 157
Puerto Rican Academy of History, 36, 196n50
Puerto Rican Institute of Culture, 186
Puerto Rico: agricultural systems of, 13–14, 63–64, 96–97, 114; class hierarchies in, 11–18; colonial and imperial violence in, 3–6, 8–18, 22–23, 29–39, 52–53, 56–57, 88–89, 98–99, 127, 139, 160, 164–65; Commonwealth status of, 186; gender and, 3–4, 9, 47, 77, 84–87, 100–101; global networks and, 54–66; historiography and, 6–11, 18–20; literacy rates in, 34, 98, 116, 186; "modernization" discourses and, 16–18, 76–81, 176–79; national mythology of, 2–4, 7–12, 17, 159–61, 183–89; racialization in, 3–4, 9, 32–33, 71–73, 77–81, 126–27; slavery in, 11, 96; status question and, 10, 13, 88–89, 137–38, 160, 218n21; US citizenship and, 16; US universities' ignoring of, 9–10. See also specific parties, people, places, and publications
Puerto Rico Federal Relations Law, 188
Puerto Rico iliustrado (magazine), 137
Pure Labor Party, 159, 182

Quebradillas, 27
¿Quiénes somos? Organizaciones obreras (Iglesias Pantín), 62

Quijano, Aníbal, 192n32
Quiñones, Julio, 40
Quiñones, Norberto, 25

Rabasa, Magalí, 43
race: "civilization" discourses and, 9–10, 124–26; colonialism and, 71; gender and, 86–87, 100–101; international labor movement and, 18; racism and, 32–33, 46–48, 100–102; rational education and, 72–73; religiosity and, 98–99, 104; silencing of, 3–4, 9–10, 73, 78–80, 176–79; Socialist Party and, 124–26. See also Eurocentrism; modernization discourses
Racionalismo científico (Vilar), 76
Rafael Cordero Casino, 125
Rama, Ángel, 7–8, 195n17
Ramírez de Arellano, Rafael, 160
Ramón Marín, Julia, 46
Ramos, Julio, 37, 91, 94
Ramos Perea, Roberto, 72
Rancière, Jacques, 10
rational education, 69–73, 87
Ravachol (newspaper), 93
Rebelión (newspaper), 56
Reclus, Élisée, 69, 75
Redención (Limón de Arce), 47
Reily, Emmet Montgomery, 117
religion and spirituality, 98–99
Republican Party (in Puerto Rico), 13–14, 42, 58–59, 109, 116, 128–29, 165. See also Coalición (Socialist + Republican Parties)
Revista obrera (newspaper), 27
Revoltado (newspaper), 50
Revolución (Balsac and Valle), 48, 60
Revolution cosmopolite (newspaper), 50
Reyes Torres, Adolfo, 101
Rice, Graham, 56
Río Piedras, 135, 140, 150
Ríos, José A., 128–29
Ríos, Vidal, 106
Rivera, Esteban, 48
Rivera, José, 25
Rivera, Prudencia, 67
Rivera Martínez, Prudencio, 121–27, 149, 151–52, 181–82, 185
Rizal, José, 38, 168
Roberts de Romeu, Martha, 134

Torres, Concha, 177
Torres, Wilson, 98
Tostoy, Leo, 87
To the Young (Kropotkin), 48
trade unions. *See* labor unions
transnational subjectivities. *See*
    internationalism
Travieso, Martín, 183–84
Trece de octubre, 49–50, 65, 70
Trouillot, Michel-Rolph, 4–5, 27, 84
Trujillo, Rafael Leónidas, 113
Tufiño, Rafael, 186

Una idea (pamphlet), 50
Unión obrera (newspaper), 38, 40, 42, 48, 59, 75,
    95, 101, 109, 129–30, 145, 156, 212n10
Unión Obrera Central, 114
Union of Carpenters, 59
Union Party, 14, 16, 49, 68, 110–12, 134, 156, 165
Unión y fuerza (Balsac), 60–62, 70
United States: citizenship and, 16, 57, 115–16, 162;
    Puerto Rico's occupation by, 5–6, 8–10, 12–13,
    22–23, 29–39, 52–53, 56–57, 88–89, 98–99, 127,
    160, 164–65; rational schools in, 69. *See also*
    New Deal; *specific governors and presidents*
UPR (University of Puerto Rico): department
    of history in, 157, 160–61; development of,
    17; gender and, 124–25; honor discourses
    and, 137–38, 141–42, 144, 148–49, 152–55;
    social sciences in, 44–45; student strike and,
    19, 127–28, 132, 134–50
Uruguay, 112, 139
Utuado, 41, 57

Valle, Santiago, 37, 48, 60
Vázquez, Diego, 78
Vázquez, Elena, 95
vda. de Braschi, Olivia, 152–53
Vega Santos, Pablo, 64
Venezuela, 56
Verdad (newspaper), 56
Verne, Jules, 35
Veve, Santiago, 117, 209n44
Victoria Theater, 135, 140, 150
Vidal, Juan, 182
Vilafranca, Soledad, 74
Vilar, Juan, 65–66, 73–81, 87, 91, 203n97
Villa de Coamo, 27

Villafranca, Soledad, 51
Voz humana (newspaper), 42, 64–66, 69, 75

Washington, Booker T., 126–27
whiteness: "civilization" discourses and, 9
Wilson, Woodrow, 108–11, 115
Winthrop, Beekman, 114
women: counterarchives of, 4, 18, 91–93; em-
    ployers' uses of, 96–97; labor organizations
    and, 15, 82–85, 121–23, 206n63; marriage ex-
    pectations and, 90–92; paternalistic tenden-
    cies toward, 85–89, 97–98; silencing of, 2–3,
    83–84, 176–79; strikes and, 96–97, 99–101,
    104; suffrage and, 91, 121; workingmen's
    beliefs about, 71, 84–85. *See also* gender;
    silencing (historical); workingwomen
Women Tobacco Stripper Union, 15
Worker (newspaper), 164
"Workers' Manifesto" (Maldonado), 86
workingmen: archive creation by, 3–4, 10,
    25–29; *centros* and, 3, 28–29, 48–53, 73–76,
    174, 198n109, 201n54; colonial systems and,
    10–11; cultural projects of, 12–13; "culture's"
    opposition to, 137–38, 144–55; knowledge
    production by, 75–81; mobility of, 57, 71;
    party politics and, 7–8, 14, 17, 19, 114–18;
    paternalistic attitudes toward, 29–39, 47,
    77, 85–89, 94–96, 118; police abuses against,
    108–9; Puerto Rico's national mythologizing
    and, 2–3, 181–88; racialization and gendering
    of, 9, 32–33, 45, 72, 177, 186; rational educa-
    tion and, 69–81; silencing and, 7–11, 188–89;
    transnational subjectivity and, 54–57, 69–81,
    181–82; workshops as education sites for,
    2–3, 34–35. *See also centros*; education; inter-
    nationalism; labor unions; *obreros ilustrados*
workingwomen, 82–85; census data on, 206n63;
    international solidarity among, 91–93; So-
    cialist Party participation and, 121–23
workshops: labor organizing and, 174–76; as
    sites of education, 2–3, 34–35, 90–91
World War I, 121

Yager, Arthur, 108–10, 121
Yuya (workingwoman), 102

Zeno Gandía, Manuel, 46
Zola, Émile, 21, 35, 181

CPSIA information can be obtained
at www.ICGtesting.com
Printed in the USA
JSHW010006090123
35873JS00004B/15